Introduction to Personal Computers

3rd Edition

KATHERINE MURRAY

REVISED BY

ROSE EWING AND
KATHERINE MURRAY

Introduction to Personal Computers, 3rd Edition

Copyright © 1992 by Que® Corporation.

All rights reserved. Printed in the United States of America. No part of this book may be used or reproduced in any form or by any means, or stored in a database or retrieval system, without prior written permission of the publisher except in the case of brief quotations embodied in critical articles and reviews. Making copies of any part of this book for any purpose other than your own personal use is a violation of United States copyright laws. For information, address Que Corporation, 11711 N. College Ave., Carmel, IN 46032.

Library of Congress Catalog No.: 92-64026

ISBN 1-56529-029-1

95 94 93   4 3 2

Interpretation of the printing code: the rightmost double-digit number is the year of the book's printing; the rightmost single-digit number, the number of the book's printing. For example, a printing code of 92-1 shows that the first printing of the book occurred in 1992.

Hardware illustration of PS/1 computer, courtesy of IBM Corporation. Some screens in this book were created using Collage Plus from Inner Media, Inc., Hollis, NH. Additional illustrations created by Bill Hartmann.

Publisher: Lloyd J. Short

Associate Publisher: Rick Ranucci

Product Development Manager: Thomas H. Bennett

Book Designer: Scott Cook

Production Team: Jeff Baker, Claudia Bell, Paula Carroll, Michelle Cleary, Brook Farling, Laurie Lee, Caroline Roop, Linda Seifert, Johnna VanHoose, Lisa Wilson, Phil Worthington

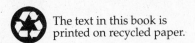

The text in this book is printed on recycled paper.

Product Director
Shelley O'Hara

Production Editor
Donald R. Eamon

Editors
Louise Lambert
Joy Preacher
Bill Barton

Technical Editor
Nancy Mingus

Composed in Cheltenham and MCPdigital by Que Corporation.

Rose Ewing, who performed the lion share of the revision for this edition, is employed as a professional computer trainer and instructional designer at MacDonnell Douglas Space Systems Company, where she developed the course design for 17 Macintosh courses, which she also instructed. Rose also is a faculty adjunct instructor at Coastline Community College, where she has developed and currently teaches word processing, desktop publishing, spreadsheet, and graphics courses.

Katherine Murray is the president of reVisions Plus, Inc., a writing, editing, and desktop publishing company that deals primarily with the development and production of microcomputer-related materials. Author of *Using WordStar 7*; *Using Professional Write*; *Using PFS: First Choice*; *Using PFS: First Publisher*; *Using Publish It!*; and *Que's PS/1 Book*. Katherine also was a contributing author to *Using HyperCard: From Home to HyperTalk* and *1-2-3 QuickStart*. Kathy has published many family-related articles in national general interest magazines.

TRADEMARK ACKNOWLEDGMENTS

ACKNOWLEDGMENTS

Introduction to Personal Computers caused a ripple effect that was felt in many lives, and with the 2nd edition, the circles widened. What an experience this book has been! I want to thank (*thank* is not a strong enough word, but what is?) the following people who contributed to the quality of the information in this book, the accuracy of the material, the strength and clarity of the book, my sanity (or lack thereof) during the course of the project, and lessons we all learned in the process.

Katherine Murray wants to thank:

My family, for understanding that I tend to be somewhat compulsive about writing and for not discouraging me when the going got tough.

Don Eamon, production editor of this edition, for the long hours and late nights when deadlines loomed.

Shelley O'Hara, who shepherded all three editions of this book.

Lloyd Short, Publisher, for all he's done throughout this book's evolution, both for the authors and for the authors' work. Sometimes, the unseen, intangible efforts go farther than all others. Thanks, Loid.

In addition, Rose Ewing wants to thank:

Editors **Joy Preacher, Louise Lambert, and Mike Barton**, for their outstanding editing skills and adherence to the rigid conventions used in Que's books.

Patty Brooks, who tied up loose ends in this revision, no matter how tedious the task.

Nancy Mingus, technical editor for this edition for her superb technical review of this book.

Granger Westberg, for his technical assistance with the DOS portion of the revision of this edition and for capturing many of the screens, both DOS and Windows.

Chris Beck, for his knowledge of the IBM and for his substantial contributions to the revision of this book.

CONTENTS AT A GLANCE

II Purchase Considerations

IV A Software Review

Conventions Used in This Book

Introduction to Personal Computers, 2nd Edition uses several conventions of which you should be aware. These conventions are listed here for your reference.

Information you are to type (usually found in examples with numbered steps) is indicated by bold type. For example, "At the prompt, type **CD**." Terms used for the first time are indicated by italic type. For example, "A *modem* is an add-on device that you use to communicate with other computers."

Special tips, notes, and cautions are highlighted by a box.

Icons also are used to call attention to the different kinds of computers. The following icons, for example, are used in this book:

 This icon tells you the information in this area refers to PCs.

 This icon tells you the marked information relates to Macintosh computers.

 This icon tells highlights information particularly important for Windows software users.

 This icon indicates where you can find Amiga information.

Introduction

Computers are everywhere. In the office, the grocery store, the library, wherever you look, computers are making life easier for others.

In the office, personal computers automate dull and repetitive tasks, such as filing, scheduling, and creating form letters. Also, personal computers can reduce errors by performing calculations, searching for and finding needed items of information, and reminding you of appointments.

At home, personal computers are becoming more personal. Today, finding family members competing for computer time is not unusual. Because schools now use personal computers, kids are not intimidated by the changing technology of the personal computer. Adults who become proficient with computers at work also carry over the benefits into the home as well. After you learn how to compose correspondence on a computer, writing longhand becomes difficult. Checkbooks seem much easier to balance when the computer does the balancing. Planning a budget seems less painful when the budget is displayed on-screen.

Computer programs are created to fulfill all kinds of needs. Are you creating a list of potential clients? Do you need to send follow-up form letters to clients you previously contacted? Do you want to create a graph that shows projected sales? No matter what task you want to accomplish—whether the job involves words, numbers, pictures, or sounds—the chances are good that you can find a computer program to do the trick.

Introduction to Personal Computers, 3rd Edition, can be your guide if you are planning to buy your first computer, if you already have a computer, or if you use computers in work. If one of these categories describes your situation, this book can be a wealth of information about the variety of available computers and software.

If you have no previous computer experience, this book gives you the chance to learn how to master the fascinating capabilities of computers. If you previously worked with computers, and particularly if your first introduction was confusing or frustrating, the organization of *Introduction to Personal Computers*, 3rd Edition, can lead you through the steps you need to take to become comfortable with your new workmate.

Why an Introductory Book about Personal Computers?

Computers can intimidate new users. Although personal computers now are commonplace in offices, homes, and schools, the learning curve for a new user can seem disheartening, even insurmountable. You don't have the time to sit down and learn everything about a computer before you produce a letter. If you haven't purchased a computer, you may be unsure of the system that may best serve your needs. How much training are you going to receive before the boss asks you to produce a printed report? You seem to have a great deal to learn in a short time. Why buy a tool to improve productivity if you must become *less productive* while you learn to use the tool?

Introduction to Personal Computers, 3rd Edition, addresses the most important questions asked by new computer users. For users who recently inherited a computer at work or at home, answers to the following questions are important:

- What does the computer do?

- What programs come with the computer?

- What makes the computer work?

- What do I do with the computer now?

For users investigating which computer to buy, the following questions are important:

- What can a computer do for me?

- What computer equipment do I need?

- How do I set up my system?
- What software do I need?

This book takes you from a basic introduction to the system, inside and out, to a hands-on section that shows you how to set up and perform a few basic operations with the new machine. Several major kinds of personal computers, such as PC, Macintosh, and Amiga, are covered.

Who Should Use This Book?

If you are new to computers, you should use this book. Serving as a nonthreatening introduction to the workings and capabilities of the personal computer—without jargon and computer buzz words—*Introduction to Personal Computers*, 3rd Edition, provides basic information in an easy-to-follow format. Specifically, this book speaks to the following people:

- Office workers who recently inherited a computer system
- Business people responsible for all varieties of tasks that can be computerized
- New computer consumers investigating available options before buying a system
- Home users who want to understand the basic workings of computers
- Students learning about the kinds of available computers
- Users and hobbyists who want to know more about the optional equipment and software available for specific kinds of computers

How Is This Book Organized?

Whether you plan to use a computer to accomplish specific tasks, such as planning a budget, or to perform a variety of tasks, *Introduction to Personal Computers*, 3rd Edition, leads you through a basic course from general ("What is a computer?") to specific ("Which kind of monitor do I need?").

This book is organized in four parts:

Part I: Computer Basics

Part II: Prepurchase Considerations

Part III: A Computer Primer

Part IV: A Software Review

In Part I, "Computer Basics," you find the information you need to know (and probably a little more) about the basic workings of the computer, inside and out. What does a computer do? How does a computer work? What kinds of computers are available? Part I addresses the questions most often asked by new users.

Part II, "Prepurchase Considerations," is important if you are still exploring options before you buy a computer. The chapters in this part are divided according to hardware category (system, monitor, printer, and so on). Each chapter helps you determine the most important features for your computer needs. Checklists help you analyze the most important aspects of the hardware you plan to purchase.

Part III, "A Computer Primer," provides a hands-on introduction to assembling and working with a computer. PC and Macintosh users find information for setting up the system, starting the computer, performing basic disk and file operations, and shutting down the computer. Also in this section, Quick Starts offer you *steps only* versions of getting started with the DOS, Windows, and System 7 basic computer procedures.

The last section of the book, Part IV, "A Software Review," introduces you to the variety of available software. Each major category of software is represented: spreadsheets, word processing, data management, integrated software, desktop publishing, graphics, communication, educational programs, recreational software, and utilities. Besides an explanation of the available kinds of software, Part IV introduces some of the most popular software packages within each category.

If you run into a word or phrase you don't recognize, look in the glossary at the back of the book for the definition. Usually, new terms are defined when introduced within the text. These terms are printed in *italic* type. Where appropriate, chapter references are provided, indicating that you can turn to another part of the book for more information on the referenced topic.

Because this book includes information important for IBM, Amiga, and Macintosh users, special symbols highlight information about each of these computers. These symbols call your attention to the hands-on procedures in Part III and to the general information in the chapters found in Parts I and II. These symbols also are used in Part IV to indicate which software can be used with which kind of computer. The following list shows the symbols, or *icons*, used for each computer:

This icon calls attention to PC-related information and procedures.

 This icon highlights information of particular interest to Windows users and related programs that run on PCs.

 This icon shows where you can find information about the Amiga computer.

 This icon highlights particularly important information or procedures for Macintosh users.

What This Book Covers

Although this book is organized so that you can proceed from a general description of computers to a more specific application-oriented approach, you can read through the book in any order. If you are investigating purchase options, you can begin with Part II. If, however, you inherit a computer at work, you may not want to read Part II at all. Use the icons, tips, and checklists to guide you. This section provides a breakdown of the individual chapters in this book.

Part I: Computer Basics

Chapter 1, "What Is a Computer?," helps you determine your present level of computer knowledge, dispels computer myths you may have, and helps you to understand the history and range of computer differences involved in today's computer industry.

Chapter 2, "What Can a Computer Do for You?," shows the benefits of using a computer for work, home, or school tasks. This chapter serves as an overview of all categories of computer applications: you are bound to find these tasks in this chapter, whether the tasks involve writing, working with numbers, publishing, managing information, or playing Space Invaders.

Chapter 3, "The Computer: A Closer Look," introduces the various kinds of computers available. By first discussing the computer as a whole and then by explaining the various components (disk drives, printer, monitor, and a variety of optional equipment), this chapter explains how the computer (and all the computer's parts) function.

Part II: Prepurchase Considerations

If you plan to purchase a computer (or are thinking about adding to a system you already have), Part II can help you make an educated decision. The chapters in this part cover basic considerations about hardware and software. Specifically, the chapters in Part II include the following areas:

- Purchasing considerations
- Purchasing a computer system
- Purchasing a printer
- Purchasing computer add-ons
- Purchasing software

Chapter 4, "Purchasing Considerations," provides questions specific to your computer needs. These questions help you determine the computer and computer peripherals that best suit your needs.

Chapter 5, "Purchasing a Computer System," builds on Chapter 4 by helping you identify the kind of system you may want to buy. Features of several kinds of personal computer—PC, Amiga, and Macintosh—are examined, and basic monitor information is included.

Chapter 6, "Purchasing a Printer," helps you analyze the print quality you need for your applications and introduces the different kinds of printers available.

Chapter 7, "Purchasing Computer Add-Ons," covers important computer components that don't fit in the stand-alone chapters. Information is included to help you determine the keyboard options you need and whether you also need a mouse, modem, scanner, or other optional equipment.

Chapter 8, "Purchasing Software," explains the major software categories. This chapter also answers software-related questions often asked by new users. (More detailed information about software is given in Part IV.)

Part III: A Computer Primer

Starting the hands-on section of this book are three quick starts designed to get you going quickly with procedures specific to each particular computer. The quick starts in this section of the book cover the following topics:

- Using DOS (PC)
- Using Windows (PC)
- Using System 7 (Mac)

Chapter 9, "Setting Up Your Computer," explains what to do after the computer comes home and still is in boxes. Basic instructions are given so that you can unpack, assemble, and connect the system. Information for the PC and Macintosh is included.

Chapter 10, "Familiarizing Yourself with the Operating System," introduces you to the *language* the computer uses to communicate with you and to accept your commands. This language is the operating system. From a basic explanation of the various operating systems to a discussion of how the operating system affects the way you work with a computer, this chapter provides the basics of how the computer and operating system work together.

Chapter 11, "Using Your Computer," includes all you need to know for the first computer session. From start-up procedures to basic information about preparing disks to store data, running applications software, making backups, and turning off the computer, this chapter gives you hands-on experience with the new system. The chapter concludes with a troubleshooting section to help you.

Part IV: A Software Review

Part IV concludes the book with chapters that provide a basic introduction to each category of software and by providing a library of popular applications software within each category. Each chapter in Part IV is organized in the same way: at the beginning of the chapter, the software category is discussed in general terms. After the general category discussion, several popular examples of software are explored.

Chapter 12, "Spreadsheets," introduces you to several popular spreadsheet application programs.

In Chapter 13, "Word Processing," you learn more about word processing programs and explore some of the available popular programs.

Chapter 14, "Data Management," details how database programs work and presents information about available database programs.

Chapter 15, "Integrated Software," highlights some of the most popular integrated software packages.

In Chapter 16, "Desktop Publishing," covers the desktop publishing market from a basic introduction of page layout to a specialized program-by-program account of popular desktop publishing software.

Chapter 17, "Graphics," introduces simple and powerful paint programs, presentation graphics packages, and the highly specialized and complex world of CAD (computer-aided design) programs. You also learn about the software available for one of the most recent and fastest growing categories of computing: multimedia.

In Chapter 18, "Communications," you learn about the various kinds of available communications software, and you are introduced to the basics of telecommunications.

Chapter 19, "Educational and Recreational Software," presents a brief look at some educational and recreational programs available for PC, Amiga, and Macintosh computers.

Chapter 20, "Utility Programs," introduces software that makes file management, backing up files, recovering accidentally deleted files, and keeping your computer running efficiently a less painful job.

Introduction to Personal Computers, 3rd Edition, concludes with a comprehensive glossary of computer terms for new computer users.

One More Thing...

The first step toward learning anything new—whether you are learning to drive a stick shift or learning to speak French—is to relax and realize that you cannot absorb everything at one reading. Even if you feel that you need to learn everything as quickly as possible, accept the fact that you need to learn, and relearn, as you go.

Computers don't have to be intimidating. This book will help you learn about the inside of the computer and about the kinds of software that you can buy, dispelling some of the mystery! Remember that a computer—any computer—is only as good as the person sitting at the keyboard.

Computer Basics

Part I provides you with basic information about computers—whether you are considering the purchase of a system or are pondering how to use the system you already have.

What Is a Computer?

A *computer*, according to Webster's dictionary, is "a programmable electronic device that can store, retrieve, and process data," a true but extremely basic definition. This chapter takes this definition a little further by introducing you to the computer from several perspectives. If this experience is your first exposure to a computer, you are probably asking some of the following questions:

- What does a computer do?

- How do you use the computer?

- What kinds of tasks can the computer perform?

- How does the computer work?

Although the nuts-and-bolts discussion of how a computer works is reserved for Chapter 3, this chapter examines computers from a conceptual, *how can you use it* perspective. This chapter also helps you identify the knowledge you already have about computers and introduces you to some basic computer terms used throughout this book and throughout the computer industry.

Introducing... Personal Computers

Computers are too widespread to deny their power any longer. Ten years ago, you could run errands to the market, to the library, to the bank, and you were surprised if you saw a personal computer anywhere. In the last decade, computers found their way into the irreplaceable heart of many businesses, keeping client lists, cataloguing inventories, and printing paychecks. Even the quick-change oil service center on the corner can't get by without a 386 PC.

So, whether you are beginning your computer education begrudgingly or are excited to learn about the new and ever-expanding technology, you first must realize that you have a great deal to learn. However, you can start with some basics. You probably know what a computer looks like, even if you don't know how to use one. You've seen the monitor, a quietly humming box beneath (or beside) the monitor, and the typewriter-like keyboard.

These three components, known as the *monitor*, the *system unit*, and the *keyboard*, vary in appearance, but the function is the same from computer to computer.

The following sections introduce you more formally to these elements.

Figure 1.1 shows a typical personal computer. The monitor usually sits atop the system unit. (Although this location isn't mandatory, most systems are set up in this way.) The keyboard, logically enough, is placed in front of the system unit.

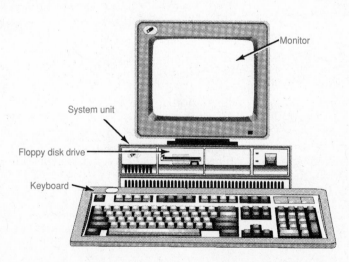

Monitor

System unit

Floppy disk drive

Keyboard

FIG. 1.1

A typical desktop personal computer system.

In Chapter 3, you learn about the functions of each of these computer components. For now, you need only to understand the basic functions of the individual parts. The *monitor* is a vital part of the system that enables you to see what goes on as you work with software. The *system unit* houses the computer's brain (the *microprocessor*), a special computer chip that performs all the "thinking" behind the scenes. In most systems, the system unit contains one or more disk drives, which you use to store and retrieve and to save programs and data. Finally, the *keyboard* provides you with a means of communicating commands to the computer. By typing information and using both the function and the arrow keys, you tell the computer—and more specifically, the computer program that you use—the actions that you want performed.

In the last few years, computers known as tower systems have become increasingly popular. *Tower* systems, such as the hardware shown in figure 1.2, are manufactured so that the system unit sits vertically on the desktop (as opposed to a horizontal system unit beneath the monitor, as shown in fig. 1.1). Many users prefer to place the tower unit on the floor, freeing more desk space and keeping the system unit away from the usual desktop hazards, such as spilled coffee or melted M&Ms.

Yet another design of personal computer is shown in figure 1.3. The early Macintosh was almost one piece: the monitor and system unit were housed in one unit, and the keyboard was connected to the system unit by a cable.

These examples are by no means the only computers available. From small to large, simple to complex, beefed up to bare bones, all kinds of systems are available. In addition to the desktop personal computer systems, you can choose the size you want: portable, laptop, notebook, and even *palmtop* computers are available. (Chapters 3 and 4 explain more about the sizes and kinds of computers available.)

Understanding the Basic Computer Types

Usually, when you are learning a new concept, the easiest way is to start at the most basic level. The preceding section covered three basic components all personal computers have. Now, you explore some of the most obvious differences among the computer groups.

Not all computers are created equal. In fact, very few computers *are* equal. In this book, you find information that relates to three distinctly different kinds of computers:

- IBM personal computers or IBM compatibles (referred to as PCs throughout this book)
- Amiga computers
- Macintosh computers (created by Apple Computer, Inc., but different from the Apple II)

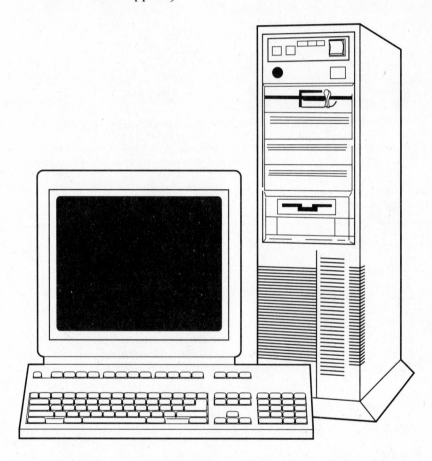

FIG. 1.2

The system unit of a tower computer sits vertically.

Within each of these categories of computers, you find many different models with varying capabilities and prices. With a little research, for example, you can find IBM compatibles that range in cost from a few hundred to several thousand dollars. The capabilities that you get with these price tags extend from working with simple data-entry and editing routines to creating massive multidimensional presentations in *realtime* (live video displayed on the computer screen and stereo sound).

FIG. 1.3

A Macintosh personal computer.

Each of these kinds of computers has a dedicated following. In subsequent sections of this chapter, you learn that the Apple II was the first major personal computer on the market, and many Apple II enthusiasts remain strongly devoted to this machine. The first IBMs, thrilling in particular to hobbyists and programmers, also remain first in the hearts of many people. Today, IBMs are widely considered to be the standard for business computers. The seeming complexity of the IBM and a perceived lack of professional use of the original Apples led to the development of the Macintosh, a machine that combines ease of use with power for professional applications. Currently, Macintosh computers are popular for business, home, and school uses and are particularly helpful for meeting graphics design needs.

Other computers, such as the Commodore 64, 128, and the Amiga, have been around for some time and continue to hold a share of market popularity. Where applicable, this book covers these computers.

The following section takes a brief detour so that you can examine any preconceived ideas you bring to your new computing experience. Take a few moments and mull over the true-or-false questions in the following section.

Testing Your Computer IQ

Before you start adding to your store of computer knowledge, you can find out how much you already know by answering true or false to the following statements. This quiz gives you an idea of your present knowledge about computers or can give you an estimate about how much more information you need to learn. If you run across a term that you don't understand, look at "A Computer Glossary" in this chapter.

1. Any computer can run any program.

   False. Unfortunately, the computer world never is this simple. Throughout this book, you learn how to match a computer with the features you want in a program that you want to use, which is an important step in automating office, home, or school-related tasks. To match hardware and software, make sure that you have the right computer to run the program (you cannot run Macintosh programs, for example, on an IBM computer); that your computer has enough memory to run the software (memory requirements are listed on the side of the software's packaging); and that you have all optional equipment necessary to run the program, such as a mouse or a joystick.

   Part II of this book deals specifically with issues related to finding and purchasing the equipment you may need for specific applications.

2. After you purchase a computer, you have everything you need to get started.

   False, unless you plan to use a computer as an expensive doorstop. A computer is worthless without software, the program (or programs) that makes the computer run. To use a computer, you need a disk operating system that acts as the link between you and the computer—you tell the computer what to do by using the operating system. The operating system you use with a computer depends on the kind of computer you buy. Operating systems are explained in Chapter 3.

   Armed with a disk operating system, you are two-thirds of the way home. You have the hardware and the operating system, but you still cannot perform specific applications, such as writing letters, analyzing data, and storing information, without an applications program. An overview of the basic kinds of applications programs is presented in Chapter 8. Also, in Part IV of this book you find chapters that include software listings of various popular applications programs.

3. All computers are basically the same.

   True and false. Depending on how you look at the subject, all computers perform the same basic function: process information. No computer thinks for itself; a computer is only as good as the person sitting at the keyboard.

The capabilities of individual computers, however, vary widely from machine to machine. Computers at the low end of the scale may be slow and inexpensive and have a limited amount of software available; more popular but expensive machines may process data with lightning speed and have a seemingly unlimited supply of software.

In a following section of this chapter, you review the differences and similarities among the different kinds of computers.

4. The smaller the computer, the less expensive the cost.

   Logical, but false. Because fewer materials are used to construct the smaller machines, you may conclude that savings are passed on to the user. Usually, however, the smaller the parts, the more expensive the technology. Creating the smaller machines costs more money, especially if you are considering the purchase of a laptop or a notebook computer (see Chapter 4).

5. All monitors work with all system units.

   False. As you learn in Chapters 3 and 5, a wide variety of monitors exists for a wide variety of computers. Often, you can purchase the monitor as part of the entire computer system. In some cases, however, you may want to select the monitor separately from the computer. Different kinds of monitors display characters and graphics by using different technologies. Although you can use many available monitors on several different personal computer systems, all monitors *do not* work with all computers.

   After you find the monitor you want for your system, does the software work with the monitor? Chapters 4 and 5 present various points to consider when you shop for hardware and software items.

6. You don't need a computer unless you use the computer in your work.

   False. At one time, this statement was usually true, back in the days when computers weighed a ton or more and required a major monetary endowment to purchase and support. With the advent of personal computers came portability, and the beginning of home computing. Now more than ever, you may need to take the computer from home to the office and back again. Today, computers can make a variety of tasks easier and more entertaining, whether you are at work, home, or school.

7. Computers come already assembled; just plug in the machine and get started.

Doubtful. Unless you purchase a computer that comes all in one piece, such as a laptop or portable computer, chances are, you must perform some assembly when you unpack the system. Usually, the system unit comes in one box, and other components—disk drives (unless the drives are included as part of the system unit); the monitor; the printer; and extra equipment (known as *peripherals*), such as a mouse, joystick, or hand scanner—are packaged separately. Assembling the computer means positioning the components and connecting a few cables.

How did you do? If you missed more than one or two questions, don't worry. After you read this book, you will be able to answer these and other computer quiz questions.

Taking a Brief Look Back

The original electronic computers were immense dinosaurs that required space the size of a small room and the constant attention of a team of engineers. Far from being personal, the large mainframe computers were used primarily in large corporations and required the entry and maintenance of large volumes of data.

In the early 1970s, companies and hobbyists alike began to experiment with assembling a smaller, more personal computer. Early computers were built from electronic bits and pieces only a techie could love—capacitors, chips, and LCDs. Only the electronically gifted could assemble, troubleshoot, and operate the first true personal computers.

In the mid-1970s, the collaborative effort of Steve Jobs and Steve Wozniak led to the introduction of the first *real* personal computer, the Apple I. This first computer was built as a kind of toy that performed only a limited number of tasks. The introduction of the Apple I, however, excited hobbyists and enticed budding computerists; everybody wanted an Apple.

The success of the Apple I led, expectedly, to the Apple II. Almost overnight, the popularity of the machine exploded. A huge empire, Apple Computer, Inc., was established. Apple computers became extremely popular in schools, providing a new curriculum in computer literacy. Teaching and reviewing important concepts for reading and math and basic decision-making skills became an important goal in educational software created for the Apple.

During this success period, other companies developed personal computers. IBM got into the game, as did Atari, Radio Shack, and Commodore. IBM was the first on the market with a major personal computer outside of the Apple realm, the IBM Personal Computer, which became known as the PC. The IBM Personal Computer took a major step toward bringing the power and flexibility of personal computers to the average user; however, because the operating system used by the IBM required users to learn a number of commands, new users found the technology intimidating. At the outset, few programs were developed that made the computer easy for novices to understand and use.

The Macintosh was designed and manufactured by Apple Computer, Inc. Introduced in 1984, the Mac was touted as "the computer for the rest of us." Designed to enable users to work with computer files and programs in graphical terms, the Macintosh introduced a hand-held device known as a *mouse*, which enabled users to move the cursor on-screen by moving the mouse on the desktop. The Macintosh also provided a terrific display, enabling users to select files, commands, and programs with the simple click of a mouse button.

As the popularity of the IBM Personal Computer grew, other companies rushed to manufacture *clone* PCs. A long string of machines similar to the IBMs, called *compatibles*, trickled onto the market. Today, an incredible number of compatibles compete with IBM in the marketplace, drastically outselling the name-brand computers sold for business, home, and school applications. Compatibles bring to users the same power and capabilities that the computers from larger companies offer but at a lower cost. Some popular compatibles include COMPAQ, Epson, Dell, Toshiba, and NEC computers.

Because of the way Apple Computer designed the Apple II and the Macintosh, few Apple-compatible computers exist in the market. The design of these machines is copyrighted, thus protecting the basic engineering of the systems from being copied by competing companies.

Noting Computer Differences

What a computer can do depends on several factors: the kind of computer you want to buy, the amount of money you can spend, and the kind of software you purchase to run on the computer. This section introduces some variables to consider as you learn about computers. Remember that computers differ greatly in many areas, so before you buy a computer, you need to do some homework and learn about the items most important to you. (Part II of this book helps you with prepurchase considerations.)

If you previously purchased a system, use the information in this section to gauge approximately where your computer system fits in the realm of personal computers. Making this evaluation now may help you make further decisions about software and devices you may add to your system in the future.

Speed

Fast, faster, fastest. As you read the computer ads, you see terms, such as *megahertz*, *nanoseconds*, and *wait states*. These terms can be extremely important to experienced computer users, but what do they mean to you?

When you first begin using a computer, you may have doubts that you save any time at all. Speed seems relatively unimportant. As you pour over the new system and accompanying programs, you turn first to one manual and then the other, trying to wade your way through the beginning stages of the learning process. How are you saving time? How does the speed of the system affect your productivity?

At the outset, speed seems to have little or no bearing on how productive you are with the new system. After you begin to process large amounts of data, however, you start to see how the speed of the computer can figure in with your overall efficiency. As you grow more comfortable entering data in a database program, for example, you see how much time the computer saves over the old, manual method of writing out 3-by-5 cards or typing names and addresses on mailing labels. No matter *what* the speed of the computer, the time and effort you save becomes apparent.

When purchasing a new computer, processing speed *is* a major consideration, especially if you have been working with computers for a while and are always in quest of a faster, more powerful machine. The speed of the machine usually is determined by the kind of microprocessor chip used in the system unit. (You learn more about the microprocessor in Chapter 3.) Today's computers can process information more than 20 times faster than the original personal computers.

What does this incredible timesavings mean? The value depends on how you plan to use your computer. If you are a writer, you may see a noticeable difference in the length of time the computer takes to move from one end of the file to the other, save files, open files, delete blocks of text, and run spell-checking routines. If you are an accountant, you may notice that a fast computer takes less time to process changes in formulas, sort information, and open and close files.

A faster machine usually is a more expensive machine. Before you buy a computer, ask to see demonstrations of the various speeds and find out whether you can get by with a slower system. If a slower system meets your needs, you can save a considerable amount of money.

Memory

Another variable that makes one computer different from another is the amount of memory the computer has. (*Memory* is the area in which a computer stores programs and data while you work on these files.) Until recently, memory was memory. Now, if you read computer ads, you see the terms *expanded* and *extended* memory. (These terms are explained in Chapter 5.) The quest for the bigger (more memory) and faster machine continues as users explore more sophisticated applications and expect more speed and power from their computers.

Again, you pay more for a system with more memory than you pay for a system with a small amount of memory. Although you can cut corners on the memory issue, consider carefully how much memory you need in the system now and how much you may need in the future. Consider how much room the programs you want to run may need. The amount of memory in the computer plays an important part in the software you use and therefore, in your productivity.

Perhaps a consideration as important as the amount of memory a computer has is how much room a computer has in reserve for additional memory. For a relatively low cost and with relatively little trouble, you can add memory to your computer, which increases the amount of room for more sophisticated programs and data. Many computers sold today have 2M (2 *megabytes*), 4M, or more memory inside the system unit (don't worry about the technical definition of memory; this topic is discussed in Chapter 3). Depending on the model you buy, computers equipped with 2M to 4M may be expandable (you can add more memory later) up to 64M. For best results, read the ads carefully or talk to the computer dealer about a computer's *expandability* before you buy.

Display Quality

Another major difference among personal computers is the kind and the quality of the display. If you plan to use the computer every day for text-intensive or graphics applications, the quality of the monitor becomes a significant issue. Staring into a glaring screen with badly formed characters and poor resolution isn't conducive to good writing, editing, or designing—or, for that matter, to good vision.

Some computers are offered as a package deal: buy this computer, and you receive this model of monitor. More often, however, you choose the monitor you want with the system (unless the monitor is a physical part of the computer), although you may pay extra to get a higher-quality monitor than the one offered with the computer.

Among the most obvious differences is whether the screen can display color or *monochrome* (the monitor displays text and graphics in only one color, such as with black and white, amber and white, or green and white). Initially, many people equate color monitors, which may be somewhat more expensive than monochrome monitors, with higher quality. The capability of displaying color, however, has little to do with the clarity of characters or graphics on-screen. Some of the highest quality monitors are black and white, but many top-of-the-line monitors are color.

For now, you don't need to understand why this wide range of display quality options exists. A full discussion of the different monitors is given in Chapter 5. Just knowing the range exists can help you choose a system. Remember that the same cost-to-value rule applies here: the newer and more advanced the technology, the higher the price tag. If you haven't purchased a monitor, read Chapter 5, "Purchasing a Computer System."

Printer Quality

Similar to display quality, the quality of the printed output depends on the printer you choose. A wide variety of printers are available and can produce print quality ranging from low-resolution dot-matrix print to high-quality near-typeset text. Because few computer system packages include a printer, you probably will purchase the printer separately.

Remember that several different designs of printers are available; and again, the higher the quality of output, the more expensive the printer. For example, if you need to print only an occasional letter, you can get by with an inexpensive dot-matrix printer for around $100. A dot-matrix printer is a low-cost impact printer that places characters on the page by pushing pins against a printer ribbon onto the paper.

In the last few years, other relatively low-cost printers, such as ink jet and thermal printers, became popular. As more sophisticated software arrived, more and more applications called for the use of color. As a result, many printers now are available with color capability, which means that you can print in colors, not just the traditional black on white.

If you need a sophisticated printer capable of producing output in a variety of fonts that rival typeset text, you need a PostScript laser printer, which retails at around $4,000 (although some PostScript printers now are available at a much lower cost). A laser printer uses a technology similar to the technology found in a copy machine to place characters on the page. A PostScript laser printer also can produce unlimited type styles and sizes. The scope is enormous. Look carefully at your needs (and your checkbook) before you buy. The purchasing considerations in Chapter 6 can help you prepare for the printer purchase.

Computer Costs

As shown in previous sections, cost is a major difference among computer systems. For a basic, low-end computer with a system unit, one or two disk drives, a monitor, and a keyboard, you can pay about $1,000. When you start adding other features, such as a better monitor, a printer, a hard disk, or more memory, the cost of the system dramatically increases. The microprocessor in the machine also affects the speed—and the cost—of a computer.

Another item that affects cost is not the computer's insides, but where you purchase the system. Remember that retail outlets get a percentage of every sale they make; you pay for the store's overhead. From a retail operation, however, you also receive some technical support and service, which you may not get from mail-order businesses. Mail order may be the answer for some situations, but you also take a big chance when you order a system sight-unseen from a computer magazine ad. Both sides have risks and costs. Chapter 5 talks about examining your computer resources before you buy.

A Computer Glossary

This section covers some basic computer terms you see throughout this book and in any computer magazine you open. These terms are by no means exhaustive. For other, more comprehensive definitions, you can consult the glossary in the back of this book.

Application. A specific use for a computer program. For example, you plan to use the computer to write books; that is, for a word processing application. (In some places, you may see the term *application software* used to describe specific kinds of programs.)

Booting. A name for starting the computer.

Board. A shortened name for *circuit board*, a board that plugs into the motherboard inside the system unit.

Cables. The long cords that connect a computer's monitor to the system unit, the system unit to the printer, and the keyboard to the system unit. Inside each cable is a collection of wires through which the electronic signals pass.

Cache memory. Extra segments of memory the computer sees as a specialized segment.

CPU. The microprocessor of the computer.

Compatibles. A term used to refer to computers similar to IBM computers.

Disk. The medium on which you store information. Two basic kinds of disks are available, hard disks and floppy disks. Most *hard disks* are nonremovable disks housed inside the computer. The hard disk stores a large amount of information. (*Removable* and *external* hard disks also are available; for more information, see Chapter 3.) A *floppy disk* (also known as a *diskette*) stores a limited amount of information and is placed inside a disk drive for data storage or retrieval. Disks are thoroughly explained in Chapter 3.

Disk drive. The device used to read and write information on a disk.

Hardware. The actual computer and all physical parts of the system and the system's components.

Installation. The process of placing programs on a computer hard disk.

Keyboard. A device that resembles a typewriter keyboard and enables you to interact with the computer software.

Memory. The amount of available space in which the computer stores programs and data while you are working with them.

Microprocessor. The single chip that handles all data processing done by the computer.

Monitor. The display device of a computer.

Mouse. A hand-held device you use to position the cursor on-screen. Many computer programs do not require the use of a mouse.

Printer. The device that enables you to print information or graphics.

Scanner. A computer add-on that enables you to *digitize* (to turn into electronic form) a printed image or document. You then can store the scanned image or document for use in other projects.

Software. Another name for a computer program.

System unit. The element of the computer system that houses the *brain*, or the major data processing parts, of the computer.

Reviewing a Few Computer Rules

In any circumstance, learning new information is often frustrating. If you are like most people, you need to work with something for a while before you feel comfortable with the subject; don't expect working with computers to be any different. Relax and give yourself time to adjust to, and try not to be intimidated by, the new technology.

As you begin your excursion through this book and into the world of the computer literate, you may want to follow these general guidelines:

- Relax, and master one concept before you move on to the next.

- Initially, you have a great deal to remember. Keep resource materials, such as this book and the instruction manual for the software, nearby for reference when you get stuck.

- Always ask questions. Every computer user started somewhere, and you may be surprised to hear that your coworkers have computer orientation horror stories of their own to tell.

- Take a break every 30 minutes or so to allow your eyes to adjust gradually to the monitor.

- Learn in the way most comfortable for you. If you don't particularly care about how the computer works or what a component is called, you can choose to learn only about the program with which you plan to work. Absorb only the information you need to accomplish the goals you set.

Chapter Summary

In this chapter, you learned a variety of facts and philosophies about your impending introduction to computers. You saw how computers are used, why computers came to be used the way they are, and how computers differ from each other. In the following chapter, you learn how computers are used for a variety of applications.

What Can a Computer Do for You?

Whether you plan to use a computer at work, at home, or at school, you may be surprised to learn how many tasks you can automate, or at least make easier, by using a computer. If you write letters, work with numbers, draw pictures, play music, or scrunch video aliens, you can buy an application program for a computer that enables you to perform these tasks. If you currently use a pencil and paper, a calculator, a filing cabinet, or other manual tools, a computer can help you accomplish the same (or better) work in less time. After you master the learning curve (which is not as steep as you think), you have a world of programs available to help you perform all the tasks you want to accomplish.

A computer is a machine that performs only the actions you specify. To make a computer useful, you must purchase a *program*, (also known as *software* or an *application program*), which performs tasks on the computer. To create a list of clients' names and addresses, for example, you must purchase a program designed to perform this job—you cannot create and maintain the client list on the computer without the proper program.

Reviewing the Benefits of Using a Computer

You know that computer ownership has benefits, or you wouldn't be reading this book. Reviewing these benefits helps you establish why computers became an integral part of business, home, and school environments. In this section, you learn about the major perks of owning or using a computer.

Saving Time

The most obvious benefit of using a computer is the time you save when you computerize your work. At the outset, you may doubt that you actually save time. After you and the computer pass the initial getting-to-know-you stage, however, you find that your work progresses quickly and that your computer proficiency grows by leaps and bounds. Getting over this initial intimidation is half the battle.

When you begin to feel more comfortable with a computer, you can see how this information processor drastically cuts down on repetitive and time-consuming tasks. In short, a computer saves time—no matter what application you use—for the following reasons:

- All information is saved on a disk, where you can retrieve, change, and store the data. No more re-entering information, typing the same information twice, or retyping rough drafts.

- The computer performs a myriad of calculations for you at lightning speed, taking all the calculations off your shoulders and reducing the risk of error.

- You can cut down on the steps involved in a project. Suppose that you are creating a report. You write the rough draft, revise the draft, give the draft to your assistant to type, receive the final copy, mark corrections, and finally give the corrected copy back to your assistant to retype. With a computer and a word processing program, you can type the report, revise the report, and print the final copy, thereby taking the whole task off your assistant's shoulders.

- You can reduce the number of people involved in a project. Suppose that you are responsible for maintaining a manufacturing schedule for three departments. Each week, you send out three schedules, one for each manager. Each manager sends back his or her schedule, with the schedules for the department filled out. You then give the entire bundle to your assistant, who types a finished schedule, which goes through a revision, to the xerox machine, and out to the individual department workers. The entire process may involve six people. With a computer and the right software, you can compile the entire schedule in less than an hour, by first gathering input from the managers (by phone) and entering the information yourself. You then can print the schedule in a format you choose, make copies, and circulate the schedule as usual.

Saving Money

Another important benefit computer users enjoy is the money-saving aspect. Again, after spending $2,000 on the system, you may find that you are now saving money a little hard to believe. If you analyzed how much money you previously spent to accomplish the tasks that the computer now performs, you realize that the cash outlay for a computer is money well spent. For example, consider these possibilities:

■ You can limit the amount of outside costs you bring into a project. Suppose that you are writing a term paper that determines the final grade, and you want to make sure that the paper is in the best possible form, with all words correctly spelled and the format exactly as your professor wanted. Before you had a computer, you wrote the term paper longhand (an arduous task) and turned the paper over to a friend who charged five bucks an hour for the job. Then you found a mountain of typos in the finished work. With a word processing program, you can enter and revise the paper, check the spelling, control the formats, and even print a cover page and add headers and footers. You can produce a terrific-looking paper without laying out any cash (although the content is still your responsibility).

■ You can reduce the amount of material you use. Suppose that as the head of the graphics art department at a small but progressive advertising agency, you are always concerned with the amount of art supplies your staff uses. Paper, markers, paints, tape—these supplies are used and replaced every day. When you started two artists using computers and a powerful graphics program, you were surprised to see a drastic drop in the rate supplies were used. Because the artists create on-screen, as opposed to on the drawing board, waste is reduced. Because the images on-screen are modified easily rather than started from scratch time after time, the money saved in terms of hours and supplies is dramatic.

■ You can lighten workloads by reducing the number of people you pay to do a specific task, which in turn frees employees to do other, less-repetitive tasks. So, in essence, a computer saves you money or increases productivity (which saves you money). Suppose that you decided to computerize the company's personnel department. Previously, three people worked in personnel: one to maintain data records, one to keep track of the filing system, and another to serve as a troubleshooter. Now that you computerized the database system and trained the employees to use the system, you can do away with the filing position. This action reduces the personnel department to two people. Note that, before you start worrying about the computers-replacing-people argument this change frees you to move the extra employee to a new marketing position, a move that, in the long run, benefits both the company and employees.

Reducing Your Workload

Another benefit addressed here (although you also find additional benefits peppered throughout this book) is reducing workload. When combined with the programs you need, computers make life easier by eliminating a great deal of work. Consider, for example, the following aspects:

■ You enter information only once. No more retyping names and addresses on letters, labels, forms, and envelopes: just enter the information once and the computer prints the repetitive information for you.

■ You reduce the time spent performing repetitive tasks. Suppose that each month you update and print an inventory report. You must go to the warehouse, pick up the most recent sales, shipping, and ordering reports, and compile all three sheets into one up-to-date inventory report. With the right program, you can store all this information in a computer so that when you receive the reports, you can make a few changes in the numbers and print the current report.

■ You lighten the workload by telling the computer to do what it does best: compute. If numbers aren't your long suit, you can rely heavily on the computer to perform a myriad of computations for you. All you need to do is choose the program you need to get the results you want, enter the data, and choose the commands to make the program work. Let the computer come up with the answers.

■ You can significantly reduce the margin of error. Spreadsheets perform calculations by tracking equations, functions, and formulas; some word processors check spelling and grammar. Also, because you enter the data only one time, after you enter the data correctly, the information always remains available. You don't have to risk a misspelling or transposed numbers; the computer stores this corrected data for you. Suppose that, at the end of each pay period, you use a spreadsheet to calculate payroll. Rather than recalculating tax amounts and net pay for each employee, you enter the number of hours worked and let the spreadsheet handle all the calculations.

The preceding section explains only a few of the major benefits you discover as you begin working with a computer. The following section covers some specific applications in which you use a computer.

Increasing Quality

Beyond the previously listed benefits, computers give you the capability of surpassing the quality of work you may otherwise accomplish with older methods. Only a few years ago, producing a typeset-quality newsletter without using outside agencies, such as typesetting services, outside printers, and freelance artists, to produce the desired effect was an impossible task. This section lists a few examples of how computers can increase the quality of your work:

■ Desktop publishing capabilities enable you to produce professional documents. Today's layout programs, which allow you to mix text and graphics, organize text in multiple column formats, add special effects like rotated text and drop-shadow boxes, and print pages that rival typeset-quality text, can cut out many steps and much of the cost of the publishing process.

■ Remember the old overhead transparencies? Although acetate sheets are still around, creating transparencies is easier and the flexibility and creativity built into most presentation graphics programs can make presentations sparkle. Similar to the evolution of publishing software, the changes in presentation graphics software give you the option of using previously impossible special effects in presentations: you can animate the way one screen fades into the next, use wild and wonderful fonts, include artsy bullets—the list goes on and on.

■ Multimedia merges the best of the best, mixing the highest quality sound, graphics, text, and video available to create stunning presentations, learning tools, or interactive media. Years ago, a multimedia presentation may have included a projector, a narrator, charts, and text handouts. Today, on the computer screen, you can produce the same presentation in dazzling color with full-action video. Unlike the limited audience participation in the now outdated form of presentation, with many multimedia productions the participant also can use the technology to return to points of interest (or confusion) and, with help from either a narrator or context-sensitive help, go over the material as often as necessary.

Exploring Computer Uses

This section presents an overview of various ways in which you use computers, whether at home, in business, or at school. These examples are not, with one or two exceptions, brand-specific; a specific brand of computer isn't recommended over another brand for a particular application. Although certain kinds of software are explained, one particular software package may not be the ultimate package for a described use. Where possible, pictures of the screens are provided to illustrate the kind of program discussed.

Writing Letters

Writing is a common part of everyday life. Whether you write using crayons, a typewriter, a ballpoint pen, or a word processor, the writing process takes time and effort. With a computer and a word processing program, writing takes less effort than the effort you may take when using any other methods.

A *word processor* is, as you might expect, a program that processes words. A word processor enables you to type, edit, format, correct, and print documents. Word processing has many advantages over more traditional methods of writing:

- Reusable text
- Easy corrections
- Simplified formatting
- Use of different type styles
- Spelling checker

When you write a letter on a typewriter, you compose the words in your head and then type the letter on the page. This information is placed permanently on the paper. What happens if you want to send a similar letter to a friend in New Jersey and you want to use two paragraphs from a letter that you previously typed? You have to type the two paragraphs again.

If you compose the letter by using a word processing program, you can make an electronic copy of the paragraphs you want to use and insert the information in the New Jersey letter at the appropriate point.

Because the words you type are saved in a file, you can use these words over and over. If you create form letters for your business, you can type a letter once and print the letter any number of times. You also can use the text with a program that tracks names and addresses, and you then can tell the computer to insert the names and addresses at the top of each letter, a process known as *mail merging*.

Another major benefit of word processing is the ease with which you can edit what you type. Few people are perfect typists. Word processing takes some of the sting out of mistakes—no more globs of correction fluid on business correspondence, no more red-penned corrections that show rerouting of text or glaring punctuation errors. With word processing, you write, reread, correct, and print the letter. With most word processing programs, the letter you see on-screen closely resembles the printed letter (see fig. 2.1). If you find errors on-screen, simply make the corrections before you print the letter.

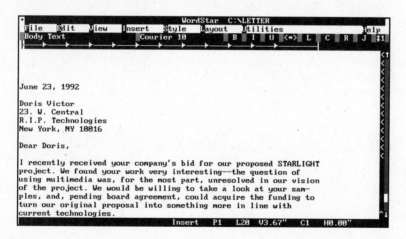

FIG. 2.1

A letter composed with a word processing program.

When you use a typewriter, the formatting aspect of letter writing is tricky. How many tabs over was the indented list? If you make a mistake, the page is messed up. You must rip out the page and start over. With word processing, you can tell the program to control many formatting features. By setting margins and indents and specifying where (and whether) you want headers and footers, you can produce a professional-looking document without the headaches and the hit-or-miss approach that using a typewriter mandates.

Many word processing programs also enable you to choose different type styles, such as boldface or italic, for the text. For some users, this option is imperative. Of course, a few typewriters also offer this option. You change a type ball to change the look and feel of the correspondence. Word processing, however, drastically reduces the time and effort involved in selecting and modifying type styles. The capability of changing type styles depends to a large degree on the capabilities of the printer. As word processors (and printers) evolve, more styles of a wider selection and better quality become available. Figure 2.2 shows a report produced with a word processing program. Notice that the headings are printed in a type style different from the body text.

Word processing programs always have been competitive with each other and continue to grow more competitive. Each year brings new and improved word processing programs that offer increasingly more powerful and flexible features. Some word processing programs can lay out the text in a variety of column formats; some word processors can import art directly into the text file; and most programs offer additional features, such as a spelling checker and an electronic thesaurus.

If you are a graduate of the phonetic school of spelling, your writing can benefit from the expert eyes of a spelling checker. A spelling checker goes through a word processing file, checking each word against an internal dictionary. When the spelling checker doesn't recognize a word or finds a misspelled word, the spelling checker alerts you and offers alternate spellings. A thesaurus also works from an internal dictionary but this feature offers synonyms for words you specify.

Maintaining Financial Records

No matter where you look, finances are an inescapable part of life. At school, you have book and tuition expenses to handle; in business, you have a mountain of financial numbers to work through; and at home, you have the household budget, taxes, and a variety of "what-if-we-buy-this-item" topics to consider.

A spreadsheet program replaces the trusty, well-worn calculator or adding machine. Like an accountant's pad, a spreadsheet program organizes data in columns and rows. Spreadsheet programs can automate calculations, which reduces the error margin and can enable you to play with theoretical financial situations.

From Agriculture to Industry:
The Social Effects of Industrialism

With the move from agricultural to industrial life, changes began rippling through society that would change the professional and personal lives of people forever. People flocked to the cities, hoping to find work in the blossoming number of mills and factories. Improvements in communications and transportation made it easier for people to move around in the world; people were no longer limited to their respective small rural towns or irreversibly separated by vast expanses of land. Improved machinery in factories promised to make life easier for the working class, and new discoveries in medicine, agriculture, and political diplomacy led to a population boom unprecedented in history.

Inhumane Humanity

These all sound like positive changes for a continent shedding the skin of old world civilization and moving into modern times. Without a doubt, the Industrial Revolution brought significant changes that changed the course of history and affected the way we live and work today. However, many of the benefits of the Industrial Revolution also brought about less-than-beneficial societal results.

With the increase in population and the exodus of people from the country to the city, housing became a problem. Small towns exploded into noisy, overpopulated cities; villages expanded to overcrowded, hazardous health traps, where the dark side of humanity was too often bred. The overpopulation and the lack of even passable housing resulted in slums spreading across major cities. These slums, inhabited by the poor, were seen to be the breeding ground of criminals.

Why did they live in such poverty? Because many of the jobs sought by the incoming workers required little or no skill and because there were so many workers available, the middle class owners were able to pay a bare minimum for their services—not even enough for a family to survive. Their

FIG. 2.2

Using different type styles in a word processed report.

Suppose that you are balancing a checkbook with the checkbook, bank statements, canceled checks, pencil, and calculator. You look over the statement, make sure that all the checks are cleared, and then total the balance.

If you use a spreadsheet program to balance a checkbook (checkbook-balancing programs also are written specifically to perform this task), you enter the check amounts, and the program figures the current balance, the average balance, and other data analyses with the push of a few buttons. Figure 2.3 shows an example of a worksheet created with a popular spreadsheet program.

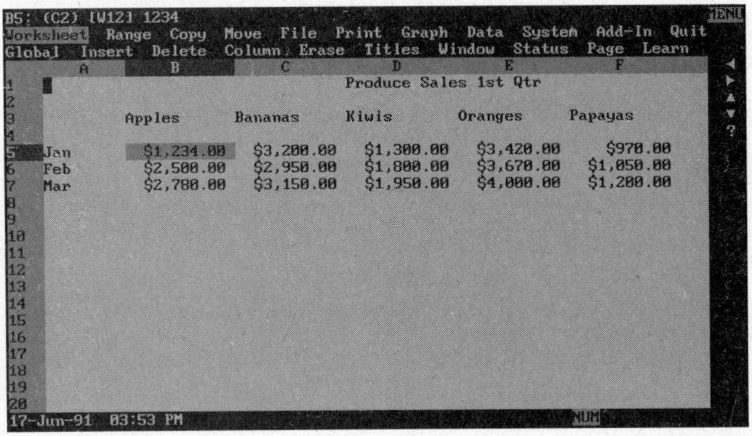

FIG. 2.3

A sample screen from a spreadsheet program.

Spreadsheet programs can be as complicated or as simple as you like. A wide range of features are available in spreadsheet programs, including the following features:

- *Reusable data.* Again, similar to word processors, data can be reused. With a spreadsheet program, you create a balance sheet only once and reuse the sheet each month by plugging in new data. The program performs the calculations for you. You also can copy sections of spreadsheet files, copy and move data, and perform a variety of other operations on the data you enter only once.

- *Automatic recalculation.* The spreadsheet program recalculates the equations each time you make a change. With a conventional accountant's pad and pencil, you must calculate the new totals manually to show how the values change when you modify a number or equation.

- *What if.* The flexibility of the spreadsheet enables you to play with numbers and work out possible scenarios. Suppose that you are trying to decide whether you can afford a new car. You can plug the payment amount, interest rate, and down payment into a monthly budget spreadsheet and determine whether you can afford another monthly commitment. With a few simple keystrokes, you can try different interest rates and see how the changes affect the monthly cash flow.

- *Automatic data entry.* The program can enter numbers for you by copying existing values or by increasing or decreasing the increment by a specified value. With the manual accounting method, you need to write repetitive or incremental values over and over by hand.

■ *Easy formatting.* By selecting a few simple commands, you can control the way numbers are displayed (in dollar format, with a certain number of decimal places, or with negative numbers in parentheses). If you are working with pad and pencil, you write all the numbers in the correct format—longhand.

Some spreadsheet programs include a feature that enables you to create a graph of the information in the worksheet (see fig. 2.4). These graphs are a great asset when you need to show your financial status in a visual format.

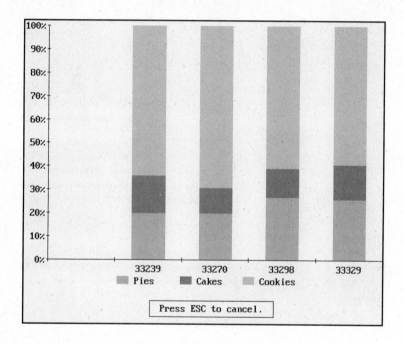

FIG. 2.4

A graph produced from a spreadsheet.

Organizing Information

Everyone needs a method of organizing data. Whether you track Little League batting statistics for the New Ulm Patriots or need to enter and maintain an elaborate system of information for a company with 1,200 employees, you need a way to organize the information you gather.

Traditionally for small organizing jobs, such as batting records, a set of 3-by-5 index cards does the trick. You write the player's name at the top of the card and then, at each game, write the date of the game and the batting statistics. In another column on the card, you can keep a running total of the batting average from week to week (see fig. 2.5). A pen, some cards, and a box to store the cards, and you are set.

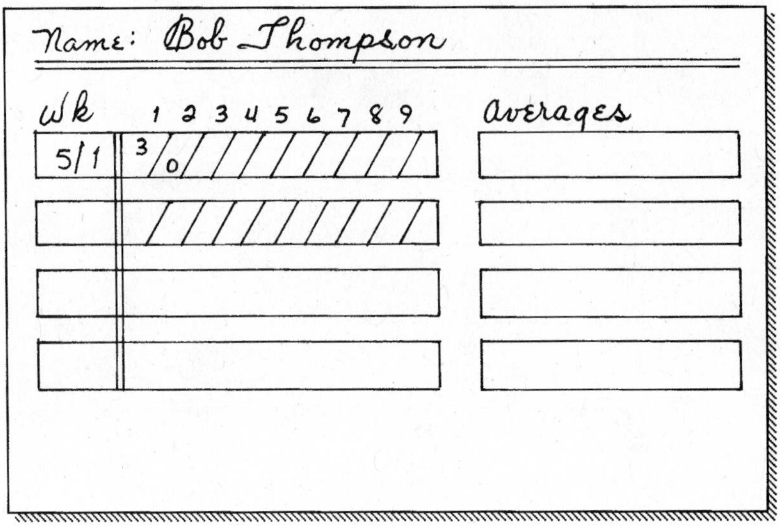

FIG. 2.5

An elementary
filing system.

For larger tasks, such as keeping personnel records for 1,200 employees, you need a far different set of tools. You need filing cabinets, file folders, and a dedication to keeping the data system organized correctly, with each paper in place. Most important, you better have an unflagging love of filing, because records for 1,200 employees confines you to running on a constant track back and forth between file cabinets.

Computers drastically reduced the work involved in setting up and maintaining all kinds of data systems, small or large. By using *database* programs (programs that enable you to enter, organize, and update information), computer users can enter the data to store and have the computer perform a variety of operations with the data.

As with any program, the features available with database programs vary greatly. You can purchase a simple program that does no more than accept names, addresses, and phone numbers, which enables you to create client mailing lists, telephone lists, and track changes in a client base (see fig. 2.6). Many, if not most database programs, however, enable you to sort the information in a variety of ways, search for specific data, use calculations in the database, and even program the database. If all these actions sound a little complicated, don't worry; just remember that the basic function of a database is to store and organize data in a manner that allows you to easily access needed information.

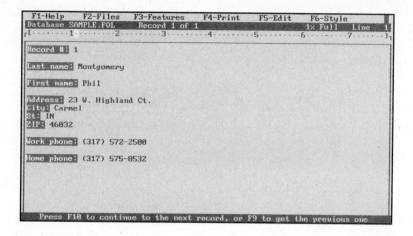

FIG. 2.6

A simple data-
base program.

Some benefits available with database programs include the following:

■ *Reusable data.* The benefit of reusable data cannot be underrated, no matter what application you use. Because you enter the information only once, you need not retype names and address, W2 forms, mailing labels, or each employee's name and address at the top of each form letter. A database program enables you to insert this data at the appropriate point in a word processing document, freeing you from retyping the same information over and over.

■ *Finding information easily.* The computerized database eases searches for specific items. Suppose that you need to change the withholding status of employee Jill Redmond. With a manual system, you go to the filing cabinet, look under R, and cross your fingers that the file is under R and not J. With a computerized database system, you type **Redmond** and the computer finds the information. Taking this example a step further, you also can tell the database program to find more than one record that meets the criteria you specify. Suppose that county taxes in Hamilton County were increased and that you need to search for the personnel records of all employees who live in this county and to show this increase on the payroll records. With a manual system, this update is quite a job. With a computerized database system, however, you tell the program to search for, find, and display the records of all employees living in Hamilton County (see fig. 2.7).

■ *Sorting capabilities.* Similar to the feature for finding and displaying information on-screen, a database program has a sorting capability. With a database program, you can sort items in a variety of ways: in alphabetical order (ascending or descending order), in numeric order (ascending or descending), by ZIP Code, by product, by county, and so on. You may want to sort data by the kind of information you are organizing, but the sorting capabilities of a database program are fundamental to the effectiveness of the system you set up.

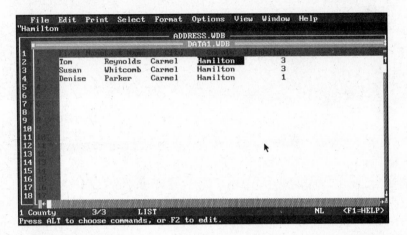

FIG. 2.7

Information displayed by county in a different database program.

- *Reporting capabilities.* All database programs have a way to get the data out of the computer. After all, what good is a method of storing data if you cannot print the results? The capability of printing the data you store, or *reporting capability*, is an integral part of working with the data you collect. To print mailing labels, for example, you tell the database program to do the printing. To insert employee names and addresses at the top of each form letter, for example, the reporting, or *printing*, feature of the program can print the information. To print a report that includes all employees in Hamilton County, the amount of county tax these employees previously paid, and the amount now paid, you use only a few keystrokes. Printing a report by using conventional filing and reporting methods literally takes hours to assemble and type.

Some truly sophisticated database programs also include a programming aspect that enables you to program the way data is entered, accepted, and accessed. These programmable databases are more complicated than need be discussed here. For now, just remember that you can find a database program—for that matter, any program—that does precisely what you want, whether your needs are simple or complex.

Generating Business Forms

Any business manager will tell you that the world is forever in search of the perfect form. Payroll forms, requisition forms, invoices, order forms, customer information forms, timesheets, inventory sheets—the list goes on forever. If your business or your job is form-laden, you may want to consider buying a program specifically designed to help you automate form-generation tasks.

In the past, if you needed to add another form to your business, you had two options: try, to the best of your ability, to design a form that included all the important elements in the correct order or attempt to cram all the information into someone else's form. If you designed the form, you had the added headache of trying to make the form look professional: with straight lines, the company logo, and well-ordered items. Before the advent of form-generation software, this task was difficult.

Today's form-generating programs mix talents from several other software departments. You may find logos or standard art similar to art found in graphics programs, text as in a word processor, and database functions, such as automatic data entry, sorting, and indexing.

Many high-end form generation programs include a library of form types that you can use *as is* or modify to create custom forms. You can find the following benefits in forms programs:

- A library of sample forms
- Easy data entry
- Support for graphics files in all major formats
- Flexibility for modifying forms
- Support for variable font sizes
- Automatic calculation within fields
- Indexing capabilities
- Sorting capabilities

If only one or two forms are at the center of your paper-pushing tasks, a form-generation program may be an unnecessary addition to your software library. As your business grows or your duties change, however, you may want to remember that this software exists, in case forms become a more important part of your business.

Publishing Materials

A major arena of computer activity involves publishing. Unforeseen on the horizon a decade ago, desktop publishing is a new force in the publishing world. The phrase *desktop publishing* refers to the capability of creating, from start to finish and on the desktop, a document that looks professionally typeset. The personal computer, along with desktop publishing software, makes this capability both possible and relatively simple.

Consider conventional publishing methods. How you publish material can range from ultra simple to extremely complex. Perhaps you create a simple church newsletter. Maybe you write the news items out by hand, type the stories on master sheets for the mimeograph machine, trace over (or draw) some, and run the master sheet through the machine. This method, now outdated, is still used (see fig. 2.8).

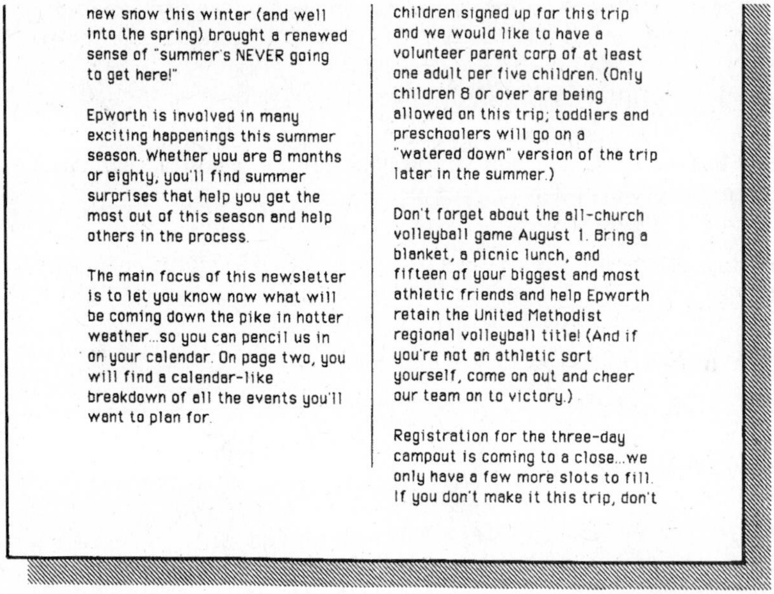

FIG. 2.8

A sample document produced by hand.

new snow this winter (and well into the spring) brought a renewed sense of "summer's NEVER going to get here!"

Epworth is involved in many exciting happenings this summer season. Whether you are 8 months or eighty, you'll find summer surprises that help you get the most out of this season and help others in the process.

The main focus of this newsletter is to let you know now what will be coming down the pike in hotter weather...so you can pencil us in on your calendar. On page two, you will find a calendar-like breakdown of all the events you'll want to plan for.

children signed up for this trip and we would like to have a volunteer parent corp of at least one adult per five children. (Only children 8 or over are being allowed on this trip; toddlers and preschoolers will go on a "watered down" version of the trip later in the summer.)

Don't forget about the all-church volleyball game August 1. Bring a blanket, a picnic lunch, and fifteen of your biggest and most athletic friends and help Epworth retain the United Methodist regional volleyball title! (And if you're not an athletic sort yourself, come on out and cheer our team on to victory.)

Registration for the three-day campout is coming to a close...we only have a few more slots to fill. If you don't make it this trip, don't

If you are involved in a more professional publishing process, you use different methods. Perhaps you are responsible for publishing the quarterly reports for a major corporation. The job involves gathering the copy, roughing out the art, hiring an artist to create the art (or supervising the artwork in-house), sending the text to a typesetter, and checking the work from the typesetter. At every step, make sure that reports are assembled properly and prepared as quickly as possible. Generally, you count on the hard work of a number of people; you also are at the mercy of these workers.

Desktop publishing takes the place of as many steps as you need in this process. You control the entire process, from writing, to designing, to printing. All desktop publishing programs can import art created in graphics programs (computerized drawing programs), and some desktop publishing programs even include a library of ready-made art (or *clip art*) that you can use in publications. (Figure 2.9 shows one of the clip art files available with an inexpensive but powerful desktop publishing program, PFS: First Publisher.)

FIG. 2.9

A sample of the clip art packaged with PFS: First Publisher.

With the correct hardware and software, you can produce publications that rival documents created with sophisticated publishing methods, at a fraction of the time and cost. You just display a predesigned template and start working (see fig. 2.10).

The power of desktop publishing programs ranges from simple to complicated. Desktop publishing basically brings to the desktop the following undeniable benefits:

■ *Controlling the project*. Each person you add to a project, each step you add, such as sending material to a typesetter, a proofreader, and an indexer, expands the length of time taken to complete the project. Desktop publishing enables you to reduce the number of steps in publishing the document. Depending on how involved you get, you can use desktop publishing to do the entire job in one basic step. You can publish a brochure from conception to printing in one day, and less if you do everything. If you rely on outside help to publish a brochure and follow the conventional publishing methods, the project can take up to several weeks.

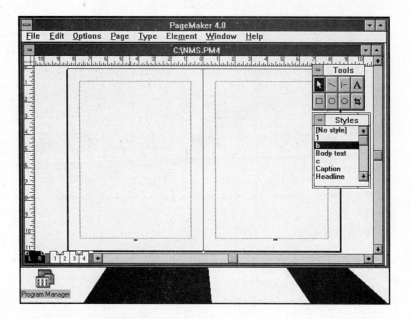

FIG. 2.10

A sample screen of a popular desktop publishing program.

■ *Designing and implementing a personal format.* With desktop publishing, you have full artistic control. Do you want 14 columns on a page? The text may be a bit difficult to read, but if you're the boss and the controller of your publishing destiny, you can produce printed material in any format. This capacity provides a wonderful freedom, particularly if, in the past, you left the design in the hands of people with less vision. With the capability of designing a personal format, you can make the publication truly your creation.

■ *Lowering publishing costs.* Although the initial cash outlay for a good desktop publishing system isn't small, the savings compared to conventional methods are astronomical. Depending on the computer and program, the costs vary. If you publish simple newsletters, purchase an easy-to-use desktop publishing program for around $100. If you need more sophisticated publishing capability and you are responsible for producing a professional-quality document as part of work or business, you want a higher-end program and a computer system that gives you power and speed. Even with the fastest, most powerful system and the most expensive desktop publishing software, the savings over conventional methods are significant.

■ *Making revisions easily.* Because the files you create and publish are stored on a disk, changing the content, layout, style, and placement of the items on the page becomes effortless.

Suppose that you don't like where a header is positioned on the page. With conventional methods, you must tell the typesetter or the paste-up person where to move the header. Depending on whether the paste-up person is in- or out-of-house, this method can require sending page proofs back and forth or at least demand a phone call. With desktop publishing, simply open the file and move the header.

■ *Achieving fast turnaround rate on published materials.* A well-known reality in publishing is that, although a project is your priority, the project may not be another employee's priority. "We will get to your project as soon as we can," is a standard, and not unfair, answer. What happens when you stay up until 3 a.m. to complete a project on time only to have the project sit at the typesetter for two weeks? If you use desktop publishing to complete the project, you may finish everything before sunup.

■ *Reusing data.* Reusable data also is an issue in desktop publishing. Because publications are stored on a disk, you can access and use bits and pieces of previous publications. Suppose that you are preparing four different reports for area hospitals. One section in the middle of the report is unique to each hospital, but another section at the beginning of the report is the same for all reports. You can use the section you created in each of the other reports without retyping or laying out the section again. You just copy the section from one file to another.

Creating Presentation Materials

Programs are now available to help you evaluate and create presentations that hit the mark. Are you working on a financial analysis that may make or break a position on the Board of Directors? With the right program, a computer can produce impressive materials that clearly communicate a point.

An effective presentation is a persuasive tool. Armed with self-confidence, an enthusiasm for the topic, and great visual aids, you can sway a group of your most dedicated detractors. (Like the person who sold the Edsel idea to the car industry. He must have put on one heck of a good show.)

Presentation materials offer yet another outlet for computer talent. In place of press-on letters and art on acetate sheets, you can now create, display, and print a variety of presentation materials that look inviting, professional, and convey the message in the clearest possible terms. Figure 2.11 shows a transparency created with a popular presentation manager program.

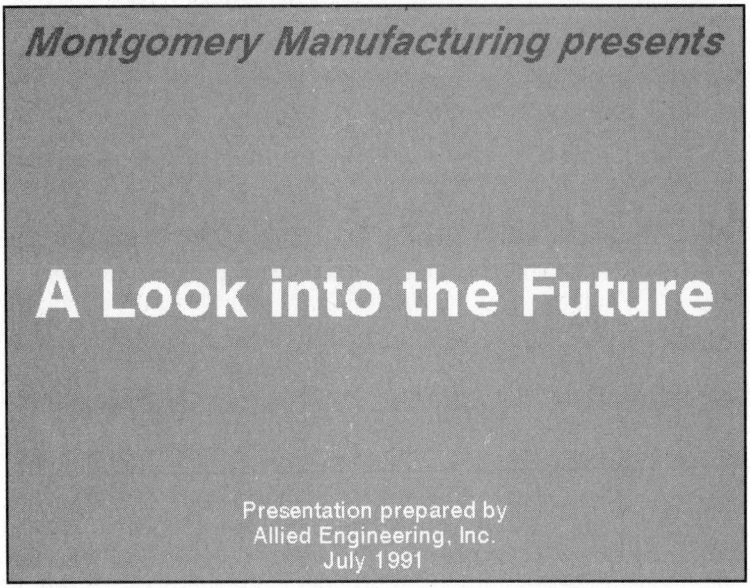

Montgomery Manufacturing presents

A Look into the Future

Presentation prepared by
Allied Engineering, Inc.
July 1991

FIG. 2.11

A transparency
created for a
presentation.

Creating Multimedia Presentations

One offshoot of presentation software is the new explosion in the field of multimedia. You now can mix sound, superb video, top-of-the-line graphics, and interactive text and sound bites to capture and hold an audience speechless to the capabilities of the technology (and your creativity). As you may expect, a platform as powerful as multimedia requires a considerable amount of memory and an extremely powerful computer. Multimedia files also take up an enormous amount of disk storage, so high capacity disk drives are necessary.

Creating a multimedia presentation puts you in the seat of director, developing the project and creating the sound, visuals, and special effects that best communicate the message. The most widely used multimedia programs are currently in the Macintosh arena but the manufacturers of Microsoft Windows and other PC supporters are rallying to bring a more representative sample of multimedia to the PC world. Figure 2.12 shows an example of a popular multimedia program for the Macintosh.

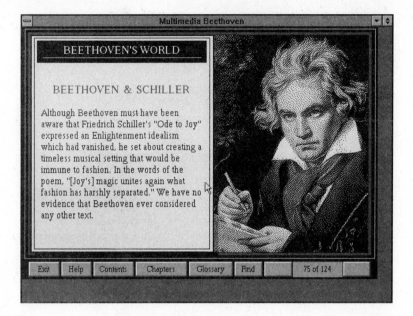

BEETHOVEN'S WORLD

BEETHOVEN & SCHILLER

Although Beethoven must have been aware that Friedrich Schiller's "Ode to Joy" expressed an Enlightenment idealism which had vanished, he set about creating a timeless musical setting that would be immune to fashion. In the words of the poem, "[Joy's] magic unites again what fashion has harshly separated." We have no evidence that Beethoven ever considered any other text.

Exit | Help | Contents | Chapters | Glossary | Find | 75 of 124

FIG. 2.12

A screen from a multimedia program.

Multimedia is still in the realm of the elite, about the same place desktop publishing was positioned on the ladder five years ago. As technology evolves and high-end computers become accessible (that is, more affordable), multimedia eventually will be in the reach of the average business computer user.

Drafting and Graphic Arts

That personal computers found yet another home in drafting, engineering, and graphic arts is no surprise. All these areas require the capability of translating creative visions on paper or on-screen.

Plans typically created with conventional drafting methods require hours of hard work, revisions, and more hard work. No matter the object illustrated, the result must show the object from a variety of angles with the highest possible accuracy. With the advent of personal computers and *CAD (computer-aided design)*, the person responsible for the design can use (in place of conventional drafting tools) the screen as a drafting board and a digitizing tablet, stylus, mouse, keyboard, scanner, and plotter. Rather than redrawing an object from different perspectives, the designer can use a CAD program to rotate the object on-screen, drastically lessening the creation time and reducing the margin for error. Figure 2.13 shows the screen of a popular CAD program.

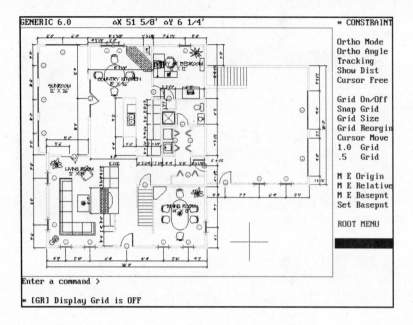

FIG. 2.13

A screen from a CAD program.

With graphics programs, the artist uses the screen as a canvas and selects from a number of tools, colors, and pattern palettes to control how items are drawn on-screen. Like other software categories, graphics programs may be as simple or as complex as you need. From a simple paint program that splashes color on the screen with a few rudimentary tools to a highly sophisticated graphics program that mixes graphics tools and CAD capabilities that give the artist supreme control over the creation, graphics programs with an incredible scope of features are available.

Figure 2.14 shows the screen of a simple paint program, and figure 2.15 shows the screen of a more sophisticated graphics program.

Accessing Information Services

A computer's capabilities do not completely rely on the insides of the system. With the right equipment and communications software, you can connect a computer to other computers across the office, the town, or the world.

Information services, such as CompuServe, are electronic databases run by huge mainframe computers. These databases store a wealth of information about a variety of topics. You connect the computer to the information service through the use of a telephone line and a special device called a modem. (A full explanation of modems is included in Chapter 3.)

By using the modem and communications software, you can hook up to an information service and get information on an incredible range of issues. Some of the following information categories are available from information services:

- World news
- Games and entertainment
- Business management issues
- Computer and technology forums
- Stock information
- Educational and reference exchanges
- Shopping networks
- Home and family information forums
- Financial, banking, and brokerage services
- Reservation scheduling
- Vacation planning
- Health information services
- Aviation forums
- Weather information

A variety of information services is available. Some services are powerful, with a seemingly unlimited storehouse of knowledge. Other services are smaller and may relate, for example, to a specific group of computer users or may answer questions only about an individual software product.

For large information services, you usually pay an initial start-up fee and then you pay an hourly rate for the time you are connected with the service. Smaller services often request a donation or charge a small initial charge for hookup. Chapter 18 explains more about information services and communications and provides a table of some of the currently available communications services.

You also can use a computer, modem, and communications software to connect to another computer in the same office or across town. Suppose, for example, that you want to send a file to the company warehouse manager on the other side of town. You can use the computer and software to send the file to the other computer (and files can be returned in the same fashion).

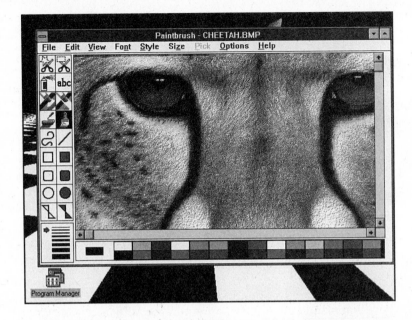

FIG. 2.14

The screen of a simple paint program.

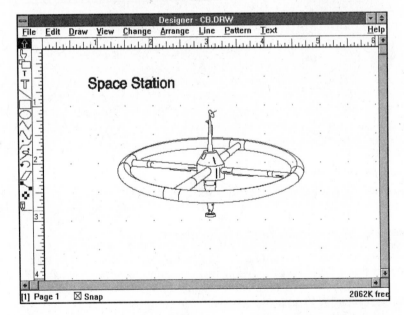

FIG. 2.15

The screen of a sophisticated graphics program.

Writing Music

A computer keyboard may not look much like a musical keyboard, but looks are deceiving. With the right hardware and software, you can write and play music by using a computer system.

Inside every computer is a speaker. The speaker makes the sound you hear when you press the wrong key at the wrong time; the computer *beeps* at you. In most computers, the capability of producing sound is very limited. A beep or a squawk is just about the limit of these computers' musical power. Two computers currently on the market—the Amiga and the Apple IIGS—handle sound far better than the average PC. These computers often are used in music writing and production.

A special kind of connection, a *MIDI* (short for *Musical Instrument Digital Interface*), can connect an electronic musical instrument to the computer. The AudioCard/Joystick option for the IBM PS/1 comes with a MIDI interface cable and music sequencing software. With the proper software, the sounds are turned into electric pulses and stored in the computer as a file. You then can edit, rearrange, and modify the music. Much of the music you hear on the radio and on television is electronically generated or edited; with a computer, the MIDI interface enables you to perform these operations in the office or home.

Music generation is a specialized area of computer use, but consider how you can enhance presentations by adding a specially written melody. If you are at all musically inclined, computerized music is another fascinating facet of a computer's potential.

Teaching with Computers

From the earliest days, personal computers were at home in schools, which is one reason why the Apple II, an ancestor of today's Apple IIe, IIc, and IIGS computers, was so successful. Educators developed an overwhelming enthusiasm for this easy-to-use computer.

All personal computers run educational software. Educational programs are available for every age, all skill levels, on almost any subject imaginable. Color graphics and cartoon characters dress up the look of the programs, and music and voice-generating routines keep interest piqued. Most educational software is designed to avoid a school-like feel. Children find that working with a computer can be fun.

Some educational software teaches basic problem-solving skills. Color, sound, and humor are used to make the child's time with the program enjoyable and productive. Many educational programs use well-known characters (such as Ernie's Big Splash, which uses Ernie and Big Bird from *Sesame Street*) to teach concepts in an environment in which a child feels comfortable.

Educational software also is available for adults. Want to learn how to type? (A useful tool if you plan to use the computer a great deal.) Are you planning a trip to France? A program is available that can help you learn basic French conversation techniques. The chances are good that, no matter what you want to learn, you can find a computer program to help you.

With the advent of CD-ROMs, a technology that enables you to read information from CDs (similar to the CDs you use in an ordinary CD player), the educational software market is bursting with new products. One of the biggest advantages of CD-ROM is the massive amount of data that can be contained on each disc. Entire dictionaries, the Bible, huge collections of geographical data can be contained on one simple slide-in disc.

Want to learn Japanese? Do your kids want to learn—direct from National Geographic—about all mammals known to man? CD-ROM technology brings you an incredible library of information accessible at your fingertips. Interactive educational tutorials combine multimedia with learning, so that students can move through the material at their own pace, reviewing necessary information and following their own inspiration into related topics.

Playing Games

Although computers are showing up everywhere, from the grocery to the bank to the gas station, these machines needn't be the serious, business-oriented tools that are all work and no play. Of course, you paid hundreds, perhaps thousands, of dollars for the computer, and you can raise productivity by using related applications software. Remember, however, that the computer also has a great capacity for fun, whether fun to you means playing electronic poker, shooting aliens, flying a fighter jet, or racking your brain over a tight-fisted game of computerized chess.

Computer games existed from the introduction of the first personal computer. A great source of skill-sharpening, mind-stretching, and just plain diversionary tactics, computer games can, just when you may need relaxation most, give you a needed break. Figure 2.16 shows a popular game, Mah-Jongg, based on the ancient game of Chinese tiles. (Some games are available with a special cloaking device. When you are at the office, playing a favorite chess game and the boss walks past, you press a certain key and a fake spreadsheet is displayed on-screen instead of the chessboard. If the boss looks over your shoulder, she may think you're working hard.)

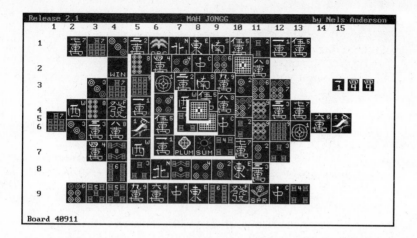

FIG. 2.16

A screen from
Mah-Jongg.

Evolving technology also is finding its way into the game market. Today's interactive games are more entertaining, more challenging, and more creative than ever before. The addition of games on CD-ROM provides you with realistic sound, voices, and an almost unlimited number of options.

Ever heard of virtual reality? No, this technology isn't available on personal computers—yet. Just arriving in mall video arcades, virtual reality games provide the user with *realistic* experiences of tracking dinosaurs, visiting friends, racing cars, and so on. By wearing a helmet and interactive gear, such as computer-sensitive gloves or boots, you react to the action displayed in the helmet by moving your body; the image shown in the headset is modified depending on your reaction. Virtual reality for PCs still is a while off: however, with the technology evolution rate accelerating, virtual reality soon may be a reality.

Chapter Summary

In this chapter you learned what computers can do, from a general discussion of overall advantages of computer use to specific ways in which computers are used. In the following chapter, you learn about computers from the nuts-and-bolts angle, and you explore what makes computers work.

The Computer: A Closer Look

This chapter is a guide to the nuts and bolts of personal computers. What makes the computer work? What are the individual pieces called, and what does each piece do? How do you tell the computer to make the programs work? This chapter takes you through a system tour, introducing you to the basic parts of a personal computer system. After you are familiar with the parts, you learn about the whole for several popular systems: the IBM, Amiga, and Macintosh computers.

In the first part of this chapter, you learn about the following parts of a computer system:

- System unit
- Keyboard
- Disk drives
- Monitor
- Printer
- Modem

Depending on the system you use (or plan to use), you may not have all these pieces. With some systems, such as the Apple II (which isn't covered here), the disk drives are not part of the system unit.

The second half of this chapter highlights the most popular personal computer systems available, including the IBM PC, Amiga, and Macintosh families. From this section, you learn to identify the important computer elements in a computer system.

Understanding Your System's Components

Every personal computer is the sum of many parts. Although some systems are housed in one unit—the monitor, keyboard, and system unit are packaged together (as in a laptop computer)—most computer systems consist of several individual pieces of equipment connected by cables.

Figure 3.1 shows an IBM PS/2 personal computer. As the figure shows, this system includes different components: the monitor, system unit, and keyboard. These components are connected by cables. For comparison, figure 3.2 shows the original Macintosh. Notice that the system unit and monitor are housed in the system unit.

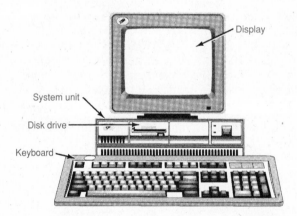

FIG. 3.1

An IBM PS/2 personal computer.

In this section, you learn the role played by each important computer element. Table 3.1 introduces each element and provides a basic idea of its function. Later sections discuss these elements in more detail.

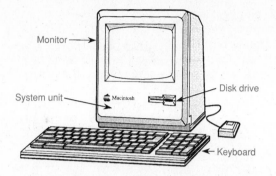

Monitor

System unit

Disk drive

Macintosh

Keyboard

Table 3.1 Personal Computer Components

Component	Function
System unit	Performs all data processing operations; houses power supply
Disk drives	Enables you to load programs and data to and from floppy disks
Hard disk	Special disk that provides a large amount of storage space for programs and data; housed in the system unit or available as an external unit
Monitor	Computer's display screen
Printer	Device used for printing a variety of computer-generated items, such as mailing labels, reports, letters, and so on
Keyboard	Typewriter-like component you use to enter data, issue commands, and generally interact with the computer and software
Mouse	Small hand-held device used for selecting commands, choosing options, indicating cursor placement, and performing a variety of other program-specific tasks
Modem	Communications device you use to send and receive data through phone lines or through a cable connected directly to another computer (depending on the computer, modems may be internal or external)

58

The System Unit

The outside of the system unit looks plain—just a simple box with a disk drive or two and maybe a reset button and a few lights on the front (see fig. 3.3). Inside the system unit, however, lies the magic of the computer. Every time you power up the computer, each time you press a key, all operations you perform with the system are controlled and processed by a single chip, the *microprocessor*, housed inside the system unit.

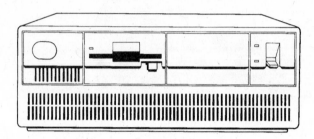

FIG. 3.3

The exterior of the system unit.

No doubt, if you look through computer magazines, you see many system units with shapes different from the one shown in figure 3.3. Some systems stand vertically on the desktop (or the floor) and are known as tower systems. Some systems have wide and thin units that take up more room on the desktop; other units are narrower at the base and taller. Computer developers are generally moving toward a smaller *footprint* (system units that take up less room on the desktop) designs, freeing space for other important things, such as graphics tablets, mouse pads, and other peripheral device needs.

If you pop off the cover of the system unit (not recommended unless you are technically skilled), you see an array of boards and chips—which may mean nothing to you if you aren't technically inclined. The following section lists a few general definitions of terms used in discussions of the system unit:

> *Boards.* Originally called circuit boards, boards are used to house computer chips. Chips are mounted to the board, and the board is plugged into the appropriate slot inside the system unit. The slots are part of the most important board, the *motherboard*, which holds the computer's microprocessor chip.
>
> *Chips.* Technically known as *integrated circuits* (ICs). Although most computer chips look similar, different designs of chips perform different operations: the *microprocessor* (CPU) chip is responsible for all operations performed by the computer; the

memory chips (*RAM* and *ROM*) store programs and data; and other chips, such as a *math coprocessor chip*, enable the computer to perform other operations. One chip can contain tens of thousands of individual electronic circuits.

Power supply. This small box-shaped device in the system unit directs needed electricity to the system and converts AC power from house current to DC power for the computer.

Cooling fan. A small fan housed in the system unit that keeps the boards and chips cool.

Expansion slots. Slots built into the motherboard that enable you to expand the system; you expand the system by adding a printer, a mouse, a modem, or a graphics tablet.

Expansion ports. These plug-in receptors in the back of the system unit enable you to attach other devices, such as a printer, modem, and other external items.

Figure 3.4 shows the inside of the IBM system unit shown in figure 3.3. (If you have an IBM-compatible, Amiga, or Macintosh computer, the inside of the system may look different.) The following sections examine these items in greater detail. Table 3.2 lists the system unit elements and indicates what systems contain what items.

FIG. 3.4

Looking inside the system unit.

Table 3.2 System Unit Elements

Element	Computer
Microprocessor (CPU)	All computers
Motherboard	All computers

continues

Table 3.2 Continued

Element	Computer
Expansion slots	Most IBM and IBM-compatibles, and all currently available Macintoshes
RAM chips	All computers (amount of RAM depends on the system)
ROM chips	All computers (amount of ROM depends on the system)
Power supply	All computers (strength of the power supply varies, depending on system type)
Cooling fan	Most IBM and IBM-compatible systems (some Macintosh computers do not include fans)
Disk drives	At least one internal drive included with all IBM, IBM-compatible, Amiga, and Macintosh computers
Expansion ports	All computers

The Microprocessor

The computer's "brain" is the *microprocessor* (or *CPU*—an acronym for *central processing unit*). The CPU is a small electonic-circuit chip responsible for all the data processing done by a computer.

Figure 3.5 shows a typical CPU. For an idea of the size of the chip, consider that the CPU which runs a computer is no bigger than the size of your thumbnail.

The microprocessor is attached to a computer's *motherboard*, the main circuit board in a computer. Different computers use different microprocessors. Generally, older personal computers, such as the IBM XT and the early Macintosh, have older and slower microprocessors. As the technology evolves, faster and more powerful microprocessors are introduced. Table 3.3 lists the microprocessors in various models of personal computers. (This list of personal computer models is incomplete. These examples were chosen to show only the range of differences.) For more information about microprocessors (CPUs), see Chapter 5.

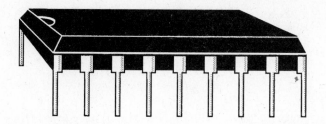

FIG. 3.5

A typical central processing unit (CPU).

Table 3.3 Personal Computer Microprocessors	
Computer Model	**Microprocessor**
IBM PC	8088
IBM PC XT/286	80286
IBM PS/1	80286
IBM PS/2 Model 25	80286
IBM PS/2 Model 80	80386
IBM PS/2 Model 90	80486
Macintosh Classic	68000
Macintosh Classic II	68030
Mac LC II	68030
Mac SE/30	68030
Mac IIsi	68030
Mac IIci	68030
Quadra 700	68040
Quadra 950	68040
PowerBook 100	68000
PowerBook 140	68030/16
PowerBook 170	68030/25
Amiga 2000	68000
Amiga 3000	68030

When the first edition of this book was published, machines with 386 microprocessors were extremely expensive, and machines with the anticipated 486 microprocessor had not yet entered the market. To-day, 386 machines are no longer the top of the line; 486 machines are now the norm. Prices of both 386 and 486 machines have dropped drastically (retail costs on 486 machines have dropped as much as $2,000 for some models). Intel is already looking forward to the introduction of the 586 microprocessor, speculated to arrive sometime before 1993.

Memory

Another important element found inside the system unit is the computer's memory. *Memory* is a term used to describe the chips in the computer where information is stored. Technically, memory is any one of the following categories:

■ *Random-access memory* (RAM). Random-access memory chips store the programs and data you load during the current work session. When you turn off the computer, the information in RAM is lost.

■ *Read-only memory* (ROM). Read-only memory chips contain important information that a computer needs to perform basic functions and run built-in programs, such as the program the computer uses at start-up. This type of memory is permanent and retains the information recorded on the chip when power is turned off.

When you shop for a computer, you may see various machines with various amounts of random-access memory. You also may see a variety of terms used to describe the amount of RAM included with the system. The following list discusses the meaning of the terms used most often:

Term	Example	Definition
Bit	Bit	The smallest measurement of data. Taken from the term *binary digit*, a bit is an electrical representation of either 0 or 1.
Byte	Byte	Roughly one character, equal to eight bits.
Kilobyte	640K	1,024 bytes of information; 640K is read as "640 thousand bytes."
Megabyte	4M	Approximately one million bytes of information; 1M is read as "one megabyte" or "one meg."
Gigabyte	1.6G	Approximately one billion bytes of information; 1G is read as "one gigabyte."

What's the Difference between RAM and Disk Storage Space?

New users are often confused about the difference between RAM (or memory) and hard disk or floppy disk storage space. If RAM stores the programs and the data, what does the hard disk store? If a hard disk offers 20M of space for program and data file storage, why is 640K or 1M of RAM so important?

An analogy best answers these questions. Imagine that you are at the library, doing research for a new educational product currently under development. You find a file of 100 manila folders from which you need to gather the necessary statistics. You also have five sheets of instructions from the boss on how to refer to various research facts. You sit at a library table, open several folders, and lay out only the instruction sheets needed for this part of the research. After all, a library table holds only so much information.

When you finish gathering data from the first set of folders, you put these folders back and pick up the second set. Similarly, when you complete the instructions on the first pages of instructions, you put these pages back and get the remaining pages.

Consider the library table as the RAM in a computer. RAM stores only the instructions and the data you need during a specific portion of a work session. RAM is the work area you use as you work with files in the program.

The 100 manila folders are stored in *disk storage*—whether on a hard disk or floppy disks. In the program, when you ask to see another file or section of a file, the data is retrieved from storage and loaded into RAM. Sometimes, depending on how much RAM space is available, the computer may discard a currently unused file to make room for the incoming file. By keeping in RAM only the files needed for the current work session, you can work much faster than if you retrieved the data from disk storage every time you used the files.

Before you leave the library, of course, you clear the table and return all the folders to the shelves. In the same way, when you finish a work session on a computer, you return all the files to disk storage.

Because a computer stores in RAM the actual program you run and the data with which you work, the amount of RAM in the machine must be large enough to hold the program you want to use. If the computer has 256K of RAM and you want to use a program that requires 640K, you must add enough memory chips for the computer to run the program. Whether you must add memory chips directly to the system or add a memory board (with memory chips plugged in) depends on the system you use. Check with your local computer dealer before you purchase or install additional memory.

Another term you may see is *cache memory*. As computers evolved and microprocessors became increasingly powerful, users wanted to access programs and data in memory faster than before. High-speed memory chips solved the speed problem but introduced another effect: exorbitant cost. To keep costs down and still give users of high-end machines faster access times, developers introduced cache memory.

Cache memory is a special RAM segment available in addition to the basic amount of RAM packaged with the system. This special section runs off of a few high-speed memory chips, but RAM uses the traditional, low-cost memory chips. The result: significantly increased processing speed without a large jump in price.

If you look at IBM or IBM-compatible computers while investigating the different types of systems available, you undoubtedly will see the terms *extended memory* and *expanded memory*. Put simply, *extended memory* is a kind of memory similar to RAM. Introduced with the IBM PC AT, extended memory enables you to set aside an extra amount of RAM space in the form of a *disk cache* (a separate segment of RAM you can use for programs and data in the current work session). *Expanded memory*, on the other hand, uses a different memory-addressing technology to give users more available RAM. To use expanded memory, you must have a program that supports Expanded Memory Specifications (EMS). To find out whether the software supports EMS, consult the program's documentation or contact your dealer.

ROM is the place where a computer stores the programs and data needed to start the computer when you turn on the power. The information in ROM is burned onto the memory chip—this information is permanent and cannot be erased. When you turn on the power, the computer reads the information in ROM to find instructions for loading the operating system or locating a particular file or program. These instructions are often known as the boot program.

Compact discs (or *CDs*) store large amounts of data. Mac, Amiga, and PC computers all have the capability of supporting compact disc, Read-Only Memory (CD-ROM) devices. Typically, you purchase a CD with programs, information, or games already on the disc, which you can access over and over, however, you cannot yet erase and reuse the CD for other data. Similarly, optical storage devices, also known as *WORM* (write-once-read-many times) drives, are used for storing massive amounts of information. For more information about CD-ROMs, refer to Chapter 4.

CD-ROM drives use an optical scanning technology to read data from CDs (similar in appearance to the CDs in a standard audio CD player). CDs can store an incredible amount of data—over 500M (megabytes)— compared to the 1.2M on a floppy disk or 240M on a high-end disk drive. One downside to the CD-ROM technology is that the CDs cannot be erased and rewritten; that is, you cannot save files to the CD in a CD-ROM drive. CDs, however, can provide you with an unlimited number of resources, storing complete dictionaries; reference works, such as *The Family Doctor;* or volumes of inspirational work, such as the Bible.

If writing data to CDs is important to you, you can investigate *WORM* (write-once-read-many) drives or optical erasable drives. The WORM drive is an enclosed platter (similar to a hard disk) that stores up to a gigabyte of information (one thousand megabytes). When you first get the WORM drive, the disk in the drive is blank, and you can save information to the disk as you would a hard disk. However, you cannot erase the information once the data is saved to the drive (although you can update information and assign information to different locations on the drive). Optical erasable disks provide you with the ability to erase the information on the disk and rewrite new data. However, both WORM and optical erasable disks are much more expensive (ranging from approximately $3,000 to $7,000) than having a comparable amount of memory available in hard disk space.

Understanding the distinction between memory and disk or mass storage is important: memory chips inside the computer store the programs and data you use during a current work session, and data storage devices—disk drives, hard disks, tape units, CD-ROMs, and WORM drives—store the programs and data you load into the computer's memory (RAM) when you need to use the information.

Suppose that you start the computer, and you want to use a particular program. You need to get that program into the computer, to load the program into RAM. How do you accomplish this objective?

The way in which you load the program depends on the method of data storage you use. If you use a hard disk, which is actually housed inside the system unit, you usually just type a command or click the mouse button. If you use a disk drive system without a hard disk, you must insert a disk that stores the program in the appropriate disk drive and then type a specific command or click the mouse button (see fig. 3.6).

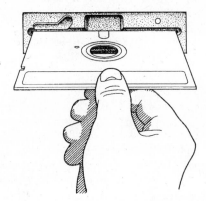

FIG. 3.6

Loading a program into RAM through the floppy disk drive.

After you enter the command (or click the mouse button), you may hear a bit of chunking and whirring as the computer reads the program from the hard disk or the floppy disk. When the computer is finished, the opening screen of the program is displayed. The program is loaded in RAM, and the first part of the program has been executed.

NOTE   Depending on the size and kind of the program you use and the amount of available RAM in the computer, all of the program may not be stored in RAM at any one time. Some software packages swap parts of the program in and out as necessary. With some computers and programs, this swapping is transparent—you may not notice anything except the light on the drive clicking on and off occasionally. With other computers, the system may prompt you to remove one disk and insert another so that the computer can access the necessary information.

Expansion Slots, Power Supply, and Fan

Some categories of computers have expansion slots inside the system unit on the motherboard. These slots provide places to plug in additional boards that run other pieces of the computer system. You may plug in an expansion board when you add a printer, a modem, a mouse, or a graphics tablet.

Also inside the system unit is the power supply (which channels electricity to the computer) and, in some systems, a fan to keep the boards cool.

The Disk Drives

In the front of the system unit, you see the disk drive (or drives) of the computer (see fig. 3.7). Depending on the type of system you use, the drives may look different from the ones shown here.

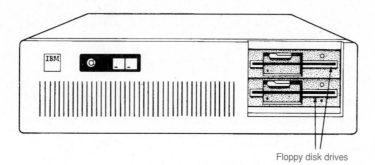

Floppy disk drives

FIG. 3.7

Floppy disk drives.

What is a disk drive? Basically, a disk drive is a device that reads information into and writes information from the computer. You can think of a disk drive as a kind of tape recorder—you push the Record button, and the recorder captures sounds on the tape; you push Play, and the recorder plays back the recorded information. Similarly, a disk drive writes information on a disk and reads information from a disk. The disk drive doesn't store any information; the data is written (recorded) on a disk prepared to receive the data.

The mechanism inside the disk drive that reads and writes data is the head. Floppy disks have two heads; hard disks have two heads for each platter. This read/write head sends and receives electrical impulses to and from the disk, reading both the top and bottom portion of the disk at the same time.

The following definitions help you learn about disks and disk drives:

Floppy disk drive. A device that enables you to store and read programs and data to and from a removable, flexible (floppy) disk that you place in the computer.

Hard disk drive. A device that enables you to store and read programs and data on a nonremovable, inflexible (hard) disk, housed inside the drive unit (see fig. 3.8).

NOTE When first introduced, the term *hard disk* meant exclusively nonremovable and internal. In the last few years, manufacturers introduced both external and removable hard disks. External hard disks—independent of the system unit—are attached to the computer by a cable; removable hard disks are hard disks you slide into a slot in the front of the system unit.

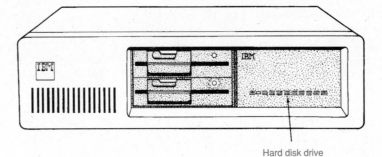

FIG. 3.8

A hard disk drive.

Hard disk drive

In a later section, you learn how floppy disks work. The following two sections discuss the disk drives.

Floppy Disk Drives

Most computers have at least one floppy disk drive. To use this drive, you insert a disk and close the drive door. What happens then depends on your objective. To load a program, type the command necessary to start the program; the computer then reads the program from the disk you inserted in the drive and places a copy of the program in RAM. If you want to save information to the disk, you issue the necessary commands from within the program, and the computer writes the file to the disk. Either way, you know that the computer is reading from or writing to the disk because the access light located on the front of the drive is on (see fig. 3.9).

Floppy disk drives come in two sizes to accommodate 5 1/4-inch disks (known as *minifloppies*) and 3 1/2-inch disks (known as *microfloppies*). Original PCs were equipped with only the 5 1/4-inch disk drives, but early Macintoshes started the trend toward 3 1/2-inch disk drives. As computers evolve, more and more PCs use 3 1/2-inch disk drives.

Some IBM computers and compatibles have *half-height* drives, named as such because the disk drive is only half the height of the disk drive introduced in the first PCs. Half-heights come in 5 1/4-inch versions only, but offer two capacities: 360K and 1.2M.

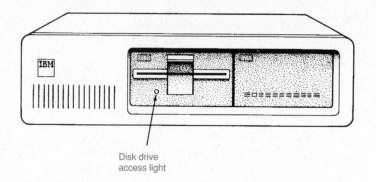

FIG. 3.9

The disk drive
access light.

Disk drive
access light

Another difference in floppy disk drive types depends on where the
drive is placed. Your system, when purchased, probably comes
equipped with at least one disk drive. This drive is housed in the system unit is an *internal* drive. *External* disk drives also are available,
providing the option of adding a floppy disk drive if necessary. Suppose
that your office is automated with a variety of PC computers. Most PCs
have 5 1/4-inch drives but newer models have 3 1/2-inch drives. What
happens when you want to use a 5 1/4-inch disk on a machine with a
3 1/2-inch drive? One option is to purchase a 5 1/4-inch external drive,
which enables you to swap compatible files as necessary from one disk
drive to another. Figure 3.10 shows an example of an external floppy
disk drive. You use the disk drive the same way whether the drive is
internal or external: you insert the floppy disk into the drive and close
the drive door.

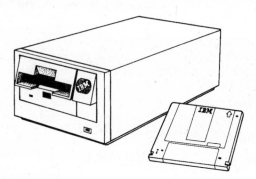

FIG. 3.10

An external
floppy drive.

The following list shows some popular computers and the disk drives
used with these machines:

IBM PC, XT, AT	5 1/4-inch
IBM PS/2	3 1/2-inch

Macintosh	3 1/2-inch
COMPAQ	5 1/4-inch
Amiga	3 1/2-inch

Hard Disk Drives

A hard disk drive stores and retrieves information from a disk in the same way as a floppy disk drive. Both kinds of disks are divided into tracks and sectors. The main difference is that in a hard disk system, the computer stores data on a nonremovable circular disk permanently housed inside the drive, instead of reading and writing information on a removable disk. The entire hard disk unit may be internal (inside the system unit), external (outside the system unit), nonremovable (permanently housed inside the system unit), or removable (capable of being removed from the system unit). Figure 3.11 shows the inside of a hard disk unit.

Hard Disk Facts

1. Most computers today come equipped with a hard disk built into the system unit.

2. Hard disks provide considerably more storage space than micro- or minifloppies.

3. Hard disks provide faster access to programs and data than micro- or minifloppy disks.

4. You can purchase hard disks with capacities from 10M to 300M; although hard disks are available with capacities of up to 1 gigabyte, drives larger than 300M are specialized and therefore expensive.

As technology advances, hard drives are getting physically smaller, yet faster in access time. Some hard drives, such as the drives produced by La Cie for the Macintosh, fit in the palm of the hand and store between 40M and 80M. Today, with the falling prices of hard drives and the possibility of data overload, a standard system having either a hard drive with huge storage capacity (many new systems are sold with 240M drives) or multiple hard drives is not unusual. In the last few years, external and removable hard drives have become increasingly popular.

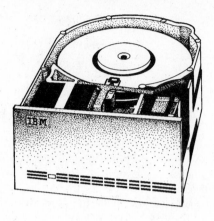

FIG. 3.11

The inside of a
hard disk unit.

A major advantage the hard disk has over the floppy is speed. With
some hard disks, you can retrieve and store information almost 100
times faster than you can using floppy disks, resulting in enormous
timesavings when you work with large volumes of data or many different files. The speed difference exists in part because hard disks are
always spinning, but floppy disks must be started for each new access.
This constant spinning is the reason you should not move the computer when the power is on—any movement can damage a spinning
hard disk.

Because you don't actually *do* anything to the hard disk, in the form of
opening and shutting drive doors, removing a disk, and so on, you may
have difficulty telling when the computer is using the hard disk. No
matter what kind of computer you use, you should see the disk access
light, which indicates when the hard disk is active. You also may hear a
soft churning noise, which tells you that the computer is reading from
or writing to the hard disk.

The Disks

A disk is the medium on which you store the programs and data for the
computer. Similar to the voice on a cassette in a tape recorder, the disk
holds information that you can play back when necessary.

Basically, personal computers use two kinds of floppy disks: minifloppy
disks and microfloppy disks. *Minifloppies* are 5 1/4-inch disks encased
in a flexible jacket; *microfloppies* are 3 1/2-inch disks housed in a hard
plastic casing. Figure 3.12 shows a typical minifloppy disk.

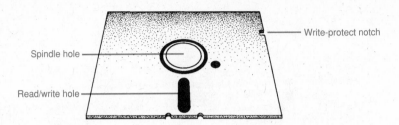

FIG. 3.12

A minifloppy
disk.

The read/write hole is the only place on the minifloppy where the recording heads in the disk drive actually touch the surface of the disk.
This place is sensitive to outside elements. If you touch this exposed
portion of the disk, you risk losing or damaging the data.

On a 3 1/2-inch microfloppy disk, the read/write hole is covered by a
metal piece known as the *shutter* (see fig. 3.13). When you insert a 3 1/2-
inch disk into the disk drive, the shutter slides back and opens the
read/write hole so the computer can read and write on the surface of
the disk. When you remove the disk, the cover slides back into place.
Because of the plastic casing and the shutter, the 3 1/2-inch disk is less
vulnerable to damage than a 5 1/4-inch disk.

Other elements on the disk include the *spindle hole*, which the disk
drive uses to hold and spin the disk (visible only on the back of the
3 1/2-inch microfloppy); the *index hole*, which the disk drive uses to
count revolutions of the spinning disk and to make sure the disk is
spinning properly; and the *write-protect notch*. This notch, as you can
see in figures 3.12 and 3.13, looks different on the two kinds of disks.
On the 5 1/4- inch disk, the notch is in the upper-right corner of the
disk. The notch appears to be "cut out" of the disk. On the 3 1/2-inch
disk, the write-protect notch is a switch you can move to the desired
position.

You write-protect a disk to preserve the data or programs the disk
stores. Suppose that you write an extensive report and save the work
to disk. You want to keep the report for the files, because you plan to
use parts of the report again later in another report. To keep someone
else from inadvertently overwriting the report you stored on the disk,
you can write-protect the disk. This procedure enables you to read
data from the disk but protects the disk from receiving more information. You can remove write-protection at any time.

When you purchase data disks, these disks are not write-protected. If
you use 5 1/4-inch disks, you write-protect the disk by placing a small
sticker-like tab over the write-protect notch. (These tabs are included
in the box of disks.) If you use 3 1/2-inch disks, hold the disk so the
shutter is pointing up and the spindle hole is facing you; then slide the
write-protect switch down. The tab or switch protects the disk so that
data cannot be written to the disk.

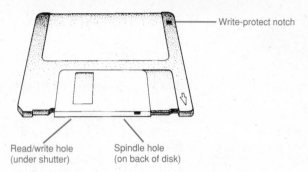

Write-protect notch

Read/write hole
(under shutter)

Spindle hole
(on back of disk)

FIG. 3.13

A microfloppy
disk.

Floppy Disk Facts

1. Two kinds of floppy disks—*microfloppy* and *minifloppy* disks— are available. Minifloppies are 5 1/4-inch disks, and microfloppies are 3 1/2-inch disks.

2. Both micro- and minifloppy disks are removable disks that you place in a disk drive, which reads information from and writes information to the disk.

3. Both microfloppy and minifloppy disks hold a limited amount of information. This size limit is known as the disk's *capacity* and is measured in kilobytes (K) or megabytes (M).

4. Microfloppies (3 1/2-inch) can store 720K or 1.44M of data (depending on the kind of microfloppy you buy). Recently, a new microfloppy disk, the ED (Extra-Density) disk, was announced. This disk can hold 2.88M of data.

5. Minifloppies (5 1/4-inch) can store 360K or 1.2M of data (depending on the kind of 5 1/4-inch disk you buy).

Defining Storage Capacities

Different disks have different storage capacities. (The *capacity* of a disk is the amount of storage space on the disk. A disk with a capacity of 360K can store approximately 360 kilobytes of data.) No visible difference alerts you to the different capacities of disks, so make sure you keep all similar disks together or use a logical labeling system to indicate the capacity of the disks you are using.

Minifloppies are the older of the two disk sizes, offering 360K (or low density) or 1.2M (or high density) capacities.

The term *density* refers to the way the disk stores data. In the same amount of space, high-density disks store more information than low-density disks.

Microfloppies are available in 720K, 1.44M, or 2.88M capacities. Make sure you purchase disks designed to work with your disk drives. A disk drive with a higher capacity can read from and write to a lower capacity disk, but a low-capacity drive cannot read a high-capacity disk. If the system has a 1.44M microfloppy disk drive and you want to read a 720K microfloppy disk in this drive, you have no problem. If you use a 1.44M disk in a 720K drive, however, the computer cannot read the information.

The increase in the amount of data stored by a hard disk is significant when compared to microfloppy and minifloppy drives. Although one microfloppy can store up to 2.88M of data, a hard disk stores anywhere from 10M to more than 160M of information (depending on the capacity of the individual hard disk).

Writing Information to a Disk

As you learned in the preceding section, the disk drive writes information to and reads information from the disk through the read/write hole.

The recording heads read data from and write data to the disk in rings—somewhat (although not exactly) like a phonograph record Each ring, or *track*, is separate and tracks are numbered from the outside of the disk inward. The track on the outer edge of the disk is track 0, and the innermost track (on a 360K floppy disk) is usually track 40. Each track is further divided into *sectors*, which helps the computer identify where information is stored on the disk (see fig. 3.14).

FIG. 3.14

A diagram that shows the division of a disk into tracks and sectors.

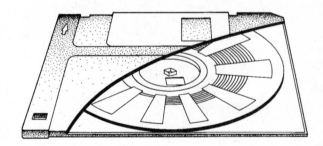

Different computers divide disks into different numbers of sectors, which is why you may have trouble reading disks from one computer in a different (but similar) machine. You may have trouble, using a disk from an IBM PC AT with a Tandy 1000, although the Tandy is IBM-compatible. You overcome the problem by formatting the disk on the same computer in which you plan to use the disk. (*Formatting* is a special procedure that prepares a disk to accept data; see Chapter 12.)

The Keyboard

The keyboard is perhaps the most vital link to a computer. You perform a variety of operations with the keyboard from simple typing tasks to selecting menu options, entering commands, and carrying out a wealth of actions with a few keypresses.

Again, different computers use different keyboards, but basically all keyboards have the same general keys, as indicated in the following list:

- *QWERTY keys*. The alphabetic keys on a computer keyboard similar to the keys on a typewriter keyboard.

- *Arrow keys*. Directional or cursor-movement keys ($\uparrow$, $\downarrow$, $\rightarrow$, $\leftarrow$), which may or may not have a separate keypad. The Home, End, PgUp, and PgDn keys also move the cursor.

- *Numeric keypad*. A keypad of numbers usually located at the far right side of the keyboard. On some keyboards, this keypad can be toggled between numeric and cursor-movement mode. When the keypad functions as a numeric keypad, pressing a key types a number; when the cursor-movement function is toggled on, pressing a key moves the cursor in the direction of the arrow shown on the key (see fig. 3.15).

- *Function keys*. Extra keys on the keyboard labeled F1 through F10 (or through F12, depending on the number of function keys available). Most programs assign specific features to function keys, which are usually located along the top or left side of the keyboard.

Figure 3.16 shows the IBM Enhanced Keyboard. Each key area is clearly defined; each group of keys is positioned in a special area of the keyboard. On other computer keyboards, however, this division may not be the same.

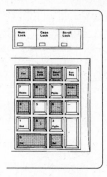

FIG. 3.15

A numeric and cursor-controlled keypad.

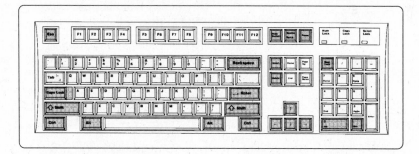

FIG. 3.16

The IBM Enhanced Keyboard.

Not all keyboards have function keys, which are special-purpose keys you can program to carry out specific tasks you perform repeatedly. Suppose that you often underline text in the letters you type. Depending on the software you use, you can assign the underline to a function key so that each time you want to start underlining, you press the key. Function keys also can be used for a variety of other tasks. All IBM and IBM-compatible computers have function keys, although the location and number of function keys vary from machine to machine. The function keys are labeled F1, F2, F3, and so on, and usually are placed across the top or along the left edge of the keyboard. Apple computers (as a rule) lack function keys, although later-model Macintoshes offer full-featured keyboards with function keys. (You purchase these keyboards separately.)

Table 3.4 highlights the important keys on IBM-style keyboards. Table 3.5 explains some of the extras available on Macintosh keyboards.

Table 3.4 Special Keys on IBM-Style Keyboards

Key	Description
Enter or Return	Serves as an action key; press to tell the computer to carry out an action or read and respond to command-line input
Esc	Backs out of a menu or cancels an operation (dependent on software)
Ctrl	Used in combination with other keys to select commands and perform actions
Shift	Raises typed letters to uppercase
Alt	Used in combination with other keys to select commands and perform actions
Tab	In word processing, works similarly to typewriter tab; in other applications, moves cursor forward or backward
Backspace	Moves cursor back one space
Caps Lock	Produces all letters as capitals; affects only the letter keys
PgUp	Scrolls page display up one page
PgDn	Scrolls page display down one page
Home	Dependent on software, may move cursor to the upper-left corner of the screen or, in some programs, to the start of a line
End	Dependent on software, may move cursor to lower-right corner of the screen or, in some programs, to the end of a line
Ins	In most applications, changes computer to insert mode, enabling user to insert information without overtyping existing characters (in some programs, inserts characters from a Clipboard on which data is stored)
Del	Deletes character at cursor position (dependent on software)

Table 3.5 Special Keys on Macintosh Keyboards

Key	Description
Return	Serves as an action key; press to tell the computer to carry out an action
Arrow keys	Similar to keys on the IBM-style keyboards (↑, ↓, →, ←), arrow keys move the cursor on-screen and usually do not have a separate keypad
Clear	Clears the number most recently typed; located on the numeric keypad
Command key	Used in combination with other keys to select commands and perform actions; shows the open-apple (⌘) symbol and the cloverleaf (⌘) symbol.
Enter	Functions the same way as the Return key for most applications; positioned in the lower right corner of the numeric keypad
Option	Used in combination with other keys for selecting commands

Although all keyboards may appear alike, some keyboards may have features you like and other features you dislike. The sensitivity of the keys to the touch is one area of concern for many typists. Do the keys feel *loose*, rattling as they are pressed? Is sufficient firmness built into the keys so that a light keypress produces the desired result? Do you hear a reassuring keyclick each time you press a key?

Other considerations include the basic layout of the keyboard. Does the keyboard have Ctrl keys on both sides of the space bar? (If your programs, such as WordStar, require the use of the Ctrl key, the accessibility of the Ctrl keys may be important to you.) Is the Enter key big enough for you to reach easily as you type? Are the function keys arranged the way you like them?

In recent years, keyboard manufacturers have developed some new ideas about keyboards. Today, a new curving keyboard exists (the center of the keyboard being at the *bottom* of the curve and the ends curving outward, toward your computer). This curved keyboard is supposed to make typing easier because the keyboard shape is based on the shape of the user's hands.

Another kind of keyboard was recently introduced on which a membrane that covers all the keys replaces independent, pressable keys.

(Remember the early Atari computers?) This keyboard is spill-proof and dust-proof, and one manufacturer (Genovation) claims that the keys respond to even the lightest touch.

The Mouse

The mouse scurried into the business world at a speed that surprised many people. First viewed as a device akin to a joystick (used mainly for games), the mouse grew in popularity to become an important part of many applications.

Originally designed to supplement the keyboard, the mouse accomplished tasks not easily done with keys (see fig. 3.17). The mouse is used most often for moving objects on-screen—moving the cursor, moving a graphics object, or dragging a block of text. You move the mouse in the direction you want the object to move, and the object moves correspondingly on-screen.

FIG. 3.17

The Microsoft mouse.

The first mouse was introduced with the Macintosh (which was unusable without a mouse). Gradually, the mouse made inroads into other applications and eventually into the PC environment. Most applications dealing with graphics, layout, or design are enhanced by adding a mouse. You can streamline spreadsheets, word processing, and databases by using a mouse to select menu options and move data on-screen.

All applications designed for the Macintosh are created to use the mouse, but adding a mouse to a member of the Apple II or IBM families is optional. When you buy software for the computer, check to see whether the software requires a mouse.

The mouse has grown in popularity and evolved technologically. Trackballs (a mouse cousin) and cordless mice are new devices you may find useful if you ever wrestle with the tangled tails of various desktop components.

The graphics tablet, another input device, has grown dramatically in use. A graphics tablet enables you to use a stylus (a special kind of special pen) on the electronically sensitive tablet to draw images, graphics, schematics—anything—on-screen. Graphics tablets are most popular in applications that involve art, such as CAD design, graphic arts, desktop publishing, and presentation graphics.

The Monitor

The monitor is a window to the workings inside the computer (see fig. 3.18). Computer users spend a great deal of time looking at the glassy face of the monitor; when you consider purchasing the display for a system, be sure that you get a sharp and comfortable-to-view monitor. (For more information about purchasing considerations, see Chapter 5.)

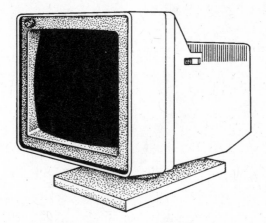

FIG. 3.18

A typical monitor.

A myriad of monitors is available (green screen, amber screen, paper-white, LCD, ELD, analog, digital). The following listing describes the various kinds of screens you can use:

■ *Analog* and *digital*. Terms that describe the way in which the monitor receives video signals from the computer. These terms are explained in greater detail in Chapter 5.

■ *Amber, green,* or *paper-white* screen. Some one-color monitors (monochrome monitors) are available in amber, green, or paper-white (which produces gray tones) as well as in black-and-white.

■ *CGA*, *EGA*, and *VGA*. Acronyms for graphics display cards, placed inside a computer so that when the computer is connected to a compatible monitor (CGA, EGA, VGA, or multisync), the graphics on the monitor are displayed correctly (see Chapter 5 for more information).

■ *ELD* (Electro-Luminescent Display). This kind of screen is available in many popular laptop and portable computers, such as the COMPAQ 386.

■ *Color monitor*. A monitor capable of displaying text and graphics in color. Color monitors range in capability from displaying eight colors to displaying millions, depending on the monitor, card type, and software.

To further complicate monitor selection, you can choose from a variety of monitor sizes and features. Similar to television sets, monitors come in numerous widths and sizes, different signal intensities (resulting in better or poorer on-screen quality), and various shapes. Full-page monitors are taller than ordinary monitors, enabling desktop publishing enthusiasts to display an entire publication page while working on layout. Two-page monitors, which are wider than the average monitor, enable the display of two pages side by side. Figure 3.19 illustrates an example of a two-page monitor. (In Chapter 5, you learn more about monitor features.)

FIG. 3.19

A two-page monitor.

The Printer

Think of a printer as an optional necessity; if you need a printout of data, you need a way to print this information. Many kinds of printers and printer options are available. Figure 3.20 shows a typical low-cost dot-matrix printer. Because printers are explored in Chapter 6 and you need only a surface knowledge of printer technology at this point, only the basic differences in printers are defined in this section.

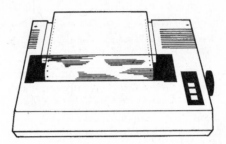

FIG. 3.20

A dot-matrix printer.

You can break down (loosely) the main categories of printers into the following four sections:

- Dot-matrix printers
- Inkjet printers
- Laser printers
- PostScript printers

If you scale the printer categories from 1 to 10 in terms of output quality and cost, dot-matrix is a 1, and PostScript is a 10. On output produced on a dot-matrix printer, the letters are formed by individual pins pressing against a printer ribbon. Some dot-matrix printers offer good quality at a low cost, but you still can see the dots when you look closely. For this reason, if you need high-quality output, choose a printer farther up the scale.

At the top of the scale is the PostScript printer, a machine capable of producing near-typeset-quality copy at a fraction of the cost of typesetting. Besides high quality, however, you get a high price tag. Figure 3.21 shows the difference between output produced on a dot-matrix printer and output produced on a PostScript printer.

The other two printer categories (inkjet and laser printers) are in the middle in terms of quality and cost. Inkjet printers smooth out the dots produced by dot-matrix printers but still lack the quality of a laser printer. A laser printer hits the quality mark but, without PostScript, a laser printer is limited in the number of different fonts you can produce. Again, these printers are explained here in general terms only; Chapter 6 explores printer technologies in more detail.

```
This text was printed on an EPSON FX-286e dot matrix printer.
This text was printed on an EPSON FX-286e dot matrix printer.This
text was printed on an EPSON FX-286e dot matrix printer.This text
was printed on an EPSON FX-286e dot matrix printer.This text was
printed on an EPSON FX-286e dot matrix printer.This text was
printed on an EPSON FX-286e dot matrix printer.This text was
printed on an EPSON FX-286e dot matrix printer.This text was
printed on an EPSON FX-286e dot matrix printer.This text was
printed on an EPSON FX-286e dot matrix printer.This text was
printed on an EPSON FX-286e dot matrix printer.This text was
printed on an EPSON FX-286e dot matrix printer.
```

This is an example of type printed on a QMS PS810+. This is an example of type printed on a QMS PS810+. This is an example of type printed on a QMS PS810+. This is an example of type printed on a QMS PS810+. This is an example of type printed on a QMS PS810+. This is an example of type printed on a QMS PS810+. This is an example of type printed on a QMS PS810+. This is an example of type printed on a QMS PS810+. This is an example of type printed on a QMS PS810+. This is an example of type printed on a QMS PS810+. This is an example of type printed on a QMS PS810+.

FIG. 3.21

Output produced on a dot-matrix printer and a PostScript printer.

The Modem

A modem is another optional piece of equipment you may not need at first. The word *modem*, short for *mod*ulator/*dem*odulator, refers to the process of changing (modulating) data into electronic pulses, sending the pulses through a phone line, and then changing (demodulating) the pulses back to usable data at the other end of the line. As the name describes, the modem transmits data from one computer to another computer in a far part of the office or the world.

When you start using computers, modems may seem a little beyond you. Unless the applications software specifically requires that you hook up to another computer via modem, you may choose not to use this equipment until you need this capability. A world lingers, however, just beyond your phone jack—waiting for you to tap into an endless computer bank of information.

Numerous electronic services can provide you with almost everything you want to know about a given subject—instantly. These services are known as *bulletin board services* or *information services*, and many major services are available throughout the world—no matter what kind of computer you use. A modem can link you to any number of small local bulletin boards that may advertise hardware specials, display user group information, or trade new computer games and routines. With a modem, you also can perform a wide variety of financial functions, such as electronic check writing, stock trading, and so on.

Most computers aren't equipped with a modem; you probably need to add the modem separately. For more information on selecting a modem for your system, see Chapter 7, "Selecting Computer Add-Ons."

Understanding Operating Systems

The last stop in this tour of hardware doesn't involve hardware. Without an operating system, a computer is no more than an expensive paperweight. An *operating system* is the liaison between you, an applications program, and the computer. When you want to use the computer, you tell the operating system by entering or selecting certain commands. The operating system translates these commands into electronic code the computer can understand, and the request is carried out.

You can use various operating systems depending on what kind of computer you have. The following list presents an overview of the most popular operating systems available:

MS-DOS or PC DOS

OS/2

Apple DOS

Finder

System 7

UNIX or XENIX

AmigaDOS or MegaDOS

The first two operating systems, MS-DOS and PC DOS (developed specifically for IBM PC computers), are the most popular operating systems for PCs. The Amiga computer uses a different kind of DOS—known as MegaDOS—which is incompatible with PC DOS or MS-DOS machines without a hardware and software add-on. In the last two years, OS/2, an operating system for IBM computers, has grown in popularity; although OS/2's capabilities are being explored, OS/2 2.0, the latest version, doesn't yet rival MS-DOS or PC DOS in use. Apple DOS and ProDOS are the operating systems developed for the Apple II family of computers, which makes these two operating systems by default among the most widely used operating systems in the personal computer world. The Macintosh uses the Finder operating system; a primary advantage of Finder is the option of having several applications open on-screen at one time. High-end Macs (and some low-end Macs, with memory upgrades) now use System 7, Apple's long-awaited new operating system. UNIX and XENIX are two high-level operating systems used primarily on larger computers programmed and run by experts. (For more detailed information on the various operating systems, see Chapter 10.)

In the following section, you learn how all the elements discussed in the preceding parts of this chapter come together into a computer system—IBM, Amiga, or Macintosh.

Reviewing Basic Computer Categories

The most popular and easily identifiable computers are the Amiga, IBM (or IBM-compatible), and Macintosh systems. In this section, you learn—from a hardware standpoint—why these systems are different.

Although this section deals only with three brand-name computers, remember that an incredible range of IBM-compatible computers exists in the marketplace today. Many IBM-compatible companies that started off as small producers of DOS machines have now grown to huge corporations, making their names almost as well known as Apple or IBM. Some of the extremely successful computer manufacturers are Compaq, Zenith, Leading Edge, NEC, Tandy, and Epson.

The Amiga

Early in the search for low-cost, user-friendly personal computers, a company called Commodore created a small, almost toy-like computer for hobbyists. These early computers (which first appeared sometime between the IBM PC and the IBM AT) were equipped with small amounts of memory, used cartridges or tapes to store programs and data, and were never considered a business power machine.

Commodores sold strongly for several years to home computer users and people looking for an easy-to-use machine that ran popular games as well as educational and applications software. New models of the early Commodore, such as the C64 and the C128, evolved with more memory and more features, but eventually the market dried up for low-end computers. Today, the original Commodore is no longer available (although you can find these systems in the computer portion of the classified section of a newspaper).

Commodore—the company—continues to go strong, in part because of the success of the Amiga family of computers. The Amiga is a stand-alone system, similar in looks to a PC, with a separate monitor, system unit, 3 1/2-inch drive, and detached keyboard and mouse (see fig. 3.22). Known for incredible graphics and animation capabilities, Amiga is a favorite among users involved in creating presentation material and interactive or animated displays. The downside for some users is that the Amiga isn't IBM-compatible unless you purchase a *bridge board*, an add-on card that plugs in a slot inside the Amiga system unit. A bridge board makes the system compatible with an IBM XT or IBM AT. Without the bridge board (available for high-end Amiga systems), however, you cannot share files between the Amiga and an IBM computer.

FIG. 3.22

The Amiga computer.

Like other computer families, the Amiga is available with a wide range of capabilities, from a low-priced machine that has only 500K of memory to a high-end machine with a whopping 9M of memory. For the serious Amiga user, a video production switcher turns a computer into a full-scale video production studio for a $10,000 investment.

The newest Amiga, the 3000T, was designed primarily for taking advantage of the growing multimedia market. The Amiga 3000T, running AmigaDOS 2.0, offers four-voice, two-channel sound and several thousand different colors. A graphics and video integration utility called AmigaVision allows you to mix your own multimedia presentations right on your desktop.

By adding a UNIX board and more memory, both the Amiga 3000 and 3000T can be made UNIX-compatible.

PCs

As you learned in Chapter 2, the IBM PC arrived in the market as the first major personal computer in the wake of the shock wave of the Apple I. The IBM is different from the Apple computers because the IBM uses different software, includes different internal parts, and processes data differently.

This section introduces some of the popular IBM models. Remember that, besides regular desktop models, the line includes laptop and portable computers (see Chapter 4 for a discussion of laptops and portables).

The IBM PC

The original IBM Personal Computer was introduced in 1981. With a monochrome monitor, two full-height 5 1/4-inch disk drives, and an 8088 microprocessor, the IBM was quickly adopted as the standard personal computer for business applications.

The original PC's keyboard looks cluttered by today's standards. The function keys formed two rows along the left edge of the keyboard, and the numeric keypad (which also served as a cursor-control keypad) was scrunched up next to the standard QWERTY keys (see fig. 3.23).

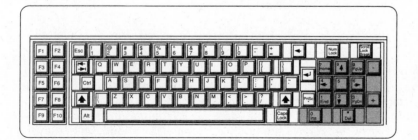

FIG. 3.23

The original IBM PC keyboard.

The IBM XT

The next generation of the PC was the XT, a PC with more power and a hard disk drive. The XT was equipped with 256K of memory, a floppy disk drive, and a 10M (and later, a 20M) hard disk drive. The hard disk was a major feature for PC users, providing a substantial jump in storage capacity (from 360K floppies to 20M hard disk). The IBM PC XT used the same keyboard as the original PC.

T   I   P In advertising, the terms *PC-compatible*, *XT-compatible*, and *AT-compatible* mean that you can run the software or use the hardware device with all compatible machines.

The IBM PC AT

The IBM PC AT soon followed, with 256K or 512K of memory. The greatest differences from the original PC were the 80286 microprocessor and the addition of a half-height floppy disk drive, capable of working with 1.2M disks. This system included a 20M hard disk, a floppy disk drive, and a slightly different appearance. The PC AT also introduced a new keyboard, which separated the cursor-control/numeric keypad from the standard QWERTY keyboard. This new keyboard also added three indicator lights in the top right corner of the keyboard to show when the Num Lock, Caps Lock, and Scroll Lock keys were active.

The IBM XT/286

IBM then introduced a machine based on both the AT and the XT, the XT/286. Although this computer offered the new 80286 microprocessor, making the XT/286 the new standard beyond 8088 power, the IBM XT/286 was a big machine that made a little splash. The XT/286 was actually a redesigned AT motherboard in an XT case. This system had 512K memory and a 20M hard disk.

Although the XT/286 was the last of the IBM XT and AT computers to be marketed, PC-compatible manufacturers built millions of computers based on the IBM designs and continue today to build more systems, such as the Compac DeskPro. Also, the PS/2 computers, which use the new MicroChannel bus architecture, created a second, higher level of computing power (for more information about MicroChannel bus architecture, see the following section).

The IBM PS/2

IBM formally introduced the Personal System/2 in April of 1987. Not satisfied with announcing one machine, IBM again blazed onto the market with the introduction of an entire family of computers with new monitors, printers, and a desktop publishing package.

The PS/2 is different for several reasons. All models—and many exist— have a small footprint design, which gives users maximum desk space with desktop models and even more space with floor-standing models. Figure 3.24 shows the PS/2 Model 30 (a desktop model), and figure 3.25 shows the system unit of the PS/2 Model 65 SX, a floor-standing unit. Table 3.6 describes some of the PS/2 computers currently available and provides information about each system.

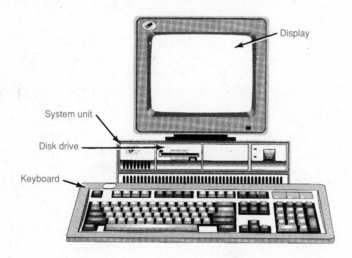

FIG. 3.24

The PS/2 Model 30.

FIG. 3.25

The PS/2 Model 65 SX floor-standing system unit.

Table 3.6 PS/2 Models

Model	Type	Description
25	Desktop	Low-end system with 8086 microprocessor, 512 to 640K RAM, MCGA display, one 720K 3 1/2-inch disk drive, and two expansion slots
25/286	Desktop	Same as 25 but with 80286 microprocessor, 1 to 4M RAM, VGA, one or two 1.44M disk drives, two expansion slots, and optional 30M hard disk
30/286	Desktop	80286 microprocessor, 1 to 4M RAM, VGA, one or two 1.44M disk drives, three expansion slots, and optional 30M hard disk
L40 SX	Laptop	80386SX microprocessor, 2 to 18M RAM, VGA, 60M hard disk, and one 1.44 drive (no expansion slots)
50 Z	Desktop	80286 microprocessor, 1 to 2M RAM, VGA, two 1.44M drives, 30 or 60M hard disk, and three expansion slots
55 SX	Desktop	80386SX microprocessor, 2 to 8M RAM, VGA, one 1.44 drive, 30 or 60M hard disk, and three expansion slots
55 LS	Desktop	80386SX microprocessor, 2 to 8M RAM, VGA, optional 1.44 drive, optional 60M hard disk, and two expansion slots
65 SX	Floor-standing	80386SX microprocessor, 2 to 8M RAM, VGA, two 1.44 drives, 60 to 320M hard disk, and seven expansion slots
P70 386	Laptop	80386SX microprocessor, 2 to 8M or 4 to 8M RAM, VGA, one 1.44 drive, 30 to 120M hard disk, and two expansion slots
70 386	Desktop	80386SX microprocessor (486 available for this model), 2 to 6M or 2 to 8M RAM, VGA, two 1.44 drives, 60 or 120M hard disk, and three expansion slots
70 486	Desktop	80486 microprocessor, 2 to 8M RAM, VGA, two 1.44 drives, 60 to 120M hard disk, and three expansion slots
P75 486	Laptop	80486 microprocessor, 8 to 16M RAM, XGA, one 1.44 drive, 160 to 400M hard disk, and four expansion slots

Model	Type	Description
80 386	Floor-standing	80386 microprocessor, 2 to 4M or 4 to 8M RAM, VGA, two 1.44 drives, 80 to 320M hard disk, and seven expansion slots
90 XP/486	Desktop	80486 microprocessor, 4 to 32M RAM, XGA, two 1.44 drives, 80 to 960M hard disk, and three expansion slots
95 XP/486	Floor-standing	80486 microprocessor, 4 to 32M RAM, XGA, two 1.44 drives, 160M to 1.6G (gigabytes) hard disk, and six expansion slots

The PS/2 family brings new flexibility to personal computing. The low-end system, Model 25, uses the early 8086 microprocessor and the basic internal design (slot architecture) of the older generation of IBM PCs. The Model 50Z introduces MicroChannel Architecture (MCA), a new technology that enables the high-end PS/2s to move data faster than is possible with the slot architecture of PCs. All models higher than the L40 SX (which includes the Models 50Z, 55 SX, 55 LX, 65 SX, P70 386, 70 386, 70 486, P75 486, 80 386, 90 XP 486, and 95 XP 486) use the MCA. You can expand the high-end machine—the Model 95 XP 486, which includes an 80486 microprocessor—to 32M of RAM, and you can have from a 160M to a 1.6G hard disk.

The IBM PS/1

The newest computer introduced by IBM, the PS/1, is an easy-to-use machine specifically developed for the home market. Far from a toy, the PS/1 is a computer you can use at home, whether you plan to bring work home from the office, computerize home inventory, or perform a variety of other personal, educational, and business uses.

A major strength of the PS/1 is the ease with which you put together and use the system; even a beginner can set up the computer in minutes. You go through no complicated software installation procedures; the PS/1 is equipped with several programs: Microsoft Works, PRODIGY communications service, and Promenade (a communications service specifically for PS/1 users). In addition, and depending on the model of PS/1, you may receive other software. If you purchase the joystick add-on, you receive two popular computer games, Where in the World is Carmen San Diego? and Silpheed. Finally, if you purchase the Audio

Card/Joystick option, the PS/1 adds a MIDI interface cable and Cakewalk, a music sequencing program that enables you to record, edit, and play back songs on a MIDI instrument.

Smaller than any PS/2, the tiny PS/1 is a modular design; for this system, you need desk space only slightly larger than the size of a notebook. The PS/1 system unit, keyboard, mouse, and monitor all fit together to give you maximum space on the desktop.

The first feature you notice when you power up a PS/1 is the computer's System Menu, a four-part screen that shows the options. With built-in tutorials, powerful software packages, an included modem and communications software, the PS/1 is a terrific investment for the home or the in-home office. Table 3.7 highlights the various PS/1 models and explains the features found on each model.

Table 3.7 PS/1 Models	
Model	Description
M01	80286 microprocessor, 512K RAM, black-and-white VGA display, and one 1.44 drive
M34	80286 microprocessor, 1M RAM, black-and-white VGA display, one 1.44 drive, and one 30M hard disk
C01	80286 microprocessor, 512K RAM, color VGA display, and one 1.44 drive
C34	80286 microprocessor, 1M RAM, color VGA display, one 1.44 drive, and one 30M hard disk
Options:	A second 1.44 drive
	512K memory expansion (M01 and C01)
	Adapter card unit with three expansion slots
	Audio card add-on
	Audio card and joystick add-on
	Second joystick add-on
	PS/1 printer

Macintosh Computers

In the years following the introduction of the first Macintosh in 1984, several new models were introduced. The first Mac had 128K of memory, one 400K disk drive, and a built-in 9-inch monitor (see fig. 3.26).

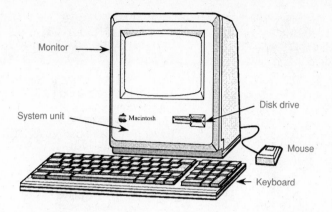

Monitor

System unit

Macintosh

Disk drive

Mouse

Keyboard

FIG. 3.26

The original Mac.

Recently, the entire line of Macintoshes was revamped. Some systems went through little more than cosmetic surgery, but others were re-worked and modified to give users more power for less money. Table 3.8 highlights the current Mac models and explains each machine's capabilities.

Table 3.8 Macintosh Models

Model	Type	Description
Classic	Compact	8MHz 68000 microprocessor, 2 to 4M RAM, 3 1/2-inch SuperDrive, 40M hard disk, 9-inch monochrome monitor
Classic II	Compact	16MHz 68030 microprocessor, 4M RAM, 3 1/2-inch SuperDrive, 40-80M hard disk, 9-inch monochrome monitor
SE/30	Compact	16MHz 68030/68882 microprocessors, 1 to 8M RAM, 3 1/2-inch SuperDrive, 40 or 80M hard disk, 9-inch monochrome monitor, optional Direct Slot expansion cards, A/UX and DOS operating system options
Mac LCII	Desktop	16MHz 68030 microprocessor, 2 to 10M RAM, 3 1/2-inch SuperDrive, supports three displays (RGB, monochrome, and high-res RGB), 40M hard disk, MS-DOS and ProDOS operating system options

continues

Table 3.8 Continued

Model	Type	Description
Mac IIsi	Desktop	20MHz 68030/68882 microprocessors, 2 to 17M RAM, 3 1/2-inch SuperDrive, supports five displays (RGB, monochrome, high-res RGB, portrait, and two-page), 40 or 80M hard drive, A/UX and DOS operating systems option
Mac IIci	Desktop	25MHz 68030/68882 microprocessors, 4 to 32M RAM, 3 1/2-inch SuperDrive, supports five displays (RGB, monochrome, high-res RGB, portrait, and two-page), 40 or 80M hard drive, A/UX and DOS operating systems option
PowerBook 100	Laptop	16MHz 68000 microprocessor, 4M RAM, 3 1/2-inch SuperDrive, 40- to 80M hard disk, Supertwist LCD display
PowerBook 140	Laptop	16MHz 68030 microprocessor, 4M RAM, 3 1/2-inch SuperDrive, 40- to 80M hard disk, Supertwist LCD display
PowerBook 100	Laptop	25MHz 68030 microprocessor, 4M RAM, 3 1/2-inch SuperDrive, 40- to 80M hard disk, Supertwist LCD display
Quadra 700	Tower	25MHz 68040 microprocessor, 4M RAM, 3 1/2-inch SuperDrive, 80- to 400M hard disk, supports five displays: monochrome, RGB, high-resolution RGB, portrait, and two-page monitors
Quadra 950	Tower	33MHz 68040 microprocessor, 8M RAM, 3 1/2-inch SuperDrive, 80- to 400M hard disk, supports five displays: monochrome, RGB, high-resolution RGB, portrait, and two-page monitors

The Macintosh Classic

A new machine with an old look, the Macintosh Classic resembles the original Mac, with the familiar 9-inch built-in monitor and attached system unit. The Classic is available for less than $1,500 and is equipped with 2 or 4M RAM. The Classic bumped the popular Mac Plus from the Macintosh line-up, but it offers all the features and the faster access rate (by 25 percent) of the Plus.

The Macintosh Classic II

The Mac Classic II was introduced for users who want the portability and low cost of the Classic but demand more speed and greater processing power. The Classic II uses Motorola's 68030 and runs at 16MHz—twice as fast as the clock speed of the original Classic. The Mac Classic II has a retail list price of $1,699.

As a system on a network, the Classic is extremely popular and because of its small size and compact design, this machine is easy to cart to and from home and office. The Mac Classic comes with one 1.44M Super-Drive, built-in monitor, keyboard, and mouse. The new Macintosh Classic can read from and write to MS-DOS and OS/2 disks, which makes the Classic a PC-compatible computer for some applications.

The Mac SE/30

The Mac SE/30 is a newer version of Mac, taking some of the best features of the Mac Plus and the SE, which added an expansion slot and room for an internal disk drive, and combining these features with additional power in the form of a Motorola 68030 CPU for a high-speed, flexible machine (see fig. 3.27). You can load the system with 1M to 8M RAM, select a 40M or 80M hard disk, and—if you add the 3 1/2-inch previously-mentioned SuperDrive—read from and write to MS-DOS and OS/2 3 1/2-inch floppy disks.

FIG. 3.27

The Mac SE/30.

The Macintosh LCII

The Macintosh LCII is a new machine of the traditional desktop Mac design. (Apple calls these computers *modular* machines.) The LCII offers full-color capability and supports three different monitors. The

16 MHz 68030 microprocessor is a fast, powerful chip that makes the system more than 100 percent faster than the Classic. The body of the Mac LCII is more squat than other modular Macs; the system unit is short and wide enough to accommodate a 12-inch monitor (see fig. 3.28). The standard Mac keyboard and mouse are included in the basic package.

FIG. 3.28

The Macintosh
LCII.

Possibly the greatest benefit of the LC is the inclusion of an expansion slot that accommodates an Apple IIe board, making the LC the first Macintosh that runs the myriad of Apple IIe software still available on the market. For this reason, the LC is popular for home and education uses and for many low-end business applications.

The Mac II Computers

The last few entries in the Mac family all are variations of the Mac II computer: the Mac IIsi and the IIci. Both Mac IIs are fast machines with superior display quality and expansion capabilities. The Mac IIs run the innovative new System 7.0 operating system.

The Mac IIsi is the low-end system, equipped with an internal expansion slot, support for four Apple monitors, a sound-input feature, and a 20 MHz 68030 microprocessor capable of processing information at an incredible rate. Figure 3.29 shows an example of a typical Mac II.

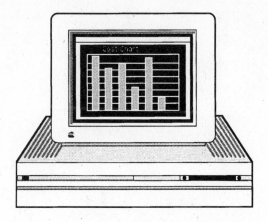

FIG. 3.29

A member of the
Mac II family.

The Macintosh IIci is even faster, cutting processing time by up to 50 percent in many applications by using a 25 MHz 68030 microprocessor. This system also gives you the option of adding even more memory than the IIsi (up to 17M) and adds an 80M (rather than 40M) hard disk.

The Macintosh PowerBook Computers

Early in 1992, Macintosh introduced yet another computer, which caused quite a ripple in the way users work with Mac systems. After being a relative "no show" in the laptop computer market—despite the limited success of the original Macintosh LC—Apple created a computer destined to be a success: the lightest, smallest Macintosh ever made. This computer is the PowerBook.

Three PowerBook models are currently on the market. The 100, weighing a little more than five pounds, is based on the 68000 microprocessor and includes 4M of RAM and a 40M hard drive. The 140, weighing just less than seven pounds, runs on the 68030 microprocessor, offers 4M to 8M of RAM, and a 40M or optional 80M hard drive. The top-end model, the 170, also weighs less than seven pounds and is based on the 68030/68882 microprocessor. This model comes equipped with 4M of RAM, a 80M hard drive, and an internal modem. Figure 3.30 shows an example of a PowerBook.

A built-in trackball in the center front of the PowerBook makes mouse operations easy without the distraction of a mouse. Additionally, all the PowerBooks are based on System 7 and can run IBM software seamlessly if you add a program, such as Soft PC.

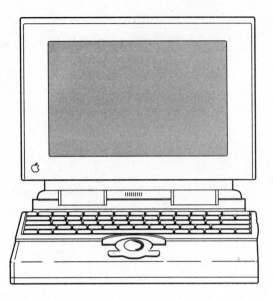

FIG. 3.30

The new
Macintosh
PowerBook.

The Macintosh Quadra Computers

The Quadras are sleek, sophisticated-looking tower machines (the first
Macs to break the horizontal mold) that make the most of System 7 and
offer the latest in technology. Figure 3.31 shows an example of the high-
end Quadra.

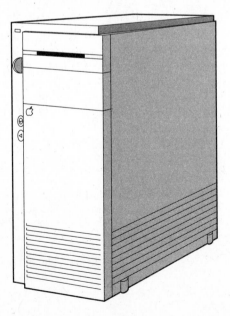

FIG. 3.31

The new Quadra
950 computer.

The Quadra 700, which is based on the 68040 microprocessor, operates at 25 megahertz, and comes with 4M of RAM (expandable to 20M) and nine expansion ports. The Quadras 950 is a similar, but faster, machine with more room to grow. Based on the 68040, the 950 runs at 33MHz. The standard 950 comes with 8M of RAM (expandable to 64M) and has 10 expansion slots. The Quadra computers, like the PowerBooks, use only the System 7 (or higher) operating system and cannot operate with previous Macintosh operating systems.

Chapter Summary

In this chapter, you took a step-by-step journey through the hardware components in a computer system. You learned important details about the popular personal computers in today's market and explored the many facets of computer hardware. The following chapter, the beginning of Part II, analyzes your computer needs.

PART II

Prepurchase Considerations

If you are planning to purchase a computer (or are thinking about adding to the system you already have), Part II can help you make an educated decision. The chapters in this part cover basic considerations about hardware and software.

OUTLINE

Purchasing Considerations

I f you have been shopping for a computer, you are probably over-whelmed with the mass of equipment available. With such an intimi-dating range of systems and features from which to choose, how do you know what hardware to buy? Every dealer claims to have the best system. How do you decide on the computer that best fits your needs? How do you choose one software product from the thousands of available programs?

Starting with a basic "How can I use a computer?" approach, this chap-ter helps you analyze and identify your computer needs. Although this first chapter of Part II serves as a general guide to evaluate your com-puter needs, the remaining chapters in this part focus on purchasing considerations for computer components.

Determining Your Needs

This section presents a list of questions to mull over as you begin the computer hunt. Perhaps you already answered some of the following questions. If so, you can read only the chapter sections that apply to your needs.

This section helps you find answers to the following questions:

- Do you buy the system or software first?

- What can you use the computer for?

- How much must you spend?

- Where will you use the computer?

- What size system do you need?

- Who else is going to use the computer?

- Must the computer be compatible with other computers at work or home?

- Will the computer meet all your future needs?

- Do you want a PC, Mac, Amiga, or PC clone?

- What components come with a computer? What extra components do you need?

- Where is the best place to purchase extra components?

- Do you buy a new or used computer?

Do I Buy the System or the Software First?

You need to decide whether to first purchase a system and then the software, or the reverse. How you answer this question depends greatly on your previous experience. Usually, the best plan is to consider the software and then choose the machine that runs this software.

Make sure that the computer system you purchase isn't outdated or so limited that you can run only the single software program you purchase. You may consider a system that enables you to expand your software library and build on your present computer applications. If you like a particular spreadsheet that enables you to quickly and easily calculate taxes, purchase the software and the computer on which this spreadsheet program runs.

You also need to ensure that the system can handle a variety of software. You may work only with taxes now, but eventually you may want to write letters, play games, and balance a checkbook. Make sure that the system has room to grow. Usually, unless you are forced to conform to a certain hardware standard—if all systems in the office are

Macs or IBMs—first find the software you like and then choose the system that runs the software.

What Can My Computer Do?

The answer to this question may be one word or several paragraphs. From the practical side, you purchase a computer to automate one task, such as tracking only monthly expenses, writing correspondence to clients, organizing student names and addresses, or publishing simple newsletters.

With imagination, you can envision even more uses. With a computer, you can produce routine correspondence in one-fourth of the typing time required. You can produce graphs to enhance spreadsheets and print mailing labels from a computerized database, which saves hours you previously lost to this necessary but boring task.

The best thing you can do before you start shopping is to think seriously about what you want from a computer. In the best of all possible worlds, what do you want the computer to do? If you're like many people, a first answer to this question may be "Do my job, answer my phone, and take care of my life while I go to Hawaii." After the fantasy clears, however, you realize that computers can perform hundreds, if not thousands, of real-life tasks. The following list shows you the wide variety of business tasks a personal computer can help you achieve:

■ Writing and publishing

Writing and editing business and personal letters
Producing reports, proposals, and contracts
Publishing training materials
Creating advertising copy
Laying out and typesetting ads
Printing fliers and brochures
Creating company logos, letterhead, and business cards
Writing and publishing invitations

■ Managing financial tasks

Performing general ledger accounting
Tracking accounts payable
Tracking accounts receivable
Preparing tax worksheets
Preparing payroll worksheets
Performing cost analysis
Preparing profit-and-loss statements
Preparing balance sheets

  Preparing year-end reports
  Balancing a checkbook
  Planning a major purchase

■ Managing data

  Creating and maintaining client lists
  Recording personnel information
  Maintaining inventory
  Creating an ordering system
  Organizing a CD collection
  Tracking names and addresses of friends and relatives

The preceding list covers only a few applications that personal computers can perform. Besides writing, crunching numbers, and managing data, businesses can use computers to create sophisticated graphics, connect to other computers, create presentation materials (including music and animation), and handle a variety of other tasks.

Remember that not all programs run on all computers. After you find a software program you are happy with, you need to find a computer to run the software.

How Much Do I Have To Spend?

No matter what you buy, cost is always a consideration. The money you can afford to spend significantly affects your choice of system. No matter what demanding tasks you want the computer to perform, if you lack the funds to back up your needs, you may have to compromise.

As you write your want list, keep an eye on your budget. Remember that the faster and newer the technology, the higher the price tag. If you know what you need before you buy, you can be in the right place at the right time to pick up a powerful system for a relatively low cost.

The first step in buying a computer is to rid yourself of purchasing myths you picked up along the way. Consider the following points as you begin this planning stage:

■ Bigger isn't necessarily better.

  Once upon a time, people believed that the bigger the system, the more capabilities it had. This adage was applied to computers (mainframes compared to personal computers) and peripheral devices, such as printers, hard disks, and monitors. Based on this belief, to get a top-of-the-line system you filled the office or desktop with computer equipment. Fortunately, as technology evolved, computer equipment was developed with a smaller *footprint*, which means the computer takes less space on (or under) a desk.

■ Smaller doesn't mean less expensive.

Along with this movement toward smaller equipment came an increase in the technology and, therefore, the cost of computers and peripheral equipment. If you have ever checked the pages of the *Computer Shopper*, hoping to find a laptop for next to nothing, you probably were unpleasantly surprised. Laptops, particularly the more powerful models, cost as much as or more than a comparable full-sized personal computer. No matter which model of computer you purchase, you pay more for the smaller, more streamlined models than you do for an older, larger, heavier machine because the technology in the scaled-down components costs more to produce.

■ Brand-name computers aren't the only computers worth buying.

When personal computers were first introduced, the main competitor in the market was Apple, with Tandy, Commodore, and Texas Instruments not far behind. Because these computers were the only systems available, the manufacturers expected a hefty price for their machines. Not long after the IBM PC took off, other computer companies began developing computers that emulated the IBM technology—at a lower price. These computers are known as *clones* because the technology, but not the expensive price, was cloned. Clones are available in abundance for the IBM personal computers, but because of the *closed* technology of Apple computers (other manufacturers cannot copy the designs), few computer manufacturers tried to develop a Macintosh clone. For more information about clones, see the section "Do I Want a PC, Amiga, Mac, or PC Clone?" that follows in this chapter.

Table 4.1 highlights some costs to consider as you think about budgeting a personal computer purchase.

Table 4.1 Computer Setup Costs

Before Purchase

Cost (in hours) of researching which equipment to buy.

Cost (in dollars) of hiring a consultant to evaluate your computer needs and to recommend hardware and software purchases.

At Purchase

Initial outlay for hardware, including system unit, monitor, printer, and extras (peripherals), such as a modem, scanner, or mouse.

continues

Table 4.1 Continued

At Purchase

Initial outlay for software, including the operating system, applications software, such as word processing, spreadsheet, database, or graphics programs.

The optional purchase of an extended warranty plan. (All new computers include some kind of warranty, but many companies offer an extended warranty for an additional cost.)

After Purchase

Cost (in hours) of downtime while you set up and check out the computer. (Downtime usually is more important in business and school environments than in home use.)

Cost (in dollars and time) invested in hardware and software training (whether you hire a consultant to do the training or you explore the system and programs).

Productivity cost while you and your employees get up to speed with the new equipment and software.

The minimal costs of supplies and upkeep, such as electricity, printer paper, printer ribbons, and toner cartridges (used with laser printers).

Where Will I Use My Computer?

Before you buy a computer, decide where you want to set up. If you plan to use the computer at the office, you have one set of considerations; at home, you have other considerations:

■ At the office

Think about where in the office you may work. At a desk? If so, depending on the size of the desk (and how often you use the desk), select a small-footprint machine so that you can place the PC on the desktop and still have the maximum amount of desk space available for the usual desk clutter. If you are extremely protective of desk space, select a tower computer system in which the system unit stands vertically on one end (see fig. 4.1). In the office, you may have a separate desk or workstation for computing. If so, the size of the system isn't a big consideration.

NOTE You can place the system unit of almost any PC-style computer vertically. For extended periods, however, this position may cause wear and tear on the hard disk. You can buy stands designed specifically to hold the system unit.

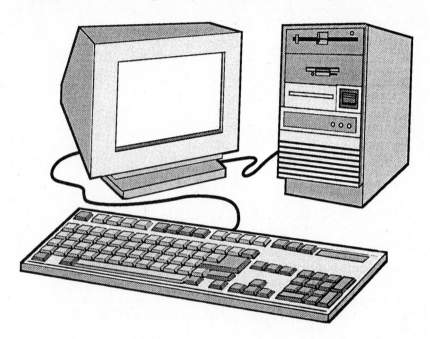

FIG. 4.1

A tower system.

■ **At home**

Do you need a computer you can move around easily, or do you plan to install a workstation and work consistently at one location? Do you plan to take the computer back and forth to work?

If you are setting up a workstation, you can buy any size system that suits you. If you need to move the computer from room to room or if you plan to take a computer back and forth to work, you need a system small enough to travel. A portable computer, such as the COMPAQ 386 or an NEC laptop, is small and light enough to easily tote around. The following section explains more about portable and laptop computers.

What Size System Do I Need?

Computers come in a variety of shapes and sizes: small and smaller, large and larger, portable and immovable. From the largest mainframe computer to the smallest personal computer (eventually the Wrist Mac, a wrist-attachable Macintosh with a one-inch monitor), you can find a system with the footprint and the capabilities you need.

The following computer types are explained in this section:

- Desktops
- Portables
- Laptops
- Notebooks
- Palmtops
- Pen computers

Desktops

Chapter 1 introduced you to the personal, desktop-sized computer. The desktop computer is available in many sizes, from a large desk-hogging model to the newer small-footprint models that require less space on a desk, such as the IBM PS/1. Figure 4.2 shows a typical desktop computer.

FIG. 4.2

A personal computer.

The trend now seems to move toward tower technology, where the system unit is designed to stand on end, giving you more elbow room and freeing up desktop space (although you still need a place to put other equipment, such as the monitor, printer, and mouse). The IBM PS/2 Model 60 was one of the first big systems to use tower technology (see fig. 4.3). Macintosh recently introduced tower units, the Quadra 700 and 950 computers. These computers are the most powerful Macintoshes, yet these systems fit easily under a desk and out of the way.

FIG. 4.3

The IBM PS/2 Model 60.

Portable Computers

A portable computer, shown in figure 4.4, enables you to take work with you—for a small cost in time and effort. Most portable computers are truly portable, although not as easy to tote as the newer, smaller laptops.

Several good portables are available, the forerunner of which was made by COMPAQ, a leading IBM-compatible computer manufacturer.

Technically speaking, every personal computer is portable. Most computers, however, are not *easily* portable. One of the first popular portable computers (the now defunct Osborne) was designed as an all-in-one unit: the system unit, mini-monitor, and keyboard all fit together in one nice (although heavy) portable unit, complete with handle. This design enabled the dedicated computer user to take the computer on an airplane, to the races, anywhere. If you owned an Osborne, you needed only a hefty power outlet and a great deal of desktop space at the destination. The small footprint standard was a only gleam in the manufacturer's eye.

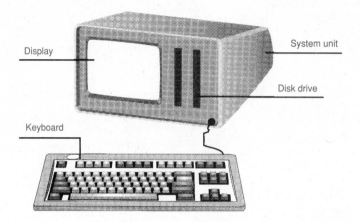

FIG. 4.4

A portable computer.

Today, several popular portable computers are on the market. COMPAQ Computer Corporation is a longtime leader in portable, desktop, and laptop computer manufacturing. Apple provides the Mac Classic II and Mac SE/30 as their portable computer line. Both of these systems have the monitor and CPU in one unit complete with a carrying handle on the back. Although the keyboard and mouse are separate, they fit nicely in a Mac carrying bag available through most retailers.

Portable computers are growing more powerful, lighter, and easier to manipulate but for real bite-sized power, however, look at laptops.

Laptop Computers

The laptop computer rose to superstardom because this design represents the best aspects of portability. At 9 to 12 pounds, with capabilities ranging from a bare-bones, one disk drive, LCD display to a beefed-up system powerful enough to rival an expensive 486 deskbound system, the laptop computer enables you to take the office with you.

Laptops are created for people who choose not to—or cannot—leave the computer behind. Going in the car? Plug the system in the cigarette lighter. Heading to the beach? Take the laptop along and use the battery pack. A laptop computer travels wherever you do, whether you are in a cramped subway or on a cruise ship at sea.

Whether the journey involves a subway, boat, train, or plane—whether you fly to North Dakota or Fiji—a laptop computer can accompany you with minimum fuss and bother. You can operate the laptop computer from batteries, so even AC current is not mandatory. (You do, however, need a considerable supply of batteries. Batteries last eight hours or less of consistent computer use before recharging.) Figure 4.5 shows both the older, luggable and popular laptop computers.

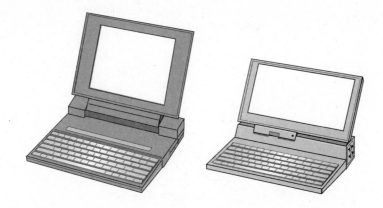

FIG. 4.5

A luggable computer (left) and a laptop computer (right).

If you need real portability, consider a laptop. With a modem, access to a printer, and software (on 3 1/2-inch disks), you can build a laptop into a workstation as powerful as any desktop system. You also can hook most laptops to standard monitors so that you don't lose display quality for the sake of portability.

With laptop computers, however, appearances may deceive you. To the untrained eye, these machines seem simple and inexpensive: you don't see much hardware, so laptop computers shouldn't cost much. Technology, however, doesn't work this way. You pay as much and perhaps more for a powerful laptop as you pay for an equally powerful desktop computer.

Notebook Computer

Due to the sweeping success of the laptop computer, an even smaller cousin, the notebook computer, is making a niche in the market (see fig. 4.6). Here, the name *notebook* is an accurate description: weighing in at 4-6 pounds and roughly 8-1/2 x 11 inches, you can tuck these small computers under your arm like a notebook.

The PC notebooks offer a wide range of capabilities, from one-drive systems with liquid crystal displays to power-user systems with 80486 microprocessors, high-capacity hard drives, and VGA displays. Macintosh also offers a line of notebook computers called *Powerbooks*. The Powerbook 100, Mac's low-end notebook computer is the lightest of the series and retails for under $2,000. However, with no internal floppy disk drive and only 20M of hard disk, the low-end 100 has limitations. The high-end Powerbook 170 runs five times faster than a Mac Classic and comes complete with an internal floppy drive, a math coprocessor for speedy calculations and a built-in fax modem. You find no savings in price here; average notebooks cost from $650 for a low-end system to $4,600 or more for a high-end machine.

FIG. 4.6

A notebook computer.

Palmtop Computer

Packing more power into ever-smaller packages continues beyond the notebook computer. Hewlett-Packard and Lotus combined technology to produce a palmtop computer (see fig. 4.7). The Hewlett-Packard 95LX, which looks more like a checkbook than a notebook computer, offers a day planner and a financial calculator. Built into ROM are Lotus 1-2-3 Release 2.2 and DOS 3.2. The 95LX comes with 1M of memory and costs less than $700.

Pen Computer

If you want the latest cutting-edge technology, you now can buy the Pen computer. The Pen computer provides an alternate method of data input. Information is written directly on-screen with a Pen (often referred to as a *Stylus*), and your handwriting is then translated to typed text by a handwriting recognition program. Current Pen computers are roughly the size of a notebook computer but lack a keyboard or mouse. Data is entered with the pen only.

FIG. 4.7

The HP palmtop
computer.

One popular Pen computer is the NCR 3125, which lists for $4,795 and includes a 20M hard disk drive. IBM soon plans to release their own Pen computer, the ThinkPad, which will list for around $5,000. Both the NCR 3125 and the ThinkPad include a floppy disk drive and both run standard Windows software.

Some possible uses for Pen computers may include inventory control (a Pen computer makes marking off items as you go through a truck-load or isle of merchandise an easy task). Sales or other traveling professionals may find the Pen computer easier to handle than a portable, laptop, or notebook computer.

As Pen computing advances, the physical size of the computer is shrinking. Apple has introduced the Newton, available in January 1993, which is the size of a standard palmtop computer. Although not as powerful as its competitors—the ThinkPad and NCR 3125—the Newton's $500 to $700 list price should bring a sigh of relief to hopeful Pen computer owners. The Newton currently provides only the simplest of applications, such as a note-taking program, a calendar and scheduler, and a bare-bones graphics program.

Although Pen computers are clever and useful tools for on-the-fly computing, these computers will not soon replace standard keyboard computers in terms of speed, power, efficiency, and versatility.

Who Else Will Use My Computer?

One major consideration to consider before you buy is who else may use the computer. If you are purchasing a computer system for a large company, select a system that best fits the needs and learning curves of all users. Although you may prefer an IBM system, you may be in a position to purchase systems for many people who, until now, were never exposed to computers.

Think about the other people who will use the computer or computers you purchase. To also consider the applications with which these people may work, look at the following example:

Jeff needs to purchase computers for his small advertising agency. Although he wants a computer for desktop publishing to reduce the cost of laying out and producing advertising copy, he realizes that other people in the office also can benefit from computers. Consequently, he decides to purchase a computer for the bookkeeper, a computer for the layout person, a computer for the graphic artist, and a computer for the administrative assistant.

Each of Jeff's employees performs a different task with a computer. The following partial list of the potential applications explores the factors Jeff needs to consider:

- The bookkeeper needs to use a spreadsheet program to track accounts receivables and payable, create balance sheets, publish weekly and monthly reports, supply tax information, and compute and print payroll checks.

- The graphic artist must use a sophisticated graphics program to create artwork for the ads.

- The layout person needs to combine the art generated by the graphic artist with text written by the copywriter. These elements form an effective layout.

- The administrative assistant plans to use a database program to track all client information, a scheduling program to record and display information related to project tracking and client meetings, and a word processor to generate letters to clients.

Only the graphic artist has previous computer experience. Jeff worked with computers for years, is comfortable with DOS commands, and is familiar with a variety of programs. Which computer should he buy? Should he purchase systems (and software) built around the easy-to-learn-and-use philosophy or the just-simple-enough-so-I-can-decipher-it philosophy? Because he runs a small business that relies heavily on the productivity of his employees (and he cannot spend a great deal of time and money in training), going for easy-to-use is a good move. The best solution for Jeff is to consider the software he needs and purchase easy-to-use systems to support this software. For his purposes, Jeff purchases Macintosh SE/30's with Microsoft Works for the administrative assistant and bookkeeper, and Mac IIci's with Aldus PageMaker 4.2 for the layout person, and Aldus Freehand for the artist.

Does My System Need To Be Compatible with Others at Work or Home?

Another consideration is compatibility. Does your company already use a specific brand of personal computer? If so, you may want to stick with this computer (IBM, Amiga, or Mac) to retain compatibility with the programs and data on existing machines. (However, particularly with IBM and Mac, several popular programs exchange data—and newer Macintoshes can read files created from several leading operating systems.)

In the early PC days, if you created a file on an IBM, you used this file only on an IBM. If you worked with a Macintosh, the file stayed on the Mac, unless you went through all kinds of hoops to convert the data to a format that a non-Mac computer can use. Today, the sharing gap is slowly closing. With the advent of the new Macintoshes and the sprouting of operating systems other than those chosen previously by IBM and Apple, applications are becoming more generous about sharing files between machines.

Suppose that your company, a major software developer, produces a Macintosh product that becomes so popular that IBM users want a version. You don't benefit by keeping the product in only one arena. Rather, you lose an incredible marketing opportunity and miss the chance of appeasing thousands of people. Consequently, you develop the software so different-yet-compatible versions of the program run in both Macintosh and IBM environments, and you can use the files created in these programs on either machine. This compatibility makes file sharing easier. Certainly, this trend is the wave of the future.

Leading this wave is Aldus Corporation's PageMaker, a successful desktop publishing program that runs on either a Macintosh or an IBM (or a clone). Although different versions of the program exist for the two different machines (to make use of the different operating systems), the files are usable in either machine.

For many applications, however, the program is available for only one genre of machine. A program that runs under DOS on an IBM cannot be understood by a Macintosh. Likewise, an IBM cannot read a file you created on a Mac. For more information about operating systems and software, see Chapter 10, "Familiarizing Yourself with the Operating System," and Part IV, "A Software Review."

Does the Computer Meet My Future Needs?

The advice here is simple: don't buy a dinosaur. The deal that says, "Buy this computer for $99 and get a free car wash," sounds good for the pocketbook, but odds are high that the system is obsolete and may not be around in a year—with no replacement parts in sight. Such clearance sales seem great deals now, but with a product as complex as a personal computer, a lack of technical support down the road can devastate you. Be sure that you purchase a system from a company you can depend on to be around for a long time (particularly if you have no technical skills). Don't purchase a system from a computer company that wasn't here yesterday and therefore may not be here tomorrow.

Another computer question involves system expansion. Although you may limit computer use to one or two applications right now (such as spreadsheets and word processing), you may later want to start desktop publishing. Can you add memory to the system? Does adding a board to the computer present a problem? Be sure that you know what you want the computer to eventually do, and purchase a system that enables you to expand the computer's capabilities.

Do I Want a PC, Amiga, Mac, or PC Clone?

Deciding which computer to buy is a difficult question to answer. People tend to gather under the banner of one computer model or another. Each category of computer has large and passionate fan clubs. Thanks to the shrinking compatibility gap, however, this decision is becoming less ominous.

Getting Around the Incompatibility Issue

In the past, when you chose one system over another, you were stuck with your decision. When you chose one computer, you became limited to using only software that runs on this computer. If you bought a Macintosh, you have all the great qualities of the Mac but you can't use

IBM programs. What if a company introduces a program that runs under DOS and solved every software need you ever had, but you have a Macintosh? What do you do?

With today's computers, one or more of the following methods may help you to get around the incompatibility problem:

- A file-transfer program, which enables you to read a DOS file on a Macintosh (and vice versa).

- A hardware fix that installs a *bridge board* inside the computer that enables the computer to run and work with data from both PC and Mac applications. These boards also are available for Amiga computers.

- Rely on the progressive thinking of software manufacturers and hope the makers of the desired software develop versions for your computer.

- Purchase a system, such as the Mac SE/30, which is capable of reading data produced under a variety of operating systems. All new Macintoshes are equipped with a SuperDrive, which reads from and writes to disks formatted with MS-DOS or OS/2.

- Purchase a Reduced Instruction Set Chip (RISC) computer (the first versions are planned to be released at the end of 1993). Apple and IBM currently are collaborating on RISC-based computers that will run DOS and Mac software, with no special hardware or software additions.

Choosing IBM, Amiga, or Mac

Which system do you choose? Much of the decision is determined by personal preference. Have you ever used DOS? Do you feel more comfortable with a graphical interface that enables you to select programs and files by clicking on the file name or on an icon (Macintosh)? Do you find the graphics interface restrictive because you prefer to control a computer by typing various DOS commands? Is the software you want to use available for both types of systems? If not, is a comparable program available for the system you prefer?

Some people prefer the IBM for writing and the Macintosh for graphics. The Amiga seems to be a hands-down favorite of people who work heavily in electronic visual arts. Other die-hard users believe the IBM is great for everything. On the flip side, some Mac enthusiasts claim their fingers might wither and fall off if they touch an IBM keyboard. The Amiga, although a great computer, seems to work best in the home, and in small-businesses, and the Amiga usually isn't considered for sophisticated business use. Power users tend to gravitate toward IBMs, IBM compatibles or Macintoshes.

Considering a PC Clone

When IBM clones first appeared on the market, these machines emulated the limited power of the original PC and offered the technology at a lower cost.

Because of the way the Macintoshes are designed, reproducing the design of the Mac hardware and user interface is difficult or impossible. Few clones are available for the Mac, although some exist.

What do you gain when you purchase a PC clone rather than a name brand? You may reduce the cost (a pleasant advantage), and if you shop wisely you still may find all the capabilities, support, and expansion possibilities available with a brand-name computer.

What Components Do I Get with My Computer?

Often, the components included in a computer system aren't obvious. When you purchase a computer, what do you really buy? Is the computer the system unit? Does the price include the monitor and disk drives?

The answers depend on where you purchase the system. If you buy a system piece-by-piece from a mail-order outfit or if you choose hardware from the *Computer Shopper*, expect to receive the components as you ordered them—piece-by-piece. If you purchase the equipment from a retail computer store, you may be purchasing a complete system: a monitor, a system unit, disk drives, a mouse, and perhaps even a printer. As with all else, be sure that you know exactly what you order and how much each component costs.

Usually, you can buy the elements of a computer system as separate parts. You certainly have the option of doing so, even if the system you are considering is advertised as a complete deal. Check around and make sure that you get exactly what you need in each component. If you buy all pieces separately, make sure that you purchase most of the following items:

- The system unit (which may or may not include a floppy disk and a hard disk, or two floppy disks)

- Disk drives (if necessary)

- A hard disk (if not included with the system unit)

- The keyboard

- The monitor

- Extra memory

- A modem

- A mouse

- A printer

- Extra devices, such as a scanner, plotter, or graphics tablet

- The operating system

- The applications software

If you plan to purchase these items separately, be sure that you also get the cables needed to assemble the system. Make sure that each item that attaches to the system unit includes the required cable; if any cables are missing, contact the dealer right away. For more information about assembling a system, see Part III "A Computer Primer."

What Extra Components Do I Need?

You can buy just the basic system—system unit, monitor, disk drives, operating system, and software. You also may need a printer (almost everyone needs a way to print the information entered into the computer). You also may decide to buy a modem, which enables you to connect, through the phone lines, to other computers and to information services, such as CompuServe, GEnie, Dialog, and Prodigy.

A scanner is great for getting logos and other artwork into a computer so that you can work with and include original art in brochures, newsletters, and advertising fliers. Although you may not need these capabilities in the basic system you purchase, these options are available.

Whether you need a mouse is determined by the software you choose. Computing on a Macintosh without a mouse is unthinkable and a mouse is therefore included with every Mac. Mice also are rapidly finding their way into popular PC applications. The new PS/1 comes with a mouse as standard equipment. For all kinds of applications, from spreadsheets and word processors to games, the mouse can be a fast and efficient means of selecting commands and making menu selections.

Where Do I Purchase Extra Components?

You can answer this question by looking at the options. Can you get these extra components elsewhere at a lower price? If so, do you receive technical support in the event the component fails? Don't buy an obsolete printer from a company with one foot out the door. If the printer breaks after the company folds, you may not find replacement parts—even ribbons.

Usually, consider the following three issues when you are ready to purchase extra components:

- Cost
- Support
- Quality

Nothing is surprising in the statement "You get what you pay for." If you want a quality product, you pay for it. If you want support for the product you buy, you also pay for support. Both quality and support are essential issues when considering a computer add-on purchase.

Before you buy, check the product reviews in popular computer magazines. *PC, Byte, MacWorld, InfoWorld,* and *Computer Shopper* are excellent magazines to begin the search for information. As you think about where to buy a system and whether to buy all components in one place or to purchase pieces from the places with the best prices, ask yourself whether the cost is worth the support and quality you receive. If the answer is yes, and if you can afford the cost, you wind up with a great product and a support team to back you up. If the answer is no, keep shopping.

Do I Buy a New or Used Computer?

Most people ignore the option of buying a used computer. Even if you plan to use a computer only for home, school, or occasional business tasks, buying a used computer is a bit risky. Although buying a used computer seems the cheaper way to go, you may end up paying out more in replacement parts if a part fails in a recycled machine. If you are starting on a shoestring and you can get a warranty from the store selling the used equipment, you may solve your computer problem with a used computer. You can find used computers listed in trade papers, on school bulletin boards, or at local user groups. Be careful, however, and be sure that you have an expert check out the system. Many retail computer outlets offer technical support; you can have a licensed technician check out the system for you.

Using Your Resources

As you begin your computer education, the best advice is to use all the resources available to you and learn everything you can before you buy. You quickly discover that the information and the range of choices can overwhelm you. However, knowing is better than not knowing, even if knowing makes the choice more complex. Usually, count on these resources as you gather data to help you choose the right system for you.

■ Personal experience

The personal experience of other people can be invaluable. You can learn from, and avoid repeating, others' mistakes. Ask friends and coworkers why they prefer their systems. Find a business similar to yours and look at the systems. Why did the company select the system? How much did the equipment cost? How much does the system benefit the business? What software handles the business work?

Learning by example is always the best way. Look around and talk to other computer users, who are happy to share with you what works, or doesn't work, for them. Don't, however, make the decision based wholly on what others tell you. The final test is how comfortable you feel with a new machine and what applications work best in particular situations.

■ Computer magazines

Many publications—weekly, monthly, bimonthly, and quarterly—inform you about which system to buy. Some magazines focus entirely on PC, Amiga, or Macintosh systems, and others center on general applications. Some excellent magazines are *PC, PC World, Byte, MacUser, MacWorld, PC Computing, InfoWorld,* and *Publish!.* Many leading computer magazine publishers do an excellent job of reviewing and summarizing the features of various computer products. These magazines are probably the best source of information as you compare the capabilities of the hardware and software.

■ User groups

A computer user group consists of die-hard fans who meet to share information about one particular computer model. PC, Macintosh, Atari, and Commodore user groups (and, undoubtedly, many more than these models) abound. When you attend a user-group meeting, you can get many answers about the products you are investigating. To learn about user groups in your area, consult the phone book, ask the local dealer, contact a local bulletin-board service, or talk to other users.

■ Retail outlets

When you approach a retail computer outlet, go in with a list of questions about the products you are exploring. Ask to see demonstrations of the machines, learn about the features that interest you, and ask about the best features for the applications you plan to use. Although you pay more if you purchase a computer from a retail outlet, you usually receive technical support for the equipment and a reasonable amount of software support, as well. During the investigation stage, however, do not commit your loyalty to one store or resource.

Before You Buy...

Exhaust your information resources before you invest in a computer system. Before you commit to a specific computer brand or to a particular application program, tap into the following resources:

■ Read computer magazines that cover a variety of computers and applications; especially, read the reviews of current hardware and software.

Some of the better magazines are *PC, PC World, Byte, MacUser, MacWorld, PC Computing, InfoWorld, Publish!, Home Computing, Games,* and *Personal Publishing.*

■ Talk to friends and business associates about computers and how satisfied (or dissatisfied) these people are with each kind of system.

■ Find a computer user group in your area and attend a meeting. Groups are available almost everywhere for all popular computers. Remember that although you may hear about the strong points of each group's computer of choice, you may not hear objective viewpoints at these meetings.

■ Go to a local computer store and ask a salesperson to demonstrate each category of computer. Ask to see how different operating systems work, and don't be afraid to ask more questions.

After you gather together all the information you need to decide on whether to buy an IBM, Amiga, Mac, or PC clone, the final decision comes down to one factor—personal preference. Just find the software you need to do the job, the computer with which you feel most comfortable (and that runs the software that interests you), and write the check.

Chapter Summary

In this chapter, you studied a variety of elements to consider before you purchase a computer system. From a basic section on how to determine what you want from a computer to more specialized discussions on budgeting, finding the system you want, and using your resources, this chapter also took you a few steps closer to purchasing a system. In the following chapter, you learn more about the similarities and differences of the basic system, and you explore the various kinds of available monitors.

Purchasing a Computer System

B y now, you probably made some preliminary decisions about the basic system you want (Amiga, Mac, or PC). You also may have decided on the programs you need for the computer (word processing, spreadsheet, or database programs), and the general price range that fits your budget.

After mulling over the various purchasing considerations, you are ready to ease into a serious investigation of specific computer systems. This chapter helps you narrow the field of possibilities by focusing on the qualities you need most in a system.

As you think about putting a system together, you need to decide what this system can do for you or your business in the future. Consider the kinds of software you *want* to own and more important, what categories of programs you *need* most for your business or personal use. Be sure that you also find out which machines run the software you plan to purchase.

You can make informed decisions about the model of computer you need for specific applications by answering the following questions:

- What model do you want?

- Should you mix and match components?

- How fast should the computer be?

- How much memory do you need?

- How much hard disk storage do you need?

- How many disk drives do you need?

- What kind of monitor do you want?

- What programs can you run?

- Do you need to connect the system with other computers?

- What support is offered?

Deciding Whether To Choose Software First

When you are buying a computer, should you *first* choose the software and *then* pick the computer to run the software? Some experts say yes and some say no.

The best approach is to consider all these options and make the choice that best meets your needs. However, choosing software first can help you reach a decision.

Suppose that you need an accounting program to help organize the bookkeeping system in your office. If the office is a stand-alone business that shares no files or data with another office, you can make a software choice by deciding which program you like best and then get the hardware that runs the software.

If you are part of a large chain of offices that shares information and programs, however, the choice may be limited to software the other offices are using. In this case, compatibility between programs is important: you must purchase a program—and a computer—that enables you to swap files with the other offices. You must either buy the same software and hardware or buy programs and computers that give you the compatibility you need.

Some people prefer to choose the software first. Finding a Macintosh program that meets your needs is a good argument for investing in a Macintosh. Discovering you are a born-to-publish Ventura Publisher user may prompt you to spend the computer budget on an IBM-compatible system.

When making computer choices, many people are born into one camp or the other. "I like the way IBM does things—always on the leading edge," or "The Macintosh makes learning and using the computer a nonthreatening and friendly task. This computer is the best choice for my office."

Other people haven't formed decisions, and the process of eliminating systems can be long and complicated. If you are having trouble deciding which computer to buy, your software preference can serve as a tie-breaker. Suppose that you are the new products publications specialist and must produce desktop-published materials on each new product the company introduces. You are told to find a computer on which to publish the materials. The company wants to spend only a small amount of money to produce these simple one-page fliers.

You are torn between purchasing an IBM AT clone or a Mac Classic II. You've weighed every factor, and although the Mac is a little more expensive, you are leaning in this direction. In the midst of the confusion, a friend tells you about an easy-to-use desktop publishing product, PFS: First Publisher, which has all the features you need for publishing the new-product fliers. The program, however, runs only on IBM (DOS) computers. The choices are to purchase the IBM system and First Publisher, to choose the Mac and purchase a different desktop publishing product with similar features, or to wait and shop around for additional hardware and software to further complicate your decision.

If you aren't required to purchase a particular software program, and you find no software that meets all your needs, decide on the hardware first and then find software that runs on the computer you chose.

Deciding on a Basic Computer System

Most small-business and home applications can be handled by a single desktop (or floor-standing) computer used by one person (see fig. 5.1). The basic structure of the system is a box (the *system unit*) that houses the memory chips, a hard disk drive, a floppy disk drive or drives, and other special devices. Attached to the box are a keyboard and perhaps a mouse. The display screen, or *monitor*, enables you to see what the computer and the software are doing. (Both the system unit and monitors are discussed in following sections of this chapter.) Because you need printed output (printed reports, mailing labels, newsletters, balance sheets, and so on), you also need a printer.

All desktop computers are a combination of the previously mentioned components. However, the speed at which computers process information, the amount of memory included, and the design of the components distinguish each computer. In the PC, Amiga, and Macintosh worlds, an evolution toward greater speed and storage has taken place since each of these machines was introduced.

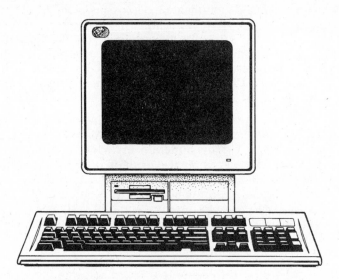

FIG. 5.1

A basic computer system.

If all this information sounds like an overwhelming smorgasbord of computer bits and pieces, don't be alarmed: buying a computer can be easy. Buying a computer takes one of two approaches. For new users, the package deal is best: you purchase a specific model of computer that comes with a system unit, monitor, disk drives, and occasionally, the printer (see the following section, "What Model Do You Need?"). On the other hand, many experienced users mix and match components by purchasing a monitor from one manufacturer, a system unit, drives, and memory from another, and so on.

If you are a new user, search for a manufacturer or retailer who sells and services complete systems. Then, after exploring this route, if you can't find a system with the capabilities you want and can afford, you can do a little more research and buy different components from different manufacturers. (For more information about putting systems together, see "Should You Mix and Match Components?" in a following section of this chapter.)

What Model Do You Need?

Putting together a computer system is no longer a process only for the electronically sophisticated user. Before the first real personal computers, the only way you could assemble a desktop computer was to build one from a variety of electronic parts. Today, you can walk into a computer store and walk out with a complete system. If you prefer, you can purchase a computer by mail order, or you can telephone the order directly to a manufacturer and have the computer delivered to your home or office.

When you walk into the neighborhood retail computer store, you see a variety of systems on display. Depending on the models of computers the store carries, you may see Macs, IBMs, and a variety of IBM-compatible computers, such as COMPAQs, Epsons, and Toshibas. With each major brand-name computer, however, you still have a few choices to make. Suppose that you want an IBM computer, but you aren't sure which IBM is the best choice. As you look around, you can see that IBM offers many different computer models.

Most major computer manufacturers build several computer models. This variety eliminates the need for shopping for various components and piecing computers together bit-by-bit (or chip-by-chip). You purchase the model that offers the components you want. In the IBM PS/2 line, for example, many models are available, each with different components. Consider the following comparison of two IBM PS/2 models:

IBM PS/1 Model B82	IBM PS/2 Model 80-041
System unit	System (tower) unit
VGA adapter*	VGA adapter*
2M memory	1M memory (expandable to 16M)
One 1.44M 3 1/2-inch drive	One 1.44M 3 1/2-inch drive
101-key keyboard	101-key keyboard

The monitor is sold separately.

The Macintosh also is available in several different models. The following list compares two of the more popular Macintosh models:

Macintosh SE/30	Macintosh IIci
System unit	System unit
2M memory	2M memory

continues

Macintosh SE/30	Macintosh IIci
One 1.44M floppy disk drive	One 1.44M floppy disk drive
One hard disk drive (40 or 80M)	One hard disk drive
Built-in 9-inch monitor	External color monitor*
Mouse	Mouse
Keyboard	Keyboard

*The monitor is sold separately.

Should You Mix and Match Components?

Some experienced computer users prefer to assemble or add to their computers by purchasing components from a variety of sources. Most people who mix and match get the parts by mail order—ordering a system unit, keyboard, and perhaps memory chips from one manufacturer; choosing a monitor from a second manufacturer; and perhaps buying disk drives from a third company. Some people build the basic system unit from components—a motherboard, box, power supply, and so on. Other people purchase entire systems (either by mail or from a retail outlet) and then later add other items, such as a printer or a mouse.

Two major caveats apply when you consider the mix-and-match approach to purchasing a computer system:

■ If you are inexperienced, have an experienced user or technical support person check your list before you order. Make sure that all the items you order work together and that you order everything you need.

■ Check out the manufacturer before you buy, especially if you are purchasing sight-unseen. Has the seller been in business long? Where does the company get equipment? Does the seller offer a warranty? If so, how long is the warranty effective? Several years ago, retail computer stores were a can't-lose choice; you saw and worked with the system before a purchase, and after you got the system home, you could call the store for help if something didn't work. Today, most retail stores continue this same service, but a great number of users prefer to cut out the retail costs and buy systems through wholesale catalogs or order by mail from ads in popular computer magazines. Whether you buy a complete system from one manufacturer or put together a system by purchasing parts from different manufacturers, be sure that you find out about the suppliers before you order.

Whether you decide to purchase an entire system or assemble a computer from various components, you still have several questions to answer. Which model do you need? Which components make up an ideal system? The following sections help you decide which features are important. For example, before you can decide between a particular model with 512K of RAM or one with 1M of RAM, you need to know how memory affects computer use.

How Fast Should Your Computer Be?

Inside the system unit is the brain of the computer system, the CPU (central processing unit), or microprocessor.

At the most basic level, the *microprocessor* controls the speed of the system, although other factors also affect the speed. (These other considerations, such as the data path, are explained in a following section of this chapter.) A microprocessor's speed is measured in *megahertz* (MHz), or millions of cycles per second.

To you, the speed issue means how quickly a computer starts a program, calculates numbers, or performs a variety of other tasks. The faster the speed of the microprocessor, the quicker the machine.

The computers discussed throughout this book—PC, Amiga, and Macintosh—use different CPUs. Each CPU has a unique way of processing information, runs at a different speed, and provides different capabilities. This section explains CPU considerations.

How Does the CPU Work?

The *central processing unit,* or CPU, is the single chip that makes a computer work; without this chip, the system is nothing more than an expensive paperweight. The CPU controls all the calculating and processing that happens within the computer; the CPU also regulates and communicates information internally (running memory cards, communicating with RAM, and so on) and externally (controlling external devices, such as the printer, mouse, modem, plotter, and so on).

The CPU sends the information along a data path to the various components—internal or external. The instructions on the chip tell the computer how to send the data. How quickly the CPU processes information is related to two factors: the speed at which the CPU is capable of operating (in MHz) and the width of the path along which the data is sent. Data paths can be 8 bits (the computer can send 8 bits of data at once), 16 bits, or 32 bits wide (see fig. 5.2).

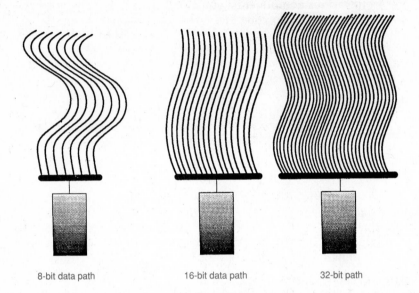

FIG. 5.2

The differences in data paths.

8-bit data path   16-bit data path   32-bit path

Think of the speed of the computer in terms of the amount of water (gallons per minute) that runs through a garden hose. An 8-bit data path simultaneously uses 8 garden hoses to fill a pool; a 16-bit data path uses 16 hoses, and a 32-bit data path uses 32 hoses. If all the hoses operate at the same speed, which data path works faster? Obviously, the 32-bit (or 32-hose) data path gets the job done more quickly.

If you are new to computers, the term *CPU* may sound too much like computer jargon for comfort. You should know more about the CPU, however, before you purchase a computer. The capabilities of the CPU in a system have a great effect on the speed of the computer and also can affect the kind of software you use.

PCs and CPUs

The first PCs, equipped with 8088 microprocessors, are slow by today's standards. The IBM PC and the XT operated at between 4 and 10 MHz, and the 80286, introduced with the PC AT, was capable of speeds of 8 to 16 MHz. The difference between the data transmission times in these two processors involved many elements, but at the most basic level, the processing was faster in the 286 machine because of the speed of the chip and the width of the data path. Table 5.1 shows the CPUs used in popular PC models.

Table 5.1 PC CPUs

Model	CPU	Speed (MHz)
PC/XT	8088 (8086)	4.7-10
AT	80286	8-16
386	80386, 80386SX 80386DX	16-33
486	80486, 80486SX, 80486DX	16-50

The 80386—and now the 80486—microprocessors further increased the speed of the chip and the size of the data path. With the 386, the data path was expanded to 32 bits; the 386 machines can process information up to four times faster than the original PCs.

Computers with 80486 microprocessors are setting new standards in speed. Although you can pay dearly for this state-of-the-art technology, you can find a 486 system for less than $3,000. Some mix-and-match computer stores can provide the 486 system for about $2,000. In a recent issue of *Computer Shopper,* one popular mail-order company, Gateway 2000, offered a complete high-end 33 MHz 486 system for $2,655 (and if you need only 4M of memory, the cost is $2,495). This system has the following components:

33 MHz 486 (the CPU, an 80486, operates at 33 MHz)

8M RAM

A 1.2M 5 1/4-inch drive

A 1.44M 3 1/2-inch drive

200M hard disk drive

VGA adapter with 512K video RAM

14-inch super VGA color monitor with 1,024-by-768 resolution

124-key keyboard

Mouse

MS-DOS 5.0

Windows 3.1

PS/2 CPUs

The IBM 80386 machine was introduced into the PS/2 line with the PS/2 Model 80. The PS/2 also introduced a new kind of data path, which enables the data to be transmitted independently of the CPU operation. This technique lightens the load on the processor and enables the data to flow faster.

This new technology, known as Micro Channel Architecture, is a revolutionary new concept from IBM and sets a new standard independent of the PC data bus. Only PS/2 Models 56 and above include Micro Channel Architecture; if you plan to purchase an MCA system, be sure that you investigate the effect MCA has in terms of add-on boards and other devices. Because MCA is a relatively new technology, traditional PC expansion boards do not work in MCA machines. Make sure that you talk to the dealer or to the board's manufacturer before you buy components that may be incompatible with MCA. Table 5.2 lists the CPUs in each PS/2 model.

Table 5.2 PS/2 CPUs		
Model	CPU	Speed (MHz)
PS/2 Model 25	8086	8
PS/2 Model 25/286	80286	10
PS/2 Model 35	80286	20
PS/2 Model 40/SX	80386SX	20
PS/2 Model 56	80386SLC	20
PS/2 Model 57	80386SLC	20
PS/2 Model P70	80386	20
PS/2 Model 70	80386 or 80486	25
PS/2 Model 80	80386	20
PS/2 Model 90 XS	80486	25
PS/2 Model 90	80486	33
PS/2 Model 95	80486	20
PS/2 Model 95	80486	33

A problem with the PS/2 Micro Channel Architecture is that most higher level machines (computers with 80286, 80386, or 80486 CPUs) use the new data bus design. Although these machines are software compatible with previous PCs, you cannot use the same hardware inside a PS/2 Model 50 that you use in a PC AT. This design also affects how data transfers. This situation is one reason IBM introduced the PS/1. The PS/1 retains the standard PC AT-style data bus and uses the 80286 microprocessor.

Understanding the Ads

You may see the following terms when you are computer shopping:

Bus:

        PC-compatible
        AT-compatible

CPU:

        286
        386
        486

ISA (AT bus)

EISA (standard for extending 16-bit AT bus to 32-bit [386+] machines. PC bus is 8-bit [8088]; PC/AT bus is 16-bit [80286]; EISA is 32-bit [80386+]).

The term *PC-compatible* means that the computer uses the 8088 CPU and is compatible with hardware and software sold for the IBM PC. The term *AT-compatible* means the computer uses the 80286 CPU and is compatible with hardware and software for 286 machines. Finally, when you see a machine referred to as a 286, 386, or 486, you know the computer runs on the 80286, 80386, or 80486 microprocessor, respectively.

Macintoshes and CPUs

Similar to the PC generation, different Macintoshes use different CPUs. The CPU in the Macintosh is housed on the motherboard inside the system unit of the computer. Table 5.3 shows the different Macintosh CPUs and operating speeds.

138

Table 5.3 Macintosh CPUs

Model	CPU	Speed (MHz)
Mac Classic	68000	7
Mac Classic II	68030	16
Mac SE/30	68030	16
Mac PowerBook 100	68000	16
Mac PowerBook 140	68030	1
Mac PowerBook 170	68030	25
Mac LCII	68030	16
Mac IIsi	68030	20
Mac IIci	68030	25
Quadra 700	68040	25
Quadra 950	68040	33

Macintosh computers use a chip designed by Motorola, Inc. Some users argue that the chips themselves are better designed and more powerful than their Intel cousins, used in PCs and PS/2s. The result is that the Macintoshes are powerful computers available in different models that can fit into a variety of applications, from home and school use to high-end business operations.

In 1994, the first *RISC*-based (Reduced Instruction Set Chip) Macintosh 88000 CPU-based series is scheduled for production. These chips transfer data faster because the instructions contained on the CPU are less complicated and are therefore easier for the computer to process. This new technology also will provide a platform for innovative programs, such as voice processing and cursive handwriting recognition.

What Do Differences in CPUs Mean to You?

To a new computer user, all this technical talk about CPUs may seem overwhelming. When you go computer shopping, be aware of the CPU each computer uses for the following reasons:

■ If you are buying a PC, you need to know whether the machine runs the software you want to use. For example, if you decided to work with a program available only for 286 machines, don't buy a PC-compatible computer with an 8088 CPU.

■ The faster the CPU you can purchase for the money, the better. If you can find a 486 system for the same amount of money as a 386, for example, purchase the 486. The newer technology offers you more power and speed and is compatible with the software for earlier machines. If you can purchase a Macintosh with a 68040 CPU for the same price you may spend for a 68030 Mac LCII, you are better off with the more powerful computer.

How Much Memory Do You Need?

For new users, memory can be a perplexing term. Many people confuse computer memory with storage. Remember that *memory* is what the computer uses to hold programs and calculations while running the application. *Storage* is the area where the programs and data files are kept when the computer is turned off.

Throughout this book, and throughout any hardware or software manual, you see three letters used to tell you how much memory or storage is being discussed. These letters are K (kilobytes), M (mega-bytes), and G (gigabytes). The most basic measurement of data is a bit. A *bit* is one electronic pulse, eight of which make up a byte of information. (One *byte* is roughly equivalent to one text character of information.)

One K, or *kilobyte*, is equal to about one thousand bytes (or characters) of information. (You can think of a 1K file as being about as long as a double-spaced, one-page letter.) One M, or *megabyte,* is equal to about one million bytes of information. One G, or *gigabyte,* is equal to about one billion bytes (1,000 megabytes) of information.

A computer's memory is measured in either kilobytes or megabytes. You may see a system's memory shown as 640K or 1M, 2M, 4M, and so on. You also may see the terms *expanded*, *extended*, and *virtual* memory. The following section introduces you to the memory issue. The sidebar "Understanding Expanded, Extended, and Virtual Memory" elaborates on this subject.

Understanding Memory Basics

The application (software) you use can be affected by the speed at which a computer processes information. Similarly, the application influences the amount of memory you need in a system.

The first generation of PCs were equipped with only 64K. The original PCs were capable of expansion to 576K, but many users started with and stayed with 64K until newer models appeared. Programmers, therefore, wrote applications needing only 64K to run. These software products didn't do much by today's standards: usually, the software filled only a specific need, such as tracking employee information or creating an electronic spreadsheet. At the time, however, even limited software programs were regarded as revolutionary.

How Much Memory?

If you already purchased a computer and are trying to figure out how much memory the system has, you can use one of the following options:

- ■ If you use a DOS 5.0 machine, type **MEM**, which displays on-screen the memory information.

- ■ On a Macintosh, go to the Apple menu and select "About the Finder" for available RAM information.

- ■ Some utility programs for both the PC and Mac can display the amount of available memory.

For more information about performing the preceding procedures on each computer, see Chapter 10, "Familiarizing Yourself with the Operating System."

Because of memory requirements, some programs are too large to run on older model computers. Today's applications are written to use memory more frugally, but because the capabilities of the programs grew, these programs require more and more memory. The more capabilities built into a program, the more memory the program requires. Powerful programs are bigger than their less-muscled counterparts.

In Chapter 3, memory was compared to the top of a library table. You placed on the table at a particular time only the files you needed to accomplish a specific task. After you completed the task, you put the files away and opened different files for the next task. Memory handles data and programs in a similar manner; only the programs you need at a particular time use the RAM you have available.

Suppose that your work requires two different DOS-based programs: one spreadsheet program and one word processing program. The manufacturers of both programs recommend that systems have at least 640K of RAM to run the programs. Do these requirements mean you must have 1280K to run both programs—640K for each program? Thankfully, the answer is no. Because you run only one program at a time, a computer needs this available RAM for only one program at a time. 640K is all you need.

NOTE You can find out how much memory a program requires by reading the information on the software packaging (the requirement should be shown on the back or the side, or in the first few pages of the program's documentation) or by calling the manufacturer.

Understanding Expanded, Extended, and Virtual Memory

As you investigate the different kinds of systems available, if you are looking at IBM or IBM-compatible computers, you run into the terms extended and expanded memory. If your path leads toward the Macintosh line of computers, *virtual memory* is an important key term.

Extended memory is memory similar to RAM. Introduced with the IBM PC AT, extended memory enables you to set aside an extra amount of RAM space in the form of a disk cache (a separate segment of RAM, which you can use for programs and data in the current work session). Extended memory is memory above 1M in address; this memory can be accessed only by 286 and higher machines running in a special mode known as *protected* mode. DOS doesn't run in protected mode. Therefore, the only use of extended memory under DOS is as a special storage area for printer data or as a RAM disk or disk cache. DOS then is fooled into "seeing" the extra memory as another disk drive.

Expanded memory, however, uses a different memory-addressing technology to give users more available RAM. Expanded memory is a paging scheme where a window of, say, 16K is opened up in memory below 1M (that DOS can see as memory). DOS uses this window to point to successive 16K pages in memory above 1M. To use expanded memory, you must have a program that supports *EMS* (Expanded Memory Specifications). To determine whether a software package supports EMS, consult the program's documentation or contact your dealer.

Virtual memory is not a new concept; however, Macintosh has only recently provided this memory expansion option for the Mac II line of computers. Virtual memory enables you to run more applications by using part of the hard disk as an extension to your physical RAM. If you have 4M RAM, therefore, running virtual memory makes the computer appear to have 8M. Virtual memory is currently available only on Mac II computers that use Operating System 7.0 and installed with a *PMMU* (paged memory management unit).

The amount of memory in a system also affects the speed of the computer. If a program uses the computer's entire memory allotment, the processing is slower than if a smaller percentage of the computer's memory is used. If a 128K program runs slowly in a 128K machine, the program may run faster in a 256K or 640K machine.

The original Macintosh had 128K of user memory. The next generation of Macs upgraded memory to 512K and then to 1M. Now you can get a Macintosh with anywhere from 2M to 256M of available memory.

If you already know the software you want, determine how much memory the system needs to run the program. If the system you are considering lacks this much memory, you can have the computer dealer add more memory before you take the system home. (This procedure is known as upgrading the memory.) You also can add memory to the system at a later time.

Upgrading Memory

The way you add memory to a system depends on the kind of system you buy. You can add memory to some systems by plugging in additional memory chips on the motherboard (although you shouldn't add memory chips yourself unless you really know your way around the inside of a system unit).

The best information resource for upgrading memory in a system probably is the manual packaged with the system. If you are unsure whether the computer requires additional memory chips or boards, call the manufacturer of the computer. If you prefer, you can take the system to a local technical support department and have the technicians investigate upgrade options and install the extra memory.

The cost of upgrading the memory in a computer varies. Older, slower computers can use older, slower memory chips, which cost less than newer, faster chips. Conversely, the new, faster machines use faster memory chips, which are more expensive than the older chip designs.

How Many Disk Drives Do You Need?

You need some means of permanently storing information; otherwise, the computer is just an expensive typewriter. The most common form of storage is the disk drive. The two kinds of disk drives are the *floppy disk drive* and the *hard disk drive*. The following sections explain these components in detail.

Floppy Disk Drives

A floppy disk drive stores less data and works slower than a hard disk drive. If you have the option of using a hard disk drive almost exclusively, is a floppy disk drive even necessary to the computer? Although reducing the number of floppy disks that seem to accumulate in a computer work area would be nice, the answer definitely is yes, you do need a floppy disk drive.

All software comes on disks. When you buy a program, you need some way of getting the program into the machine, so every machine must have at least one floppy disk drive. With most computers, you can add a second floppy disk drive. For either drive, the size of the drive—5 1/4 or 3 1/2—is up to you, the makers of the computer you choose (the IBM PS/2 uses the 3 1/2-inch disk drive, although the 5 1/4-inch drive is available), and the developers of the software you purchase.

Until recently, most programs were packaged on standard 5 1/4-inch floppy disks (see fig 5.3). This practice meant having a 5 1/4-inch disk drive was an absolute requirement for a computer. Other considerations, however, still exist. The older disk drives format disks by using a scheme of 40 tracks of data organized in 9 sector groups, for a total capacity of 360K bytes of storage per disk. The older disk is labeled *2S/2D*, which means *2-Sided, Double Density*. However, AT class machines use a disk drive that fits 80 tracks with 15 sector formats on the same 5 1/4-inch surface. This disk is the *2S/HD*, or *2-Sided, High Density* disk, which can hold 1.2M of data.

FIG. 5.3

A 5 1/4-inch floppy disk.

One of the major uses of the floppy disk drive is for backing up the hard disk drive and copying programs and data in case something goes wrong with the computer or the original disks. The high-density disk drive means fewer floppy disks to purchase and track. Floppy disk drives that store 1.2M of data can read the lower density 360K disks, but the 360K disk drives cannot read 1.2M disks. Buy the disk drive with the highest density within your budget. Remember that when you share files with other computers, you need to format high-density disks at a lower capacity so that systems with low-density drives can read the data on the disk. (This formatting procedure is explained in Part III of this book.)

The next standard drive was for the 3 1/2-inch disk (see fig. 5.4). This new disk is a small hard-shell floppy disk, which is harder to destroy, which makes the disk easier to care for and use. These drives also have two rated capacities: 720K and 1.44M. Again, remember both disk capacity and disk and drive compatibility. A disk drive that can read and write to high-density disks can save you some time and trouble, but if you need to share data with other computers in the office, make sure that you get a drive that also reads from and writes to disks from the other machines.

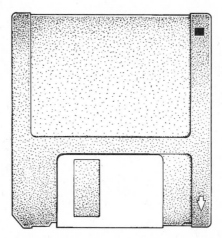

FIG. 5.4

A 3 1/2-inch
floppy disk.

With many popular programs today, you have the option of purchasing the program on either 5 1/4-inch or 3 1/2-inch disks. If you think you need both sizes of disks (if you plan to use files created on an older computer equipped with only 5 1/4-inch drives), buy two disk drives for your computer, one drive of each size. Otherwise, you may be forced to hunt for a friend's machine that enables you to copy the information from the disk size you have to the disk size you need.

For many simple applications, you can get by with two floppy disk drives. For most applications that process a substantial amount of data, however, a hard disk is becoming the standard data storage unit. A small hard disk drive costs around $200. The cost of a single floppy disk drive is $59 to $99. But here's the clincher: the smallest hard disk drive is at least 20M, which is equal to 17 HD (1.2M) floppy disks. And if you are using a system with only two floppy disk drives, you must insert and remove disks many times just to work with one program.

Hard Disk Drives

A hard disk drive has greater speed and greater capacity than floppy disk drives. A hard disk drive usually is housed inside the system unit and cannot be removed. (For this reason, you may occasionally run across a reference to a hard disk as a *fixed disk*.) Although in the past, a hard disk drive was a luxury, this device is required for most of today's larger application programs. Figure 5.5 shows a hard disk inside an IBM computer.

Hard disk drive

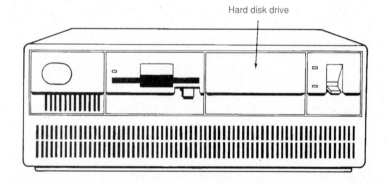

FIG. 5.5

A hard disk inside the system unit.

At the most basic level, a hard disk is a storage device—similar to a floppy disk—that stores substantially more data than a floppy disk and is inside a housing of some kind. This housing can be the system unit of the computer, or with an external hard disk drive, the housing can be the hard disk drive's case. Unlike a floppy disk, you cannot remove a hard disk from the housing.

Several different kinds of hard disks are available. Most people use an *internal* hard disk. This kind of hard disk is housed within the system unit of the computer. *External* hard disk drives also are available, which enable you to add hard disk storage to a computer without buying an entirely new system. *Removable* hard disk drives also are available, but these units are used primarily by advanced users and usually are more expensive than either internal or external hard disks. Internal hard disks are the best buy, although many users add external hard disk drives when storage capacity needs exceed the capacity of the existing hard disk.

Hard disks are popular for the following reasons:

- You can store more information (from 20M to more than 1.6G) on a hard disk than you can on a floppy disk.

- You can store and retrieve information from a hard disk much faster than you can with floppy disks.

- Because the hard disk is enclosed, you are less apt to damage the disk (or the data). Enclosed within the housing, the hard disk is safe from coffee, smoke, and other environmental dangers that can harm floppy disks.

- Many programs now require a hard disk. Even though programs are available that can be run from floppy disks, this process is extremely slow and limited, unless transferred to a hard disk. Additionally, if you are dealing with large amounts of data, such as organizing data in an extensive database or working with large spreadsheets, accessing the data from a floppy disk can be painfully slow.

Hard disks are available with varying amounts of storage space. The smallest hard disk drive you can buy now is 20M (megabytes). As you may recall, a megabyte is equal to one million characters, which is a great deal of storage space. As programs get bigger and require more storage space for the program and data files, hard disks with more storage space are becoming the standard. In the IBM PS/2 family, you can purchase a system with a hard disk in sizes ranging from 40M to 1.6G.

How much hard disk space is enough? If your applications are fairly limited, if you delete those one-time letters from the word processing files, if you don't try to keep ten years of customer information in the computer, and so on, you can manage with almost any size hard disk drive. The key word is *manage*. Some application data files can be stored on floppy disks until needed. Other files can be compressed with special programs so that the files take up less space when not in use. Different programs take up different amounts of space. The files you create with various programs also produce files of different sizes. A short letter you compose in a word processing program may use only a small amount of storage space, say, 6K. A one-page newsletter created in a desktop publishing program, however, can take many times this amount of disk space.

When you purchase software, the manufacturers tell you the minimum space requirements for the program, but remember that these requirements are for *the program only*. You need more space for storing the files that you create. Talking with someone who uses the program regularly may help you to learn how much storage space you may need for intensive work with this software.

When you buy a hard disk, apply the same rule of thumb you used for the other components: buy a hard disk with as much storage space as you can afford.

The amount of storage space isn't the only consideration. Speed also is a major factor. Disk drives are rated by how long they take to find data (the *average seek time*) and the time required to send the information to the microprocessor (the *transfer rate*). The average seek time is measured in milliseconds, and the transfer rate is measured in bytes per second. These two specifications mean more than any others when you compare the speeds of hard disk drives. The following list shows the basic ratings of hard disk speeds:

Rating	Seek time (in milliseconds)	Transfer rate (bytes per second)
Good	40ms	250K bps
Fast	25ms	500K bps
Ultra fast	12-20ms	700-900K bps

Disk controllers are the other half of a hard disk drive system. The *controller* is a board mounted inside the computer. The controller actually communicates information from the hard disk drive to the CPU and from the CPU to the hard disk drive. The controller is the single biggest contributor to the overall speed of the drive. A bad controller on a good drive makes a bad drive. An excellent controller can overcome some of the shortcomings of a slower drive. Make sure that the controller works with the machine and the drive. If you are unsure about the controller, ask your local dealer or consult the manufacturer for more information.

When you purchase a hard disk drive independently of the system, you can purchase either a hard disk drive kit or a bare drive. A hard disk drive kit contains the controller, cables, mounting hardware, and the drive. A bare drive is only the drive, and you must purchase all additional items separately.

As with all other components of the system, the faster the drive, the higher the cost. And the larger the storage capacity of the drive, the more it costs as well. If you can't afford all the size you need, opt for speed. Paying a little more for a faster controller also improves the overall performance of the system.

Before you make a decision, find all the information you can about the drives you are considering and ask the opinions of other computer users to find out what drives they recommend and why.

Choosing a Monitor

The choice of monitor is important, especially if you stare into the monitor's amber or green face day after day. Like all else related to computers, wide ranges of features and capabilities are available with monitors. In this section, you learn about the various monitors, decide what features are most important in the monitor you purchase, and find out about graphics adapters.

Evaluating Your Display Needs

Figuring out exactly what monitor features are important to you is a good way to focus on a particular monitor. As you think about the features you want in a monitor, consider the following questions:

■ *Will you work primarily with text?*

If the program or programs you plan to use deal primarily with text, be sure that you get a monitor with good *resolution*. (Resolution, when discussing monitors, is the number of dots per inch used to display characters and graphics on-screen.) In particular, when working with small characters hour after hour, the capability of the monitor to display text in well-formed, crisp characters is important. Poor screen resolution results in blood-shot and tired eyes. For text-intensive applications, stretch the purse strings and buy the monitor that gives the best resolution.

■ *Do you often use graphics in your work?*

Some monitors and graphics adapters are better suited than others for displaying graphics. As you learn in this chapter, different monitors and graphics adapters deliver varying levels of display clarity.

■ *Do you prefer a color or a monochrome monitor?*

You can let the software mandate whether you purchase a color monitor. Even if the program you plan to use displays screens in color, however, you may still have the option of disabling the color feature and showing the screens in black and white. Most programs that have color capability also can display in monochrome, so you don't lose anything from a software standpoint by choosing monochrome. Monochrome monitors offer a good display, with clearly formed characters and good screen resolution. Color can be both fun and functional, enabling you to add personality to your on-screen work, set the screen displays you find most pleasing, and customize applications.

■ *Is the size of the screen display important?*

Monitors are available in different sizes. From a small 9-inch to a 21-inch, 23-inch, or whopping 2-page display to a rather strange-looking vertical monitor, you have a variety of sizes and shapes. The special monitors, such as extra large sizes, 2-page, or vertical monitors, are expensive, so if you are working within a budget, you may want to see whether a conventional monitor offers you the features you need most.

■ *Is speed a critical issue?*

Similar to hard disks, monitors and graphics cards work at different speeds. Some monitors and graphics cards update the screen faster than others; if this feature is important for you, be sure that you shop around to find a monitor with a quick screen-update speed.

Understanding Different Monitor Types for PCs

The most obvious difference in monitors is whether the display is in color or monochrome (single color). Other differences include the size and shape of the monitor, the model of graphics adapter you can use, and the kind of circuitry used in the monitor. Like hard disk drives, a display is a combination of a controller (a *display adapter*) and the monitor.

With every monitor, you must have a display adapter to send information from the system unit to the monitor. Each model of display adapter has a built-in character set to display standard printable characters—A through Z, 0 through 9, *, %, $, and so on. Every display adapter also can switch to a graphics mode, in which patterns (or graphics) can be drawn based solely on the placement of individual dots on-screen. For more information about a particular display adapter, consult the manual that comes with the adapter or consult your dealer.

Monitors, like printers, are rated by the capability of using dots (*pixels*) to create patterns. The more pixels on-screen, the better-looking the picture. Curves appear more rounded, and lines are displayed as very thin or very bold. Some monitors are better than others. Some screens provide clear, accurate representations of the images and characters, but others show characters and graphics that you may find jagged-looking and sometimes hard to read. This difference in display quality is because of differences in the *resolution* of the display. Good, or high, resolution uses a greater number of pixels to display the image. Low resolution uses fewer pixels, which results in an image that can appear slightly distorted or choppy.

For some people, choosing a monitor is the easiest part of this whole task. Many people simply choose the software they want, see what kind of monitor the software manufacturer recommends, and shop for this particular monitor. This approach is fine, provided that the monitor fits in your budget and works with all the software you plan to purchase.

Monochrome Monitors

The world of monochrome monitors is uncomplicated. The first computers used only a one-color display, usually green on the early PCs. When you use this kind of monitor for an application, such as word processing, the monitor displays green characters against a black background.

IBM released a monochrome text monitor with the original PC. The *character cell* (the matrix of dots in which a character is displayed) was 9-by-14 dots; this matrix made the text easier to read than text on the CGA (IBM's first color adapter), which had an 8-by-8 character cell. This difference between the character cells (9-by-14) and graphics cells (8-by-8) is the real distinction between text mode and graphics mode for all PC monitors. Text mode sees cells in which characters are displayed; graphics mode sees dots.

Then Lotus released 1-2-3. IBM monochrome monitors were unable to display 1-2-3 graphs, and the text was hard to read on CGA color monitors. Hercules introduced another standard, a high-resolution text monitor that displayed graphics. Hercules monitors require Hercules cards, and sales took off after Lotus 1-2-3 supported Hercules.

The original IBM monochrome display had a resolution of 720-by-350 pixels. This designation means that the monitor displays 720 pixels across the screen (horizontally) and 350 pixels down (vertically). This resolution is acceptable for one screen. The characters on the IBM monochrome display were crisp and clear, which made the display popular in business use where basic text operations were needed. The monitor didn't display graphics, and this one major drawback was overlooked because many applications didn't require graphics capability. Today, however, so many programs use graphical menu systems, the original IBM monochrome monitor cannot display all the modern software.

Monochrome monitors are available in three varieties: green, amber, and white (or *paper white*) screens. The green-screen monochrome monitor was the first of the bunch. Then the amber monitor appeared, which many people found easier on the eyes. The paper-white monitor is the current popular monochrome, offering high resolution and a sense that what you see on-screen looks similar to the final printout.

Color Monitors

Color monitors open even more possibilities. On a simple word processing display, you can display an underlined word in red, a boldfaced word in green, and a boldfaced underlined word in cyan. A quick glance at the screen gives you a great deal of information, just by the colors used to display the words. Color costs more, however, and if you purchase a low-end color monitor, you may be purchasing poorer resolution than a comparably priced monochrome monitor offers.

The following section explains the various display adapters that work with the different kinds of color monitors. The monitor and adapter greatly affect the quality of the resolution you see on-screen.

Display Adapters

The major kinds of color display are Color Graphics Adapter (*CGA*), Enhanced Graphics Adapter (*EGA*), Video Graphics Array (*VGA*), a higher-resolution VGA (*Super VGA*), and variations of multisync monitors. The differences are in how many colors can be displayed at a time and how many pixels are displayed by the monitor. Some monitors are specific to one kind of display adapter, such as CGA. Other monitors are designed to take advantage of all color output, including boards not yet designed. These monitors are *multisync monitors*, which adjust automatically to the synchronization frequency of the display board. Multisync monitors usually are VGA monitors, which work with VGA adapters, that also act like EGA monitors and work with any graphics adapter you may use.

 NOTE With multisync capability, you can use the monitor to display software designed to run on systems equipped with CGA, EGA, VGA, or Super VGA monitors.

On IBM PCs, CGA was the first design to offer color. This adapter displays characters in an 8-by-8 character cell; as a result, text characters are slightly rough around the edges. In graphics mode, the CGA can display text and graphics in two resolutions: a medium-resolution color mode (320-by-200), which displays four different colors, and high-resolution mode, which displays two colors. In text mode, the CGA can display in 40- or 80-column character widths (the larger the number, the smaller the character) and in 16 different colors. CGA adds color to the display of many programs but the quality doesn't come close to the definition of a color photograph. Some color, however, is better than none at all and, depending how the program uses these colors, the result can be quite good.

EGA, or Enhanced Graphics Adapter, adds more dots per inch and has more colors available at a given time. The character cell for the EGA adapter is 8-by-14. Resolution for EGA goes up to 640-by-360 and displays 16 colors at a time from a palette of 64 colors. The bottom line is that EGA produces a better picture than CGA, with a wider variety of sharper colors.

The introduction of VGA not only advanced but also changed color technology. The VGA adapter interacts with the monitor in a different manner than the technology of EGA or CGA. With a VGA card and monitor, the video signals are *analog* signals, and each signal is a separate color (red, blue, or green). The signals then are mixed and changed in intensity to give a wide spectrum of colors. This signal mixing allows even more colors and sharper images on-screen. With VGA, the screen is composed of 800-by-600 pixels (Super VGA has a resolution of 1024-by-768 pixels), with up to 256 separate colors displayed at the same time, and offers a color choice (a *palette*) of 262,144 shades and tones.

The PS/2 models 25 and 30 use another display technology: *MCGA*. The Multi-Color Graphics Array is a display adapter built into the motherboards of Models 25 and 30. Although similar to the CGA, the MCGA can display several colors and provide text and graphics resolution better than CGA standards.

When you purchase a color monitor, expect to pay two prices. The first price is in dollars: the better the monitor and adapter, the higher the price tag. If you watch for special offers from manufacturers (by reading the industry magazines), however, you may pick up a VGA card and monitor as cheaply as you can buy EGA equipment.

The second price you pay is in speed—or, rather, the lack of speed. For the screen to display so many dots with so many colors, the adapter must use a better video processor and even come with special memory to track each pixel and the color the pixel represents. Some cheaper display cards offer the highest resolution available but may offer this resolution with a lack of speed or even a little flicker when a screen clears and redisplays. Because the makers of adapter cards often re-engineer and update their cards, the best way to make a selection is either to see the display card and monitor combination in action at a local store or to read magazine reviews of this combination before you buy.

Another trick you can use when choosing a monitor is to see how many different mail-order houses sell a particular model. These companies do *not* want these boards or monitors returned and don't sell only the cheap stuff. If only one company sells a display or card, wait until the hardware is reviewed in a major computer magazine.

Multisync monitors offer a good choice in display technology. These monitors are designed to handle a large variation in the kinds of signal the monitor processes. A multisync monitor is expensive but if your color needs to change or evolve, the investment is worthwhile. Multisync monitors also have tiny pixels. Because this monitor creates sharp on-screen images even at lower resolutions, the overall quality is better than the displays of single-sync monitors.

A final note on PC displays. The price differences among the classes of monitors continue to shrink. Most good adapters can be switched to display even monochrome images. If you buy a flexible display card and an expensive monitor, you leave room for easy future upgrades.

Understanding Macintosh Monitors

With PC technology, the monitor and display adapter you choose determine the quality of the on-screen image. The basic category break also holds true for Macintosh monitors, both color and monochrome. Beyond this decision, however, complications exist because of the differences between Macintosh and PC technology.

The basic difference between PC and Mac monitors is in the way the signals are sent to the display. With PCs, the quality of the display is mandated by the monitor model and display adapter. On the Macintosh, the quality of the display is controlled by both the software and the monitor's features.

All Macs use analog monitors that receive video input from the separate signals. The red comes in as one signal, the blue as another, and the green as yet another. (These monitors are often referred to as RGB monitors—Red, Green, Blue.) You can produce an almost unlimited number of hues by varying the strengths of the three signals.

In terms of display quality, the monitor doesn't control the formation of characters as much as the computer's internal character generator ROM does. Because of the separate signals in the analog color monitors (you also can purchase analog monochrome monitors), however, the distortion often present in the color composite monitors doesn't occur, because of the variety of hues available with analog monitors, users can achieve greater contrast and better blending and shading, which creates effects that appear to offer better screen resolution.

The first Mac monitor was built into the system unit (see fig. 5.6). The monitor was small, 4 1/2-by-7 inches, giving only a 9-inch diagonal viewing area, yet the resolution was superior to most standards available at the time. Since then, Mac monitors were introduced in a variety of shapes and sizes—from 12- to 21-inch screens (measured diagonally) to elongated full-page monitors that can display an entire page.

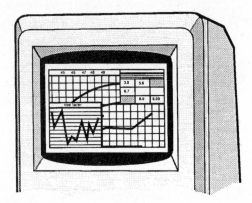

FIG. 5.6

The original Mac, showing the integrated monitor.

Figure 5.7 shows a more recent Mac system. The basic shape of this system more closely resembles a PC than the original Mac. The monitor, system unit, and keyboard are individual pieces connected with cables.

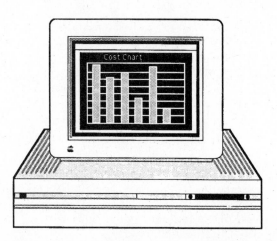

FIG. 5.7

A Mac IIsi.

You may prefer the original 9-inch Mac monitor over the more recent designs, and unless you are working with an application which requires that you see the entire page, such as a desktop publishing or CAD application, you may be so happy with the resolution of the display that the small size won't bother you. All Macs have the option of adding or selecting a stand-alone monitor. (The Mac Classic, Classic II, SE/30, LCII, and PowerBook packages include the monitor; the Mac II line lists the monitor as a separate option.)

> **NOTE** If you are fond of the Mac screen but find that you are leaning forward and squinting more than feels natural, you can buy a screen extender program, which magnifies the display shown on the traditional Macintosh screen. Several products currently available give you good resolution and a larger picture. One popular screen extender is Stepping Out II, from Berkeley System Design, available for about $95.

Many monitors are available for the Macintosh. Beyond the color or monochrome decision, you have size and shape options. Do you want a 2-page monitor? A full-page monitor? A monitor with a 19-inch diagonal width? 24-inch width? Like the monitors available for PCs, you can choose the style and size of the monitor you need. A screen wider than tall (the typical monitor design) is a *landscape* monitor, and a screen taller than wide, such as a full-page monitor, is a *portrait* monitor. You see these terms, which coincide with the same terms to describe printing orientation, used in Macintosh forums, although these phrases also can refer to any monitor.

Table 5.4 lists several popular monitors currently available for Macintoshes.

Table 5.4 Popular Macintosh Monitors

Monitor	Size	Resolution
Apple High Resolution RGB	13 inch	840-by-480
E-Machines ColorPage E16	16 inch	1024-by-768
Sony Corporation Sony CPD-1304	14 inch	1024-by-768
Radius Color Pivot	19 inch	640-by-870
RasterOps 8LC	19 inch	1024-by-768

When you add a monitor to a Macintosh, you also need to add a separate video card, which enables the system to communicate with the monitor. The video card is included with the purchase of the monitor. Usually, a different video card is needed to connect each member of the Mac family. If you decide to add a monitor to the Mac, be sure that you tell the dealer or manufacturer the model of computer you are using.

If you are purchasing a Macintosh computer, be sure that you find out everything you need to know about available monitors before making a decision. Read articles, talk to salespeople, and sit down and try out a few monitors before making a final choice.

Discussing Some Final Considerations

So far, this chapter has introduced purchasing considerations you need to consider as you shop for a system and monitor. You have looked at computer speed, storage capacity, hard disk features, and display considerations. This section raises a few final questions to address before you make a final decision.

Your Personal Comfort Zone

One major issue not yet addressed in detail is probably the decision that affects you most in day-to-day use. Are you comfortable using the monitor? The following agents can affect comfort level:

- A monitor with a nonglare screen can reduce headaches and eyestrain.

- A monitor with a tilting base enables you to turn and angle the monitor for more comfort and less eyestrain.

- A monitor that provides contrast and brightness controls gives you more choices about how text and graphics are displayed on-screen.

- A monitor with a slow screen refresh speed can be agonizing for graphics applications. (The screen refresh speed is the *scan rate*.)

- A monitor with a long cable enables you to place the monitor where you like: beside the system unit, on the desktop, or (in the traditional location) on top of the system unit.

Available Software

One consideration that may be important when you purchase a computer is the kind of software available for the computer. If you need a computer to perform a specific task, finding the computer that works with the needed software makes sense. Some software runs only on the PC, some programs run only on the Mac, and yet others run only on the Amiga. You also find programs that run on a Commodore 64, Apple II, or Atari. Be sure that you choose the computer that runs the programs you want to use in home, business, or school applications, and that enables you to expand the kinds of applications you plan to use. In other words, purchase a computer for which many programs are available, and when your needs change or expand, you won't be limited by the programs written for the computer.

Many programs exist for the different kinds of computers. Part IV of this book contains a software library that introduces you to many of the more popular applications software packages and provides examples for each of the major computers. Icons provided in the margins in Part IV also help you easily identify the software that runs on your computer.

Remember that different programs may require different features in a monitor. If you work primarily with Lotus 1-2-3, you don't need a two-page monitor. If you work intensively with desktop publishing, you may find that a two-page or a full-page monitor makes your work easier. When you find a monitor you like, ask the dealer for a demonstration by using the programs you plan to use, so that you can see how the monitor displays text and graphics with each particular application.

If you are purchasing the monitor by mail order, make sure that the monitor works with your software. If you use Aldus PageMaker at work, ask the maker of the monitor how the monitor works with PageMaker and whether you need to be aware of any bugs or of other special considerations.

As you investigate all the options, also read the reviews and the ads in popular industry magazines, such as *PC World, Byte,* and *MacWorld.*

Networks to Other Computers

Are you planning to connect the computer you purchase to a network or link to other computers that share common resources, such as printers or hard disk drives? If the computer is scheduled to be part of a team, don't invest the time and money in it until you make sure that your computer can talk to the other systems on the network. Can the hardware you plan to purchase talk to the other systems?

Available Technical Support

Technical support is a major issue for most new computer users. Technical support also can be a new user's nightmare. You bring the computer home, set up the system, turn on the monitor, see a flash of light—and then nothing. Who do you call? If you bought the computer from a reputable dealer who offers a technical support service, you can return the defective monitor and exchange it for a new one. If you are unsure of the cause of the trouble, you can call one of the support technicians and have him talk you through the setup procedure to see whether you connected a cable wrong or forgot an important step.

Most computer outlets also offer an extended technical support plan that gives you months of support for an additional fee. For most people, this additional support is worth the money, if for nothing more than the peace of mind from knowing that if something goes wrong, a technician is around to fix the problem.

Reviewing Purchasing Decisions

Use the following checklist to put on paper the purchasing considerations you are tossing around:

I want _____ (IBM, Mac, Amiga, PC clone).

I want _____ in the computer (8086, 80286, 80386, 80486, 68000, 68020, 68030, 68040).

I want _____ of RAM.

I want _____ storage space:

        a. Hard disk?_____Size?_____

        b. Floppy disk drive? _____
           Number?_____

        c. Other?_____

I want _____ monitor (CGA, EGA VGA, Super VGA, multisync, Mac).

These special features are important:

_____

_____

_____

_____

Chapter Summary

This chapter introduced many of the points to consider as you get ready to purchase a system. Whether you are already leaning toward the PC or Mac camp or you still are unsure which computer is best for your needs, be sure that you identify how important speed, storage capacity, display quality, and compatibility are to you. In the following chapter, you explore some printer purchasing considerations.

Purchasing a Printer

If you are new to computing and are reading this book from the beginning, you have learned the basics about computers and have taken the following important steps:

- Analyzed your computer needs

- Determined the model of computer for your needs

- Learned about the differences in computers and determined the features, such as speed and storage capacity, you need

- Considered the kind of monitor you need

Now, you must select a printer for the new computer. You can use a computer *without* a printer, but you probably need printed copies of the information you enter and use on the computer. If you produce letters, reports, financial statements, graphs, or any kind of printed output, you need a printer.

In this chapter, you learn about the various kinds of printers available. The span of printer capabilities is almost as wide as the range of needs; you can buy a simple, inexpensive printer to get the information on paper, or you can pay a substantial amount of money to purchase a printer capable of producing typeset-quality text and graphics. Many printers exist between these extremes.

Analyzing Your Printer Needs

Start by analyzing your needs. Use the following questions to help find the kind of printer that fits your application:

■ *What kind of quality do you need from printouts?*

The answer to this question is probably the most important factor in determining the kind of printer you need. Who reads the print-outs? Is your work circulated only among others in the department or do you need a high-quality printout to send to clients?

■ *Is speed an issue?*

If you need to print documents quickly or spend a great deal of time printing a large volume of information, you need a printer capable of producing with some speed.

■ *Do you need high-resolution graphics?*

With the advent of desktop publishing and computerized graphic arts, you can design and create highly sophisticated artwork. To get acceptable final output, however, the printer must provide the necessary quality.

■ *Do you need to print in color?*

Many applications don't require color in printouts; however, if you need color, you can choose among several printers.

■ *Do you need a variety of fonts and type styles?*

If you are happy with simple printouts in one basic typeface with a few enhancements, such as boldfaced headlines or italicized words, you can use a relatively low-cost printer. If you need a variety of typefaces and fonts in a wide spectrum of sizes and styles, you may need a PostScript printer.

Introducing Different Printer Types

This section introduces the kinds of printers currently available. Some printers fall outside the categories listed here. One area of confusion is the number of different terms used to describe different items. The following list defines some of the most frequently used printer terms and explains the basic functions of the printers and parts:

Daisywheel printer. A category of impact printer. The characters are cast on a wheel-shaped disk, which presses against the printer ribbon and then against the page.

Desktop typesetter. Produces the highest print quality currently available in a desktop printer; uses laser technology to print characters and graphics on a page at the highest possible resolution.

Dot-matrix printer. A category of impact printer that forms letters by creating characters from a cluster of dots. Rather than pre-formed letters, such as the wheel of a daisywheel printer, the print head of the dot-matrix printer is a cluster (matrix) of pins that push against the ribbon and onto the page to form the desired character. If you look closely at most output produced on a dot-matrix printer, you see the matrix of dots that create each character.

Impact printers. Places characters on the page by pressing the print head against a ribbon onto the paper.

Inkjet printer. Forms characters by squirting dots of ink onto the page (using the same matrix technology the dot-matrix printer uses but without the impact).

Laser printer. A printer technology, similar to the technology of an office copier, used to place text and images on the page.

Letter quality. The quality achieved from a good office typewriter. Letter quality is not the highest quality available but for many office uses, letter quality is a sufficient standard.

Plotter. A specialized printer that produces high-quality output by moving ink pens over the surface of the paper. Plotters are used for computer-aided design and presentation graphics.

PostScript printer. Category of laser printer that uses a special page description language known as PostScript to communicate with the printer. PostScript offers a wide range of fonts you can scale to any size possible within the amount of RAM available in the printer, which enables the printer to produce high-resolution graphics.

Print head. The printer mechanism that forms characters by pressing characters against the printer ribbon and onto the page.

Print modes. Most dot-matrix printers can print in more than one quality level (mode). Draft mode produces a quick printout, but the quality is poor. Near-letter quality (NLQ) mode produces text with more clearly formed characters but takes longer to print. Condensed mode prints twice as many characters within the same amount of space used for draft or NLQ mode. (Not all printers support all modes.)

Printer memory. The amount of memory in the printer. The printer's memory stores all external fonts and, in laser printers, stores fonts you download during a work session.

Printer ribbon. The ink ribbon used in impact printers.

Resolution. The number of dots per inch (dpi). The greater the number of dots, the higher the resolution and the clearer and crisper the characters or graphics.

Toner cartridge. The cartridge that stores the toner used in laser printers. Toner is a powdery substance, used in place of ink to place text and graphics on the paper.

Impact Printers

The most popular category of printers is the impact printer. The major players in the impact category are dot-matrix printers. Daisywheel (or formed-letter) printers are another kind of impact printer, holding a small share of the impact printer category. In both kinds of printers, the mechanism is a simple, print head and a ribbon that the print head strikes against, or impacts, the paper. The impression left is affected by the quality of the paper, the amount of ink in the ribbon, and the overall design of the printing mechanism. Both kinds of impact printers offer advantages, but the dot-matrix printer clearly offers the greatest flexibility within this category.

This section discusses the differences among impact printers and how the technology works. Figure 6.1 shows the inside of an impact printer. Notice the location of the print head. (The appearance of the print head depends on whether you use a daisywheel, ball or thimble, or standard dot-matrix impact printer.) This illustration was based on a dot-matrix printer. The roller bar positions the paper, the tension arm holds the page in place, and the ribbon receives the impression from the print head and transfers the characters to the page.

Daisywheel and Other Formed-Letter Printers

The idea of a formed-letter printer dates back to the first typewriters (see fig. 6.2). An individual letter is molded onto an arm. The arm strikes against the ribbon, and the impact makes the letter on the paper. Rather than a series of long, spindly arms attached to a keyboard, a daisywheel has the letters spread around the edge of a flexible wheel-shaped disk (see fig. 6.3). The wheel looks like a mechanical, many-petaled daisy. The disk spins; when the proper letter is in place, the hammer (the print head) pushes the letter onto the ribbon.

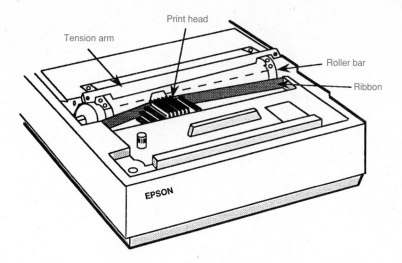

Tension arm

Print head

Roller bar

Ribbon

EPSON

FIG. 6.1

Inside an impact printer.

This striking motion creates a distinctive *click* each time a letter is printed. Depending on the shape and materials used in the enclosure, a daisywheel printer can be quite loud. Just think about hearing a typewriter going at constant speed for several minutes to get an idea of the noise these printers can make.

Popular Daisywheel Printers

NEC Spinwriter

IBM QuietWriter

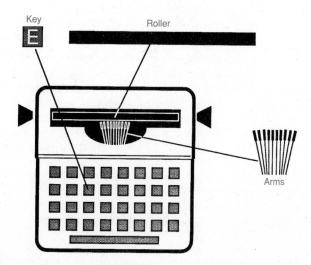

Key

E

Roller

Arms

FIG. 6.2

Typewriter technology.

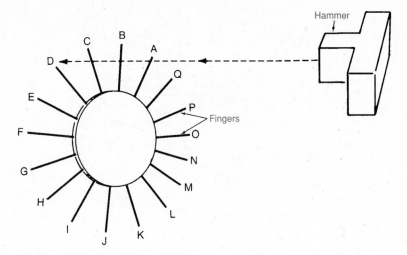

FIG. 6.3

The print wheel from a daisy-wheel printer.

One buzz word in the printer world is *letter-quality*. This term means that you want the final output to look as though you typed the page on a typewriter. Because the daisywheel printer essentially is a typewriter without a keyboard, you can produce only letter-quality output. This same feature, however, also is the downfall of the daisywheel printer. Because the wheel spins to line up the proper character for printing, the time required for each letter to be printed is relatively long (in computer terms). A daisywheel printer certainly prints faster than most typists, but the printer still is much slower than other kinds of printers. Even if the quality of the type may be acceptable within the application, the printer speed may not be acceptable.

To measure speed, printers use the rating *characters per second (cps)*. A typical daisywheel printer has a print speed of 15 to 55 characters per second. Because the price of the printer usually determines the speed, you may pay a premium price to get a fast daisywheel printer.

Translating characters per second into usable time results in *throughput*. How long does the printer take to print the letter or report? For a one-page letter with 350 words and an average of six characters per word, a 15 cps daisywheel takes 140 seconds (or 2-1/3 minutes) to print the entire page. A 55 cps daisywheel takes 38 seconds to print the same page. Compare these times to the speed of a laser printer rated at 8 pages per minute (or roughly 8 to 9 seconds) for the same letter. Daisywheel printer results are letter perfect, but the time may be too costly. To put this comparison into perspective, consider your specific needs. Do you plan to print several pages an hour or only a few pages a day? If you print sporadically and are happy with the quality, a daisywheel printer may be acceptable. If you print large amounts of information, the lack of speed becomes a great handicap.

The most limiting factor for daisywheel printers is the fixed size of the letters. You cannot, for example, change the size of a capital A on the daisywheel. The letter is molded in plastic or metal on the end of a spindle. Changing *spacing*, or the pitch of the type, is not possible without changing the wheel. If the final draft needs small print *and* normal size letters, you must stop in the middle of printing, change the wheel, start again, stop again, and so on. Because you cannot, on demand, change the shape of the letter, you also must change style or fonts by changing wheels.

Many people still use a daisywheel printer where the lack of speed presents no problem because the quality of the output is high. Brother makes good low-cost daisywheel printers and also offers some typewriters with built-in computer adapters that you can use as either typewriters or printers.

The Spinwriter is another kind of formed-letter printer. A product of NEC (Nippon Electric Company, Japan), the print head in the Spinwriter looks more like a thimble than a wheel. If you fold the daisywheel arms upward, away from the center, you have a spinning thimble. Spinwriter thimbles take less vertical space inside the printer and therefore can be used in desktop printers with lower profiles.

The ball-style print head is used in a formed-letter printer manufactured by IBM. Similar to the technology used in IBM's line of typewriters, the IBM ball print head is a metal globe moved in various directions by the ball holder. Unlike the other two kinds of full-impact print heads, the entire ball is moved against the ribbon (see fig. 6.4). With the full mass of the ball behind the strike, an even impression is made every time. (This kind of head is found only on typewriters with special adapters that allow the typewriter to be used as a printer.)

FIG. 6.4

The ball-style
print head.

Dot-Matrix Printers

Dot-matrix printers have the widest variety of models and manufacturers. Dot-matrix printers differ from the older-style impact printers in the fundamental design of the print head. Rather than having each character as a formed letter (on a stick), the print head is a cluster of wires or pins that push against the ribbon to form the character. The number of pins in the head determines the speed and quality of the final printout. Usually, two kinds of dot-matrix print heads are used: 9-pin and 24-pin (also referred to as 9-wire and 24-wire).

With both kinds of print heads, the pins are aligned in columns. As the print head moves across the page, the printer fires the pins needed to form a letter or image. With the 9-pin character, the *matrix* that defines the letter is a grid made up of individual dots 9 high and at least 9 wide. A 24-pin head produces the same character with a grid 24 dots high and 9 to 24 dots wide. Notice that, in the same space, the 9-pin head creates a character that consists of 81 dots, and the 24-pin uses 216 dots. The more dots per inch (dpi), the higher the resolution and, therefore, the more clearly formed the letters.

Most 9-pin printers overcome their dpi deficiency by using a multiple-pass technique to add more dots to the letters. Rather than going from left to right and printing the character in only a 9-by-9 dot matrix, the printer moves the paper slightly and on the way back adds a second set of dots between the already printed dots, forming an 18-by-18 dot matrix. This technique is the basis for the term *near-letter quality* (NLQ). Printers advertised as NLQ can print so many dots in the characters that the final product is hardly discernible from the perfect letter-quality output of the formed-letter printers. Dot-matrix printers can print normal or draft-quality characters as well as NLQ letters.

Popular Dot-Matrix Printers

Apple ImageWriter II

EPSON FX-286e

IBM ProPrinter

NEC LC-090

Okidata 390

Toshiba P1351

IBM PS/1 Printer

Again, speed is a consideration. The 24-pin printer doesn't need to make a second pass to fill in dot gaps. In one pass, the printer produces a better overall result than the output produced by the 9-pin in two passes. Assuming that the two printers can move the print head across the page at the same speed, the 24-pin printer is actually twice as fast. Typical cps ratings on dot-matrix printers range from 150 cps to 300-cps, but the 9-pin printer usually carries a slower NLQ rating along with its typical draft rating.

Because the grid, or matrix, of dots can change as needed, dot-matrix printers can print more than one type size or pitch. (*Pitch* is defined as characters per inch or cpi.) By changing the width of the character, the printer creates different pitches. All dot-matrix printers can print 10 cpi. This pitch is the same as the typewriter standard—*pica*. Ten-pitch type prints 80 columns of characters in a standard 8-inch wide format.

Many dot-matrix printers also can print in condensed mode. This mode prints up to 132 characters in an 8-inch wide format. Condensed mode usually can print 16 to 17 characters per inch and 20 cpi is available on some printers. Another mode available on most dot-matrix printers is condensed mode. In condensed mode, a dot-matrix printer can produce 12 cpi. This pitch is the same as the *elite* typewriter font and results in 96 characters in the 8-inch-wide format.

Some dot-matrix printers also print a variety of different fonts. A font is one size and style of type within a particular typeface (for more information, see the sidebar "Understanding Typefaces"). A dot-matrix printer usually comes with two different type styles available in the printer, and you may be able to get additional fonts with the appropriate software from other vendors. If having a variety of fonts is important, ask your dealer about adding fonts before you buy a printer.

The range of possible fonts in a dot-matrix printer grows constantly. Some printers have a special area of memory for storing fonts that are not part of the standard package. These added fonts, or *downloadable fonts*, are available through third-party vendors. Downloadable fonts usually are used by companies needing greater variety in printing styles for newsletters or varied publishing requirements.

Graphics are the other strong suit of a dot-matrix printer. Daisywheel printers have no, or very limited, graphical capabilities. Because dots can form lines, curves, and almost anything else imaginable, as well as letters and numbers, dot-matrix printers are great for printing graphs and charts. The limiting factor again is dpi (dots per inch). If the printer can print only a few dots both vertically and horizontally, the smoothness of a curved line is jeopardized. The result is a series of straight lines trying to turn a corner, a condition known as *jaggies*. The only cure for jaggies is higher resolution (more dpi). Because 9-pin printers are limited by the print head, 24-pin printers are certainly a better choice for printing graphics (and 24-pin printers are faster because they don't make as many passes to fill in the gaps between dots). Don't expect graphical printouts to be fast in either case. Dot-matrix printers slow down to keep the dots as close together as possible. If you need many graphs and pictures, you may be happier with the quality from a laser printer.

Understanding Typefaces

Not long ago, the typeface used to print characters offered little choice. As you become more accustomed to controlling the look of documents, you become more selective about typefaces. The early standards of pica and elite typefaces (usually seen on typewriters) are no longer enough. Users want distinctive typefaces to help convey the meaning of the message, whether the message is loud, light, or languid.

A typeface is a type *family*: letters and characters created using a specific type. Following is a sample of text in the Helvetica typeface:

This is an example of Helvetica type.

Each typeface family has different sizes and styles of type. The size of the type in the preceding example is 10 points (a *point* is a standard measurement equivalent to 1/72 of an inch). The style of the example is normal; no special style, such as boldface or italic, was added. The word *font* is used in multiple ways; basically, a font is one particular size and style within a typeface family. Following are some examples of different fonts:

This is an example of the Avant Garde 8-point font.

This is an example of the New Century Schoolbook 14-point italic font.

This is an example of the Helvetica 10-point font.

Inkjet Printers

In execution, the inkjet printer lies somewhere between impact printers and laser printers. The choice of inkjet printers is more limited than all other printer categories. As the cost of laser printers drops, inkjets may disappear completely (unless an extremely economical inkjet printer is created). Inkjet printers, however, do have both merit and a following.

Unlike a standard impact printer, the inkjet printer uses no mechanism to physically strike a ribbon and then the paper. The image of a letter, however, is formed by a similar dot pattern that dot-matrix printers use. The print head of an inkjet printer moves across the page, spraying the dots of ink onto the paper. Rather than ribbons, the inkjet uses ink cartridges. Because this spray-gun head uses no hammers or pins, inkjet printers make far less noise than dot-matrix printers. Like a laser printer, an inkjet printer cannot create multiple copies using carbon or carbonless paper.

When first introduced, the inkjet printer seemed like a good idea. The printer's major advantage—silence—helped promote the idea of a printer on every desk in an office. The quality of the type, however, was this printer's downfall. The first versions produced a poor-quality print-out, and a more expensive, specially treated paper was suggested for the best quality.

The recent generations of inkjets from IBM and Hewlett-Packard are a far cry from the first versions. You can use almost any plain paper; ink cartridges are easier to find; and the print quality is improved. The latest HP ThinkJet Plus printers print graphics that rival laser printers. The cost of inkjet printers lies between the cost of high quality 24-pin printers and slower low-end laser printers.

Popular Inkjet Printers

Hewlett-Packard ThinkJet

Hewlett-Packard DeskJet

Apple StyleWriter

Panasonic InkJet

Okidata InkJet

Thermal-Transfer Printers

The thermal-transfer printer uses a technology similar to the inkjet printer's technology. The thermal-transfer printer creates characters and images by melting wax-based ink off the printer ribbon and onto the paper.

This printing technology produces a higher quality of text than the quality obtainable with dot-matrix printers. Known as *resistive ribbon thermal transfer*, this process is used in both color and black-and-white printers in business applications when good-quality text is needed and the amount of noise in the office environment is a consideration. Like the inkjet, the thermal-transfer printer is quiet, which makes thermal-transfer printers a good choice for large offices.

The thermal printer is surprisingly fast. Often, the thermal printer rivals low-end laser printers for speed. Thermal printers also are expensive; when you buy a good thermal-transfer printer, such as the IBM QuietWriter III, you pay for the extra speed, high quality, and silence. Figure 6.5 shows the IBM QuietWriter III.

Popular Thermal-Transfer Printers

IBM QuietWriter III

Apple Silentype

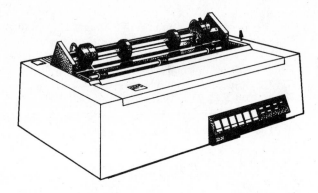

FIG. 6.5

The IBM
QuietWriter III.

Laser Printers

The laser printer is a specialized version of the office copier machine
that has been around for years. Laser printers print with greater speed,
better quality, and less noise than impact printers. Laser printers also
are the newest technology and carry the highest price tag of all the
printers available. This section looks at the differences between lasers
and impact printers and between old lasers and new lasers.

The formation of characters with the laser still relies on a pattern of
dots. Rather than being limited to a head that moves across the page,
however, these dots are created by electrically charging particles of
toner and the paper so the toner sticks to the page in the chosen pattern. With an office copier, the pattern is determined by reflected light:
from a lamp to the original and back onto a charged drum. Laser printers also use a charged drum but, rather than bouncing light off an original document, the information is digitized onto the drum by a signal
sent from the computer to the printer through a standard printer cable.

Impact printers use 9 or 24 pins to create a pattern, but laser printers
create a pattern limited only by the amount of memory in the printer
and by the physical size of the toner cartridge. The resolution of a standard laser printer is rated in dots per inch (dpi). The potential pattern
of dots created by a laser is 300 dots in one vertical inch by 300 dots
horizontally, which makes possible a one-inch square that contains
90,000 individual dots.

Laser results are more consistent because the printer has no ribbon to wear out or dry up. Only when the toner gets low does a real difference between the first copy and the last (4,000th!) copy become apparent. The drawback to the laser is in paper handling. Only one sheet at a time can pass through the printer. This limitation means that reports of several pages come out as several *individual* pages rather than a chain of pages, as with impact printers.

If you need more than one copy of a report, you must reprint the information. This method is fine for reports; the second and third copies are as good as the original. Because the speed of the printer is exceptional, you can print two reports from a laser printer as quickly as one report from an impact printer.

Perhaps the largest number of users of laser printers is in the field of desktop publishing. Because of the high resolution and speed of these printers, mixing text and graphics for newsletters and brochures becomes economical. You can make several versions of a publication for comparison before you send the final copy to a print shop for duplication. If you distribute materials in-house, you may be able to eliminate the print shop completely.

Differences in Laser Quality

How does a laser's speed relate to quality? At the 300-dpi resolution offered by most laser printers, most graphics look good. On a quality scale of 1 to 10, the graphics rate a 6. The biggest problem with laser printers is in forming curves; often, you may see rough edges on graphics or large type. The laser cannot produce halftone images because all the dots are the same size. Gray scaling (the capacity to change colors into printed shades of gray) also may not look good at 300 dpi. Both halftones and gray scaling are better on a laser printer than on impact printers, however, because of the tiny dots of the laser and the consistent blackness of the output.

Today, some laser printers are rated at 400 by 400 dpi, 600 by 600 dpi, 1,000 by 400 dpi, and even 1,000 by 1,000 dpi. At 600 dpi, images look professional, but at 1,000 dpi, the final output rivals typeset quality. (The 1,000 dpi laser printers, *desktop typesetters*, are covered in a following section of this chapter.) The final application determines how good the laser must be. For writing letters, creating in-house reports, quick newsletters, and a variety of other products that don't demand the highest quality typeset text, the older 300 dpi printers are fine. When pictures and scanned images call for higher quality, the newer 600 or 1,000 dpi printers may be more appropriate.

Differences in Laser Printer Types

You may notice a significant price range in laser printers. In the *Computer Shopper*, you can find one laser printer for less than $650 and another for $4,900 or more. The prices in laser printers vary because two different technologies (or languages) are used. One category of laser printer, the PCL laser printer, sells for $650 and up; the other printer category, the PostScript laser printer, usually costs between $1,800 to $3,000.

Although not strictly laser printers, some PostScript printers that offer color can exceed all other printers in cost. Tektronix offers a thermal-transfer color printer known as the Phaser II PXe, which lists for $4,995.

PCL (*printer control language*) and PostScript are printer languages that communicate information from the computer to the printer. These languages control the way data is sent and received and affect the capabilities found in each category of printer.

Early versions of PCL were simple languages that contained only basic instructions necessary for printing. PCL evolved, but PostScript always was an elaborate page description language that communicated detailed descriptions of each page to the printer. The complexity and power of the PostScript language provides substantially more control over the way each page is printed and enhances the quality of the printouts.

Usually, a PCL printer prints good quality text (at 300 dpi); in fact, PCL and PostScript produce printouts of the same quality. The two laser printers, however, differ in several ways. Obviously, cost is a major difference, and PostScript printers also provide greater flexibility in the use of fonts and in the number of fonts available. You can print high-quality PostScript graphics with a PostScript printer, but graphics output is more limited with PCL printers.

The current version of PCL appears in the Hewlett-Packard LaserJet IIIP. This popular laser printer uses PCL5, which—for the first time in any PCL revision—enables users to scale fonts. If you have the capacity to scale fonts, you can tell the printer language to create from a specific typeface (such as Times Roman Bold), fonts in a variety of sizes within this typeface. Before the advent of scalable fonts, you needed a specific font cartridge or software to produce multiple sizes: a cartridge each for Times Roman 10 point, 12 point, 14 point, and so on.

The new Hewlett-Packard LaserJet IIIP and PCL5 help to close the gap between PostScript and PCL printers. If you want scalable fonts, the new HP may be acceptable—at half the cost of a new PostScript printer. (The LaserJet IIIP is only $1,595 retail, and some new PostScript printers retail for more than $4,000.) The other qualities that separate PostScript and PCL still hold true. A PCL printer cannot produce top-of-the-line graphics quality, and PCL files aren't supported beyond the LaserJet IIIP.

PCL Laser Printers and Fixed Fonts

The PCL laser printers are the low-end laser printers. The Hewlett-Packard, long a standard in this category of laser printer technology and the first widely used laser printer, evolved through many generations. The first HP laser produced a few built-in fonts at 300-dpi quality. The fonts available were *fixed fonts*, using only the specific font in the printer or, later, in the cartridge. You couldn't change a Times Roman 10-point italic font to 12-point italic or 12-point boldface.

With a fixed font, the shape and size of the printed characters is defined by a table inside the printer. The printer produces characters of *only* the size and shape found in the printer's internal tables. For a bigger version of the same font, a different font table is required. Additions to the character tables require a font cartridge. The printer is limited to the shape and size of the characters as defined by the cartridge or internal table.

The next generation of HP printers accepted plug-in font cartridges with a small amount of memory and files that contained the font information. Each cartridge contained a few fonts, and accumulating a significant font library was costly and cumbersome.

All printers include some internal memory that stores the basic information for the system operations. In laser printers, particularly HP and PostScript printers with a variety of fonts and graphic elements, adequate printer memory is important. The QMS PS 815 is a PostScript printer with 2M of memory.

Soft fonts arrived soon after cartridges. *Soft fonts* are stored on disks (or on the computer's hard disk) and sent (*downloaded*) to the printer's memory at print time.

A soft font is neither burned into ROM chips nor hard-wired into the printer or a cartridge. Rather, the font definitions are loaded in the printer's memory; the printer is reprogrammed to make a new character set. A limitation of this method is that fonts *are* fixed at certain sizes and shapes. By loading and unloading soft fonts, you have virtually endless possibilities, but you waste time waiting for the next soft font to load. Soft fonts also can use a great deal of memory, so make sure that the printer has enough memory to support the fonts you plan to use.

Whether you use a PCL or a PostScript printer, you probably want to add fonts to the system. How you add fonts depends on the kind of printer you use. All printers, from dot-matrix to laser, have built-in fonts. A typical PCL printer, such as the HP LaserJet or the Brother HL10V Laser Printer, comes with 20 or 36 built-in fonts.

Adding fonts brings up two important considerations: the printer needs enough memory to support the fonts, and the software you use also must support these fonts.

You can purchase fonts from the following sources:

- Independent companies specializing in font technology such as Adobe or Bitstream
- Font packages available as add-on products to particular software packages, such as PFS: First Publisher's special fonts
- Shareware or public domain fonts that you can download from a bulletin board and use with some popular applications

T I P Depending on the model of PCL printer, you may need to purchase font cartridges. These cartridges plug into the printer and contain instructions needed to make and print the fonts and also supply the memory required to generate the fonts. If the printer has enough internal memory, you probably can use soft fonts.

The newest member of the HP LaserJet family, the HP LaserJet IIIP, doesn't use the PostScript page description language, but provides two built-in scalable fonts and the capacity to produce PostScript-quality text and graphics for publications. The LaserJet IIIP uses a technology known as resolution enhancement to smooth curves and jagged edges. With resolution enhancement, the dot technology used to create characters from a series of dots now includes a new twist. *Resolution enhancement* shrinks dots and places the smaller dots in curves and diagonal shapes, resulting in a smoother, more finished look in printouts.

Other important features of the new HP are the capacity to print portrait and landscape on the same page and to print reverse or angled text, spirals, and shaded text. Hewlett-Packard plans to introduce up to 300 scalable fonts for the LaserJet IIIP. An Adobe PostScript emulation package ($349 to $750) also is available.

Popular PCL Printers

Panasonic KX-P4455 Laser Printers

Brother HL8V Printer

Hewlett-Packard LaserJet series

Epson Actionlaser II

IBM LaserPrint 10

The primary difference between PCL and PostScript printers is *software* (PCL and PostScript are different languages that communicate information to the printer). The basic mechanics of the printers are similar. You can change many PCL printers into PostScript printers by adding a compatible plug-in board, more memory (depending on the amount of memory in the printer), and the correct software. The expense involved in this alteration may be less than the cost of purchasing a new Post-Script printer. Depending on memory requirements, you can turn an HP into a PostScript printer for about $1,200.

Another addition to the upgrade-to-PostScript arena is UltraScript PC, a software program that changes almost any printer—laser or dot-matrix—into a PostScript-compatible printer for $195. Early reviews of UltraScript PC were favorable, although output takes a long time to produce, and the output quality is limited by the capabilities of the printer. You cannot get 300-dpi output from an Epson dot-matrix printer, but other PostScript benefits are available, including the capacity to print lengthwise (*landscape orientation*).

PostScript Laser Printers

The greatest feature of PostScript laser printers is scalable fonts. Although PCL printers can print at the same quality as most PostScript printers (300 dpi), PCL printers offer only fonts fixed in typeface, size, and style. With scalable fonts, you can print *any* size and style of type by using only one definition of the character set in the printer's memory. This definition includes mathematical formulas for changing the size and orientation of the characters. One of the first scalable fonts was developed by a company named Adobe. Adobe invented a language that manipulates the mathematics of a font to make the font scalable. Called *PostScript*, this definition of scalable text became the first standard for unfixed font formats. You now can buy several variations of scalable fonts, some of which are PostScript-compatible.

The major advantage of scalable fonts is the capacity to change the size and the orientation of the characters without loading a new definition of the character or plugging in a cartridge. Suppose that you create a newsletter and the main text is in Bookman 10-point normal type. For the banner, you want to use Bookman 48-point. With a PCL printer, you must have the Bookman 48 font built in (which isn't), on a cartridge (unlikely), or on a soft font disk. With a PostScript printer, the font (Bookman) is built-in; you can just set up the document and go.

The same benefit applies to graphics. You can resize, rotate, and manipulate images captured or imported in Encapsulated PostScript (the same page description language used to explain graphics to the printer) without loss in the quality of the image (no jaggies appear on a PostScript art file).

Popular PostScript Laser Printers
Apple Personal LaserWriter LS
Apple LaserWriter IIF
Okidata OL830
QMS PS815MR

One more difference exists between PostScript printers and desktop typesetters: enhanced-resolution printers, which print at a higher resolution than 300 dpi. Several variations of enhanced printers are available: 600-by-400 dpi, 800-by-600, and 600-by-600. These printers are high-end PostScript-compatible and use a special board installed in the system unit of the computer.

Desktop Typesetters

Top quality in laser printer technology rests with *desktop typesetters*. Desktop typesetters use a technology similar to PostScript for scaling fonts and graphics that provides the highest quality currently available for personal computers: 1,000-by-1,000 dpi. Seeing the difference between the output from most desktop typesetters and output from a conventional typesetter is almost impossible.

Popular Desktop Typesetters
Raster Devices TurboSetter 1000
LaserMaster 1000

Laser Maintenance Costs

The final consideration with laser printers is operating cost. With an impact printer, a single ribbon is replaced at a cost range of $3 to $20. The disposable item from a laser printer is the toner. The laser printer engines are made by two major manufacturers: Ricoh and Canon.

With the Canon engine, a drum and toner are contained inside one easily changed cartridge. Depending on the model of printer, cartridges are rated from 4,000 to 10,000 pages, and the price is approximately $89 to $179. With the Ricoh, toner is separate and is good for roughly the same number of pages (about $25 to $35), but you must replace the drum every 10,000 to 20,000 pages. Both systems, therefore, cost about the same amount to operate.

You can use any good grade of copy machine paper for these printers. You also can purchase special paper for higher quality printers (600 to 1,000 dpi). Most manufacturers recommend the better paper for high-resolution output. Basically, the laser printer costs more to operate each time you purchase disposables. This cost is spread out over a much longer time, but laser printers still cost about 50 percent more to maintain than the maintenance costs of desktop impact printers.

Considering Other Printer Factors

You now know more than you did about printers; what you may not know is the right printer to buy. Your budget always limits purchases, so this section discusses other factors besides costs and budget.

If you plan to place the printer on the desk, a short cable works well. If you feed the paper into the printer from the back, you need enough space for the paper both before and after printing and may require a simple wire stand ($15 to $24). If you feed more than one form into the printer, such as checks and invoices, the stand needs slots to hold the different forms. How the paper feeds into the printer and where the printer sits determines whether you need a floor stand or a desk stand and the length of the cable.

If you plan to change forms frequently, you may need two printers! If your software does not support two printers, you need two printers, two cables, and a switch box to control which printer you use (the switch box also needs a cable). If you plan on more than one person accessing the printer, and if the printer doesn't have a multiple-user adapter built in, you may need a controller that enables several computers to access the printer. Depending on the number of users and the features needed, this controller costs $300 to $600. You must decide whether all users need separate printers. (Remember that when you first select and then decide where to place the printer, the number and location of users may change.) Finally, consider paper, forms, and paper storage. If you use many multipart forms, a laser printer probably isn't the best choice. The printer also must handle multipart forms *easily*. Examine the paper path; if the paper makes a 180-degree turn when traveling through the printer, this major turn may jam multipart forms.

If you often switch from continuous-feed paper or forms to single sheets or letterhead stationery, look for a printer with a paper parking feature. This feature leaves the continuous-feed paper attached to the feed mechanism while accepting a single sheet, which prevents loading and unloading the printer when you switch from continuous-feed to single-sheet operation.

If you write confidential reports, if you need a shredder for old reports, or if you bind reports for storage, find a good paper supply house to help with these considerations. If the forms aren't special or don't demand a customized design, you can use off-the-shelf forms from one of the national forms supply companies.

Remember to heed the *Buyer Beware* warning. Don't take the word of the salesperson. Try out the printer before you buy. Insert paper, ask about the ribbon (or toner cartridge), and ask about service. Don't be afraid to shop around. Printer prices may vary by up to 40 percent for the same model. Find the best price; the printer is the same no matter where you buy.

Deciding Where To Buy Your Printer

Assume that you know the printer you want. Now, think about a few more questions. Do you buy at the local computer store or by mail order? Service is an important deciding factor; who is going to fix this printer?

If a small problem arises (suppose that you don't understand how to change the ribbon or you're not getting the right font), can you call the printer manufacturer's customer support line? (All reputable manufacturers have a support line.) No matter where you buy the printer, a technical support specialist can answer these kinds of questions.

If a major disaster occurs, (someone drops a bowling ball on the cover), or something mysterious goes wrong (the printer prints backward for no apparent reason), you can take the printer to a repair technician. If the store is an *authorized* service facility that stocks parts and if the technicians are knowledgeable, the local retail store can fix the printer. You probably need the printer every business day, so repairing the printer quickly is important. Does the retail store provide a loaner machine? Does the store send the printer elsewhere for repairs?

Buying from mail order firms changes the equation. (You definitely save money buying mail order.) Ask the following important questions before you buy. Ask about turn-around time. Does the mail order company ship a replacement printer or fix the one you send in? How fast? Overnight? Who pays shipping? Is an on-site service contract available?

Does the on-site company have parts, or does the company order them?

A printer is a commodity; good printers work well right out of the box and continue to work for a long time. When a printer breaks or fails, however, what happens? When service is necessary, find a repair center that loans a printer in exchange for your machine and make sure you register the equipment so that the warranty is in effect.

Chapter Summary

Printing is an important part of working with computers. Whether you publish materials for a living or just want to document the spreadsheet that took a week to build, the capacity to provide printed output from the computer is important. In this chapter, you learned about the options in printing machinery, quality, and speed. In the following chapter, you learn about other add-on devices for the computer.

Purchasing Computer Add-Ons

Now that you have made some of the major decisions about your computer needs, the computer system you want to purchase, and the printer you need, you are ready to investigate additional options for your system.

This chapter introduces you to the following computer add-ons:

- Keyboard
- Mouse
- CD-ROM
- Modem
- Scanner

Depending on the kind of application you plan to use on the computer, you may not need all these add-ons. You undoubtedly need a keyboard but the mouse, modem, scanner, and joystick (a pointing device mainly used with games) may be unnecessary. If you are purchasing a Macintosh computer, the mouse is a necessity; if you are purchasing a

PC, whether or not you buy a mouse depends on the software you plan to use. If you use a PC with WordStar (a word processing program that requires no mouse), for example, you don't need a mouse. If, however, your near-term purchase plans include a program that recommends or requires a mouse, you may want to invest in a mouse.

This chapter takes a close look at computer add-ons and provides examples of when to use each item.

Understanding Available Keyboard Options

With most computer systems, the keyboard is included as part of the package. You also can purchase the keyboard separately or buy a keyboard other than the one included with the system. With all Macintoshes more recent than the Mac Classic II, you must buy the keyboard separately.

You also can buy keyboards from places other than the computer manufacturer. Many independent computer companies make keyboards for both PCs and Macintoshes. Most people prefer the following features in keyboards:

- A key layout design easy to use with the most-often used software.

- Function keys in a familiar and accessible location. Some people prefer function keys (special keys labeled, for example, F1 to F10) along the left side of the keyboard; others prefer these keys across the top.

- Separate numeric keypads and arrow keypads.

- A click mechanism that makes a sound when you press a key.

- The capability of angling the keyboard to the best angle for the typist.

- Enough weight so that the keyboard doesn't slide under heavy typing.

- A key action that works for you. You may prefer light responsive key action or keys that you must press firmly.

The following sections introduce the basic keyboards for IBM and Macintosh computers. Remember, however, that other manufacturers (called *third-party vendors*) make keyboards, so if you don't see a keyboard that appeals to you, many other models are available.

IBM Keyboards

The original IBM PC keyboard was in essence a long block of keys and 10 function keys to the left of the block (see fig. 7.1). This IBM keyboard, one of the first attempts at a professional keyboard for personal computers, was criticized for a mushy feel, the confusing layout of the keys, and the size of the keys. Users felt that important keys, such as Enter and Shift, were too small, and that the dual role of the numeric keypad (as arrow keys and as a numeric keypad) was confusing.

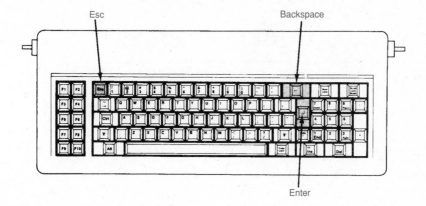

FIG. 7.1

The original IBM PC keyboard.

With the IBM PC AT, IBM introduced a new keyboard (see fig. 7.2). Solving many problems of the original layout, the PC AT keyboard had larger Shift and Enter keys. IBM also moved the numeric keypad away from the text keys and added indicator lights to show when the Num Lock, Caps Lock, and Scroll Lock keys were toggled on.

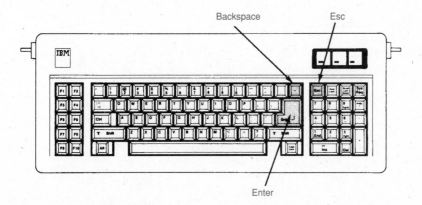

FIG. 7.2

The PC AT keyboard.

Several of the keyboard's real problems, however, still weren't addressed. The double-featured numeric keypad still confused users, and the location of the function keys limited how easily these keys were used.

When the IBM Enhanced Keyboard was introduced (shortly before the first PS/2s popped into the market), IBM addressed all the issues and came up with a solid, functional keyboard that pleased many users (see fig. 7.3).

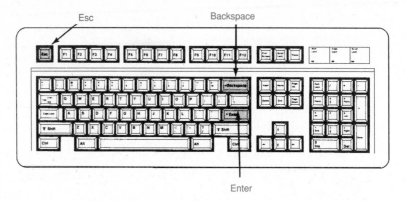

FIG. 7.3

The IBM Enhanced keyboard.

The Enhanced Keyboard located the function keys across the top of the keyboard, reducing the chance of pressing the wrong key. Users now had a choice of using the numeric keypad as a cursor-control keypad or as a numeric keypad. A separate set of arrow keys occupy a space between the numeric keypad and the regular text keys. Also, Ins (insert), Delete, Home, End, PgUp, PgDn (page up and page down), and Pause keys were added.

The Model 25 brought another standard to the IBM keyboard series. The 84-key Space-Saving Keyboard packaged with the Model 25 was in keeping with the small footprint size of the Model 25. Model 25, however, still gave users the choice of getting the larger Enhanced Keyboard at a nominal cost.

Third-party vendors also sell a wide variety of keyboards. Many of these keyboards vary slightly from the IBM Enhanced Keyboard design, perhaps offering special features, such as an increased number of function keys, or special purpose keys, such as a macro key.

Macintosh Keyboards

The first Macintosh keyboards were petite—much like the Mac itself—compact and without many extras. Although the keyboard had all the keys most users needed, the small size and compact feel of the keys perpetuated the game or toy image from which the company was trying to escape.

With all Macintosh purchases at a higher level than the Mac Classic II, you're on your own for the keyboard. You can, however, purchase the optional Apple Extended board directly from Apple.

The Extended Keyboard has the standard alphabetic keys, 15 function keys, the usual arrow keys, and a full numeric keypad.

Other Keyboards

You don't have to purchase a keyboard from the big names in computerdom, and you don't have to use the keyboard you receive as part of the package you purchase. If you are unhappy with the present keyboard, look through popular computer catalogs or magazines, such as the *Computer Shopper*, to find other keyboards compatible with your system.

The LOGOS 5001 130-key PC keyboard (see fig. 7.4), for example, offers 130 keys, eight (rather than four) cursor-movement keys, two sets of function keys, and a stand-alone macro key. This keyboard also has a built-in calculator so that you can perform calculations without interrupting the processing of your computer. The manufacturer of this keyboard, American Computer Technologies Corp., offers the LOGOS 5001 for $119.

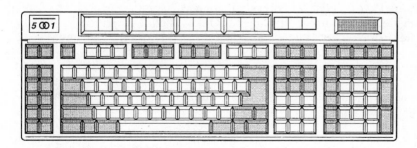

FIG. 7.4

The LOGOS 5001 keyboard.

Be careful when you consider buying a third-party keyboard. Before you buy, make sure that the keyboard is compatible with your system and offers an acceptable warranty.

Choosing a Mouse

Whether you use a mouse depends on two major considerations: the system you use and the application programs you plan to use with your computer. Before exploring applications and systems that use the mouse, consider how the mouse works.

A *mouse* is a pointing device that you use to select menu options, open files, choose commands, move graphics, and perform a variety of other operations either cumbersome or slow on the keyboard. You can use the mouse to quickly and accurately move the cursor on the screen. You press the mouse button(s) to open menus and select items.

Consider the time you take to move the cursor from one end of the screen to the other by pressing one of the arrow keys. Then imagine how quickly you can reach up and point to the place on the screen where you want the cursor. The second procedure—*pointing*—takes the same amount of time that moving the cursor by using a mouse takes. The faster the pace of your business or application, the more agonizing the wait as the cursor crawls across the screen in nonmouse-based programs.

Which Computers Use a Mouse?

Not all computers and programs can use the mouse. The Macintosh was shipped with a mouse from its first generation; in fact, the Mac literally was unusable without a mouse. The mouse is used for virtually all file and document management tasks, such as opening and closing files, running programs, and selecting menu options. The keyboard also is used for a variety of tasks, such as entering data, renaming files, and other operations that require keyboard input. The reason the Mac interface is so easy to use (operators just used the mouse to point to and click applications, files, and commands) is due in large part to mouse technology.

The Amiga computer also includes a mouse as standard equipment. Many Amiga applications, especially applications related to graphics and animation, are unusable without a mouse.

IBM PCs and compatibles were pretty slow to move into the mouse market. Introduced as a primarily Macintosh device, the mouse has lost out in the PC arena to keyboard selection methods. Early PC users preferred typing commands from the keyboard and pressing certain key combinations, such as Ctrl-Y, to perform operations that Macintosh users accomplished in mouse-based programs by pointing with the mouse and clicking the mouse button.

Microsoft Windows, a program designed for the IBM PC and compatibles, legitimized the mouse by giving users the capability of opening several files at a time (in on-screen *windows*) and selecting commands, programs, and various file operations by using the mouse. (For more information about Microsoft Windows, see Chapter 10.) Figure 7.5 shows a screen from Microsoft Windows, Version 3.1.

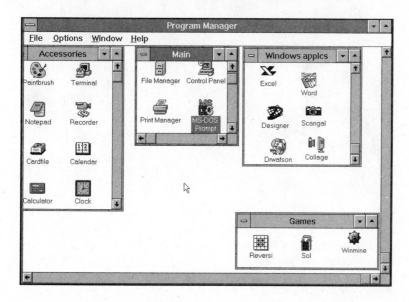

FIG. 7.5

Microsoft Windows: a mouse application for PC users.

Because the mouse was such a success, many popular IBM applications now support the mouse. IBM introduced the PS/2 with a dedicated mouse port built into the system. (A mouse port is a port on the back of the system unit which enables users to attach a mouse to the computer. Through this port, the mouse communicates actions to and from the operating system.) The IBM PS/1 is equipped with a mouse, and all the applications in the PS/1 package are mouse compatible.

Reasons To Use a Mouse

Whether you use an IBM (or compatible), a Mac, or an Amiga, the mouse enables you to point to, select, and move items on-screen. For example, in spreadsheet programs (see fig. 7.6), you use the mouse to perform the following tasks:

- Open menus

- Select commands

- Highlight spreadsheet cells

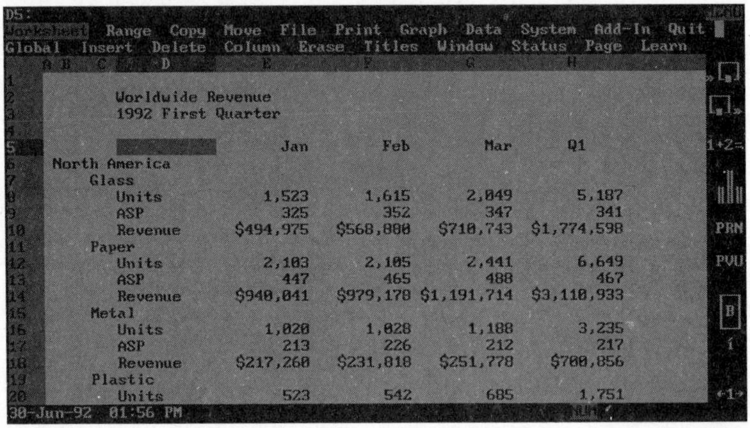

FIG. 7.6

A spreadsheet on the PC.

In the PC graphics program shown in figure 7.7, the mouse takes on a variety of personalities. When you work with text, the mouse appears as a text tool. In many programs, you may see one of two versions of the cursor: a mouse cursor (usually an arrow) or a text cursor. When you fill an area with a certain color, the mouse cursor also may appear as a paint can.

Do You Need a Mouse?

This question is answered by your response to a second question, "Do you plan to use a program that needs a mouse?" If the software you plan to use is selected by others, you may want to wait before answering this question.

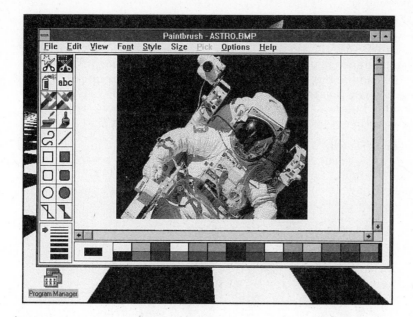

FIG. 7.7

A PC graphics
program that
uses the mouse.

Usually, people who are intimidated by the idea of using a mouse are
surprised to learn how easy using a mouse is. After you adjust to pointing and clicking, going back to selecting menu commands, options, and
operations by typing commands or by pressing keys on the keyboard
may be harder than you think.

If you buy an Amiga or Macintosh, you get a mouse, no questions
asked. For most other systems, you need to purchase the mouse as an
add-on item. The next section explains the mice available for the different kinds of computers.

What Kind of Mouse Do You Need?

If you buy a Macintosh, you don't have to worry about picking out a
mouse: Apple supplies the mouse. Similarly, if you purchase an Amiga
or an IBM PS/1, the manufacturers of these computers include the
mouse in the package. Some mice, however, are created by third-party
manufacturers. One mouse, the Turbo Mouse, is discussed later in this
section.

If you purchase an IBM PC or a PC clone, decide which kind of mouse
you want and how you want to connect the mouse to the system. Two
kinds of mice are available for the IBM: *serial* and *bus* mice. A *serial*

mouse is attached through the serial port in the back of the computer system, and a *bus* mouse requires the addition of a board that plugs into the motherboard of the computer system. Most users cannot tell the difference in performance between these two mice. Although the serial and the bus mouse work differently inside the computer (some users argue that the bus mouse is slightly faster), the only difference is that the bus mouse frees a serial port on the computer, which gives you another serial port to use for printers, digitizers, and modems.

If you work with a Macintosh computer, the choice of mice is limited: only a few third-party brands of mice exist for these computers. Unlike the PC counterparts, the Apple mouse has only one button (PC mice usually have two or three buttons). Figure 7.8 shows a two-button mouse for the PC.

FIG. 7.8

A two-button mouse for PCs.

When you shop for a mouse, you may see the following terms:

Mechanical mouse. A mechanical mouse uses a traditional design that operates on the rolling-ball concept. Inside the mouse is a small rubber ball that touches special pressure-sensitive electrodes inside the mouse housing as you move the mouse across the desktop. This action communicates the location of the mouse to the computer. The computer then knows where to display the cursor on-screen relative to where you move the mouse.

Optical mouse. Rather than the mechanical rolling-ball concept, an optical mouse *sees* where you move it by keeping track of certain coordinates. You use an optical mouse with a special pad that contains a grid of wires; when you move the mouse across the pad, the optical mouse shines a beam of light onto the pad. In the spaces between the grid lines (each line is known as a *gradical*), the light is reflected back to the mouse; when the mouse passes over a gradical, the light is not reflected back. The mouse then knows the current position and sends the coordinates to the system and the application software.

Hi-res mouse. A kind of mouse highly responsive to any movement. A hi-res mouse may be capable of resolution up to 400 dots per inch, which makes hi-res mice more sensitive to movement than a 200 dpi mouse.

A Look at Mouse Accessories

The following items may be mouse necessities for your system:

- A *mouse pad* is a cushioned surface (roughly 10 inches by 12 inches) on which you place the mouse. This pad gives the mouse an accurate tracking surface, which enables you to move the mouse smoothly. The mouse pad also keeps the mouse cleaner—bypassing the dust, dirt, crumbs, and hair that may accumulate on the desktop.

- A *mouse house* is a small pocket that attaches to the side of the system unit of your computer. This house gives you a place to store the mouse when not in use, freeing more desk space.

- For the winter months, you may want to invest in a small fuzzy *mouse suit*... (just kidding, but stores do sell these novelties).

Another kind of pointing device is climbing into the mouse arena: the *trackball*. This device is like an upside-down mouse (see fig. 7.9). The trackball is popular for games, and some CAD users prefer the feel of the trackball over the feel of the mouse. The main difference between a trackball and a mouse is the trackball unit stays in one place and you move the ball, which in turn moves the cursor on-screen. One popular trackball, from Logitech, has a list price of $119.

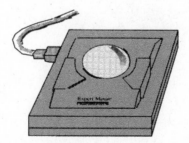

FIG. 7.9

A trackball.

The Turbo Mouse, available from Kensington for the Macintosh, is a cross between mouse and trackball technology. The ball is on top of the device (similar to a trackball) and the Turbo Mouse has two buttons with switches that enable you to set how you want the mouse to respond when you click the buttons.

The Expert Mouse, a device similar to the Turbo Mouse and also from Kensington, is available for IBM PCs and compatibles for $110.

Another mouse alternative is the UnMouse from Microtouch. Rather than rolling the device, you move your finger or a stylus across the 3-by-4-1/2-inch pressure-sensitive pad. To select, just press downward anywhere on the pad's surface.

How Much Does a Mouse Cost?

If decide to add a mouse to the computer, you may see a few differences in price. First, some popular mice are packaged *with* a program, such as Microsoft Windows or Logitech Paint. (Of course, a Microsoft mouse is packaged with Windows, and a Logitech mouse is packaged with Logitech Paint.) Second, you may see a price difference, based on whether you buy a bus mouse or serial mouse. The following listing reveals a few real-world mouse prices (*not* the manufacturer's suggested list prices):

Mouse	Price
GENIUS three-button serial mouse	$95 to $110
Logitech hi-res serial mouse	$74 to $110
Logitech hi-res bus mouse	$76 to $110
Microsoft bus mouse	$85 to $125
Microtouch UnMouse	$165 to $199

Exploring CD-ROM and Multimedia

CD-ROM (*Compact Disc-Read Only Memory*) drives are gaining in popularity as a significant computer add-on. A close relative of the audio CD player many of us have in our homes, the CD-ROM drive for your computer uses the same 4 3/4-inch plastic discs. The CD-ROM drive, however, stores up to 550 megabytes of information on a single disc and can play animated programs and games, display huge amounts of data, such as encyclopedias and popular books, and also can play sounds through the computer's speaker (an audio card is required for sound).

Depending on the type and length of the data with which you work, purchasing the compact discs for a CD-ROM drive is easy and fairly inexpensive. Most computer mail order magazines carry long lists of available CD titles, with subjects from audio Spanish lessons to full-motion windsurfing instruction.

How Do You Use a CD-ROM Drive?

Two kinds of CD-ROM drives are available: internal and external. An *internal* CD-ROM drive uses an existing slot in the computer's motherboard. The unit is installed similarly to a floppy disk drive and the disc's are inserted through a slot in the exterior of the system unit. The *external* CD-ROM drive is attached to the back of the system unit with cables and sits beside the computer. The discs are inserted in the drive through a front or top-loading caddy.

After inserting a disc in the CD-ROM drive, accessing the information is similar to accessing data from the hard or floppy disk. Most CD-ROM drives also come with utility programs that enable you to skip or manually locate tracks on the CD. These utility programs are similar to using a remote control for a home audio CD player.

After you find the track you want to play, tools are available that enable you to browse or search through the displayed data and run any animated programs. If you want to play sounds, audio cards are available for your computer that reproduce audio information. An installed audio card enables you to play even your own off-the-shelf audio CDs. Some CD-ROM drives come with audio connectors that enable you to attach external amplifiers and speakers; this feature may even be required if your computer lacks built-in speakers. Imagine hearing your favorite Mozart concerto through your computer!

CD-ROM drives are more than just mass storage and display devices though. Software is available that enables you to copy the contents of the disc and then edit the data in other programs. This capability enables you to use quality artwork, sounds, and so on in your work with only a small amount of time invested.

Suppose that you are writing a book on gardening and you decide to provide pictures and illustrations. You can purchase a CD filled with thousands of different vegetable, herb and insect pictures. As you are writing, imagine that you need a picture of the 3-ringed dog snail. Prior to the CD-ROM you would have to consult an entomology encyclopedia, manually locate the dog snail in the book, scan the picture, make touch-ups, and then insert the picture in your document. With the CD-ROM drive you just insert the CD with the gardening pictures in the CD-ROM drive and perform a search for the dog snail. After you find the snail picture, you can use a copy command to place the picture in computer RAM. Now you are ready to go back to the document and use an insert or paste command to place the snail picture in the text document.

What once potentially took hours, you now can complete in minutes and because most picture and sound CDs are sold with the intention that you use the information in your work, you are committing no copyright violation by copying and changing the data.

What are the Benefits of a CD-ROM Drive?

The following list details the benefits of a CD-ROM Drive:

Mass Storage
More than 550 megabytes of information fit on one disc (the equivalent of 700 floppy disks).

Low Cost
Disc duplication only costs the manufacturer about $5-20, so depending on the type and length of the data, this savings can be passed on to you.

No Cost
Many free programs, demos and shareware products are available on CD through major hardware and software manufacturers.

How Much Do CD-ROM Drives Cost?

Several firms manufacture CD-ROM drives, and the cost of any one drive is directly related to the features the drive may include. Both internal and external drives are available; the external drive is slightly more expensive. Some popular CD-ROM drives are the Sony CDU 535 Internal, which lists for $420, and the Sony CDU 7205 External, which lists around $625. Apple computer makes the Apple CD-ROM 150, which is available as an external unit only and retails for $599. Many other CD-ROMs are available, ranging in price from $200-$700. Check computer mail order magazines, such as *Computer Shopper, PC World,* and *MacWorld* to ensure that you get the best buy.

What are Multimedia PCs?

Now that you are familiar with CD-ROM drives, you can more easily see the attraction of the new multimedia PCs, which come with CD-ROM drives as part of the base system. *Multimedia* just means that the computer uses audio and video media to communicate information.

In the past, information was displayed only as text on-screen, which forced you to read to absorb the data. With multimedia capabilities, you now can display this information in a variety of ways.

Visually, information can be presented in text, graphics, 3-D graphics, animation, still video and full-motion video. The audio capabilities that accompany multimedia computers enable you to reproduce speech, music, and other sounds. Because of these interactive and positive feedback capabilities, multimedia computers have proven to be an innovative and effective tool for trainers, educators, advertisers, marketing reps, and people in the entertainment industry, to name just a few. Figure 7.10 shows a multimedia program.

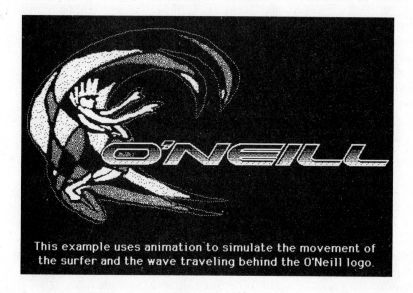

This example uses animation to simulate the movement of the surfer and the wave traveling behind the O'Neill logo.

FIG. 7.10

An example of the work done a multimedia program.

What Hardware Do You Get with a Multimedia PC?

Multimedia PCs are equipped with everything you need for adding and editing stereophonic sound, photo-quality graphics, still and full-motion video, and also standard text and graphics.

Starting with a 80286 (or more powerful) CPU, the multimedia PC also supports a full-color VGA monitor. An internal or external CD-ROM drive is included and an audio card is installed in the system unit to reproduce audio information. Completing this package is the Windows 3.1 software with built-in multimedia extensions. (Earlier versions of

Windows required the purchase of a separate multimedia extensions.) The entire package enables you to play CDs with full-motion video or animated programs; listen to the sounds and music that accompany these programs or create custom programs and sounds.

How Much Does a Multimedia PC Cost?

After you decide to purchase a multimedia PC, remember that you are buying an entire computer system, so you have many choices regarding speed and power. Because multimedia PCs come with standard equipment and minimum speed requirements (usually at least 10MHz), the cost is a little higher than the cost of an average computer.

Tandy, for example, offers a 2500 SX/20 multimedia PC for around $5,000. This price varies, depending on hard disk size, RAM and monitor. The IBM PS/2 Ultimedia Model M57SLC is equipped with an 80M hard drive, 4M RAM and an XGA monitor, in addition to the multimedia standards. This computer retails for around $5,500. Before you buy, check the industry magazines, such as *Multi-media* magazine and *Computer Shopper*, for the best prices.

Buying Multimedia Upgrade Kits

The convenience of buying a multimedia PC is unparalleled, but what if you already own a PC? Fortunately, you don't have to scrap the machine and buy a new one, as long as your current computer can be upgraded to—or already has—the minimum processing and speed requirements necessary to support multimedia.

Manufacturers now distribute multimedia upgrade kits that run on a 80286 (or better) IBM or compatible computer. These kits come complete with a CD-ROM drive (internal or external), an audio card, and the Windows 3.1 software with built-in multimedia extensions.

You can have an authorized dealer install the package or, if you know your way around the inside of your computer, you can install the equipment and software. Upgrade kits cost from $850 for internal packages to over $1,300 for external packages. Some of the more popular manufacturers are CompuAdd, Creative Labs, and Media Vision. Always check a local computer store or industry magazines for the best price available.

Understanding Modems

Similar to the mouse, the modem in the early days wasn't used by the popular computer applications. Today, modems are extremely popular, linking users through phone lines all over the world. The IBM PS/1 comes with a built-in Hayes modem and two different communications packages: PRODIGY and Promenade.

The term *modem* is short for *MOdulator/DEModulator*, which is the process the modem uses to turn data into audio signals (modulation). These signals are sent through the phone lines and are received by another modem that changes the data from audio signals to the electronic form that the computer can use (demodulation).

The earliest modems used *acoustical* couplers, which required you to place the handset of the phone in the modem, which sent and received data through the cup-like receptacles into which the handset was placed.

Today's modems can be either external or internal. An *external* modem is placed outside the computer and connects to both the system unit and the telephone jack with telephone lines (see fig. 7.11). An *internal* modem is a board plugged into the motherboard of the computer system, and the telephone wire is connected to the board. Internal and external modems are available for Macintosh, Amiga, and PC computers.

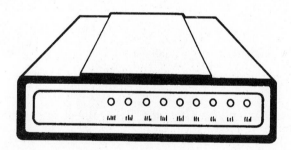

FIG. 7.11

An external modem.

Reasons To Use a Modem

Initially, you may have to use your imagination to picture why you may use a modem. After you step into the communications arena, however, going back is hard. Some uses for a modem are suggested in the following listing:

■ *Computer-to-computer communications*

With the significant increase in the number of offices in homes, the process of linking computers via phone lines (*communications*) has become a new wave in personal computing. Imagine that you are working on a report to be presented at a corporate meeting on the 14th. Two days before the meeting, you have to travel to Georgia to handle a major breakdown. With communications, you can take a laptop computer to Georgia (assuming that this laptop model has a modem), finish the report, and then use the modem to send the file to an administrative assistant. Your assistant then can print and then duplicate the report in time for the boss's approval and inclusion in the report packet assembled for the meeting.

■ *Retrieving information from information services*

A modem gives you access to a world of information previously available only in the most up-to-date libraries. Through the use of *information services*, or large main-frame computers that store an incredible amount of information on an exhaustive list of topics, you have at your fingertips information on almost any subject. From an information service, you can perform the following information-gathering activities:

Find out about cruises to Alaska

Check for up-to-date stock information

Talk to users about your favorite software package

Ask for advice on publishing a corporate newsletter

Retrieve a new game publicly distributed for your computer

Leave a message on a bulletin board about a computer you are selling

For information on how to subscribe to these information services, see Chapter 18.

■ *Electronic Mail*

The electronic mailbox is similar to the answering machine, but done through the use of computer technology. With an electronic mail system, you can leave messages for other users and read messages left for you.

With electronic mail, you can use either a private or public system. Public systems, such as the MCI or AT&T services, charge a monthly subscription fee and a per minute (or per message) rate. Private electronic mail is used within corporations to transfer messages and memos from department to department and from person to person. A variety of private electronic mail software currently is available.

Do You Need a Modem?

When you purchase a computer system, consider whether the capability of linking to other computers is important to you. A modem is easy to add at a later date. If you are unsure whether you need a modem, you can delay this purchase. When you are considering the purchase, ask yourself the following questions:

- ■ Do you ever plan to transmit data to or from a remote place?

- ■ Do you plan to use an information service to look up information or to contact other companies?

- ■ Can your business benefit from electronic mail?

- ■ Do you plan to contact the bulletin board services run by software manufacturers?

If you answer yes to any of these questions, look further into finding a modem that can operate with your system. The following section introduces you to the cost of modems. Chapter 18 explains the differences in communications software for various computers.

How Much Do Modems Cost?

Like anything else related to computers, the cost of the modem is directly related to the features of the modem. The greater the number of features, the greater the cost.

Modems have many differences besides the internal or external features. Another variable is *bit parts per second* or *bps* (also referred to as *Baud rate*) which is the speed a modem sends and receives data. Some modems send and receive data at 1200 bps; others are capable of 2400 or even 9600 bps. The earliest transmission speed standard—300 bps— is seen only rarely, now that faster transmissions are available. The following list shows how the difference in transmission speed can affect the transfer times of a 16K file (a 16K file is comparable to a 7-page single-spaced document):

Bps	Transfer Time
300	2 minutes
1200	30 seconds
2400	15 seconds
4800	7.5 seconds
9600	3.75 seconds

A modem is a relatively low-cost addition to a computer system. Some modems also are sold with communications software. Modems that transmit data faster usually cost more (a 2400-baud modem costs more than a 1200-baud modem). Because of the number of additional parts (the housing, cables, and so on), you also pay slightly more for an external modem than you pay for an internal modem. An external modem is more expensive to manufacture. The following list shows the costs of a few popular modems:

Modem	Bps	Type	Cost [*]
Hayes	1200	Internal	$149
Hayes	2400	Internal	279
Hayes	1200	External	265
Hayes	2400	External	350
Everex	2400	Internal	69
Everex	2400	External	165

[*] *Real-world prices, according to* Computer Shopper, *April, 1992; these prices do not reflect suggested retail prices.*

Arguments exist for both internal and external modems. An internal modem takes up a system expansion slot, eats some CPU speed, and costs less (two minuses and one plus). An external modem stands alone on the desktop, includes indicator lights on the front to show when data is sending and receiving, but costs more (two minuses and one plus). The indicator lights are a nice feature—particularly if you want to send and receive data while you are working on something else; the lights show you when your system is at work in the background. If you don't have an external modem, however, you can rely on the software to tell you how the data transmission is going.

Different models of modems offer different features. Although modems are relatively inexpensive, you often can get a few extras when you purchase a modem from certain manufacturers; when you buy an

ATD/Zuckerboard 2400E Internal Modem, for example, PC Talk 3 communications software comes with the modem. The ATD/Zuckerboard 2400E also offers the following features:

- Full Hayes compatibility
- Pulse or tone dialing
- Auto-answering and auto-dialing features
- Built-in speaker with volume adjustment control
- Capability of monitoring the progress of a call
- Full or half duplex operation
- Dual phone jacks
- Automatic error detection

When you are ready to purchase a modem, be sure that the following capabilities are supported:

- Transmits at a speed acceptable for your present and planned uses
- Is compatible with modems in computers from which you plan to send and receive data
- Includes additional features that you feel are important (special dialing features, error detection features, volume control)

What Is a FAX Modem?

To use a FAX, you insert the sheet of paper you want to send, and the FAX reads the sheet (like a scanner, which is explained in the following section); changes the data on the sheet to transmittable signals (like a modem); sends the data to the receiving modem, which reconverts the signals; and prints the data (like a printer).

FAX modems, or FAX plug-in boards, are now available. These modems enable you to send and receive files directly from a computer without a separate FAX machine. Some manufacturers also offer a scanner and FAX board combination that enables you to scan text and graphics and then transmit the data to another FAX machine. A major advantage of a FAX board is that you can FAX a file from the background (while working on another application) without interrupting your work. You also can keep a log of frequently used FAX numbers and perform a variety of other timesaving tasks by merging the power of the computer with FAX capabilities.

Although most stand-alone FAX systems range in price from $500 for a low-end machine to $1,000 and more, you can get a FAX board for between $250 and $400. Of course, you don't get many of the bells and whistles of a stand-alone FAX, such as a dual function as a copier, data/voice switching option, or automatic printout capabilities, but you do have the option of using the received FAX data in your computer application and printing the information.

Buying a Scanner

As computing needs change, users want better and faster ways of getting information and graphics into computers. After you type a 40-page document, you can use the text again and again, but *getting* the information entered the first time can be a real headache. If someone approached you with an option that might free you from hours of mindless typing, you would be interested.

Suppose that you are working with a client who insists that you use a logo on all the client's publications. The problem? The logo is decades old and therefore is difficult to reproduce. How can you get the logo into desktop publishing software so that you can work with the image easily?

Scanners—or scanners and OCR software (explained in the following section)—come to the rescue. A *scanner* is a device that enables you to convert data on paper—text or graphics—into a computer-usable file. How you use the scanner depends on the kind of scanner you purchase. If you buy a hand-held scanner, you scan the image by moving the scanner across the page. If you buy a flat-bed scanner, you place the page in the scanner, similar to inserting a page into an office copier.

When do you use a scanner? Suppose that the client wants you to place the logo on each page of a special publication you are producing and that the client insists on using only this logo. "No fancy artwork," he says. "We've used this logo for 75 years and it suits us very well, thank you." How can you use the logo on every page but avoid manually cutting and pasting the logo into the publication?

The solution is to use a scanner to read the logo into electronic form so that you then can place the client's graphic in documents. This step keeps you from using the X-ACTO knife and wax (or the scissors and glue) and appeases your client by keeping the same logo.

When you scan text, the scanner turns the words into a graphic image; you cannot edit, retype, or correct misspellings in this text. The computer sees the text as a graphic because the scanner essentially took a picture of the text. To turn the graphics image of the text into real text again—characters that you can edit, modify, and change font styles— you need OCR (optical character recognition) software. This category of software is used with scanned files to convert the graphics text into true text that you can use in applications. OCR software costs any- where from $150 to $1,000. Many scanner manufacturers, such as Logitech, offer OCR software as an option when you purchase a scanner.

What Kinds of Scanners Are Available?

Scanners come in many shapes and sizes. High-end powerful color scanners can scan color images, retaining the densities and slight color differences of up to 16 million colors. (The number of colors available is limited only by the scanning software.) Low-end hand scanners black-and-white scan only a portion of a page and offer a resolution of 200 to 400 *dpi* (dots per inch). In the middle ground, you find the gray- scale machines, so named because these scanners convert the scanned image into images displayed and presented in shades of gray. Depend- ing on the capability of the gray-scale scanner, you may reproduce up to 256 different gray tones in an image. Gray-scale scanners are ad- equate for many graphic scanning needs.

The resolution of the scanner determines how many dots per inch the scanner picks up when converting the image into electronic form. A 300 dpi scanner reads more dots than a 200 dpi scanner. Like other devices that use resolution as a standard, such as monitors and printers, the more dots, the better resolution the device is capable of producing. Most scanners have a switch that enables you to set the resolution of the scan.

Besides the color or gray-scale question, you have the question of the basic size of scanner: hand-held, half-page, or full-page. A hand-held scanner gives you about four inches of scanning width, a half-page scanner is a wider version of the hand-held unit, and a full-page (*flatbed*) scanner enables you to place an entire page in the scanner and capture all text and graphics shown in a one-page file. The flatbed scanner offers the best quality scanned image because nothing moves during the scan process—you don't move the scanner (you move hand- held and half-page scanners). Often, when the page or the scanner moves, the output is wobbly. Figure 7.12 shows a hand-held scanner, and figure 7.13 shows a flatbed scanner.

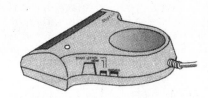

FIG. 7.12

A hand-held
scanner.

FIG. 7.13

A flatbed
scanner.

How do you use a scanner? You install the device (or have the device installed), load the scanning software that comes with all scanners and—with a hand-held scanner—pull the scanner over the image you want to scan.

If the image you scan is a graphic, save the image in a file format usable in other applications, such as PCX or TIFF (the two most common PC graphics file formats). You then can import this graphic into other programs, such as PageMaker or First Publisher, to add the scanned artwork to your publications.

If the image you scan is text, the computer recognizes the image as a graphic. All text and graphics digitized by a scanner are converted into a graphics format. Until you use special software known as *optical character recognition (OCR)* software with the captured text, the computer and applications see the text as a graphic element. Therefore, you can't edit, change the style, or work with the text (as text) until you use OCR software to convert the text from a graphic element into *real* text.

Some OCR packages are clumsy. Although you can transform text the output choices are limited. Not all OCR software enables you to set different font types; some high-end OCR software packages can recognize the font in an original scanned image and automatically match this font for the output. OCR software can cost from $150 to more than

$1,000, depending on the speed, accuracy, and flexibility you want. Some of the lower-cost OCR packages produce so many errors that retyping the entire document can be less work; on the other hand, a powerful OCR package can convert hand-written text into usable electronic text. Besides requiring a sizable investment, high-end OCR programs demand large amounts of memory, often up to 4M.

When Do You Use a Scanner?

The question of need again arises with scanners. How often are you going use the scanner? Which scanner is best for your needs? The following list can help you determine when to use a particular kind of scanner:

Use	Scanner Type
For scanning small logos	Hand-held
For importing pages of text	Flatbed or full-page with OCR software
For importing color images	Color scanner that must stay color
For scanning columns of text	Half-page scanner with OCR software

The following listing shows some examples of times when a scanner may come in handy:

- *Desktop publishing*

  Suppose that you produce newsletters for three small companies. In each case, the company wants you to use a logo in the design of the newsletters. You *can* use a graphics program to draw the logo on-screen, or you can construct the rest of the publication in a page layout program and then manually cut and paste the logos onto the appropriate locations. A simple hand scanner can electronically copy and import the logos into an easy-to-use paint program. In the paint program, you can smooth rough edges. Finally, you can pull the logos into your page layout program. You also can reuse the same file.

- *Text-intensive data entry*

  Suppose that you are cataloging the documentation of more than 1,400 photo shoots taken in your company since 1985. The work from all these years has culminated in more than 300 pages of text; each in a certain format including information like subject, photographer, date, and other important facts. Rather than spending several weeks typing this material, you can purchase a full-page scanner and OCR software. Then, after running the pages through the scanner, running the text through the OCR program, and cleaning up the errors, you have a complete set of computer files.

■ *Getting rid of half-tones*

Each year, you produce your department's annual report. The annual reports have become competitive, with all departments vying for the "Best Publication" award at the annual dinner. Last year, after adding PageMaker to your software repertoire, you thought you had the title but you took some criticism for that lousy photograph of the president you used. This year, you won't be caught unaware—with the help of a scanner and a good paint program, such as PC Paintbrush IV Plus, you make the president's photo look better than he does.

Cleaning Up Scanned Images

In the best of all worlds, scanners can scan images so that they look as good as, if not better than, the originals. Unfortunately, because you are limited to 300 dpi, most images scanned on low or mid-range scanners have a case of the jaggies (the edges are jagged, and you can see the individual dots that make up the image). To smooth graphics, you can use either a paint program or an autotrace program, such as Adobe Streamline, that traces the image and smooths jagged edges.

What Does a Scanner Cost?

Again, the cost of scanners is directly related to the features of the scanner you buy. The prices of color flatbed scanners top the chart, running from a street price of $2,294 for an Epson scanner (for IBM or Mac) to a list price of $7,995 to $9,915 for the Howtek Scanmaster (for IBM or Mac).

You can purchase a scanner from a retail outlet, from a mail-order business, or directly from the manufacturer. Make sure that you read about current models and prices in popular industry magazines, such as *PC, Byte, MacWorld,* and *Computer Shopper.*

The next step down is on the gray-scale level. Gray-scale flatbed scanners also offer a variety of features, including file output in many popular formats (such as PICT, EPS, PCX, and TIFF); different scale controls; and variable dots per inch resolution. The HP ScanJet is an industry standard, available for both Macs and PCs at a real world cost of around $1,700.

The lower level is adequate for many users and consists of hand and half-page scanners. These small devices can scan a variety of logos, graphics, and text at significantly lower costs than more elaborate models. The Logitech Scanman Plus comes with Logitech Paintshow Plus and retails for $199. This scanner gives you everything you need to scan, touch up (with Paintshow Plus), and export an image in a file format usable in other applications.

Chapter Summary

In this chapter, you looked at several add-on devices that you may want to add to your PC, Mac or Amiga system. You saw options and learned more about the kinds of keyboards available. You also learned about the pros and cons of mouse ownership and explored the more specialized functions of CD-ROM drives, multimedia computer systems, modems, FAX machines and FAX boards, and scanners. In the following chapter, you learn more about evaluating your software needs.

Purchasing Software

I n previous chapters, you considered the kind of computer you want and identified important features and add-on components that give you the power and flexibility you need in a Mac, Amiga, or PC system. In this chapter, you learn about the various categories of software available.

Most software companies today create common home and business applications with multiple platforms in mind. One company is the Microsoft Corporation; the majority of the software Microsoft develops is available for both the Mac and IBM (DOS and Windows). The software has the same features on both computers, the only difference is in how the commands are accessed: using DOS commands, using the menus in the Windows environment, or using the menus in the Macintosh operating environment.

This chapter first introduces you to each of the major software categories and then asks a series of questions that can help you identify the software you need for your particular computer uses. Which computer you choose is based on software compatibility with the computer (not *all* software is multiplatform), your company's hardware standard, or your own personal preference.

First, however, you need to distinguish between software for operating systems and software for applications. A computer's operating system serves as the link between the application programs, the computer, and you. This chapter explores applications software. In Chapter 10, you learn about the various available operating systems.

Defining Software Categories

If you have shopped for software for any length of time, you know the wide range of available programs. This section provides a brief introduction to each of the major software categories; in Part IV of this book, examples of each category of software are listed in respective chapters. The following list introduces the software categories and shows where you can find more specific information about each category:

Software category	Chapter
Spreadsheets	12
Word processing	13
Data management	14
Integrated software	15
Desktop publishing	16
Graphics	17
Communications	18
Educational and recreational software	19
Utilities	20

Spreadsheets

One of the first uses for canned software (programs packaged and sold for personal computers) was the spreadsheet. The spreadsheet is a computerized version of an accountant's pad and pencil, which replaces the traditional adding machine or calculator with automated functions and formulas. This replacement saves the user much work and significantly reduces the error margin. Perhaps best of all was the reusable data aspect: users have an on-disk version of the spreadsheet they can modify and rework as needed. Chapter 12 explores many of the most popular spreadsheet programs.

Whether you are comfortable working with columns, rows, and pages of financial data or you break out in hives at the thought of balancing a checkbook, you may find the electronic approach of the spreadsheet reassuring. Just plug in the numbers and tell the spreadsheet to do the rest. Suppose that you want to calculate whether you can afford a new car.

First, start by determining how much money you have left each month:

Monthly income:	$2,100
Monthly expenses:	$1,400
Monthly income remaining:	$700

Then, determine how much you would pay to finance the car:

Total price of car:	$8,900.00
Number of months financed:	48
Interest rate:	13.75
Total amount financed:	$13,795.00
Total monthly payment:	$287.40

Subtract the monthly payment from the amount of money left over each month (minus $76.49 in expenses, which includes license plates, taxes, and the increase in insurance premiums):

Monthly net income:	$700.00
Monthly car payment:	$210.91
New net income:	$489.09

The formulas involved in the preceding calculations are found in the spreadsheet program manual. Suppose that you want to finance the car for only 36 months and that you want to make a down payment. If you can scrape together $2,000 toward a down payment for the car, how does this change affect your monthly budget? What happens if you try a different interest rate?

With conventional bookkeeping methods, you must recalculate all the figures by plugging in different numbers to get different results. With an electronic spreadsheet, however, you change a number or two and the program handles the calculations. Compare figures 8.1 and 8.2. Figure 8.1 shows how you are forced to refigure the calculations based on the items that changed (number of months, down payment, interest rate). Figure 8.2 shows how easily a spreadsheet program can calculate the different results.

The layout of the electronic spreadsheet closely resembles the layout of a traditional accountant's pad. Columns and rows store the data, enabling you to work with columns of numbers and set up the spreadsheet in whatever way works best for the task. The intersection of each column and row is a *cell*, and each cell stores a number, formula, or text that you enter as you create the spreadsheet.

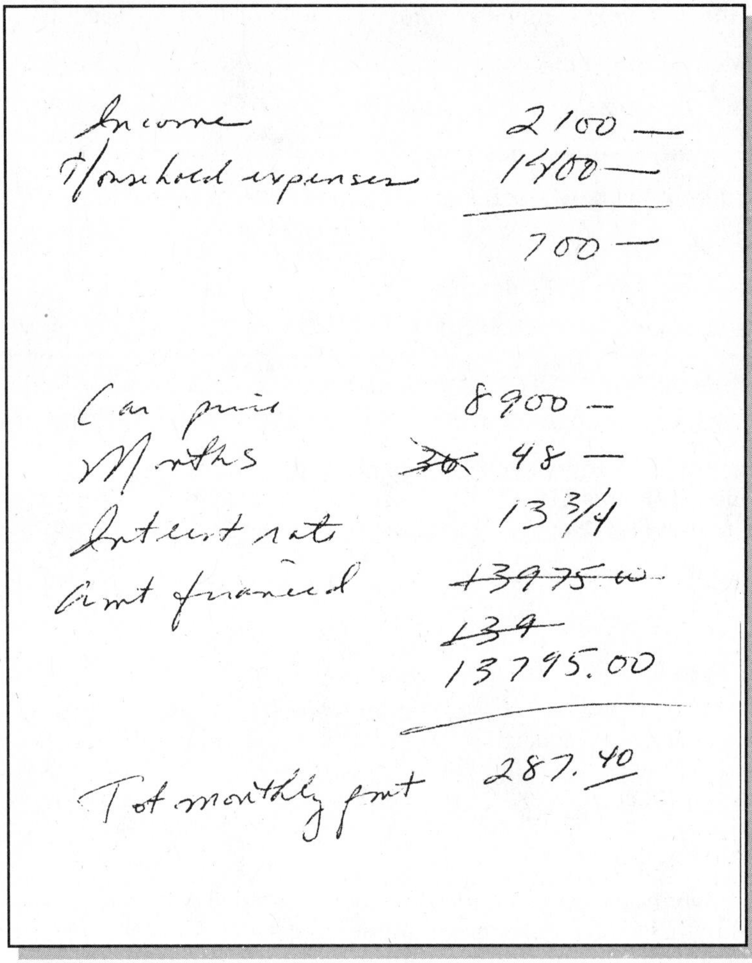

FIG. 8.1

Calculating the
conventional
way.

The spreadsheet also contains built-in functions, which are like
prewritten formulas the program uses to perform calculations on data
you choose. Suppose that you want to add the values in column A, as
shown in the following example:

	A	B	C	D
1	123.45			
2	234.56			
3	345.67			
4	456.78			
5				
6				

Rather than telling the program to add all four of these values (such as typing **123.45+234.56+345.67+456.78**), you can tell the program to @SUM(A1..A4). @SUM is a function that tells the program to add the numbers you specified. The (A1..A4) part of the function is known as the range of cells you want to add. You place the function in the cell in which you want the result to appear. Cell A6 in the preceding example displays the actual result 1,160.46, but the program stores the function. Then, if you change the number in cell A3, the program recalculates the total in A6. Figure 8.3 shows an example of using a spreadsheet function.

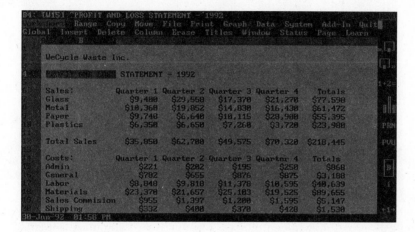

FIG. 8.2

Getting the spreadsheet to work for you.

The Benefits of Spreadsheet Programs

■ The columns and rows format of the spreadsheet is easy to understand and use.

■ You can perform calculations on the data you enter; formulas are saved with the spreadsheet.

■ Data entry can be automated and checked for errors.

■ The format used to display numbers can be changed easily.

■ Columns and rows can be sorted, copied, and moved with formulas intact.

■ The spreadsheet can be printed in a variety of formats for financial reports.

■ Most spreadsheet programs have a built-in graph generator that enables you to create simple graphs from the data in the spreadsheet.

```
 F1-Help    F2-Files   F3-Features      F4-Print     F5-Edit      F6-Style
Spreadsheet                                       1% Full    Row    6  Column    1
400 By 200       C1      C2      C3      C4     C5      C6      C7      C8      C9

R1            123.45
R2            234.56
R3            345.67
R4            456.78
R5
R6          1,160.46                              ▐
R7
R8
R9
R10
R11
R12
R13            Name:                         Formula R6C1:
R14            tot(c1r1..c1r4)
R15
R16
R17
R18
 Press Esc to cancel changes, or press Alt-F or any cursor key to save changes
```

FIG. 8.3

Understanding
spreadsheet
functions.

Word Processing

Word processing was another major step in applications software.
From the first versions of software, word processing took away from a
generation of typists the typewriter, carbon paper, and correction fluid
and replaced these tools with on-screen editing, formatting, and simple
printing procedures.

What can you do with word processing? You can type letters, reports,
novels—anything you can type on a typewriter. If you make a mistake,
you can use the Backspace key to erase the error and type the word
again correctly. If you decide that you don't like the opening of the report and want to move two or three paragraphs around, you can mark
and then move the text with a minimum of trouble. The best thing
about the word processing program is that after you have entered and
saved the text, the program is in a file, ready to be edited, used again,
or printed. After you type a 10-page document, you never have to type
the file again, no matter how many words you misspell, how many paragraphs you want to move, or how much of the document you rewrite.
Chapter 13 introduces you to several of the most popular word
processing programs. Figure 8.4 shows a popular word processing
program, Microsoft Word.

At the most basic level, word processing enables you to work with text.
Instead of typing text over and over, you can use a word processing
program to store your words until you again need them. The fact that
you *can* reuse documents is a major benefit of word processing. You
type, save (in a file), and reuse the text when you need the data. You
also have at your disposal a number of editing features, such as a spelling checker, a thesaurus, and a built-in grammar checker that helps you
produce text not only quickly but accurately.

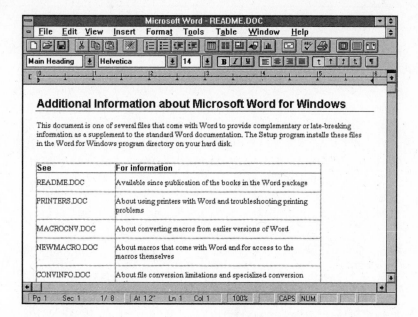

FIG. 8.4

The Microsoft
Word for
Windows word
processing
program.

The variety of word processors is staggering. Some basic word processing programs enable you only to enter, edit, save, and print text. Other programs perform all these tasks and more. You can think of the range of word processors as a pyramid. At the bottom are features common to all word processing programs: typing, editing, simple formatting, and printing procedures. At the next level is a more specialized but still common group of features: help menus, special function or quick keys, easy formatting features, and screen functions that you can customize. The next level grows more specialized, with built-in spelling checkers, thesauruses, grammar checkers, address books, file-exportation utilities, and so on. At each new level, some word processing programs drop out. A select group continues building toward the apex of this pyramid, however, in the race for the definitive word processor.

At the apex of this pyramid are highly specialized features, such as the capability of integrating text and graphics, creating special effects, working with special legal dictionaries, and myriad other individual features. Most users who purchase even the highest level word processing programs may still work with low- and medium-range features.

Be aware of the features you are purchasing before you buy a word processing program. If you need a mid-range word processor, don't purchase a top-of-the-pyramid program. If you need a simple program that everyone in the office can learn quickly, avoid word processors so powerful (and so expensive) that the learning curve looks like Mount Everest.

The Benefits of Word Processing

- You type the document only once and then store the file on disk to be used again.

- Most programs provide easy text entry and editing features.

- Most programs include on-screen formatting capabilities that enable you to control tabs, indent paragraphs, format columns, and place special codes for the printer.

- Most word processing programs have spelling checkers, and some also have additional features, such as a thesaurus or grammar checker.

- Most programs offer a variety of printing options, enabling you to customize the program for your printer.

- Some word processors enable you to change the font and style of text.

Data Management

Data management software manages data—whether this data includes cataloging a CD collection, maintaining an elaborate database of clients, or keeping up with the newest additions to the PTA list.

A database program enables you to store, sort, and retrieve information. Each database is built on the concept of records and fields. Each *record* stores similar information about one particular item, whereas each *field* is the individual information item that is part of a record.

Suppose that you want to create a database to organize a massive seven-rack CD collection. Here, each CD may be represented by a record in which you store four pieces of information (fields) about the CD:

Field	Stores this information
Category of music:	Whether the music is Popular, Classical, or Instrumental
Artist or composer:	Name of group, artist, or composer
Location of CD:	The rack where the CD is stored (or if you loaned a CD to a friend, which friend)
Number of CDs by the artist:	The number of CDs in the collection by the same artist

The following listing shows the kinds of records you can enter in this database. Remember that each row is a record (each CD) and that each column represents a field (information item about each CD):

Record	Category	Artist	Location	Number
1	Classical	Bach	Rack 5	3
2	Popular	Boston	Rack 1	2
3	Instrumental	David Lanz	Rack 3	2
4	Popular	Bad Company	Rack 1	1
5	Classical	Mozart	Rack 5	3
6	Popular	Rush	Rack 3	2
7	Classical	Vivaldi	Rack 5	1
8	Classical	Beethoven	Rack 6	4
9	Popular	Def Leppard	Rack 2	2
10	Popular	Aerosmith	Rack 2	2
11	Instrumental	George Winston	Rack 7	2

Although you enter the data in no specific order, you can tell the database to organize the information in any way you choose. Suppose that you want all the CDs in the list arranged alphabetically, by category. The result looks like the following list:

Record	Category	Artist	Location	Number
1	Classical	Bach	Rack 5	3
8	Classical	Beethoven	Rack 6	4
5	Classical	Mozart	Rack 5	3
7	Classical	Vivaldi	Rack 5	1
3	Instrumental	David Lanz	Rack 3	2
11	Instrumental	George Winston	Rack 7	2
10	Popular	Aerosmith	Rack 2	2
4	Popular	Bad Company	Rack 1	1
2	Popular	Boston	Rack 1	2
9	Popular	Def Leppard	Rack 2	2
6	Popular	Rush	Rack 3	2

Notice how the records changed sequence. The change happened because the database sorted the records, placing each item in order by category and then alphabetizing each category within the field. (The database also arranged the categories—Classical, Instrumental, and Popular—alphabetically.)

The way a database program enables you to sort records depends on the program you use. A wide range of other features also is available in different database programs. You can find a database program that can help you organize all the little data fields in your life. You can choose from a simple enter-and-organize-the-data approach to a multilevel complex database program that enables you to link databases, perform a variety of sophisticated functions, and even program the way users enter data. Figure 8.5 shows a screen from dBASE IV, one of the most popular database programs currently available.

The Benefits of Data Management Programs

- You can reuse data; you enter data once and then sort, search, and arrange the information to your heart's content.

- You can arrange data easily by using the database program's sort feature.

- You quickly can find the data you need by using the program's search capabilities.

- You can use printing features that enable mailing label and report generation.

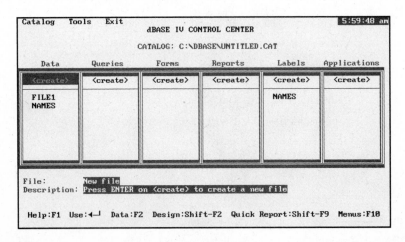

FIG. 8.5

A popular database program, dBASE IV.

Integrated Software

Integrated software is a term used to describe a program that actually is several programs in one. Many popular integrated packages include the following application programs:

- Spreadsheet
- Word processor
- Data manager
- Graphics
- Communications

The integrated package is popular for users who need a variety of different programs. Figure 8.6 shows a popular integrated program for the PC, PFS: First Choice. Users can enter data in one application and then use the information in other applications, a process that saves time and trouble and protects the accuracy of the data. Suppose that you entered a list of employee names in the filing (*data management*) portion of the program. You then set up a spreadsheet, and instead of typing all the employee names a second time, you can copy and paste the names into the appropriate spreadsheet row. Then, when you are ready to send out information about a change in policy, you can have the program plug the names and addresses of the employees into a document. You can see how the feature of reusable data comes into play in integrated packages.

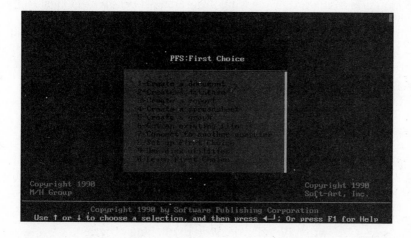

FIG. 8.6

The PFS: First Choice integrated program.

The Benefits of Integrated Software

■ Data is compatible among applications.

■ The menu system usually is the same, lessening the number of menus and options the user must learn.

■ Having everything in one package means less time loading programs and opening and closing files.

■ Purchasing an integrated package costs less than purchasing the same number of applications individually.

Popular integrated packages are available for the Mac, the Amiga, and the PC. Chapter 15 highlights several of the most popular integrated programs.

Desktop Publishing

Desktop publishing software is a relatively new addition to the gallery of software available for Macs and PCs. Desktop publishing enables you to produce documents, such as newsletters, company reports, and other publications, by using the capabilities of the computer and page layout software.

The difference between desktop publishing and word processing programs is that word processing programs process words; desktop publishing programs can combine text and graphics to produce the publications you need. Some desktop publishing programs include clip art (individual art items you can use in publications). Chapter 16 includes specific information about desktop publishing programs.

Desktop publishing takes the publication of your documents a step farther than does word processing. Although some word processing programs enable you to perform many desktop publishing features (remember the top-of-the-pyramid word processors?), most do not offer features that enable you to create publications more complex than simple reports, letters, and manuals. For more complicated projects that require multiple columns, integration of graphics, a variety of fonts, and special effects, desktop publishing software gives you the power and flexibility you need to arrange the page elements any way you want. Figure 8.7 (and this book as well) are examples of documents created with a popular desktop publishing program.

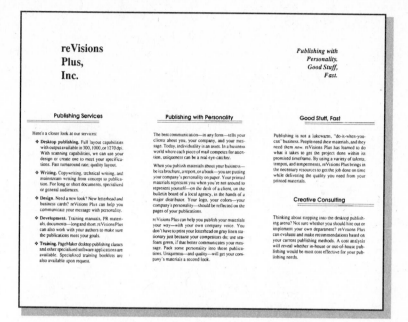

FIG. 8.7

A document created with desktop publishing software.

Desktop publishing has high-end and low-end programs. You can purchase a simple program for less than $100 that enables you to publish newsletters, brochures, and a variety of other publications. Similarly, you can get powerful programs for about $600 that enable you to create massive documents, complete with index, table of contents, and automatic page numbering.

The Benefits of Desktop Publishing Programs

■ You arrange text and graphics on-screen.

■ You can assemble documents quickly and make changes easily.

■ You can import text from word processors or type the text directly in the program.

■ You can print on a variety of printers, from dot-matrix to PostScript laser printers.

Graphics

A graphics program is handy when you need to create a logo, clean up a scanned image, or create an art element. Graphics software comes in different shapes and sizes. Like other categories of software, graphics programs range from a high end to a low end. Low-end graphics programs are sometimes called paint programs, and they often provide a good range of artwork. Paint programs usually create bit-mapped graphics, meaning that each art element you create is only a pattern of dots on-screen. This kind of graphic is easy to edit: you just magnify the size of the graphic and change the color of a few dots. The printed output may look choppy, however, and sometimes the individual dots can be seen.

Graphics software comes in different shapes and sizes. You usually see the terms *paint* and *draw* programs when you are investigating graphics. The following paragraphs explain these two kinds of applications programs.

You use *paint* programs to paint the screen, creating artwork from a pattern of dots. This kind of graphics is easy to edit: you magnify the part of the graphic you want to work on and change a few dots (how you make changes depends on the program you use). Although easy and fun to use, paint programs don't offer users the highest quality graphics available. Because each item is actually a picture made from dots, you often see the individual dots that make up each graphic, resulting in a choppy or jagged printed output.

Draw programs, however, use a different technology to create graphics. Draw programs, which usually are more complicated to use than paint programs, see the items as objects you create and manipulate as necessary. You can select individual items that you can resize and work with as necessary.

To illustrate the difference, compare two popular PC graphics programs: PC Paintbrush IV (a paint program) and Micrografx Designer (a draw program). PC Paintbrush IV is an extremely popular paint program for the PC, available for about $110. Micrografx Designer, which costs about $450, is a popular draw program for the PC, offering among the highest quality standards currently available for the PC.

To create a rectangle in either of these programs, the procedure is the same:

- With PC Paintbrush IV, you select the rectangle tool, select a place on-screen, and draw the rectangle.

- With Micrografx Designer, you select the rectangle tool, select a place on-screen, and draw the rectangle.

The difference comes when you alter the rectangle you just created:

- With PC Paintbrush IV, if you want to change the shape of the rectangle, you must either erase the rectangle you just made and create another or magnify the display and, dot by dot, change the shape of the rectangle (see fig. 8.8).

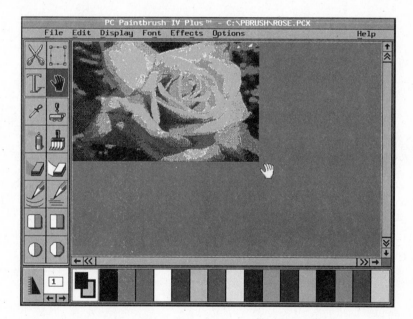

FIG. 8.8

Working with a paint program.

- With Micrografx Designer, you click on the rectangle, then drag one of the handles that appear until the rectangle is the size and shape you want (see fig. 8.9).

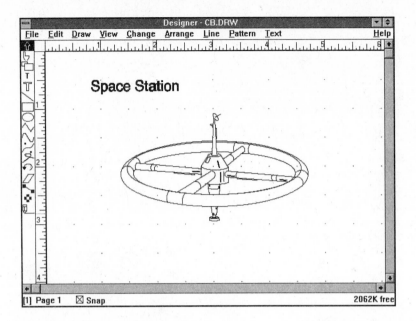

FIG. 8.9

Working with a
draw program.

The main difference between these two programs is in how each program sees the graphics. Because Micrografx Designer recognizes the rectangle as an object and not as a series of dots, you can work with the rectangle as an object. This capability makes the draw program more powerful and flexible. Also, because the graphics are communicated to the printer in a language that understands the object-oriented descriptions, the printed quality of the graphics can far surpass the print quality of paint programs.

Draw programs are more expensive than paint programs, however, and usually are more complicated to learn. Before you invest in a graphics program, be sure that you think carefully about the degree of quality you need from the graphics and the kind of program that best suits your needs.

Throughout this book, you see the terms *high end* and *low end* to describe various graphics packages. Usually, *low end* refers to paint programs because these programs give an overall lower quality of printout and offer fewer features. A hierarchy of programs exists within each category (paint and draw), however, so don't discount any program until you investigate the features of all the programs.

High-end graphics programs usually incorporate some CAD features and provide high-quality images that you can export in a variety of formats. These sophisticated graphics programs usually offer an incredible range of features.

Chapter 17 highlights some of the most popular low-end and high-end graphics programs available.

The Benefits of Graphics Programs

■ With on-screen graphics, you don't have to go back to the drawing board every time. You can make small modifications to the original art until you arrive at the design you want.

■ Use of the art tools in a graphics program gives you more control over the precision of your creations.

■ You can reuse the art you create without losing any of the quality.

■ With many graphics programs, you can export art directly to popular desktop publishing programs.

Presentation Graphics

Presentation graphics is a kind of software that has been around for a short time but is rapidly climbing in popularity. Developed for people who use computers to produce charts and presentations, presentation graphics software enables you to enter data easily, create various kinds of charts, and add special enhancements to customize presentations.

The difference between graphics and presentation graphics programs in part depends on the capabilities of the presentation graphics software. Many high-end presentation graphics programs include graphics capabilities so that not only can you create and produce charts easily, you also can use the graphics part of the program to add custom logos, draw art for the background, or create buttons that link one chart to the next.

The presentation graphics program Harvard Graphics 3.0 includes an extensive number of features that enable you to create pie, text, XY, and organizational charts. You can use the Chart Gallery to create a chart type (just pick the chart design you like and plug in the data); with the Draw feature you can add specialized logos, buttons, and background art; the program's file maintenance features help you to organize and work with files; and you can add programs to a special Applications menu so that you can move among other programs without leaving Harvard Graphics. You also can print, plot, or record a chart (with a film recorder), or you can display charts on a monitor in a *slide show*, or presentation, automated for the viewer. Figure 8.10 shows an example of the Chart Gallery in Harvard Graphics.

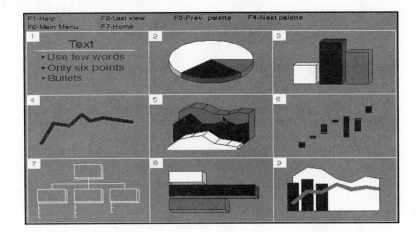

FIG. 8.10

The Harvard
Graphics Chart
Gallery.

Harvard Graphics is a high-end presentation program, retailing at about
$350. A lower end chart-generating program is Graph-in-the-Box Execu-
tive, which offers fewer advanced features but still does the job for less
than $200.

The Benefits of Presentation Graphics Programs

■ You can enter or import chart data (most popular programs
support data from spreadsheet programs, such as Lotus 1-2-3
or Microsoft Excel).

■ You easily can change chart types to find the chart that best
suits the data.

■ You can automate chart display in a slide show presentation.

■ You can print charts, display charts on a monitor, or use other
output devices, such as plotters or film recorders.

■ You can use an extensive number of options to customize the
choice of chart, text, colors, or various other settings in the chart.

Communications

Communications software is used with a modem to connect one computer to another computer, whether the computer is a stand-alone system in some remote corner of the world or a huge corporate mainframe
from which you retrieve important information.

Without communications software, you cannot use a modem. With communications software, however, you can send and retrieve files, ensure data accuracy, and check for transmission errors. Some modems are packaged with communications software, so check out the modem before you buy additional software. Chapter 18 explores individual communications programs.

Usually, good communications software offers the following features:

■ Automatic dialing features

■ A phone book feature that enables you to store frequently called numbers

■ The capability of transmitting files in a variety of formats (or *protocols*)

■ The capability of talking to many different kinds of modems

■ A help system

■ Simple commands in the form of buttons or easy-to-use menus

■ The capability of customizing a work session by setting special keys (sometimes called macros or quick keys)

■ A text editor that enables you to view and work with text you receive from another computer

Although some modems are packaged with communications software, be sure that you check out any software included with the modem. If the software doesn't include the items in the preceding list, you may want to shop around and find more powerful software for your communications sessions. Figure 8.11 shows a screen from a popular communications program.

Educational and Recreational Software

Educational software helps you learn things you need or relearn things you forgot; and recreational software enables you to get away from it all and just have fun. A wide range of software in both areas is available for the IBM, Mac, and Amiga computers. However, many educational packages are also now available on CD-ROM for the Mac and IBM (see Chapter 7, "CD-ROM and Multimedia," for more information). These educational discs are especially desirable because of their immediate data retrieval capabilities and the audio and visual interactions that contribute to a rewarding learning experience.

Recreational, or game, software is a big seller everywhere. Sure, you work with numbers during the day. Of course, the advances in word processing make life easier. Naturally, you take computers seriously. You can, for example, sit in front of a full-color screen of a Grand Prix track and race a couple of laps. Computers don't have to be all work and no play. Chapter 19 lists important educational and recreational programs you may want to check out.

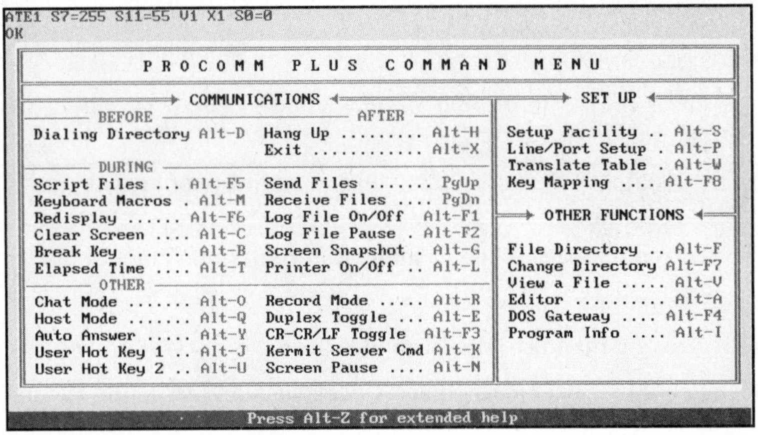

FIG. 8.11

The opening menu of a popular communications program.

Utility Software

As you become experienced with the computer, you soon learn that the basic setup of the system is a sterile work environment and that, occasionally, you encounter problems with the hard drive or with accidentally deleting files. Utility software is a wide-ranging category that covers application programs that make living with a computer faster, easier, and even more fun.

With utility software, you can make your computer run faster (by rearranging the manner in which programs and data are placed on the hard disk), make the hard disk hold more data (by using special file compression software), recover accidentally erased files (by using file recovery software), change the way the computer responds when you make a mistake (by using programs that exchange the boring computer "beep" with a digitized voice), and more. Using the programs covered in Chapter 20 can make your work both more efficient and more enjoyable.

Determining What Software You Need

Now that you learned about the various software categories, how do you tell which kind you need? Consider the following questions:

■ *What kind of tasks do you want the computer to perform?*

If you want to reduce the time spent editing text, think *word processing*. If you grit your teeth each time you are asked to do a financial statement, think *spreadsheet*. If you are tired of cutting and pasting together your organization's newsletter with an X-ACTO knife and rubber cement, think *desktop publishing*. If the tasks are not so clear cut, you may benefit from integrated software.

■ *What features do you need?*

Do you work primarily with numbers? If you currently create schedules, reports, financial statements, or any kind of project that requires the calculation of numbers, you may benefit from having a spreadsheet program at your disposal.

Do you work with words? Whether you write, type, edit, or arrange words, word processing saves you countless keystrokes in typing and retyping time. All you type—reports, letters, manuals, books, advertising copy, and banners—can be done more efficiently with a word processor. Best of all, a word processor enables you to save written work on disk; you type the document only once.

Do you organize data? If you work with data in any form, such as entering, sorting, organizing, searching for, or creating reports from data, you will love working with a database program. Designed specifically to enable users to enter, find, and retrieve data easily and efficiently, database programs take you out of the filing cabinet and back to the keyboard.

Do you publish materials? Whether you create simple advertising fliers, church newsletters, or complex multivolume reports, a desktop publishing program can make your life easier. Low-end and high-end programs exist to help you bring text and graphics together with the least possible bother.

■ *Do you need more than one application?*

Suppose that you need a word processor and a spreadsheet. Do you plan to share information between these applications? Do you plan to use text in the spreadsheet or numeric values from the spreadsheet in the word processor? If so, consider purchasing integrated software.

■ *Does the program need to be compatible with other programs?*

Compatibility is a major consideration when you purchase a new applications program. If you use PageMaker and you are looking for a graphics program, make sure that you can use the files from the graphics program you are considering in PageMaker.

■ *What are the experience levels of the people who use the software?*

If the people using the software have varying skill levels, consider purchasing a program that is easy for everyone to learn and use. Think about the learning curve involved and the various skill levels of the users before you buy.

After you answer these questions, think about the future. Do you see your computer needs growing? Are you going to outgrow a limited word processing program in a few months, causing you to upgrade to a better package (which means disrupting your staff so that they can learn the new program)? If so, you may want to start out with the higher-end program.

You also may want to add to your software library. Suppose that you need a word processing program now, mainly to create and print limited letters and reports, but you plan to move into desktop publishing in the future. You can start with Microsoft Word as your word processor (an easy-to-learn-and-use high-end word processing program) and then purchase PageMaker or Ventura Publisher at a later date (both desktop publishing programs work hand-in-hand with Microsoft Word).

Can You Run the Software on Your System?

Different programs may require different specifications from your computer system. On every software package, you find a list of hardware and software requirements. Check the following facts before you buy software:

■ The kind of system that runs the software

■ The amount of RAM needed

■ The amount of disk storage space (to hold the program and files)

■ The number of disk drives recommended

■ The kind (and version) of operating system supported

- The kind of monitor and video adapter required
- The printers supported
- The program's capability of using expanded or extended memory
- The kinds of files compatible with the program
- The need for other programs to run this software

Where Do You Buy Software?

You can purchase software from a variety of sources. You can purchase software by mail-order, although seeing the software demonstrated before buying is a wise step. You can purchase software at retail software outlets, such as Software Etc. and Egghead Software; at many bookstores, such as Waldenbooks and B. Dalton; and at computer retail stores, such as ComputerLand and MicroAge Computer stores.

Although no real disadvantage or advantage exists to buying software mail-order or retail (although with retail stores, you usually can see a product demonstrated before you buy), learn as much as possible about a program before you purchase. In addition to the hardware-related questions in the previous section, be sure that you check for the following capabilities and consumer options:

- Make sure that the software is compatible with other programs you use, if this factor is important to you. If you use PageMaker in your work, purchasing a paint program that doesn't work with PageMaker won't help you much. Be sure that you mention other programs you use to the manufacturer or salesperson so that he can make sure that you buy a compatible program.

- Is a technical support line available to call if you have problems? If you are purchasing the software from a retail outlet, find out if support is available in the event you have problems with the program.

- If you are unhappy with a product, does the retail outlet or the manufacturer refund your money?

What about Software Support?

You can get support for the software; all reputable software companies have a technical support line you can call if you get stuck or have questions. Fill out the registration card in the software package and keep handy the registration numbers of all your software. Most technical support people ask for the registration number to make sure that you are a registered owner.

You also may receive software support from the place you purchased the program. Many retail outlets offer consulting and training on the major packages. For a fee, you can purchase from some computer stores a technical support package that gives you access to a support professional when you run into problems with either hardware or software.

Reviewing Purchasing Decisions

Use the following checklist to put on paper the purchasing considerations you are tossing around:

The work I do on my computer consists of _____ .

I need _____ (Spreadsheet, Word Processing, Data Management, Integrated, Desktop Publishing, Graphics, Communications, Education and Recreational) software to accomplish my tasks.

This software requires that my computer run Operating System version number _____.

I need _____ of RAM to run this software.

I need _____ Kilobytes/Megabytes of storage space to store this software.

I need a _____ monitor (CGA, EGA VGA, multisync, Mac) to effectively run this software.

These special features are important:

_____

_____

_____

_____

Chapter Summary

This chapter, the last chapter in Part II, helped you identify the software you need for your work. The following part, "A Computer Primer," takes you through a series of hands-on sessions to help you become comfortable with your new system.

PART III

A Computer Primer

Now that you have investigated your options and selected a computer, you are ready to set up and begin working with your new system. Specially designed quick starts for the Macintosh and each of the following PC operating environments: DOS, DOS Shell and Windows—help you unpack and assemble your system. More detailed chapters then lead you through the beginning uses of a computer.

OUTLINE

Using Your PC— DOS and DOS Shell

This quick start introduces you to life with your new PC. Now that you have learned about the various types of computers available and have made a purchasing decision, you are ready to put your hands to the keyboard.

First, if you haven't selected a work area and unpacked and assembled the computer, do so now. (For help, refer to Chapter 9 for unpacking and assembly instructions.) After the system is put together, you can fire up the system.

NOTE This quick start includes steps for starting and working with a system that uses the DOS operating system and is followed by a quick start for PCs, using the DOS Shell operating interface.

This quick start walks you through the following steps:

DOS

1. Starting your PC

2. Entering the date and time

3. Formatting a disk

4. Copying a disk

5. Displaying the contents of a disk

6. Copying a file

7. Renaming a file

8. Erasing a file

9. Shutting down the PC

DOS Shell

1. Starting DOS Shell

2. Formatting a disk

3. Copying a disk

4. Displaying the contents of a disk

5. Copying a file

6. Renaming a file

7. Erasing a file

8. Exiting from Dos Shell

Working with DOS

This part of the quick start introduces you to DOS, the Disk Operating System used on the PC. You tell the computer to perform certain tasks by typing in DOS commands. The following sections describe several DOS commands, step by step, to get you started.

Starting Your PC

After you connect all the components, turn on the computer by performing the following steps:

1. Make sure that all cables are properly attached; thumbscrews are tight; and power cords are plugged in.

2. Locate the On/Off switch. This switch may be in the front of the system (such as on the PS/2 Model 50 shown in figure 11.1), or on the side or on the back of the machine.

3. If you must start the computer from a DOS disk, place the disk in drive A and close the drive door. (You must perform this step if the computer does not have a hard disk.)

4. Move the switch to the On position. The computer then starts and DOS boots. With DOS 5.0, you see the following message on the opening screen:

```
MS DOS Version 5.0

C:\
```

 NOTE If you use an IBM PS/1, powering up is a simple task. After the system is connected, press the On/Off button on the front of the monitor, and the System Menu appears on-screen.

Entering the Date and Time

DOS prompts you to enter the correct date and time. To enter a new date, type the date in the following format:

mm-dd-yy

The dates 09-18-56 and 01-13-92 are acceptable dates in DOS's date format. After you enter the date, press Enter.

When the time prompt appears, type a new time in the following format:

hh:mm:ss

The times 12:29:23 and 18:02:23 are valid. If you use DOS 5.0, you see the traditional 12-hour time with an *a* or *p*, indicating A.M. or P.M. After you enter the time, press Enter. DOS displays the current date and time, similar to the following formats:

```
MS DOS Version 5.0

C:\ date

Current date is Sat 7-14-1992

Enter new date (mm-dd-yy):
```

```
C:\ time
Current time is 14:52:00.00p
Enter new time:
```

Formatting a Disk

To format a disk on a PC, follow these steps:

1. Start the computer (place the DOS disk in drive A, if necessary).

2. Type **FORMAT A:**.

 NOTE   To format the disk in drive B, type **FORMAT B:**. (Do *not*, however, type FORMAT C: and press Enter, or DOS will format the hard disk of the system.) DOS then prompts you to put a disk into drive B.

CAUTION: If you mistakenly type FORMAT C:, press Enter, and press Y in response to the final warning message, all data on the hard drive is lost!

---

3. Insert the disk and close the drive door.

4. Press Enter. DOS then formats the disk. Some DOS versions, such as DOS 5.0, display the percentage of the disk formatted as the process is carried out. When the process is complete, DOS asks you whether you want to assign a name (a *volume label*) to the disk. Providing this name is optional. (To assign the disk a name, see the sidebar "DOS, DOS Shell, Windows and Mac Disk-Naming Conventions," in Chapter 11.) For now, just press Enter.

   DOS then asks whether you want to format another disk.

5. To end the format session, type **N** and press Enter.

Copying a Disk

When you want to copy an entire disk, use the DOS DISKCOPY command, as follows:

1. Type **DISKCOPY A: B:** and press Enter.

2. Insert into drive A the disk *from which* you want to copy (source disk).

3. Insert into drive B the disk *to which* you want to copy (target disk).

4. Press Enter.

5. When the DISKCOPY process is complete, DOS asks whether you want to copy another disk. Press N.

Displaying the Contents of a Disk

You may want to display the contents of a disk—whether you are looking for an elusive file or you can't remember what you stored on a particular disk.

To display a list of files on a disk, follow these steps:

1. Place the disk you want to use in drive A.

2. Type **DIR A:**.

3. Press Enter.

DOS then displays a list of the files that reside on the disk. The listing includes the file names, the date and time the files were last updated, and the size of the files in bytes, similar to the following listing:

```
C:\ DIR A:

    Volume in drive A has no label
    Directory of A:\

KMC16    KM    18816  6-19-92      11:34a

KMC18    KM    21120  6-21-92      3:01p

KMC20    KM    15872  6-25-92      10:41a

KMCFM    4480  3-12-92       6:41p

LESLIE   4VR   66560  5-16-92      10:22p

KMC17    KM    18176  6-20-92      12:07p

    6 File(s)    145024 bytes

           759808 bytes free

C:\
```

Copying a File

To copy a disk of files or a single file on a PC, follow these steps:

1. Insert the disk from which you want to copy (the *source* disk) into drive A.

2. Insert the disk to which you want to copy (the *destination* disk) into drive B. (You also may want to copy the files to drive C.)

3. Type the COPY command in the following format:

    COPY A:*filename* **B:**

This command copies the file you specified (*filename*) from the disk in drive A to the disk in drive B. To copy the file to the current directory of drive C, type the command in the following format:

COPY A:*filename* **C:**

You also can use the COPY command to copy the entire contents of the disk. Type the following command for this operation:

COPY A:*.* C:

CAUTION: COPY is a dangerous command that overwrites on the destination disk files whose names duplicate file names on the source disk. Always check directories for duplicate file names before you copy files.

Changing Directories

To change directories in DOS, type **CD/***directoryname* and press Enter. To move back one previous (the *parent*) directory, type **CD ..** and press Enter.

Renaming a File

To rename a file by using DOS, take the following steps:

1. Go to the directory that stores the file you want to rename.

2. Type the command in the following format:

    REN *oldfilename newfilename*

Replace *oldfilename* with the name of the file you are renaming and *newfilename* with the new name for the file. You can use the following command:

    REN LETTER.TXT LET1.TXT

This command renames the original file (LETTER.TXT) as LET1.TXT.

Erasing a File

To erase files on a PC, perform the following steps:

1. Change to the directory in which the files you want to delete are stored. (Remember that the DOS command for changing directories is CD.)

2. Type the following command:

   DEL *filename*

   Substitute the name of the file you want to delete for *filename* in the preceding example.

3. If the file is stored on a disk other than the current disk, enter the drive letter in front of the files named, as shown in the following example:

```
C:\ dir a:

        Volume in drive A has no label
        Directory of A:\

KMC16  KM      18816  6-19-92      11:34a
KMC18  KM      21120  6-21-92      3:01p
KMC20  KM      15872  6-25-91      10:41a
KMCFM  4480    3-12-92       6:41p
LESLIE 4VR     66560  5-16-92      10:22p
KMC17  KM      18176  6-20-92      12:07p
        6 File(s)    145024 bytes
               759808 bytes free
C:\ del a:kmc17.km
```

You also can use the ERASE command to delete a DOS file. Use the same format but type **ERASE** rather than **DEL**, as shown in the following syntax:

    ERASE *filename*

T   I   P   If you erase a file by mistake and are running the latest version of DOS, DOS 5.0, you can use the **UNDELETE** *filename* command to restore the file. Several utility programs also are available that have unerase options (Norton Utilities, for example).

Shutting Down Your PC

To end a work session with the PC, follow these steps:

1. If you are using an application program, first make sure that you save the currently open file.

2. Return to the operating system level. (If you are unsure how to perform this step, look in the program's documentation for instructions on how to exit the program.)

3. After the operating system prompt appears (C> for DOS on a hard disk system), you can safely turn off the system. If you use a power surge protector strip, turn off the system with the surge protector's switch; otherwise, turn off the monitor and then the system by flipping the power switches on each piece of hardware.

T   I   P   When you turn on the system, always turn on the hard disk first, then (after the beep) turn on the monitor. Don't use the power surge switch to turn on both units at the same time.

Working with DOS Shell

This part of the PC quick start introduces you to an operating interface known as *DOS Shell*. DOS Shell works with DOS, however, DOS Shell has a graphical interface that first-time users may find easier to learn than standard DOS. The commands in DOS Shell are menu driven and a mouse allows access to the commands by pointing and clicking. Because DOS Shell actually runs on *top* of DOS, the prompts and messages are the same in both environments.

This section covers the DOS Shell that comes with version 5.0 of DOS. If you are running an earlier version of DOS, these steps may not be the same.

Starting DOS Shell

After ensuring that all of the components are attached properly and you have turned on the computer; follow these steps to get DOS Shell up and running:

1. If you must start the computer from a DOS disk, place the disk in drive A and close the drive door. (You must perform this step if the computer does not have a hard disk.)

2. Move the switch to the ON position. The computer then starts and DOS boots. With DOS 5.0, you see the following message on the opening screen:

   ```
   MS DOS Version 5.0
   C:\
   ```

3. At the C:\ prompt, type **DOSSHELL** and press Enter.

The screen shown in figure QS1.1 appears.

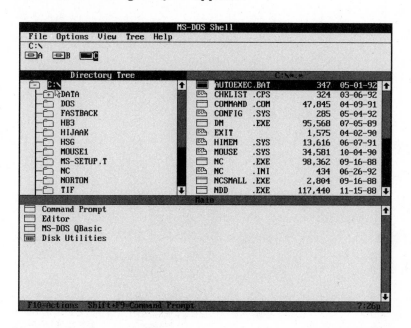

FIG. QS1.1

The Dos Shell main window.

Formatting a Disk

To format a disk on a PC running DOS Shell, follow these steps:

1. Double-click the DOS Utilities option, located in the program list area at the bottom of the screen.

2. Double-click the Format option.

3. Specify the drive that contains the disk you want to format. (Usually A or B, do not type C, which is your hard drive.)

> **CAUTION:** Formatting the hard disk drive (drive C) completely erases the contents of the hard disk.

4. Click OK.

   DOS Shell prompts you to insert a disk in the specified drive (if you haven't yet inserted the disk or if—on a 5 1/4-inch drive—you didn't close the drive's door).

5. Press the Enter key.

DOS Shell begins the format, displaying the percentage of completion.

Copying a Disk

Follow the steps below to make a backup copy of an entire disk by using the DOS Shell Utilities option:

1. Double-click the DOS Utilities option, located in the program list area at the bottom of the DOS Shell screen.

2. Double-click the Diskcopy option.

3. Specify the source drive (where the original disk is).

4. Press the space bar and specify the target drive (where the backup copy is—they may be the same).

5. Click OK.

6. DOS Shell prompts you for the source disk. Insert the disk and press any key.

7. Continue following the instructions on-screen.

8. On completion, DOS displays the prompt: `Copy another diskette?` Press Y to continue or N to exit the DOS copy command.

Displaying the Contents of a Disk

You may want to use this command to find a needed file or simply see what is currently on a disk. To find a file or view a disk's contents, click the drive icon or directory you want to view from the Directory Tree located on the left side of the screen.

The DOS Shell's file list area, on the right side of the screen, displays the files currently on the specified disk or directory.

Copying a File

Use the Copy command to copy a single file or an entire disk of files. Follow these steps:

1. Click the file you want to copy.

2. Click the File menu.

3. Select the Copy option.

4. DOS Shell asks you to specify a destination for the copied file. Type in the destination drive and directory name (if applicable).

A copy of the file is placed in the designated area.

Renaming a File

Use the following steps to assign a new name to your files in DOS Shell:

1. Click the file you want to rename.

2. Click the File menu.

3. Select the Rename option.

4. At the prompt, type the new name.

5. Click OK.

Use file names that easily identify the file. Names like DATA1, DATA2, etc., are quick and easy to assign, but in two weeks it will be difficult to remember the contents of the file.   **T I P**

Erasing a File

Use the Delete command to completely erase a file and create space on the hard drive or a floppy disk. Follow these steps:

1. Click the filename to highlight the file you want to erase.

2. Click the File menu and select Delete.

3. To erase the file, click OK.

T I P   If you erase a file by mistake and are running DOS 5.0, you can use the command **UNDELETE** *filename* to restore the file, or there are several utility programs available that have unerase options (such as Norton Utilities and PC Tools).

Exiting DOS Shell

To exit DOS Shell and return to standard DOS, perform the following steps:

1. Click the File menu.

2. Select the Exit option.

When the operating system prompt appears (C> for DOS on a hard disk system), you can safely turn off the system. If you use a power surge protector strip, turn off the system with the surge protector's switch; otherwise, turn off the monitor and then the system by flipping the power switches on each piece of hardware.

Using Your PC— Windows

This quick start introduces you to the Windows operating environment for the PC. Windows is a graphical interface similar to Macintosh in the use of windows and menus. Although Windows still requires DOS, the Windows interface is more sophisticated and easier to learn than DOS, as this quick start explains.

First, if you haven't selected a work area and unpacked and assembled the computer, do so now. (For help, refer to Chapter 9 for unpacking and assembly instructions.) After you put together the system, you can turn on the power switch of the computer.

This quick start includes the following steps for starting and working within the Windows operating environment.

1. Turning on a PC

2. Starting Windows

3. Opening the File Manager program

4. Formatting a disk

5. Copying a disk

6. Displaying the contents of a disk

7. Copying a file

8. Renaming a file

9. Exiting the File Manager program

10. Exiting Windows

Turning On Your PC

After you connect all the components, turn on the computer by taking the following steps:

1. Make sure that all cables are properly attached, all thumbscrews are tight, and all power cords are plugged in.

2. Locate the On/Off switch. This switch may be in the front of the system, similar to the switch on the PS/2 Model 50 (see fig. 11.1), or on the side or on the back of the machine.

3. If you have not loaded your DOS and Windows software onto your hard disk, do so now. (You must have a hard disk to run Windows.)

4. Move the switch to the On position. The computer then starts and DOS boots. With DOS 5.0, you see the following message on the opening screen:

```
MS DOS Version 5.0

C:\
```

 NOTE If you use an IBM PS/1, power up is a simple task. After the system is connected, press the On/Off button on the front of the monitor, and the colorful System Menu appears on-screen.

Starting Windows

Follow these steps to start Windows:

1. From the DOS prompt C:\, type **WIN**.

2. Press Enter.

The screen in figure QS2.1 appears.

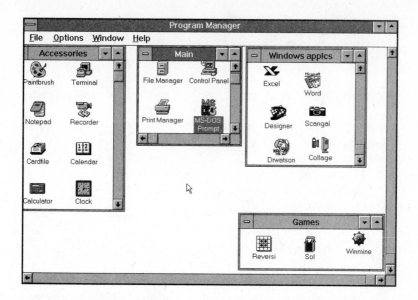

FIG. QS2.1

The Windows
3.1 screen.

The Windows application and utility programs appear as icons (pictorial representations) in the Program Manager window. To perform disk and file copy and erase procedures, you must be in the File Manager program. Refer to the following set of steps to launch the File Manager.

Opening the File Manager Program

Follow these steps to start the File Manager:

1. From within the Program Manager window, double-click the Main Window icon.

2. Locate the File Manager icon from within the Program Manager window.

3. Double-click the File Manager icon. The following screen appears (see fig. QS2.2).

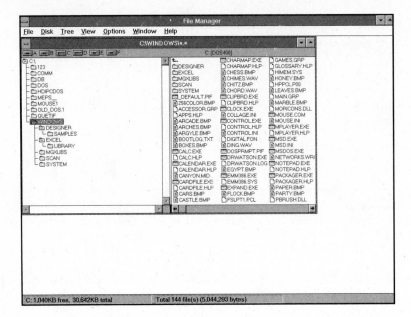

FIG. QS2.2

The File Manager
window.

Formatting a Disk

To format a disk by using the File Manager in Windows, take the following steps:

1. Click the Disk menu at the top of the screen.

2. Select the Format Disk option.

   Windows displays the Format dialog box.

3. Click the down-pointing arrow next to the `Disk In` prompt and select the drive you want to format. (Usually drive A or B; remember that C is the hard drive.)

> **CAUTION:** Formatting the hard disk (drive C) will erase all of its contents.

4. Click the down-pointing arrow next to the `Capacity` prompt and select the density the disk can be formatted at.

5. Click OK.

Windows displays an Information dialog box, which asks you to confirm the format.

6. Click Yes. Remember that this process erases all files on the specified drive.

On completion, Windows displays a Format Complete dialog box with the total bytes on the disk and the bytes available. Windows also asks: Do you want to format another disk? Click Yes to continue or No to return to the File Manager screen.

Typically, 5 1/4-inch disks are formatted as 360K for standard (double-sided) double-density disks and 1.2M for high density disks. 3 1/2-inch disks are formatted at 720K for standard density and 1.44M for high density.

T   I   P

Copying a Disk

From within the File Manager program, you can use the following procedure to copy the contents of an entire disk in Windows:

1. Click the Disk menu.

2. Select the Copy Disk option.

   If you have a two-floppy disk system, Windows displays the Copy Disk dialog box.

3. Click the Source down-pointing arrow to indicate the drive in which the original (*source*) disk is located.

4. Click the Destination down-pointing arrow to indicate where you want the copied information to go (*destination*).

5. Click OK.

   An Information dialog box appears that asks you to confirm the delete step.

6. To continue, click Yes.

   Windows prompts you for the source disk.

7. Insert the disk and click OK.

   Windows displays the percent complete dialog box and then asks for the destination disk.

8. Insert the destination disk and click OK.

Windows displays the percent complete dialog box until the copy is complete.

Displaying the Contents of a Disk

To view the contents of a disk or a directory in the Windows File Manager, click the drive or directory name from the left side of the File Manager window.

Windows displays the contents of the selection on the right side of the File Manager screen.

Copying a File

To copy a file in the File Manager of Windows, perform the following steps:

1. Click the file you want copied.

2. Click the File menu.

3. Select the Copy option.

   Windows displays the Copy dialog box.

4. Type the destination directory and a name for the file in the edit boxes provided.

5. Click OK.

Renaming a File

To rename a file using the File Manager in Windows, follow these steps:

1. Click the file you want to rename.

2. Click the File menu.

3. Select the Rename option.

   Windows displays the Rename dialog box.

4. Type the new name in the To edit box.

5. Click OK.

Exiting the File Manager Program

To exit the File Manager program and return to the Windows Program Manager, follow the steps below:

1. Click the File menu.

2. Select the Exit option.

The File Manager program closes and the Program Manager window appears.

Exiting Windows

To end a work session within the Windows operating environment on the PC, take the following steps:

1. If you are using an application program, exit from the program.

2. At the Program Manager, click the Control Box icon on the upper left corner of the window.

3. Select the Close option.

4. When the operating system prompt appears (C> for DOS on a hard disk system), you can safely turn off the system. Turn off the monitor and then the system by flipping the power switches on each piece of hardware.

When you turn on the system, always turn on the hard disk first, then (after the beep) turn on the monitor. Don't use the power surge switch to turn on both units at the same time.

T I P

Using Your Macintosh

This quick start introduces various procedures you use on a Macintosh that is running System 7.0 or later. The way you interact with the Mac is based on a desktop-like graphical environment. Much of what you do involves disk, folder, and file icons.

If you haven't selected your work area and unpacked and assembled the computer, go ahead and do so now. (If you need help, refer to Chapter 9 for specific instructions.) Then, when everything is put together, you are ready to fire up the system.

This quick start walks you through the following steps:

1. Starting your Mac

2. Accessing Balloon help

3. Turning off Balloon help

4. Initializing a disk

5. Opening disks and folders

6. Closing disks and folders

7. Creating and naming a folder

8. Copying a disk

9. Copying a file

10. Renaming a file or folder

11. Erasing a file

12. Shutting down your Mac

Starting Your Mac

When you are ready to start your Mac, follow these steps:

1. Make sure that all cables are attached properly; thumbscrews are tight; and power cords are plugged in.

2. Turn on the system. The On/Off button is located in the back left corner of the Classic II and SE/30 computers (see fig. QS3.1).

A smiling Mac icon appears, followed by the words Welcome to Macintosh, which verifies that the Mac has booted properly.

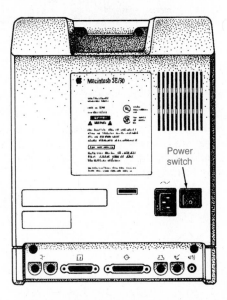

FIG. QS3.1

The On/Off button on the back of the display.

The first change you see on the Mac is the Finder Desktop. The Finder Desktop resembles a physical desktop with icons representing different objects, such as the trash can (for deleting files) and the hard disk (for storing files). The following file and disk procedures are performed at the Desktop.

Using Balloon Help

To help guide you through the operations of the computer, Macintosh System 7.0 provides *Balloon help*. To turn on Balloon help, follow these steps:

1. Go to the ⟨?⟩ icon in the upper right corner of the screen.

2. Click the mouse button and pull down to select the Show Balloons option.

Now you're ready to get information on the commands and different parts of the Desktop. Refer to the following list of possible help topics and follow the instructions. Once you are comfortable with the concept of Balloon help, feel free to get information on other commands and areas of the Desktop.

Hard disk information

1. Place the mouse pointer on the hard disk.

2. Balloon help shows information on the hard disk (see fig. QS3.2).

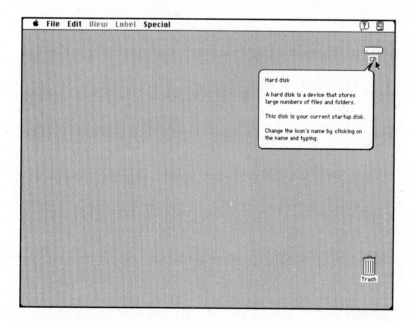

FIG. QS3.2

Balloon help information on the hard disk.

3. Move the mouse away from the hard disk and Balloon help goes away.

File menu information

1. Move the mouse on top of the File menu at the top of the screen.

2. Balloon help appears displaying information about the File menu.

3. Move the mouse away from the File menu to remove the Balloon from the screen.

Eject option information

1. Open the Special menu by pointing and clicking on it.

2. Pull down to select the Eject option.

   Balloon help appears with information regarding the Eject option.

3. Move the mouse away from the Eject option to remove the information balloon.

Balloon help can provide new users with a lot of valuable information. However, after you're ready to do some work, the balloons appearing and disappearing with your every move can also make you crazy. Refer to the steps below to turn off Balloon help:

1. Go to the ⟦?⟧ icon in the upper right corner of the screen.

2. Select the Hide Balloons option.

Initializing a Disk

To format (initialize) a disk on a Macintosh, follow these steps:

1. Start the system.

2. After the Finder desktop appears, insert the disk that you want to format in the drive.

   The Mac tries to read the disk and finds that the disk is unreadable. The computer asks whether you want to initialize the disk.

3. Select whether you want to format a one-sided or a two-sided disk.

   The Macintosh displays a warning that the initialization process will erase all information on the disk.

4. Click the Erase button to continue the format.

5. Enter a name for the disk and click the OK button. You may use up to 32 characters of any combination, except for the colon (:), which is reserved for certain system files.

The Macintosh then begins formatting the disk. After the format is finished, the Macintosh verifies the format and creates a directory. The disk is then displayed on the desktop with the name you specified.

Opening Disks and Folders

When a disk or a folder appears on the Finder desktop, you can open it by using one of the following methods:

■ Click the disk or folder icon so that you inverse (highlight) the icon (black with white lettering). Then open the File menu and select the Open option.

■ Click the disk (or folder) icon to highlight it, and then press ⌘ (the Command key and the letter **O**).

■ Double-click the disk or folder icon.

The contents of icons on the Macintosh are always displayed in windows. (See fig. QS3.3 for a typical Macintosh window.)

Closing Disks and Folders

To close a disk or folder, select one of the following options:

■ Click the disk (or folder) icon, open the File menu, and select the Close option.

■ Click the disk (or folder) icon and press ⌘-W (the Command key and the letter **W**).

■ Click the close box in the upper left corner of the window in which the disk or folder appears (see fig. QS3.3).

Creating and Naming a Folder

When you add files to the Mac, you need to add a new folder in which to keep the files. To add a new folder, follow these steps:

1. Open the window where you want the folder to appear.

2. Open the File menu.

3. Select the New Folder option. (You can bypass the menu selections by pressing ⌘-N, if you prefer.)

4. Type a name for the folder. (The words Empty Folder are replaced with your first keystroke.)

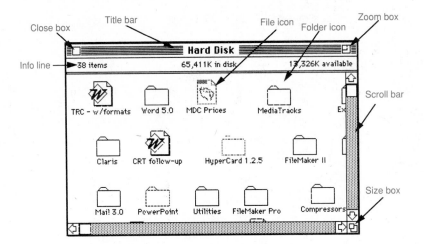

FIG. QS3.3

The parts of a typical Macintosh window.

Copying a Disk

To copy the contents an entire floppy disk to the hard disk, follow these steps:

1. Make sure that the system is on and the desktop is displayed.

2. Insert the floppy disk you want to copy into the drive.

3. Place the mouse cursor on the disk you want to copy.

4. Click and drag the floppy disk icon on top of the hard disk icon. The hard disk becomes highlighted when the floppy disk outline is positioned properly on top of it.

5. Release the mouse button. A screen appears, showing the progress of the copy procedure.

The Macintosh places the copied files from the floppy disk in a folder on the hard disk.

Copying a File

To copy a file (or files) from a floppy disk to the Macintosh's hard drive, follow these steps:

1. Place the disk from which you want to copy the file (the *source*) in the drive.

2. Double-click the disk icon to show the disk's contents.

3. Click the file you want to copy from the source disk and drag the icon to the hard disk icon.

A screen appears, showing the progress of the copy procedure. When the copy is complete, the file icon appears in the hard disk window.

Renaming a File or Folder

The graphical interface of the Finder makes renaming files and folders easy. To rename a file or folder icon, follow these steps:

1. Open the disk containing the file or folder you want to rename.

2. Click on the name of the file or folder icon. The icon becomes highlighted and a rectangular box surrounds the name.

3. Type the new name for the icon.

4. Press Enter. The Finder then saves the new name for the file or folder icon.

Erasing a File

To erase a file on the Macintosh, follow these steps:

1. Open the folder storing the file you want to erase.

2. When the mouse cursor is positioned on the file you want to erase, press and hold down the mouse button.

3. Drag the file icon out of the window and over to the trash can.

   The trash can becomes highlighted when the file is in the trash (see fig. QS3.4).

4. Release the mouse button. The sides of the trash can bulge, indicating that something was thrown away.

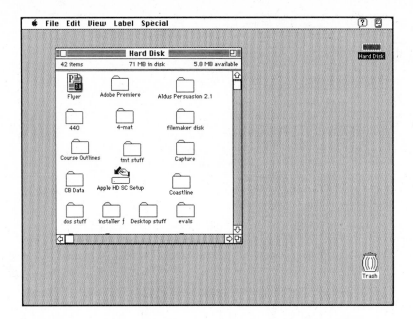

FIG. QS3.4

The trash can
when occupied.

T I P   You can retrieve files accidentally thrown away from the trash can. To display the contents of the trash can, double-click on the trash can. A window appears, showing the item(s) you threw away. To recover a file from the trash can, click to highlight the file, then open the File menu and select the Put Away option. The Macintosh puts the file back in the original location.

Shutting Down Your Mac

When you are ready to turn off the Macintosh, follow these steps:

1. If you were using an application program, quit the program now. The Desktop appears.

2. Quit all open applications and close any open folders at the Desktop. Click the close box in the upper left corner to close any open windows.

3. Point to the Special menu in the menu bar at the top of the screen.

4. Open the menu and select the Shut Down option.

Some Mac models display a message that tells you that you can turn off the Macintosh safely. If you choose, you can start another session by clicking the Restart button displayed. Other Mac models simply shut down completely after you select the Shut Down option.

You then can turn off the Macintosh by first turning off the monitor (only the Mac II line has separate monitors) and then turning off the main switch on the back of the unit.

Setting Up Your Computer

Now that you have purchased a computer, you are ready to set up a work area and put together the system. This chapter walks you step-by-step through procedures for setting up Macintosh and PC computers. (If you just worked through one of the preceding quick starts, you may want to skip this chapter and proceed to Chapter 11, "Using Your Computer.")

This chapter starts right after purchase and helps you determine whether you have all the pieces you need. You also find information on preliminaries, such as filling out the warranty card and registering the equipment, and procedures for getting ready to use the equipment, such as selecting a good work area, unboxing the system, and connecting the components.

As you learn in Chapter 3, few computers are created equal. The differences found in each computer system (and the system's appearance) depend on the age of the system, the kind of system you purchase, and a thousand other variables. As you also learned in Chapter 3, however, all personal computers contain the following basic components:

- A system unit
- A monitor
- A keyboard

If you have an IBM PS/1, you have a system unit, a monitor, a keyboard, and a mouse.

A basic Mac SE/30 system includes the following pieces:

- A system unit-monitor combination
- A mouse
- A keyboard

A basic Mac II system includes the following parts:

- A system unit
- A monitor
- A keyboard
- A mouse

You also can purchase additional components for your system, such as printers, a CD-ROM, a graphics tablet, a modem, and so on.

Whether you purchase a true-blue IBM, a Mac, or a PC clone, you go through the same basic setup procedures. Setup involves the following steps:

1. Checking the system.
2. Selecting a work area.
3. Unboxing the system.
4. Connecting the components.

The following sections explain these steps. You find illustrations, where appropriate, to help you identify key areas on the machine.

Checking Your Computer

Did you receive all the parts for which you paid? Whether you purchased the system through mail order or picked up the system at the computer store, look at the invoice to determine that all parts are present. If an important part was on back order (the part was unavailable to ship when your order was filled), you may have trouble. Reputable computer dealers tell you if a request cannot be filled. If an important item, such the monitor, is missing, perhaps you can get a loaner where you purchased the system.

Check all the components and make sure that you have all the parts you need. Write down the particulars about the system and include the serial numbers of individual units.

Writing down this system information is a good idea. When you have part of the system serviced or when a vendor calls and asks about the kind of graphics adapter you use, how much RAM is installed in the computer, and other facts, you can read the *cheat sheet* and find the answers right away. Figure 9.1 shows another example of a documentation sheet designed to hold more information.

Item Description	Serial Number	Date Purchased	Warranty? (How long?)
Mykota 286 16Mhz system	34T45571	5/23/90	Yes: 1 year
Samsumg Mono VGA monitor	SM207T-4	5/20/90	Yes: 2 years
EMK 16-bit VGA board	VGA34	5/23/90	Yes: 1 year
Logitech bus mouse	LG-MS19	5/20/90	Yes: 1 year
Hayes 2400 modem	2349-0	5/23/90	Yes: 1 year

FIG. 9.1

Example of a cheat sheet that lists important information about your computer.

Next, examine the manuals that came with the system. You probably have several different manuals for the various components in the system, such as the system unit, a monitor, a mouse (if used), perhaps a graphics adapter, a plug-in memory board, a graphics tablet, printer, and so on—you probably have a small library of manuals that tells you about the components in the system.

Make sure that you also save the warranty cards and fill out and send the registration cards to the manufacturer. Sending in these cards ensures that the equipment is under warranty, so if anything goes wrong, you can get the problem corrected in a reasonable time (and, hopefully, at no cost).

Bundle all this information together (the cheat sheet, the hardware manuals, and the warranty information) and store the bundle in a safe but accessible place. This way, you can get to the information when you need answers.

Selecting a Work Area

The area in which you work is almost as important as the machine with which you work. If you take time to set up a work area where you can concentrate, that uses the best possible light, and that makes you comfortable, you are halfway toward the goal of productive work with your system.

A good work area has the following qualities:

- Good, indirect lighting that enables you to see the monitor clearly but doesn't cause glare on-screen.

- Adequate space, giving you plenty of room to move the mouse (if you use one) and to move about between the printer and the system.

- Desktop room for working with conventional tools, such as paper, pens, and books.

- Privacy that keeps you out of the mainstream of the office or house but still gives you access to the places you need to go.

- A desk or worktable that enables you to position the monitor relatively close to eye level. This position keeps you from slouching or sitting up too straight while you work with the monitor.

- Access to a power outlet within a reasonable distance (you don't want to run power cords all over the office or room just to get to one outlet). Invest in a surge protector to guard the system against badly timed power bursts.

■ A good chair is a vital consideration. If you are hunched over or if the chair back is too high or too low, be sure that you adjust the chair (or purchase a new one) before you begin to spend eight hours a day at the computer.

Unpacking the Computer

Next, you need to unpack the computer. Keep the packing slips, packing materials, plastic wraps, and boxes from the packaging. Store the boxes in case you need to box up and move the system.

Again, make sure that all the pieces you need are in the boxes. Whether you are using an IBM, Mac, Amiga, or PC clone, you probably have the same basic pieces:

■ System unit

■ Monitor, cable, and power cord

■ Keyboard and cable

With a PC system, you have separate power cords for the monitor, system unit, and printer. Unbox all the pieces, and if anything is missing, call the dealer.

Unbox the printer too and make sure that the printer cable and power cord are packed with the printer.

Positioning the Computer

The procedure for setting up a computer depends on both the kind of system and your personal preferences. As you learned in Chapter 3, several kinds of systems are available. If you have one kind of system, such as a conventional PC desktop system, you may want to set up the system one way. If you have a different kind of system, such as a tower system or a portable, you may want to arrange your work area differently. As you position the system, make sure that you choose an arrangement with which you are happy. Remember that if you aren't totally satisfied with the system arrangement, you can rearrange items until you find a comfortable layout.

In the work area you prepared, position the system the way you want by following these steps:

1. If you bought a conventional desktop system, position the system unit so that you can easily insert and remove disks into and from the drives. If you plan to place the monitor on top of the system unit, place the system unit so that you can see the screen easily.

   If you use a tower system (the system unit is vertical), choose a location for the system that gives you easy access to the component. Whether or not the system unit was sold as a tower PC, many people prefer to place the system unit under their desks, out of the way of bumps and mishaps. System unit stands cost about $15; these stands enable you to stand the system unit on one end. Now that shorter tower systems are being designed, you may prefer to leave the system unit on the desktop.

2. Place the keyboard in front of the system unit.

3. If you use a mouse, place it to the right (or left, if you are left-handed) of the keyboard.

4. Position the printer. Make sure that you have the printer cable and the printer's power cord. Position the printer so that paper can enter and exit the printer without binding or hanging up.

5. Position all other components. Leave room to work with papers, folders, and other necessary desktop material.

6. Arrange the lighting so that you have enough light for the desktop, but not so much light that you cause on-screen glare.

Evaluating the Work Area

Now that the system is positioned, decide whether you're happy with the work area design. Ask the following questions:

- Is the lighting right?

- Is enough room available for working with hard-copy reports, files, and other extra materials?

- Is the phone within easy reach?

- Is the printer positioned so that you can print without restricting the paper either entering or exiting the printer?

- Is the monitor comfortable for viewing? Can you spend hours working at the monitor without stress?

- Are the disk drives within easy reach?

If you are unhappy, make changes now, before you connect all the components.

Figure 9.2 shows a sample work area for a PC system. This system is a traditional desktop system in which the system unit is horizontal. Figure 9.3 shows the work area for a tower system. Notice that in this figure, additional components (graphics tablet and external modem) are added.

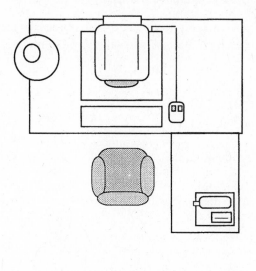

FIG. 9.2

A sample plan for a PC work area.

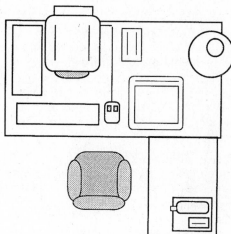

FIG. 9.3

A work area plan for a tower system.

Connecting the Components

Now that you have unboxed the system and placed the computer in a suitable working area, you now can connect the components. Before you begin, identify the cables and ports that you will use to attach the components. This section introduces ports (the plug-like receptacles on the back of the system unit) and cables, then walks you through the steps needed to connect a monitor, a keyboard, a mouse, and a printer.

Understanding Cables

Cables are the lifeline of a computer system. Without cables, nothing can be attached—all pieces of a computer system become expensive paperweights. A power cable brings the electricity the computer needs to run. A cable communicates video signals to and from the monitor. A cable connects a keyboard to the system unit, enabling you to enter data and run applications. A cable communicates information to and from the printer.

The cable looks like a simple wire encased in a plastic covering. Actually, a cable is a complicated device that can consist of 2 to 50 small wires bundled together so that some wires relay power and some wires relay data to and from the components in the computer system.

The connectors at the ends of the cable enable you to plug the cable in the appropriate port in the back of the system and in the components you are connecting. If you use a Macintosh, you plug the keyboard cable into the keyboard and into the port in the back of the Macintosh system unit. The *connectors* are small units that contain a certain number and formation of *pins*—little metal posts that fit into the Apple desktop bus (the keyboard, mouse, and so on) port in the back of the system unit (see fig. 9.4).

Different cables have different kinds of connectors. The keyboard cable may be a small round cable that fits in a circular opening in the back of the computer, and the printer cable usually is a long thin connector, rounded on the edges, and has one side slightly shorter than the other (see fig. 9.5).

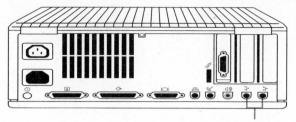

Apple desktop busports
(keyboard connectors)

FIG. 9.4

The connectors
for the keyboard
of the Macintosh.

FIG. 9.5

A printer cable
connector.

Understanding Ports

Working with a computer system requires that you gaze into the screen and work with the disk drives in the front of the system unit. In the setup phase, however, you spend most of the time at the back of the computer. Figure 9.6 shows the back of a PC-compatible computer. Labels on the figure identify where the various components attach to the back of the system.

In figure 9.6, you can see several different plug-like receptacles in the back of the computer. These receptacles are known as *ports*. When you need to add another component to the system, such as a printer, you plug the printer cable into the printer port. The computer now can send and receive information through the port and cable to and from the printer. When you print a document, the program sends the data through the port and the printer cable to the printer, and the data is printed.

FIG. 9.6

The back of a
PC-compatible
computer.

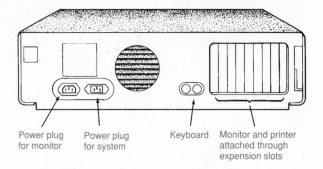

Power plug   Power plug   Keyboard   Monitor and printer
for monitor   for system   attached through
                                                expension slots

Because different computers use varying arrangements of ports, your system may not resemble the system in figure 9.6. Remember that the size of most ports differ.

As you add components to the system, such as a printer, mouse, scanner, and so on, you may notice that the cables also are different sizes and that each cable fits into a port on the back of the computer. You add new ports, such as serial and parallel ports, game ports, and ports for new equipment, by adding plug-in cards inside the computer. These cards plug into the motherboard of the system.

When you plug a cable into a port, you may notice that different cables attach in different ways. The basic procedure, however, is the same, as shown in the following steps:

1. Determine the cable that attaches to each port.

   You determine the proper port either by judging from the shape of the port and cable connector or by looking at the small icons above the ports on the Macintosh computer.

2. Align the cable with the port.

3. Push the cable connector firmly into the port.

4. Tighten the cable. Some cable connectors require that you use a small screwdriver to tighten the cable connector; others, like the Macintosh, and the PS/2 use thumbscrews to tighten the connector. Figure 9.7 shows a typical cable connector and the port to which the cable connects.

Figure 9.8 shows a rear view of the PS/2 Model 50. Note the locations of the connectors and ports.

For a comparison, consider figure 9.9, which is the back of a Mac SE/30. The Mac uses small icons above the ports and on the connecting cables. Figure 9.10 shows the Mac port icons and what each icon represents.

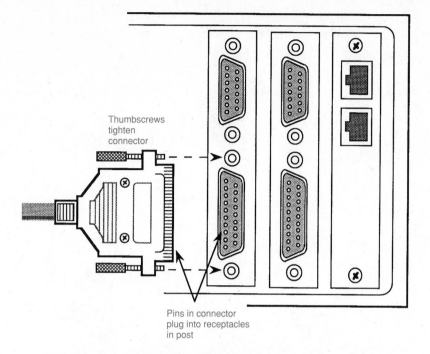

Thumbscrews
tighten
connector

Pins in connector
plug into receptacles
in post

FIG. 9.7

A typical cable
connector and
port.

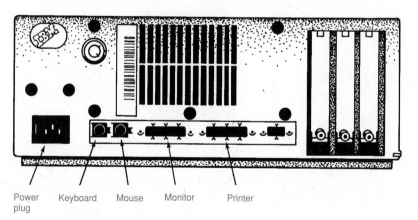

Power   Keyboard   Mouse   Monitor   Printer
plug

FIG. 9.8

The back of a
PS/2 Model 50.

Attaching the Monitor

After setting up the system unit, first decide where to place the monitor. Because you spend most of your time looking at the monitor, exact
positioning of the screen is an important decision. You may prefer the

monitor as close to eye level as possible, with a minimum of glare and the fewest possible number of distractions, such as an open window.

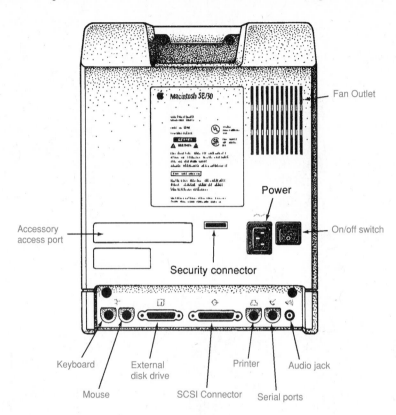

The back of a Macintosh SE/30.

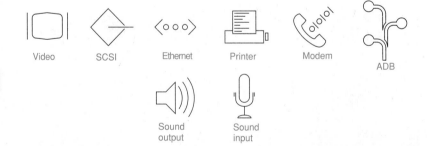

The Macintosh port icons.

Now that you understand the basics of cables and ports, attaching the monitor becomes easy. Although the system may differ slightly from examples shown in previous figures, most monitors come with a power cable and a connector cable that connects the monitor to the system unit. Usually, the connector cable is *hard-wired* into the back of the monitor (the connector cable is not detachable), but the power cord can be unplugged from the back of the monitor.

To attach the monitor, take the following steps:

1. Position the monitor at the desired location (on the system unit, on the desktop, or beside the system unit).

2. Attach the end of the connector cable to the back of the system unit.

3. Attach one end of the power cable to the monitor and the other end to the surge protector or power outlet.

If you use a Macintosh computer, you see an icon that indicates the port into which you plug the monitor cable. (If you use a Mac Classic II or an SE/30, the monitor is built into the system.) If you use one of the Macintosh II computers, an IBM or a PC clone, plug the monitor into the connector that fits the monitor cable.

Attaching the Keyboard

The IBM/PC clone keyboard comes with a keyboard cable that connects the keyboard to the system unit. Unlike the Macintosh, the keyboard cable is *hard wired* (built in) to the keyboard.

On all systems, to connect the keyboard, position the keyboard where you want and plug the end of the keyboard cable into the appropriate connector (port) on the back of the system. On Macintosh computers, you can tell the keyboard port by the icon above the port opening. On other computers, you can find the keyboard port by looking for the port that fits the connector on the end of the keyboard cable. On some systems—specifically, on Macintosh and some PC clones—you also need to plug the keyboard cable into the keyboard. Macintosh computers that use the Apple extended keyboard also have the option of connecting the cable to either the right or left side of the keyboard.

Attaching a Mouse

Depending on the system, attaching a mouse may or may not be a simple task. If you have a newer PC computer, the system probably has a mouse port. In this case, just plug in the mouse and go. (The PS/2 Model 50 includes a mouse port, but all IBMs before the PS/2 line do not.)

If the PC lacks a mouse port, or if you are using a bus mouse (in which the mouse is plugged into a card that you install inside the system unit), have a technical support person install the mouse.

If you are using a Macintosh, connecting the mouse is easy. You can plug the mouse cable into the mouse port in the back of the computer or you can plug into the open side of the keyboard. (Only Apple extended keyboards provide a mouse port on the keyboard.) You can tell the correct port by the icon above the port opening.

Attaching the Printer

The printer is all that remains to set up. (You also may have other peripherals, which you attach after you set up the printer.) After the printer is unpacked and positioned, plug the cable in the appropriate port in the back of the printer and into the printer port on the back of the computer.

Take a minute to investigate a little printer technology. Previously in this chapter, you learned that the cables enable data and power to travel back and forth between the system unit of the computer and peripherals, such as the monitor, mouse, keyboard, and printer. Computers send and receive this data in different ways, either in serial or parallel configurations. A port that sends and receives the data is a serial or a parallel port.

With a *serial port*, information is sent one bit at a time, in a single-file line. With a *parallel port*, information is sent two bits at a time, in double—or parallel—lines. Obviously, you can send information through a parallel port twice as fast as through a serial port.

When you look for a printer, you may see the terms *serial printers* and *parallel printers*. These terms refer to the way in which a printer transmits data to and from the system unit. When you purchase a printer, be sure that you find out (from the salesperson or the manufacturer) which kind of printer you buy so that you know to which port you connect the printer. (If you are unsure which port is which, ask for assistance from a technical support person or your dealer.)

T I P   Macintosh computers cannot use parallel printers without a special hardware device, such as the Grappler 9 Pin and the Grappler LQ from Orange Microsystems.

> **TIP**
>
> The printer cable and the cable connector are larger than other cables. Remember this size difference when you set up a system; the printer has a supplied power cord and cable.

A "Before You Begin" Checklist

Now, the system is together but not yet working (operating a computer is covered in the following chapter). Before you turn on the machine for the first time, make sure that you took care of everything. Ask the following questions:

■ Are all cables connected and secured? (Tighten the little thumbscrews and, if necessary, use a Phillips screwdriver to attach these connectors. Otherwise, the peripherals may not work.)

■ Is the work area comfortable? If you need to move anything, now is the best time. (You can move things later, but after you connect everything, you have more trouble moving the system.)

■ Did you fill out the warranty and registration information?

■ Did you save all the boxes?

■ Do you see any unused spare parts? (You shouldn't!)

Chapter Summary

In this chapter, you assembled a system, an operation that entails unboxing the parts, setting up a work area, positioning the computer, and connecting all the cables. The following chapter brings all this machinery to life in "Familiarizing Yourself with the Operating System."

Familiarizing Yourself with the Operating System

I n the last chapter, you put together a computer system. You chose a work area and set up the components. You connected the components with the appropriate cables. Now you want to turn everything on, but the computer cannot work without an operating system.

Before you can flip the power switch and watch the system come to life, you must learn about operating systems. Specifically, this chapter covers the following areas:

- Defining an operating system
- Understanding differences in operating systems
- Examining operating system capabilities
- Reviewing different operating systems
- Installing an operating system

Defining an Operating System

At the most basic level, the operating system tells a computer how to operate. The operating system contains instructions, or *programs*, that enable you to perform many different disk and file maintenance tasks, such as regular disk-keeping chores, to help you keep the system in order.

The operating system also interacts between you and the computer, communicating in a language the machine understands. The operating system also controls how you interact with the computer. If you use a Macintosh, you communicate with the operating system by clicking file and folder icons and by using the mouse to select options from menus. If you use a PC and DOS, you probably communicate by entering commands on a prompt line.

Depending on the kind of computer you use, you may see the operating system called by different terms. A variety of operating systems is available—different systems for different computers. If you use a Macintosh, the operating system is the Finder. If you use a PC, you may be using MS-DOS, PC DOS, DOS Shell, UNIX, or OS/2. Usually, you see one of the following names of operating systems:

- MS-DOS or PC DOS
- DOS Shell
- Finder and System 7
- OS/2
- UNIX or XENIX
- Windows[*]

[*] *Microsoft Windows is a software environment for PCs that runs on top of DOS but is often known as an operating system. Windows is examined in a following section of this chapter.*

DOS is an operating system widely used on IBM and PC-compatible computers. (MS-DOS is a version of IBM's original PC DOS, which was created by Microsoft Corporation.) The Macintosh uses the System Folder and Finder as its operating system. Other popular operating systems include CP/M, UNIX, XENIX, and OS/2. Operating *environments*, such as the extremely popular Microsoft Windows, also provide other choices in the way you interact with a computer. For more information on operating systems, see "Reviewing Different Operating Systems," in a following section of this chapter.

The following list shows the operating systems used by the most popular personal computers:

Computer	Operating System
IBM PC, XT, AT, XT 286, 386 PS/2 Models 25, 30, 60, 70, and 80	DOS 5.0, OS/2 2.0 for more recent model PS/2s and high-end PCs
Macintosh	The System Folder version 7.0 and Finder

Most computers are sold with the newest version of operating system. When you purchase a Macintosh, the current version of the operating system is part of the deal. When you purchase a PC, the dealer may or may not install the operating system, but usually, DOS is included in the sale. You also receive a manual about the operating system and disks. Be sure that you keep all manuals in a safe place so that you can refer to the documentation when the need arises.

Understanding Differences in Operating Systems

Most operating systems work on only one kind of machine, such as DOS on PCs, the Finder on Macs, and so on. Usually, computers run under one operating system only, but some new computers on the market have operating systems that read files created under other operating systems. On systems capable of running more than one operating system, such as a 486 PC that runs DOS or OS/2 (or UNIX or XENIX), you can use only one operating system at a time.

The workings of the operating systems include some of the following differences:

- The user interface
- The capability of multitasking (performing more than one operation at the same time)
- The software supported by the operating system

How Do You Determine
the Operating System a Machine Uses?

If you just purchased a system, your head may be swimming with advice and warnings from fellow computer users. You brought the system home (or to the office), unpacked the parts, connected all the cables, and—your mind goes blank. What operating system do you have?

If you use a Macintosh, do not worry. This system uses the Finder. The System Folder and the Finder come in different versions, discussed in a following section of this chapter. To find out which version of the System and Finder you have, just go to the Apple menu and select "About this Macintosh." The System software version appears.

If you use a PC, the choices are slightly more complicated. To determine whether you have a system that runs MS-DOS, PC DOS, or OS/2, first check the invoice that came with the system. The programs should be itemized, telling you specifically the operating system you have. You receive manuals with the system as well, so check the manuals that accompany the software.

If you purchased an IBM, you probably have IBM's PC DOS; if you purchased a PC clone, you have a version of MS-DOS. If you purchased another IBM-compatible computer, such as the popular COMPAQ, you may have a version of DOS created for COMPAQ computers—COMPAQ DOS, a variation of MS-DOS. Check the manuals for details related to the individual operating system. Because all DOS versions are to a large extent similar, the term *DOS* is used here to refer to all MS-DOS and PC DOS operating systems. If the machine is an OS/2 machine, you probably received a set of OS/2 manuals and software with the system. To find out which version of the DOS you have, at the C:> prompt, type **VER** and press Enter. The System software version appears.

Operating Systems and the User Interface

The term *user interface* is an overused phrase that refers to what users see and work with on-screen. You see user interface used in connection with both operating systems and application programs.

Consider the Macintosh screen shown in figure 10.1. The Macintosh interface includes icons that represent files and folders. The entire design of the Macintosh interface is visual. To move a file, you click and drag an icon to the desired location. To discard a file, you drag the file's icon to the trash can at the bottom of the screen. Because of the easily understood visual design, the Macintosh user interface is known as *user-friendly*. Other designers of operating systems and programs are working similar visual approaches into other user interface designs.

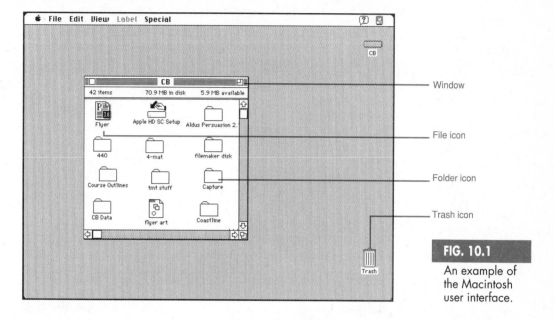

FIG. 10.1

An example of the Macintosh user interface.

By comparison, the operating system used on early PCs wasn't user-friendly. DOS, specifically versions prior to DOS 5.0, required users to enter commands at the command prompt. You need to understand the command that you use, *before* you use the command, which is a difficult task when learning DOS.

Suppose that you want to copy a file. The following example illustrates the difference in user interface philosophy:

■ With the Finder (on the Macintosh), you click on the icon of the file you want to copy, open the File menu, and select Duplicate. The copy of the file appears beside the original. You then can drag the icon to a desired location.

■ With DOS 5.0, when you see the DOS prompt, which, if you are using a hard disk, usually looks like C>, type the COPY command, using the following syntax:

   COPY *thisfile thatfile*

This command makes a copy of the first file (named *thisfile*) and names the copy *thatfile*. If you want to move the file to another directory, you indicate this desire in the COPY command with the following syntax:

COPY C:*this_directory**thisfile* **C:***that_directory**thatfile*

With the release of DOS Shell version 5.0, DOS moved closer to the user friendly status of the Macintosh. With the menu system in DOS Shell 4.x and 5.0, you can select commands from menus and bypass the DOS prompt command-entry method.

The kind of operating system with which you are most comfortable depends on your past computer experience. You may prefer the Macintosh interface because of the ease with which you can learn and use the system. You also may prefer DOS because working with icons and being unable to work at a command level with the operating system and with applications may frustrate you.

Multitasking Capabilities

Another major difference in operating systems concerns whether the systems can multitask. *Multitasking* is the capability of running more than one application program at a time.

DOS isn't a multitasking operating system; OS/2 is. For the Mac, the Finder in System 7.0 and more recent releases enable you to simultaneously open as many applications on-screen (in windows) as the memory of the computer allows. The Finder doesn't, however, work in more than one window at the same time.

The distinction between open windows and active windows is important. Although the Mac operating system enables you to *open* several windows at a time, you can work in only one window at a time. The window in which you work is the *active* window. If the Mac were a true multitasking computer, you could sort database records in one window while performing spreadsheet operations in another. Figure 10.2 shows an example of Microsoft Windows, with several applications open on-screen.

For many users, multitasking is a major issue. Suppose that you are producing a report. In this report, you need to include the department's financial data, graphics, and text from a word processor. As you write with the word processor, you realize that you forgot the statistics of a product. You need to open the spreadsheet file that stores the information, but you are in the word processor.

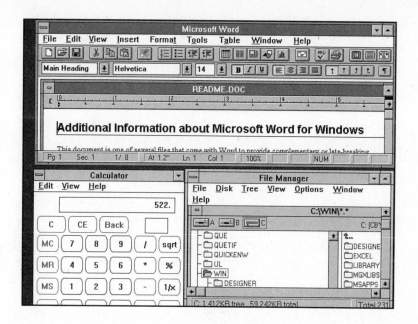

FIG. 10.2

An example of several applications open at the same time.

If both the operating system and application program supported multi-tasking, you can open the spreadsheet file, check the information you need, and return to the word processor without trouble. In a true multi-tasking environment, you also can start a search-and-replace procedure in the word processor, leave the word processor and go to the spreadsheet file, and then return to the word processor without interrupting the word processing operation. If the operating system cannot multitask and you are using a variety of stand-alone programs (as opposed to an integrated software package) to accomplish the task, you must exit from one program, load another, open the file you need, close the file, exit from the second program, restart the original program, and open the file with which you began. Simple enough, but if you repeat this scenario many times during a work session, you lose a considerable amount of time loading and exiting programs.

Examining Operating System Capabilities

Besides the internal communication the operating system carries on with the hardware, the operating system enables you to perform the following kinds of functions:

- Disk management
- File management
- Interaction with application programs

The following sections present an overview of various functions carried out by the operating system. For more specific information about using a particular operating system, see Chapter 11, "Using Your Computer."

Disk Management

Disk management sounds complex. You need a method of preparing, organizing, and working with disks. When you first begin computing, you may have just a few disks, an easily tracked number. You know every file you keep on each disk because—at least at first—you take the time to label the disks accurately. You need to know how to prepare the disk for data storage (*formatting* the disk) and, eventually, to understand more sophisticated tasks, such as copying and erasing disks.

Whether you use a hard disk or floppy disks, the operating system provides you with the means of performing the following disk management tasks:

- Formatting the disk (preparing the disk to store data and programs)
- Copying files from one disk to another
- Erasing disks
- Displaying a list of the files on the disk (displaying a directory)
- Organizing the location of files on either floppy or hard disk

These procedures are explained in Chapter 11.

File Management

As you begin working with files, you soon need a method of organizing them. The operating system helps you perform the following file management functions:

- Make copies of files
- Copy files to disks
- Set up directories to organize your files
- Rename files

■ Erase files

■ Move files from one directory to another

Chapter 11 gives more information about these procedures.

Disk and File Basics

A disk stores the programs and data you work with on the computer. Whether this disk is a floppy disk, which you insert into a disk drive—5 1/4-inch or 3 1/2-inch—or a hard metallic disk that turns inside a hard disk housing, the function is the same. The disk stores data so that you can easily retrieve and work with the data in subsequent work sessions.

A file stores a collection of information about a specific item. A file can be a letter you create in a word processor, a piece of art you draw with a graphics program, a client list from a database, or a program. You can create a file that holds a 20-word memo or a 200,000-word novel. A file can be as small as a single word, number, or line, or as large as the memory in the computer (or the disk space) allows. Throughout this book and in other computer texts, the word *file* usually refers to a collection of information you create with a specific application program. With a word processor, you open a file, enter data, and save the file. You then can reopen the file, work with the data, and perhaps print the file.

Every operating system gives you a method of working with and organizing disks and files. The more files you create, the greater the need for file and disk organization, because the greater the chances of reusing disks (you need to know how to erase the files already stored on the disks) and copy files. Chapter 11, "Using Your Computer," explains many of these basic disk and file maintenance tasks.

Interaction with Application Programs

Although operating systems are software, these systems aren't the kind of software you use to perform specific tasks, such as word processing, accounting, or managing data. A different kind of software, *application software* or *programs*, is used to help you carry out the operations you bought the computer to perform. The *operating system*, however, controls the basic operation of the system and gives you a method of working with files and disks and running the application software.

No matter what program you ultimately choose, you need some way to format disks, copy files, erase files you no longer need, rename files, and so on. Rather than having each application program to provide a means of performing disk and file maintenance tasks, the operating system gives you all the tools you need for caring for files and disks. This factor enables the makers of the application programs to write programs that use the smallest amount of RAM possible, because they don't need to create program routines to take care of operations performed by the operating system. When you purchase an application program, you need to make sure that the program runs under the operating system that you use on the computer. Some programs are available for more than one operating environment, such as Microsoft Excel, Microsoft Word, and Lotus 1-2-3, all of which are available in both IBM and Macintosh versions.

You start most applications from the operating system level of the computer, although occasionally, you may set up the system so that certain programs boot when you turn on the computer. Usually, however, you need to activate the application programs you use by doing something from the operating system level. If you use a Macintosh, you activate applications by double-clicking on a program icon, which in turn causes the program to load in memory. If you use a DOS machine, you type the file name at the DOS command prompt (*word*, for example, to load Microsoft Word). For more information about working with programs, see "Installing and Starting Programs" in Chapter 11.

Many application programs include options that enable you to rename, delete, or copy files from within the program. Other programs may include an option that enables you to return temporarily to the operating system level to perform a few commands and then return to the program. WordStar and Microsoft Word 5.5, two DOS-based word processing programs, contain a routine that enables you to escape to DOS level, carry out a DOS command, such as COPY or RENAME, and then return to the program by pressing a key.

Reviewing Different Operating Systems

Because this book focuses primarily on the two major personal computer types—PCs and Macs—you have not as yet seen equal treatment for all the popular operating systems. Different operating systems are used on different machines for different tasks. This section reviews the following operating systems:

- DOS
- OS/2
- UNIX and XENIX
- The Finder and System 7

You also learn about the operating environment, Microsoft Windows.

DOS

DOS is the original operating system designed for the IBM PC, XT, and PC AT family of computers. You see DOS referred to as MS-DOS, PC DOS, and just plain DOS. DOS (an acronym for *disk operating system* and pronounced *"doss"*) is a generic reference to the operating system used by IBMs and compatibles.

From the earliest DOS release in 1981, DOS was used by entering commands after an on-screen prompt and pressing Enter. Introduced with DOS 4.0 (and enhanced with DOS 5) is the *DOS Shell*, which gave users the option of displaying and selecting commands from a menu system rather than remembering and then entering commands after the prompt. Many new users found the original command-entry method unfriendly and intimidating, claiming that unless the users memorized many commands or kept a reference manual handy at all times, finding a way through file and disk procedures was cumbersome. DOS 4.0 and 5.0 give users the best of both worlds: users who prefer the command-entry method can use the DOS prompt, and new users have a friendlier method, the DOS Shell, to select commands and options.

Figure 10.3 shows the display after the DIR (directory) command is issued at the DOS prompt. (The DIR command displays a list of all files in the current directory on the current disk.) Figure 10.4 shows the DOS Shell available with DOS 5.0.

Que Corporation publishes several books that help you get up to speed with DOS. Specifically, you may want to consult *Using MS-DOS 5*, *Que's MS-DOS 5 User's Guide*, Special Edition; or *MS-DOS 5 QuickStart*.

OS/2

Working together, IBM and Microsoft developed a new operating system to run the IBM Personal System/2 family of computers. OS/2, an acronym for Operating System/2, was expected to burst on the market as the new operating system standard. To date, OS/2 has fallen short of this anticipated immediate success.

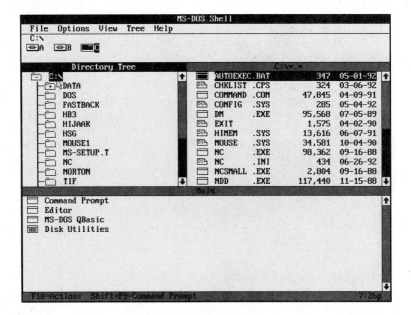

```
Volume in drive C is MAIN FOLDER
Volume Serial Number is 0252-09CC
Directory of  C:\

AUTOEXEC BAT        51 12-02-89  12:00a
CONFIG   BAK        76 12-02-89  12:00a
WORKS        <DIR>     01-01-90   2:06a
DOS          <DIR>     01-01-90   2:09a
SYSTUTOR     <DIR>     01-01-90   2:11a
PRODIGY      <DIR>     01-01-90   2:12a
SIERRA       <DIR>     03-04-91   5:09p
CAKEWALK     <DIR>     03-04-91  10:27p
CARMEN1      <DIR>     03-04-91  10:36p
PROMENAD     <DIR>     03-05-91  11:26p
PROMENAD BAT        55 03-05-91  11:27p
QDOS     LOG     10457 05-19-91  10:55a
COLLAGE      <DIR>     03-14-91  11:55a
QD2      EXE     76800 03-30-80   8:37p
WS4          <DIR>     03-21-91  11:02a
INSTALL  DOC      2560 03-21-91  11:28a
HG3          <DIR>     05-15-91  11:34a
QAKEYS   KM       2560 03-27-91  11:42a
CONFIG   SYS       128 03-24-91   3:02p
-- More --
```

FIG. 10.3

The display after the DOS command DIR is used.

```
                          MS-DOS Shell
   File  Options  View  Tree  Help
C:\
 A    B    C

          Directory Tree                        C:\*.*
   C:\                              AUTOEXEC.BAT      347  05-01-92
      DATA                          CHKLIST .CPS      324  03-06-92
      DOS                           COMMAND .COM   47,845  04-09-91
      FASTBACK                      CONFIG  .SYS      285  05-04-92
      HB3                           DM      .EXE   95,568  07-05-89
      HIJAAK                        EXIT           1,575  04-02-90
      HSG                           HIMEM   .SYS   13,616  06-07-91
      MOUSE1                        MOUSE   .SYS   34,581  10-04-90
      MS-SETUP.T                    NC      .EXE   98,362  09-16-88
      NC                            NC      .INI      434  06-26-92
      NORTON                        NCSMALL .EXE    2,804  09-16-88
      TIF                           NDD     .EXE  117,440  11-15-88
                                    Main
   Command Prompt
   Editor
   MS-DOS QBasic
   Disk Utilities

 F10=Actions  Shift+F9=Command Prompt                     7:26p
```

FIG. 10.4

The DOS Shell with Version 5.0.

Early releases of OS/2 didn't meet with instant public approval. As more and more software developers create applications that run under OS/2, however, and as the price of computers powerful enough to take advantage of OS/2's features drop to affordable ranges, the popularity of OS/2 appears on the rise.

What does OS/2 offer that DOS doesn't? One answer to this question is *multitasking*. With OS/2, you can open and work on several different applications at one time. OS/2 also recognizes an enormous amount of memory, including expanded and extended memory. DOS is limited in the way memory is recognized, and because this restriction limits the number of programs DOS can have in RAM at one time, DOS cannot support multitasking.

Similar to the latest version of DOS, OS/2 also offers users a choice of command mode or a menu system, known as the *Presentation Manager*. With the Presentation Manager, you can use the mouse to select commands and options. Figure 10.5 shows an example of the Presentation Manager.

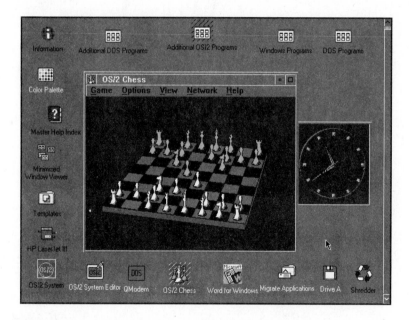

FIG. 10.5

The OS/2 2.0 Presentation Manager.

OS/2 also offers a DOS mode, which enables you to use most of the familiar DOS commands. For more detailed information about OS/2, consult *Using OS/2 2.0* (Que Corporation, 1992).

UNIX

UNIX is included in this whirlwind tour of operating systems because the UNIX operating system is designed for engineers and programmers. You may never use this operating system for the new computer (unless you are investigating the revolutionary NeXT computer, which uses UNIX exclusively). However, UNIX has important features worthy of mention here.

UNIX is a powerful operating system that requires the utmost sophistication from computer hardware and software. UNIX is not only a multitasking operating system (you can have more than one application active at one time), but also a multiuser operating system (the operating system can support more than one user at a time, as in a network of computer systems). UNIX also has sophisticated security features that enable users to protect programs and files from unauthorized access.

Microsoft Corporation (maker of MS-DOS) created a second version of UNIX, called XENIX. XENIX is now widely used and is recognized as the most successful UNIX clone in the market.

For more information about UNIX and XENIX, consult Que Corporation's *Introduction to UNIX* (Que Corporation, 1992).

The Finder and System 7.0

The operating system of the Macintosh family of computers—the System Folder (sometimes referred to as the *Finder*)—is responsible for changing the way many people look at computers. This operating system, first introduced with the original Mac in 1984, brought users a computer with a friendly face and an easy-to-understand and easy-to-use concept.

The Macintosh operating system is based on the concept of a desktop. Because the computer screen is a graphical representation of a desktop, you can easily understand the connection between disks, files, folders, and windows. You display the contents of a disk in a window that opens on the desktop. Inside the window, stored folders and program files appear. To start a program, place the mouse pointer and double-click the program icon. To open a folder, you double-click the folder icon and reveal the files inside.

These concepts are simple. The Finder is the tool responsible for this friendly on-screen interaction; the Finder is the graphics interface that gives the Macintosh today's *graphical* appearance. Although you can open several folders or windows on-screen at one time, the Finder is incapable of multitasking. You can open several windows but only one window is active at a time.

The most recent version of the Macintosh Operating System, System 7.0, has a built in multifinder, which increases the speed with which users move between applications. Unfortunately, System 7 also is incapable of multitasking. System 7, however, brings to the Macintosh revolutionary capabilities previously available only on mainframe computers hosting far more power.

The new System 7 includes multicolored icons, a customizable Apple menu, control panels and DAs (*desk accessory* programs) you can open by double-clicking, and Balloon help feature.

Other features of System 7 include the Publish and Subscribe commands, which enable you to *publish* so that other *subscribers* on the network can read the file. Changes made to *subscribed* files then are automatically copied to the original document.

System 7 also includes TrueType, a new font technology created by Apple. Unlike other font configurations, TrueType is an outline font technology that enables you to scale fonts to any desired size; no bitmapped (or blocky) characters are used. The result is a high on-screen resolution that prints at 300 dpi.

System 7 also has QuickTime, a video player and editing option that enables you to add video to any document. Using QuickTime, a video board, and a camcorder, for example, you can record live video into a Macintosh. You then can paste this recording in a standard Word document. When the reader comes to the icon that represents the video, a double click plays the video. (If you are just playing previously recorded video, the video board and camcorder are unnecessary, only QuickTime is required.)

These and other features make the Macintosh operating system a great success. New users find the point-and-click environment easy to understand and use. Even experienced users like the ease with which files are manipulated and organized. For more information about the Finder and System 7, see *Que's Big Mac Book*, 3rd Edition and *Using the Mac with System 7*, both published by Que Corporation, 1992.

Microsoft Windows

Microsoft Windows, introduced in 1985, is a special kind of software that falls more under the category of *operating environment* than operating system. Windows is a graphical interface that runs on top of DOS.

The first version of Windows provided a common interface for applications written for Windows, but failed to sweep the market because of limited power and a lack of available applications. Newer versions of Windows, however, that provided a host of improvements in speed and user interface also created a strong following of previous DOS users.

One of Windows' strong points is the capability of switching quickly and easily between Windows applications. Similar to the Macintosh environment, Windows enables you to move between applications with a minimum of trouble. Suppose that you want a paragraph of text that resides in a Word for Windows document to be added to an Aldus PageMaker document. With Windows, you can open both applications and move back and forth easily, copying and pasting the text from one program to the other. Similarly, you can open another program, such as Micrografx Designer, and copy and paste the pictures from this graphics program in the PageMaker document.

The latest version of Windows, 3.1, released in April 1992, is the most stable environment so far, offering a multitude of performance enhancements, including a new printing system and an improved disk cache feature, which uses an area of random-access memory (RAM) as a temporary storage area for often-requested program code.

Windows 3.1 also brings TrueType fonts to the Windows applications. TrueType provides scalable fonts, which eliminates bitmap versions of fonts used by previous Windows versions. The on-screen resolution is high and materials are printed at 300 dpi (dots per inch).

Another feature of Windows 3.1 is Object Linking and Embedding (OLE). With OLE, you can access one application while in another. Suppose that you decide to paste an Excel chart into a Word for Windows document. Rather than the standard paste command, you have a new paste command that pastes a link between Excel and Word. You then can double-click the Excel chart from within the Word program and Windows 3.1 automatically launches Excel and brings up the chart so that you can make changes. After you close the Excel chart, Windows places you back in Word for Windows.

Windows 3.1 is faster than previous versions, works on 80386- or 80486-based computers, and includes an automatic installation procedure. Windows 3.1 also adds several features, such as a Program Manager, which helps you organize applications and files; a File Manager, which provides powerful disk-management capabilities; a Control Panel, which enables you to control the printer and associated drivers; Record, which enables you to record keystrokes so that you can automate frequently used procedures; and complete multimedia capabilities, including sound, record, and playback options, as well as built-in CD-ROM drivers. Figure 10.6 shows an example of Microsoft Windows 3.1.

More than 400 applications programs are now written to work with Microsoft Windows.

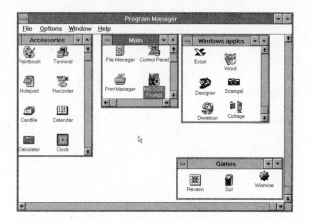

FIG. 10.6

A screen from
Microsoft
Windows
Version 3.1.

Installing an Operating System

To run properly, the computer needs access to the disk operating system. Now that you have all the pieces put together and are armed with a basic understanding of your particular operating system, you must make sure that the operating system is installed.

When you install a program, whether an operating system or an applications program, you place the files on the hard disk of the computer so that the program (or operating system) can access the needed program information. Some programs have *installation procedures* that place the files on the hard disk, so that the program knows how to find important program information.

If you don't have a hard disk system and are using a floppy disk system—a system with only one or two floppy disk drives—you must place a copy of the operating system startup disk in drive A each time you turn on the computer. The operating system is loaded into memory (or installed) when you turn on the computer.

The following sections provide an overview of installation procedures for these operating systems:

- DOS (PC)
- OS/2 (PC)
- Windows (PC)
- The System and Finder files (Mac)

Preinstallation Questions

Before you install software on the computer, ask (yourself or the computer dealer) the following questions:

■ *Is the software already installed?*

If you purchased the computer, the operating system, and the software from a retail dealer, the dealer's technicians may have set up the system and the software. Some computer stores perform this service at the store; others charge for this service. If the outlet you are working with offers installation as an option, have the technical support staff install the software and set up the system. This service lessens the learning curve and enables you to work with the system much sooner than if you installed the operating system and the software.

■ *Does the software demand that you follow a specific installation routine?*

Whether the software is an operating system or a program you plan to use on the computer, you can find this answer in the manual that came with the software. You usually find these instructions in the first part of the book or in a separate small installation manual. The manual gives you instructions that either show you how to copy the files to the hard disk or tell you how to activate the installation procedure. Many popular PC application programs enable you to start the install program by typing either **INSTALL** or **SETUP** and pressing Enter. The method used depends on the individual program and doesn't work for all programs.

Installing DOS

The methods you use to install DOS depend on whether you use a hard disk or a floppy disk system. The term *installation* doesn't really fit unless you place the files on the hard disk; with a floppy disk system, technically, you install DOS into RAM each time you boot the computer. The following sections explain how you can install DOS.

Preparing the Hard Disk

Before you place programs or data on the hard disk of a computer, you must prepare the hard disk to hold the information. This procedure is highly technical and is best left to people comfortable with this work (when in doubt, find a technical support person to help you). The process of preparing the hard disk involves the following steps:

1. Use the FDISK program (supplied with the DOS operating system) to partition the hard disk, which sets up an organization for the way the hard disk stores files.

2. Format the hard disk by typing **FORMAT C:**. (This procedure is essentially the same as formatting a floppy disk, but on a larger scale.) Use the **/S** switch to make the disk DOS-bootable.

> **CAUTION:** Formatting the hard disk erases all data on the disk.

After these steps, set up directories on the hard disk to store and organize the program and data files with which you work.

 NOTE If you have an IBM PC AT, you must run the SETUP program before you do anything else. For more information about preparing the hard disk of the computer, see *MS-DOS 5 User's Guide,* Special Edition (Que Corporation, 1991).

Installing DOS On a Hard Disk

The method you use to install DOS on a hard disk depends on the version of DOS you are using. If you are using MS-DOS 5.0, the SETUP program installs DOS.

If you purchased the computer and DOS 5.0 from a dealer, you may want to ask the dealer to help you install DOS on the hard disk. If another operating system, such as OS/2, UNIX, or XENIX, already is installed on the hard disk, you need to read the *Getting Started* manual packaged with the version of DOS.

Using the SETUP program, follow these steps to install DOS:

1. Insert the DOS SETUP disk into drive A.

2. From the C:\ prompt, type **A:**.

3. From the A:\ prompt, type **SETUP**.

4. Follow the prompts as they appear for complete installation instructions.

DOS Special Files:
AUTOEXEC.BAT and CONFIG.SYS

As you begin to read about and work with DOS, you run across references to two files: AUTOEXEC.BAT and CONFIG.SYS. These two files deserve closer inspection.

AUTOEXEC.BAT is a *batch file*, a batch of DOS commands in a file. The commands in AUTOEXEC.BAT give the computer important information, such as where the system can find certain application programs. You don't need to create an AUTOEXEC.BAT file for the computer to work but, because AUTOEXEC.BAT provides the computer with this important information each time you start the system, this file saves you the trouble of entering all the instructions manually at the start of each work session.

CONFIG.SYS is a file used by both DOS and OS/2 to give the computer important hardware configuration information. CONFIG.SYS contains statements that modify DOS. CONFIG.SYS also contains the settings for the number of files the operating system can open at one time and the number of buffers used to store data.

For more information about AUTOEXEC.BAT and CONFIG.SYS files, see *Using MS-DOS 5*, published by Que Corporation, 1991.

On a Floppy Disk System

Installing DOS on a floppy disk system (a computer with one or two floppy disk drives and no hard drive) differs only in *where* DOS finds the files needed to start the program. To work, the computer must locate the operating system files. If you use a hard disk, all the DOS files are copied to a specific directory on the hard disk, so you don't need a DOS disk in the floppy disk drive. If you use a floppy disk system without a hard disk, place a DOS disk in drive A each time you start the system so that the computer can load DOS into RAM. To load DOS in RAM, make sure that the DOS disk is in drive A when you turn on the system.

> Making copies of important disks is essential, whether the disks hold original programs or important data you use frequently or infrequently. If you use a floppy disk-based computer, you *must* make copies of all disks before using them. Create a work disk you can use every day—a copy of the original program or data disk. If the work disk is accidentally damaged, you still have the original copy of the disk. Copying disks is explained in Chapter 11.

T I P

For more information about installing and working with DOS 5.0, see *Using MS-DOS 5* and *Upgrading to MS-DOS 5*, (Que Corporation, 1991).

Installing OS/2

The procedure for installing OS/2 differs from the DOS procedures. Because this operating system is literally unusable on a system without a hard disk, you cannot boot the computer from a single disk. OS/2 comes with a full-fledged installation procedure, during which you tell the operating system the kind of hardware you are using. The following overview details the steps needed to install OS/2.

1. Insert the OS/2 Installation disk in drive A. (Make sure that you write-protect the original disk before running this installation procedure.)

2. Turn on the computer. If the computer is already turned on, press Ctrl-Alt-Del to reboot the system.

3. If necessary, turn on the monitor.

   The computer goes through a series of self-tests to make sure that the hardware is functioning properly. The computer beeps and begins reading the operating system information on the disk in drive A.

   The OS/2 installation procedure then starts. A copyright message and a welcome screen appear on-screen.

4. Press Enter and follow the installation instructions displayed on-screen.

5. After you go through all the installation screens, OS/2 prompts you to press Enter to complete the installation of the operating system. Press Enter.

6. Remove the Installation disk from drive A.

7. Press Ctrl-Alt-Del to reboot the computer.

For more information about OS/2, see *Using OS/2 2.0*, Barry Nance and Greg Chicares, published by Que Corporation, 1992.

Installing Windows

To install Windows, you use the SETUP program that accompanies Windows. This new setup procedures offers big improvements over previous versions. You may choose a *custom* or *express* installation. Custom installation enables you choose only the programs you want, saving on the amount of disk space required. Although quick and easy, Express installation, however, installs the entire package, including all accessories, help files, and a tutorial for first-time mouse users.

If you are upgrading a version of Windows, SETUP enables you to install a new directory that doesn't replace the old directory, which can be helpful if you just want to *test drive* Windows 3.1 before deciding if you want to keep the new version.

To install Windows, take the following steps:

1. Place the Window Setup disk into drive A.

2. From the C:\ prompt, type **A:** and press Enter.

3. From the A:\ prompt, type **SETUP** and press Enter.

4. For complete installation instructions, follow the prompts that appear.

Installing the System and Finder Files

The Macintosh uses a different version of the System software and the Finder. The current Macintosh system software is System 7, released in May 1991.

Most manuals don't refer to the Macintosh operating system as an operating system. The Macintosh operating system actually is a combination of several files, primarily the System files and the Finder. The *Finder* is the graphical interface you use when you work with the Mac. The Finder controls the pictures (*icons*) you click to open folders, disks, and files and controls the pull-down menus and the desktop from which you work. The *System* files include basic operational files and extra files for performing different functions, such as installing fonts, making macros, and other functions.

To install System 7 and Finder files on the Macintosh, you need at least 2M of RAM and a hard disk. To install previous system versions, you need only two floppy drives. You may ask the retailer or a technical support person to perform the installation, or you can perform the installation by taking the following steps:

1. Place the Macintosh System Tools disk in the drive. Unless you made a copy on another machine, you may have to use an original. Use the original disk only once and then make (and use) a copy. Copying procedures are discussed in the following chapter.

2. Turn on the Macintosh.

3. If you have a separate monitor, turn on the monitor.

4. Open the System Tools disk by placing the mouse cursor on the disk symbol (an icon) and double-clicking on the mouse button.

5. To open the Installer folder, double-click on the icon (see fig. 10.7).

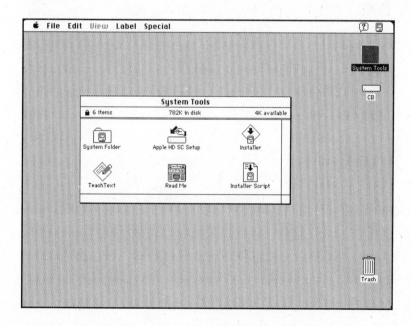

FIG. 10.7

The Installer icon.

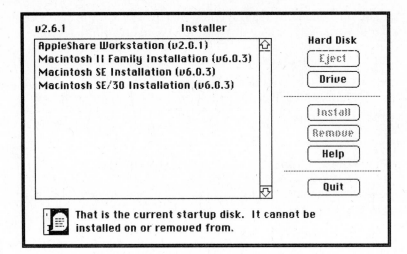

FIG. 10.8

Selecting an
Installer script.

NOTE If you don't see the Installer folder, look in the Utilities or
Setup folder.

6. Select the Installer for your model of Macintosh (see fig. 10.8).

7. Choose the drive in which you want to install the Tools files.

8. Click the Install button. The Installer transfers the important files
to the drive you specified in step 7.

For more detailed information about installing System 7, see *Using the
Mac with System 7*, Que Corporation.

Chapter Summary

In this chapter, you learned the basics about the operating system. In
the following chapter, you learn how to use the computer and operating system to perform basic file and disk maintenance tasks, such as
formatting and copying disks and viewing, copying, renaming, and deleting files.

Using Your Computer

This chapter rounds out the hands-on section of this book with some practical applications. Whether you use a PC or a Macintosh, as you begin working with the computer you may find that many short procedures make up one work session. To write a letter, for example, you need to start the computer, load the word processing program, open the file, write or edit the letter, close the file, perhaps print the file, and exit from the program. At first, each step seems yet another series of smaller steps. As you grow accustomed to working with the computer and the programs, however, the simple procedures shown in this chapter will become second nature to you.

First, you learn to start the computer. Then you learn to format floppy disks—a procedure that prepares floppy disks to store data. Finally, you find an introduction to working with files—the common denominator among all computers and computer users. Specifically, you learn the following procedures:

- Starting the computer
- Formatting and copying disks
- Displaying contents of directories and disks
- Organizing files
- Understanding and naming files

- Copying files
- Erasing files
- Renaming files
- Installing and starting programs
- Shutting down the computer

Defining Some Terms

Before you start, you need to understand a few terms you see throughout this chapter. If after reading the following listing of terms, you still don't understand these concepts, don't be too concerned. The discussions that follow in this chapter further define each concept.

Backup copy. A copy of a program or data disk that you keep for daily use to protect the originals from damage.

Boot. Starting the computer (either cold boot or warm boot).

Cold boot. Also known as *power-up*; the procedure when you initially turn on the computer for the current work session.

Default. A setting or value the program assumes if you do not supply a new setting or value.

Density. A measurement of the amount of data that can be stored in a square inch on a disk.

Directory. In the PC world, a directory is analogous to the conventional filing cabinet drawer in which you store files related to a certain subject.

DOS prompt. The on-screen indicator displayed by DOS to tell you the system is ready to accept commands. If the current disk drive is C, the DOS prompt is displayed as C>.

File. A named collection of information stored as a unit. (You first create and then save a letter in a file on a disk.)

Folder. In the Macintosh world, a folder is analogous to a conventional drawer in a filing cabinet. Each folder can store many files.

Format. Preparing a disk to store data.

Icon. An on-screen graphical element or symbol that represents a certain item, such as a file or folder.

Logged drive. The disk drive where the operating system looks for files to retrieve or save; also called *default drive* or *current drive*.

Path. The route the operating system or program takes to a specific directory or folder to locate or save a specific file.

Subdirectory. With PCs, subdirectories are directories within other directories. You can create many subdirectories and many levels of subdirectories within a single directory. (Macintosh has folders for this purpose.)

Warm boot. Restarting the computer while the power is on. You perform a warm boot (also known as *rebooting*) by pressing Ctrl-Alt-Del on DOS computers or pressing the reboot button on the Macintosh.

Write-protect. The process of protecting a disk from receiving information. Write-protecting prevents accidental erasure and overwriting of files. Especially important is to write-protect disks that store important information like programs (and operating systems).

Starting Your Computer

By now, you must be eager to see that intelligent-looking system operate. The first step is to turn on the system. The following section describes the procedures for working with a PC.

Starting Your PC

After you get all the components connected, turn on the computer by performing the following steps:

1. Make sure that all cables are attached correctly, all thumbscrews are tight, and the power cords are plugged in.

2. Locate the On/Off switch. This switch may be on the front (see fig. 11.1), on the side, or on the back of the machine.

3. If the computer system requires that you start the computer from a DOS disk, insert the disk into drive A and close the drive door. (You follow this procedure if the computer does not have a hard disk.)

4. Flip the switch to the On position.

The computer then should come to life. You hear a variety of whirring and grunting noises as the system processes the tasks the computer is set up to go through at the start of each work session.

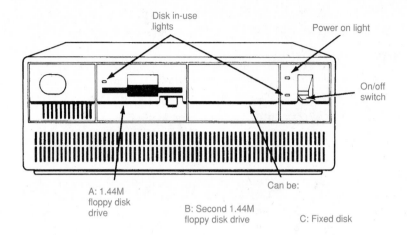

Disk in-use lights

Power on light

On/off switch

FIG. 11.1

The power switch on the PS/2 Model 50.

A: 1.44M floppy disk drive

Can be:

B: Second 1.44M floppy disk drive

C: Fixed disk

How Do You Know Which Disk Drive Is Which?

You probably saw the terms *drive A*, *drive B*, and *drive C* throughout this and other computer books. If you work around computers for any length of time, you get used to these terms and don't struggle deciding which drive is which. At first, however, the distinction can confuse you. The following list shows a few guidelines for drive names:

- In a two-drive system with the floppy disk drives arranged one on top of the other, the top drive is usually named A and the bottom is named B. For a side-by-side arrangement, A is on the left and B is on the right.

- The hard disk is usually referred to as drive C.

- References to drives D, E, F, and so on, probably are references to parts (known as *partitions*) of the hard disk set off so that the software *sees* the hard disk as a series of separate drives.

Within DOS, you can assign the disk drives any name you like. Most people use the A, B, C standard, however, to be consistent with popular software configurations and with other computer users.

If you need to place a disk in drive A but are unsure which drive is which, try putting the disk into the drive on the top (in a vertical arrangement) or on the left (in a side-by-side drive arrangement). If this drive isn't drive A on the computer, the system beeps, which tells you that the procedure cannot work until you put the disk in the correct drive.

Depending on the kinds of applications you use, the operating system you use, and the way the machine is configured, you may see different messages.

The machine probably works through a power-on self-test (POS) during which the computer checks its parts, making sure that everything is in working order. During this time, you may see System initializing or a similar message that informs you the computer is performing a self-check. The initial self-test may last from a few seconds to several minutes.

If everything is working properly, the computer then should display the C> prompt or ask you to confirm the displayed date. If something goes wrong, you may see a message like the following example:

```
The boot operation failed -- check the disk!!
                -- Press any key to reboot --
```

With other versions of DOS, you may see the following, friendlier message:

```
Cannot find operating system.
    Press any key to reboot.
```

If you get one of these messages, don't panic. The computer is telling you that the operating system files needed to carry out the basic start-up procedure cannot be found. To solve this problem, find and insert the DOS system disk into drive A and reboot the computer by pressing Ctrl-Alt-Del. This step should solve the problem. If you start the machine with DOS 5.0, you see the following message and prompt on-screen:

```
MS DOS Version 5.0

C:\
```

Next, depending on your version, DOS displays the date stored in memory as the current date. If the displayed date is incorrect, type the correct date in the format *mm-dd-yy*, such as **07-19-92** for July 19, 1992. If you make a mistake, press the Backspace key to erase the characters and retype the correct date. When the date is correct, press Enter. (With some versions of DOS, you must type **DATE**—upper- or lower-case letters—and press Enter to show or change the date setting.) After you press Enter, the time appears on-screen and you have the option of entering a new time setting, as shown in the following example:

```
C:\ date

Current date is Sat 8-14-1992
Enter new date (mm-dd-yy):
```

```
C:\ time

Current time is 11:45:03.94
Enter new time:
```

Inserting Disks

You saw several instructions to insert the disk into drive A. You now know what (and where) drive A is, but which way does the disk go when you put the disk into the drive? With a 5 1/4-inch disk, follow these steps:

1. Make sure that no disk is in the drive you are using.

2. Make sure that the disk drive door is open. (If the door is closed, the little lever is in a vertical position, blocking the slot in the drive. To open the door, move the lever to the right or up.)

3. Hold the disk so that your thumb and forefinger grasp the labeled edge of the disk. The edge of the disk with two small notches should be facing away from you toward the drive. The write-protect notch should be on the left side of the disk.

4. Slide the disk into the disk drive slot.

5. Close the drive door by moving the lever to the left (or down).

With a 3 1/2-inch disk, follow these steps:

1. Make sure that no disk is in the drive you want to use.

2. Hold the disk so that the label is up and the metal shutter is facing away from you and toward the drive.

3. Slide the disk into the disk drive slot. The disk drops down into the drive (these drives have no door to close).

Most of today's computers are equipped with a built-in battery-backed calendar and clock. The clock usually keeps correct time even when the system is not in use. With some systems, however, the time displayed by the clock may be off by a few minutes. You can accept the value displayed by DOS by pressing Enter, or you can enter a new value in the format *hh:mm:ss*. If you use a version earlier than DOS 5.0, the time is displayed in military format. If you use DOS 5.0, you see traditional 12-hour time, followed by a or p, indicating a.m. or p.m.

What If You Don't Get a Date and Time Prompt?

If the machine displays the C> prompt without first showing the time and date prompts, this may mean that the clock in the system is maintained automatically—without your intervention—or that someone changed how DOS is set up so that these prompts are bypassed. To change the date, you can display what DOS sees as the default by typing **DATE** and pressing Enter. Likewise, you can display and change the time by typing **TIME** and pressing Enter.

Starting Windows

This section takes PC users through the steps necessary to start the Windows operating environment on DOS. Windows, like the Macintosh, is a menu-driven, graphical interface. Files and applications are depicted with icons and a mouse is used to point and click for various tasks. (Most retailers can, at your request, install the Windows program on a newly purchased system.)

After all the components are connected, turn on the computer. You now should see the DOS prompt, C:\. To start Windows, take the following steps:

1. At the C:\ prompt, type **WIN**.

2. Press Enter.

After Windows loads, you see a screen similar to figure 11.2.

Overview of the Windows Operating Environment

The Windows environment provides a menu bar with a variety of choices for file and application manipulation. The following list shows the commands available in Windows:

- Opening files

- Closing files

- Launching utility programs

- Launching application programs

- Getting on-line help

- Using on-line tutorials

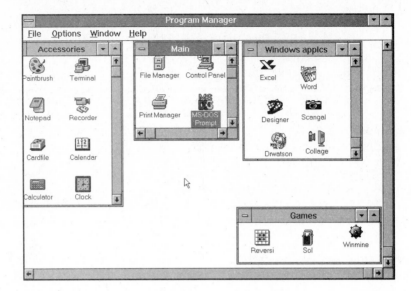

FIG. 11.2

The Program
Manager in
Windows 3.1

Starting Your Mac

This section takes Macintosh users through the steps needed to start the Macintosh. The Macintosh operating system uses the graphical interface known as the Finder, which displays all files, folders, and disks as icons on an on-screen desktop.

Many retailers install the operating system on the Mac when you buy the computer. If the operating system is already on the hard disk of the Mac, you don't need to boot the computer from a system disk. (If the operating system isn't on the hard disk or if you don't have a hard disk, follow the procedures listed in Chapter 10 for installing the System and Finder files.)

After you connect all the components, turn on the computer and follow these steps:

1. Make sure that all cables are attached correctly; thumbscrews are tight; and the power cords are plugged in.

2. If you need to boot from a system disk, insert the disk into the drive.

3. Turn on the system. The On/Off button is located in the back left corner of the computer on the Mac Classic II and SE/30 (see fig. 11.3).

You see a Welcome to the Macintosh screen and then the Finder desktop (see fig. 11.4).

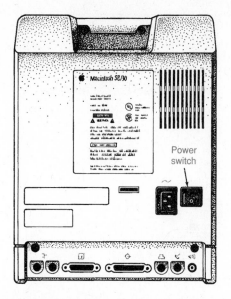

Power switch

FIG. 11.3

The On/Off button on the back of the computer.

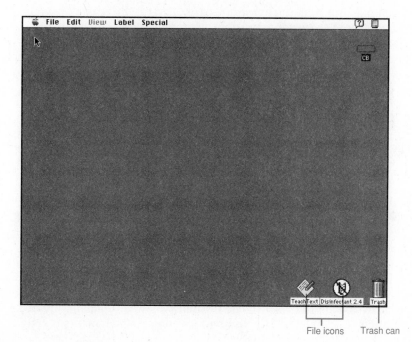

File   Edit   View   Label   Special

TeachText   Disinfectant 2.4   Trash

File icons   Trash can

FIG. 11.4

The Macintosh Finder desktop.

Overview of the System and Finder Desktop

The Macintosh desktop (the Finder) is organized to look and feel like the top of a desk. Disks appear as icons (small pictures that represent files, folders, disks, and programs).

The desktop offers a menu bar with a wide range of choices you can use to perform a variety of operations, as shown in the following list:

- Opening files
- Closing files
- Deleting files
- Creating a folder
- Getting on-line help
- Selecting all files and folders on the desktop

This list gives you just an idea of the variety of functions you can perform from the Finder desktop. Later in this chapter, you learn about performing these procedures in the Macintosh environment.

Working with Disks

The next step, now that you have the computer up and running, is preparing disks to store programs and data. This discussion starts with a section on protecting the original disks.

You see this warning made again and again throughout every computer book you ever own: *Never use original (or master) disks; always work from backup copies.* Why is this warning so important?

The answer to this question is rapidly changing. Although the 5 1/4-inch disk still is one of the disk standards, the 3 1/2-inch disk is rapidly gaining in popularity for two reasons: you can store more information on 3 1/2-inch disks, and because of the hard plastic casing, 3 1/2-inch disks are harder to destroy. The flexibility of the original floppy disks, and the vulnerability of the disk surface to outside elements through the read/write hole, demonstrate clearly the need to work from a backup copy of a master disk or any disk that stores important information you don't want to lose. As you continue through this chapter, remember that the Macintosh uses only 3 1/2-inch floppy disks, and references to 5 1/4-inch disks should be ignored if you work on a Mac.

The following sections introduce you to three basic procedures you need to know when working with disks. First, you learn to write-protect the disks so that you can keep from inadvertently writing data on disks you want preserved. Then you learn about formatting disks (preparing disks to store information). Finally, you learn about copying disks (making backups so that you can keep the original or important disks safe).

Protecting Original Disks

When possible, make copies of original disks and use only the copies for daily (or even occasional) use. (Making copies of entire disks is covered in the next section.)

Before you use an original disk for anything, you should write-protect the disk. *Write-protecting* the disk preserves the data on the disk and keeps any other data from being written to it. This process is reversible. You can "un-write-protect" a disk later. Depending on whether you are using 5 1/4-inch or 3 1/2-inch disks, the procedures for write-protecting the disk are different. To write-protect disks, follow these procedures:

■ For 5 1/4-inch disks, place a write-protect tab over the write-protect notch along the top right edge of the disk (see fig. 11.5). Most packages of disks include a set of write-protect tabs.

■ For 3 1/2-inch disks, slide the write-protect shutter, which protects the disk (see fig. 11.6).

To front of the disk drive

Write-protect notch

FIG. 11.5

Write-protecting a 5 1/4-inch disk.

Formatting Disks

Before you can place information on a disk, you must format the disk. Formatting prepares the disk and writes important information so that the computer knows how and where to place information. Specifically, the computer creates a *file allocation table* (*FAT*) and the Mac creates a

Finder, which each operating system uses as an index to help place and later find and retrieve files from the disk. Formatting divides the disk into tracks and sectors, areas that enable you to store the data when you save files on the disk. (For more information about tracks and sectors, see Chapter 3.)

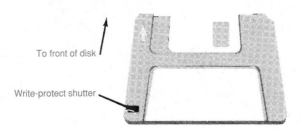

To front of disk

Write-protect shutter

FIG. 11.6

Write-protecting a 3 1/2-inch disk.

Formatting with DOS

To format a disk on a PC with DOS, follow these steps:

1. Start the computer. (Insert the DOS disk into drive A if necessary.)

2. Type **FORMAT A:** (upper- or lowercase letters) and press Enter. DOS prompts you to insert the disk to format into drive A.

If you want to format the disk in drive B, type **FORMAT B:**.

> **CAUTION:** Do *not* type FORMAT C: and press Enter, or DOS formats the hard disk of the system, and you lose all the data on your hard disk!

3. Insert the disk and close the drive door.

4. Press Enter. DOS then formats the disk.

Some versions of DOS, such as DOS 5.0, display the percentage of the disk formatted as the process is being carried out. When the procedure ends, DOS asks whether you want to assign a name (*volume label*) to the disk. This name is optional. (If you want to assign the disk a name, see the sidebar "DOS, DOS Shell, Windows, and Mac Disk-Naming Conventions" in this chapter.) For now, just press Enter.

DOS then asks whether you want to format another disk. The screen looks something like the following:

```
C:\ format a:
Insert new disk for drive A;
and strike ENTER when ready

Format complete

   1213952 bytes total disk space
   1213952 bytes available on disk

Format another (Y/N)?
```

To format another disk, first press Y and then press Enter. To abort the format process, press N and Enter.

Formatting with DOS Shell

To format a disk by using the DOS Shell operating interface, follow these steps:

1. Double-click the DOS Utilities option at the bottom portion of the DOS Shell screen.

2. Double-click the Format option. The Format dialog box appears (see fig. 11.7).

3. Specify the drive where the new (unformatted) disk resides.

4. Click OK.

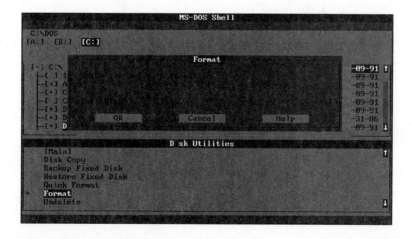

FIG. 11.7

The DOS Shell, showing the Format dialog box.

DOS prompts you to place a floppy disk in the specified drive (if the disk isn't already in the drive) and then displays the percentage of completion.

Formatting with Windows

To format a disk on the PC using the Windows operating environment, you must use the File Manager program. Follow these steps to launch the File Manager and format a disk:

1. Make sure Windows is running by typing **WIN** at the C:\ prompt.

2. From within the Program Manager, double-click on the Main Window icon.

3. Locate and double-click the File Manager program icon.

4. From within the File Manager program, click on the Disk menu.

5. Select the Format Disk option. The Windows Format Disk dialog box appears (see fig 11.8).

6. Specify the drive with the unformatted disk from the Disk In pull-down menu.

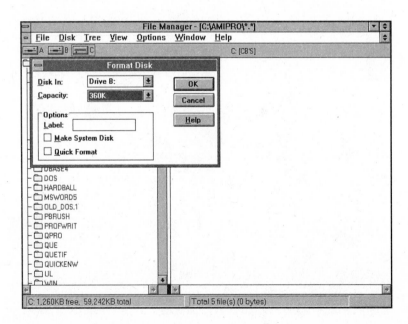

FIG 11.8

The Windows Format Disk dialog box.

7. Specify the density of the disk from the "Capacity" pull-down menu.

8. Click OK.

   Windows displays a dialog box confirming the format.

9. Click Yes. Remember that this process erases all the files on the specified drive. Clicking No aborts the format operation.

After the format process is complete, Windows asks if you want to format another disk. Click Yes to continue; click No to return to the File Manager screen.

Formatting on the Mac

To format a disk on a Macintosh, follow these steps:

1. Start the system.

2. When the Finder desktop appears, insert the disk in the drive.

   The Mac tries to read and then finds that the disk is unreadable. The computer asks whether you want to initialize the disk (see fig. 11.9).

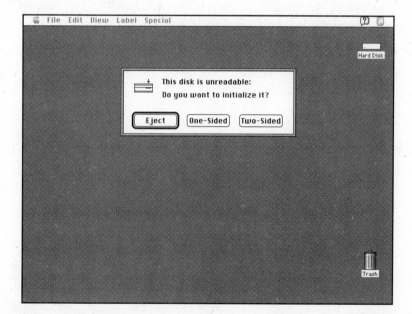

FIG. 11.9

The Mac prompts you to initialize the disk.

3. Select whether the disk you want to format is one- or two-sided. High density disks simply have the option of Initialize or Eject.

   The Macintosh displays a warning that the initialization process will erase all information on the disk.

4. Click the Erase button to continue the format.

5. Enter a name for the disk and click the OK button. The Macintosh then formats the disk. After the format process is complete, the Macintosh verifies the format and creates a directory. The disk appears on the desktop with the name you specified.

DOS, DOS Shell, Windows, and Mac Disk-Naming Conventions

Whether you use a Macintosh or a PC running DOS, DOS Shell, or Windows, you can provide a volume label for the disk after you format the disk. The following list details the conventions used by each operating system:

- Names within Windows, DOS, and DOS Shell can be 1-11 alphanumeric characters. Names cannot contain periods or slashes.

- With the Macintosh, you can use up to 27 characters, although the first character must be a letter. (Names can be any alphanumeric combination except for the colon (:), which is reserved for system files by the Macintosh.)

- Also with Macintosh and DOS, no two files in one folder or directory can have the same name.

Copying Disks

When you make a backup copy of a disk, you make a duplicate of the disk; the programs and data are written on the copy in the same way they were written on the original disk. Whether you use a PC or Macintosh computer, copying a disk is a simple and often-performed procedure.

T I P   Always create a backup copy of each new program you buy as soon as you open the package; then put away the original for safekeeping and use only the copy for day-to-day tasks.

Copying Disks in DOS

When you want to copy an entire disk on a PC running DOS, you use the DISKCOPY command in the following format:

DISKCOPY A: B:

This command tells DOS to copy the entire contents of the disk from the disk in drive A (the *source* disk) to the disk in drive B (the *target* disk). If you use a single-disk system (one floppy disk drive), type the command in this format:

DISKCOPY A: A:

DOS prompts you when to swap the disks in the drive.

Use the following DISKCOPY procedure to make a copy of an entire disk:

1. When using the source disk, place a write-protect tab over the notch (on a 5 1/4-inch disk) or move the write-protect switch to protect (on a 3 1/2-inch disk).

2. Type **DISKCOPY A: B:** and press Enter.

3. Insert the source disk into drive A.

4. Insert the target disk into drive B. (If you do not have a two-drive system, skip this step. DOS prompts you when to swap the source disk with the target disk in drive A.)

5. Press Enter. DOS begins the DISKCOPY procedure. The operating system displays information about the process as data is read from the source disk and places the information on the target disk. (If you use only one disk drive, DOS prompts you to remove the target disk and insert the source disk again.)

6. When DISKCOPY is finished, DOS asks whether you want to copy another disk. If you do, press **Y**; if not, press **N**.

Copying Disks in DOS Shell

To copy an entire PC disk running DOS Shell, follow these steps:

1. Double-click on the DOS Utilities option at the bottom of the DOS Shell screen.

2. Double-click on the DISKCOPY option.

3. Specify the source drive, followed by a space and the target drive.

4. Click OK.

Follow the prompts as they appear asking you to insert first the source disk and then the target disk.

Copying Disks in Windows

To copy a PC disk from within the Windows operating environment, follow these steps:

1. Launch the File Manager program from the Main Window.

2. Click on the Disk menu.

3. Select the Copy Disk option.

   The Windows Copy Disk dialog box appears.

4. Select the Source from the down-pointing arrow list box.

5. Select the Destination from the down-pointing arrow list box.

6. Click OK.

   The Copy Disk dialog box asks you to confirm the disk copy.

7. Click Yes. Remember this process causes the contents of the destination disk to be completely replaced by the contents of the Source disk.

8. To continue the disk copy, follow the prompts on-screen.

Copying Mac Disks

To copy an entire Macintosh disk, using a single disk drive, follow these steps:

1. Make sure that the system is on and the desktop is showing.

2. Insert the source disk you want to copy into the drive.

3. Go to the File menu and select the Eject option.

   The source disk is ejected, however, a dimmed icon of the disk remains on the screen.

4. Insert the destination disk.

5. Drag the dimmed icon of the source disk on top of the destination disk.

6. Release the mouse button. When you do so, the Macintosh displays an alert box, asking if you are sure that you want to completely replace the contents of the (destination) disk with the contents of the (source) disk. Click on Yes to continue the copy.

7. Follow the prompts on-screen that ask you to first insert the source disk and then the destination disk.

Displaying Disk Contents

Now that you have learned how to format, write-protect, and copy disks, you need a way of looking at the files on disks. You may want to display the contents of a disk because you are looking for a particular file and you didn't label the disk. The procedure for viewing the contents of a disk is known as displaying a disk *directory*. If you use a Mac, this procedure may seem obvious. But if you use a PC, you need a method of displaying the contents of disks.

Displaying PC Files

After you copy files to a disk, you need to make sure that the files were copied. Displaying the contents of a disk is known as getting the *directory* of a disk.

To get a directory of a disk, follow these steps:

1. Insert into drive A the disk for which you want to display a directory.

2. Type **DIR A:** and press Enter.

DOS displays a directory of the files you stored in the current directory of the disk. You also see the size of each file (shown in number of bytes) and the date and time the file was created or last updated. The following example shows the kind of display you see:

```
C:\ dir a:

Volume in drive A has no label

Directory of A:\

ITC16    KM     18816  6-19-91      11:34a
ITC18    KM     21120  6-21-91       3:01p
ITC20    KM     15872  6-25-91      10:41a
ITC19    KM     24064  6-24-91       6:23p
ITCFM         4480  3-12-91        10:41a
ITCH05   REV    66560  5-16-91      10:22p
```

```
ITC17     KM      18176  6-20-91        10:51a

 7 File(s)      145024 bytes used

           759808 bytes free

C:\
```

Displaying Files in DOS Shell

To display files in DOS Shell, select the drive icon or directory you want to view from the Directory Tree on the left side of the screen (see fig. 11.10). The right side of the screen then displays the contents of the selected drive or directory.

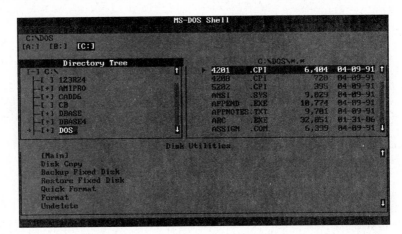

FIG. 11.10

The DOS Shell, showing the Directory Tree and the selected directory's contents.

Displaying Files in Windows

All file manipulation is done in the File Manager program while working in Windows. To launch the File Manager and display files and directories, follow these steps:

1. From the Program Manager, double-click on the Main Window icon.

2. Double-click on the File Manager program icon.

   The left side of the File Manager window displays the current directories.

3. Click on the desired directory or drive icon.

The right side of the File Manager window displays the contents of the specified directory or drive (see fig. 11.11).

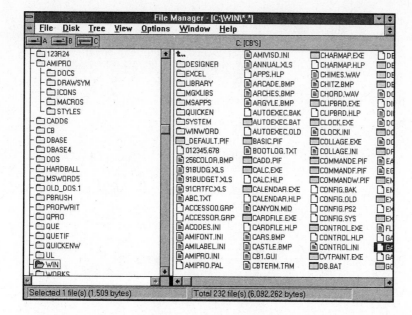

FIG. 11.11

The Windows
File Manager.

Displaying the Contents of Mac Disks

If you are using a Macintosh, you can easily see the files stored on each disk because of the graphical interface. The Finder desktop enables you to show on-screen the contents of disks by double-clicking the disk's icon; the files on the disk appear in a window (see fig. 11.12). Depending on the view you choose for displaying the files, you may see only the file icon and the file name. In another view, such as the by Name view, you see file names (listed in alphabetical order), the kind of file or folder, and the date the file was last modified. This information is important when you need to find the most recently modified file in a particular folder on the disk.

With the Macintosh, you have further control over the way the computer displays files. In the Finder's View menu (located along the upper edge of the screen), you find the following options for displaying the files in the window:

Option	Displays files
by Small Icon	Shows a smaller icon
by Icon	The default display; shows large icon with file names underneath

Option	Displays files
by Name	Displays files alphabetically by file names; also shows kind of file (or folder) and displays the date the file was last modified
by Size	Displays files from largest to smallest
by Kind	Displays files organized according to kind of file
by Label	Displays files organized according to labels you attach
by Date	Displays files organized by date last modified (from present to past)
by Version	Displays files organized by the version of software in which they were created
by Comment	Displays files organized by the comments you attach to the files

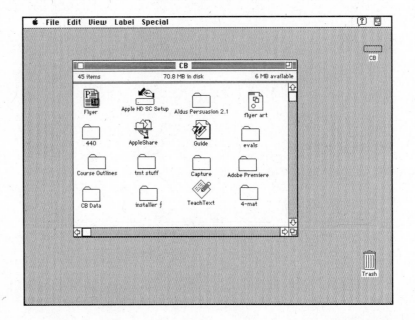

FIG. 11.12

Files viewed by icon on the Finder desktop.

The option currently selected is highlighted with a check mark. To display files by date, follow these steps:

1. Open the View menu.

2. Select the by Date option.

The Finder reorganizes the files in the window according to the date last modified (see fig. 11.13).

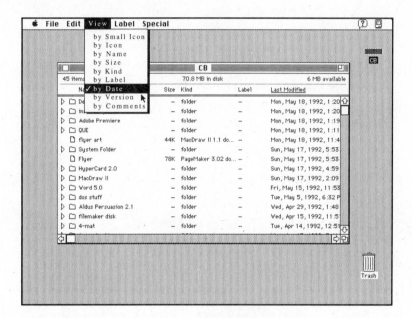

FIG. 11.13

Viewing files by date.

Organizing Your Files

No matter which computer you use, you need a method of organizing files. When you first begin working with computers, tracking files may seem easy, but as your computer experience grows (along with the number of files you use), you need a reliable method of saving files so that you can find and retrieve these files easily.

If your system lacks a hard disk and all the files and the programs with which you work are loaded from disks, the organizational method is different than if you use a hard disk.

Whether you work from floppy disks or use floppy disks only to store backups of work, adhering to the following rules of organization can help keep you on track:

- Store all data files for a particular program on one disk. If you work with Lotus 1-2-3 and Professional Write, store 1-2-3 data files on one disk and Professional Write information on another disk.

- You may prefer to store all files relating to a particular project on one disk. If you are working on a page-layout project for a client, you can store the text and art files for this project on one disk.

- Label the disks clearly so that you don't accidentally overwrite important files with other files.

- Keep the disks in a disk holder to protect your information from dust, dirt, smoke, coffee, and other hazards of office life.

- Become compulsive about backups. Make sure that you save all important files and programs on backup disks.

- Write-protect disks that you want to protect against accidental loss of data.

Working with PC Directories

If you previously worked with an IBM PC or a DOS-based machine, you may be familiar with DOS's method of helping you organize the files on a hard disk.

With DOS, you organize files by placing these files in directories and subdirectories. (A *directory* stores related files, as you specify, and a *subdirectory* is a directory within a directory.) The main directory on the hard disk is known as the *root* directory, the only directory that exists on the hard disk until you issue the command to create more directories. These additional directories are known as *subdirectories*.

Many people think of DOS's organization of directories in terms of a tree structure. Like an upside-down tree, the directories in DOS begin with one main directory (the root directory) and divide into smaller subdirectories (like the branches of a tree). Figure 11.14 shows an illustration of this concept.

Organizing the files in this manner is much like categorizing files. Suppose that you use four major programs for most of your work: First Choice, PC Paintbrush, WordStar, and Q&A. You can organize the hard disk so that you can access each of these programs from the root directory. This organization resembles the structure shown in figure 11.15.

You may want to create further subdirectories. Suppose that you are working with several different kinds of documents in Q&A. You can create more subdirectories to help keep these files organized (see fig. 11.16).

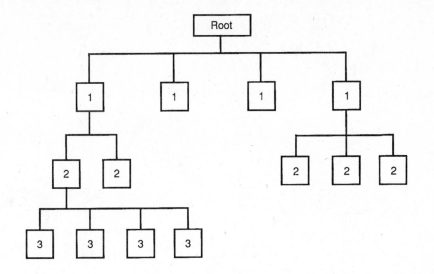

FIG. 11.14

The tree structure of DOS directories.

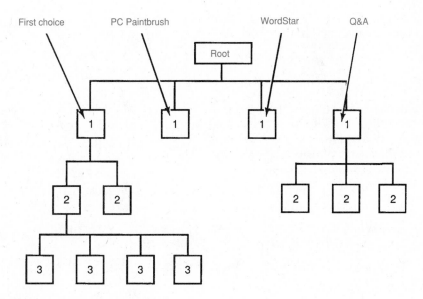

FIG. 11.15

A DOS directory tree structure with subdirectories for major programs.

Creating a Directory

Creating a directory is a relatively simple procedure. When you see the C> prompt, type **MD***directoryname* (substitute the name of the directory you want to create in place of *directoryname*) and press Enter. Directory names can be 1 to 8 alphanumeric characters, followed by a period, with 1 to 3 additional alphanumeric characters. Names cannot contain periods or slashes.

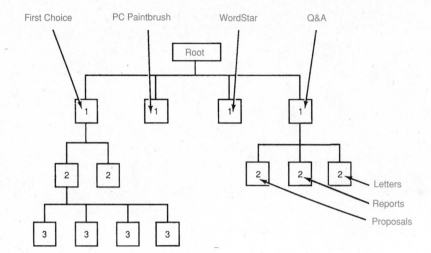

FIG. 11.16

A DOS directory tree structure with subdirectories within subdirectories.

MD stands for the *MAKE DIRECTORY* command, which tells DOS to create, in the current directory, a directory with a name you specify.

Changing Directories

You may want to change to different directories when you want to work with different programs or data files. Suppose that you were writing a letter in WordStar (in the WS4 directory) and now you want to work on a spreadsheet (in the 1-2-3 directory). To change directories, take one of the following actions:

■ To return to the root directory while in any directory, type **CD** and press Enter.

■ To change to a different directory, when the C> prompt appears, type **CD***directoryname* (here, **CD 123**) and press Enter.

■ To go back one directory level, type **CD ..** and press Enter.

T I P   CD stands for *CHANGE DIRECTORY*. This command tells DOS to change to the directory you specify if the directory exists in the current directory.

Removing a Directory

You may want to remove directories you created. Suppose that you just completed a major project. You saved all the necessary files to a disk because you no longer need these files on the hard disk. Before you can remove the directory, you must delete the files (covered in a following section of this chapter). To remove a directory, follow these steps:

1. At the C> prompt, make sure that no files are in the directory by typing **DIR** and pressing Enter. (If you try to delete a directory that contains files, DOS displays an error message, telling you that the directory still contains files.)

2. At the C> prompt, type **RD** *directoryname* and press Enter.

RD stands for *REMOVE DIRECTORY*. This command tells DOS to remove the specified directory.

> Before you can remove a directory, you must delete all program and data files in the directory. (Erasing files is covered in a following section of this chapter.)

T I P

Working with DOS Shell Directories

If you have worked with DOS, you may already be familiar with the DOS method of file organization. (See the previous section, "Working with PC Directories," in this chapter.)

DOS Shell brings a graphical interface to the same organization principles. DOS Shell enables you to organize files in directories and subdirectories. (A *directory* stores related files; a *subdirectory* is a directory within a directory.) Just as in DOS, the main directory is known as the *root* directory, and is the only directory that exists on the hard disk. Additional directories *(subdirectories)* must be created.

Performing the following steps creates subdirectories in DOS Shell:

1. Click the directory icon in which you want to create a subdirectory.

2. Click the File menu.

3. Select the Create Directory option.

4. DOS Shell prompts you for the name of the new directory. Type the name and click OK.

Working with Windows Directories

Windows enables you to create directories with the File Manager program. To create a directory or subdirectory, take the following steps:

1. From the Program Manager, double-click the Main Window icon.

2. Double-click the File Manager program icon.

3. Click the directory icon where you want the subdirectory to be created.

4. Click the File menu.

5. Click the Create Directory option.

6. Windows prompts you for the name of the new directory. Type a name that easily identifies the directory.

7. Click OK.

Working with Mac Folders

The procedure for working with Mac files and folders is less complicated than working with the PC. The Finder enables you to keep everything in order on the desktop through the use of folders. If you previously worked with DOS-based applications, you understand the connection between folders and directories: a DOS directory performs the same function as a Macintosh folder.

You can display the contents of a disk by double-clicking on the disk icon. The contents of the disk then appear in a window on the desktop. Inside the window you see folder and file icons (see fig. 11.17).

When you double-click a file icon, the operating system runs the program. Double-clicking the Word icon in figure 11.18 causes the Finder to load and run the program Microsoft Word. If you double-click a folder icon, the contents of the folder appear in another window on-screen (see fig. 11.18).

You can add a new folder in either of the following ways:

■ Open the File menu and select the New Folder option.

■ Press ⌘-N.

The Finder displays a new folder in the current window. The program assigns the folder the name Empty Folder. You then can rename the folder by clicking once on the name and typing the new name.

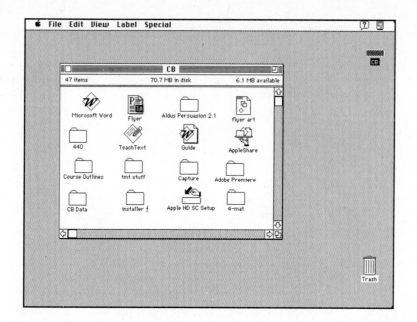

FIG. 11.17

A Macintosh window, displaying folder and file icons.

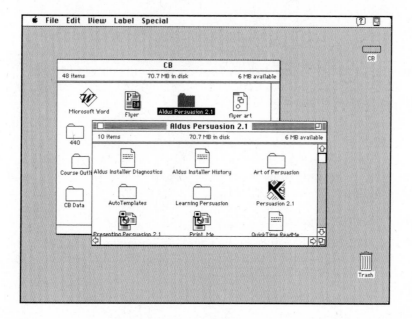

FIG. 11.18

Displaying the contents of a folder.

Working with Files

Now that you know the basics about starting the computer, working with disks, and organizing files, you're ready to learn basic file maintenance techniques. The following sections introduce you to these disk and file maintenance procedures:

■ Copying files

■ Erasing files

■ Renaming files

Copying Files

At some point, you may need to copy a file for backup purposes. A copied file also can be used when you want to produce a similar document but don't want to alter the original file. The steps shown in the following sections explain how to copy a file in DOS, DOS Shell, Windows, and Macintosh.

Copying Files with DOS

You may want to copy a disk of files or a single file on a PC, for example, if you want to give a copy of a spreadsheet to a coworker. To copy a file, take the following steps:

1. Insert the disk from which you want to copy (the source disk) in drive A.

2. Insert the disk to which you want to copy (the target disk) in drive B. (Or you may want to copy the files to drive C.)

3. Type the COPY command in the following format:

    COPY A:*filename* **B:**

This command copies the file you specified (*filename*) from the disk in drive A to the disk in drive B. To copy the file to drive C, enter the following line at the DOS prompt:

    COPY A:*filename* **C:**

You also can use the COPY command to copy the entire contents of the disk. The following line shows the command for this operation:

    COPY A:*.* C:

Copying Files with DOS Shell

You may copy a single file or multiple files within DOS Shell. Follow these steps:

1. Insert the disk from which you want to copy (the source disk) in drive A.

2. Click the name of the file you want to copy.

3. Click the File menu.

4. Select the Copy option.

5. DOS Shell displays a To:/From: dialog box, requesting a destination location for the specified file. Type the drive and directory destination.

6. Click OK.

The copied file appears in the specified destination location.

Copying Files with Windows

To make a copy of a file in Windows, you must be in the File Manager program. Perform the following steps to launch the File Manager and copy a file:

1. From the Program Manager, double-click on the Main Window icon.

2. Double-click on the File Manager program icon.

3. Click the file you want to copy from the files list.

4. Click the File menu.

5. Select the Copy option.

   Windows displays the Copy dialog box.

6. Type the destination directory name and provide a name for the file.

7. Click OK.

The file appears in the specified destination directory.

Copying Mac Files

You may copy a single file or multiple files on the Macintosh. To select more than one file for copying, click on the first file and then press and hold the Shift key while you click on the other files.

To copy a file (or files) on the Macintosh, follow these steps:

1. Place the disk from which you want to copy the file (the source) in the drive.

2. Double-click the disk icon to display the contents of the disk.

3. Click on the file you want to copy.

4. Open the File menu and select the Duplicate option.

The Mac shows the progress of the copy procedure. When the copy is complete, the file's icon appears in the same window next to the original with the name `Copy of <file name>` assigned. Drag the file icon to the desired location.

T I P   If you are selecting more than one file for copy, the files must be contained within the same window.

Erasing Files

Along with computer proficiency comes the problem of disk population. How many files can you store on a disk before the disk is full? You need a method of erasing files you no longer need. This section explains how to erase files.

Erasing Files in DOS

When you want to erase files on a PC, follow these steps:

1. Change to the directory in which the files you want to delete are stored. (Remember that the DOS command for changing directories is CD.)

2. Type the following command:

    DEL *filename*

    (Substitute the name of the file you want to delete for *filename* in the preceding example.)

You also can use the ERASE command to delete a DOS file. Use the same format, but type **ERASE** rather than DEL, as shown in the following syntax:

ERASE *filename*

CAUTION: Be careful when deleting files, especially if you are using a PC and DOS. However, if you are using DOS 5 and you accidentally delete a file, you can use the DOS command **UNDELETE** *filename* to restore the file. (Some quick-unerase utilities, such as the program included with Norton Utilities, can also retrieve some accidentally obliterated files.)

Erasing Files in DOS Shell

When you want to erase files while in the DOS Shell, perform these steps:

1. Click the file name you want to erase from the files list box.

2. From the File menu, select Delete.

    DOS Shell displays a dialog box, confirming the file delete.

3. To delete the file, click OK.

Erasing Files in Windows

The procedure for erasing files in Windows must be done in the File Manager program. To launch the File Manager and erase files, follow these steps:

1. From the Program Manager, double-click the Main Window icon.

2. Double-click the File Manager program icon.

3. Click the name of the file that you want erased.

4. From the File menu, select Delete.

    Windows displays the Delete dialog box so that you can confirm the delete operation.

5. Click OK.

Erasing Mac Files

The procedure for erasing Macintosh files is more entertaining than the PC equivalent. To erase a file on the Mac, follow these steps:

1. Open the folder that stores the file you want to delete.

2. When the mouse cursor is placed on the file you want to delete, press and hold down the mouse button.

3. Drag the file icon out of the window and over to the trash can.

   The trash can icon is highlighted when the file is in the trash (see fig. 11.19).

4. Release the mouse button. The sides of the trash can bulge, indicating that something was thrown away.

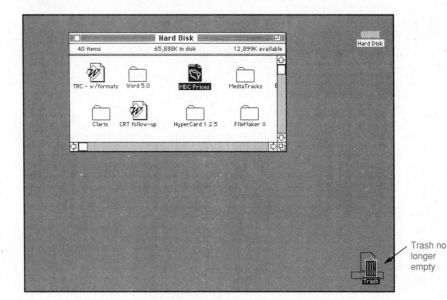

Trash no longer empty

FIG. 11.19

The trash can in use.

T I P

You can retrieve files from the trash can that you accidentally throw away. To show on-screen the contents of the trash can, double-click on the trash can icon. A window appears, showing the item(s) you threw away. To recover a file, select the file from the trash window, open the File menu and select the Put Away option.

Renaming Files

From time to time, you may want to rename files. Suppose that you worked on a report for the department's annual meeting. You revised and revised and now have a final draft. The file's previous name was DRAFT1. Now, you're ready to give the file a final name by renaming the file.

Renaming Files in DOS

To rename a file by using DOS, follow these steps:

1. Go to the directory that stores the file you want to rename.

2. Type the command in the following format:

   REN *oldfilename newfilename*

   Replace *oldfilename* with the name of the file you are renaming and *newfilename* with the new name for the file.

 In DOS, you cannot have two files with the same name in the same directory. Make sure that you use a nonexisting name when you rename files.

Renaming Files in DOS Shell

The DOS Shell interface makes renaming files easier than in DOS. To rename by using DOS Shell, follow these steps:

1. Click on the file you want to rename.

2. Click the File menu.

3. Select the Rename option.

4. A dialog box appears asking you for the new name. Type the new name (1-8 alphanumeric characters).

5. Click OK.

DOS Shell changes the name of the file to the new name you typed.

Renaming Files in Windows

Renaming files, like all other file manipulation in Windows, must be done in the File Manager program. To launch the File Manager and re-name a file, follow these steps:

1. From the Program Manager, double-click the Main Window icon.

2. Double-click the File Manager program icon.

3. Click the file that you want to rename.

4. From the File menu, select the Rename option.

   The Rename dialog box appears.

5. Type the new name in the TO: edit box. (Refer to the sidebar "DOS, DOS Shell, Windows, and Mac Disk-Naming Conventions" in the previous section for information on naming files in Windows.)

6. Click OK.

Renaming Mac Folders and Files

The graphical interface of the Finder makes renaming files and folders easy. To rename a folder, follow these steps:

1. Open the disk that contains the folder you want to rename.

2. Click on the folder name. The folder icon is highlighted and a rectangular border surrounds the name.

3. Type the new name for the folder. Your first keystroke replaces the current name.

4. Press Enter. The Finder then saves the new name for the folder.

To rename a file, open the folder, click on the file name, and follow the same procedure for renaming folders.

Installing and Starting Programs

Whether you use a Mac or PC, the operating system is the launching pad for all applications. This section explains how to load applications from the operating system.

Installing Programs

Depending on the kinds of programs you use, you may run into different installation procedures. Installation is covered as an overview of operating systems in Chapter 10. Installation of various software programs may differ, but the concept is the same, as the following listing explains:

- On a hard disk system, you install (or load) a program on the hard disk and set up the program to work with the computer's particular components (the specific printer type, monitor type, and so on).

- On a floppy disk system, you install a program in the computer's memory each time you start a work session and also set up the program to work with the system. (These settings are then saved on a floppy disk rather than saved on the hard disk.)

Some software programs use elaborate installation routines that automate the procedure so much that all you do is insert the disk into drive A and type a simple command, such as **INSTALL** or **SETUP**. The program's installation routine then leads you through a variety of screens, prompting you when to insert a particular disk and helping you make choices about the kinds of hardware you use.

Other programs offer only a simple copy-to-install procedure; you create a directory on the hard disk (remember MD for MAKE DIRECTORY), copy the files to the directory, and start the program.

To find out what kind of program you have and to find the program's specific installation instructions, consult the documentation packaged with the software. If the documentation is unavailable, check to see whether a file named README.DOC is present on the program disk. Often, software manufacturers include late-breaking news about software releases in this README.DOC file. (To learn whether this file is present on the disks, use the DIR command, or with a Mac, display the contents of the disk by double-clicking on the icon.)

T I P

If you find a README.DOC file on a DOS disk and you want the contents of the file to appear on-screen, type the following command:

TYPE README.DOC ¦ MORE

Press Enter. (If the name of the README file is different, enter this name in place of the README.DOC file name shown here.) The pipe character (¦) and the word **MORE** tell DOS to display the file one screen of the document at a time. When the screen is full, DOS pauses and waits for you to signal that you want to see the next screen by pressing another key.

Be sure that you read all installation instructions carefully before you install a program on the system. When in doubt, find a technical support person or contact a local bulletin board or user group for help.

Starting Programs

This section explains how you start programs on a Macintosh or a PC running DOS, DOS Shell or Windows. (Remember that software programs vary greatly. The procedure is different to some degree for every computer and every program. This section provides only an overview of the steps involved in starting individual programs.)

Starting Programs in DOS

The method you use to start programs on a PC differs slightly, depending on how the programs are installed. For most programs, however, the procedure is similar to the following:

1. Change to the directory where the program files are stored.

2. Type the program start-up command and press Enter. (The command you use to start the program varies from program to program. Usually, the command is a variation of the program name.) The following list shows some commonly used startup commands:

123	1-2-3
HG	Harvard Graphics
Q	Quicken
WORD	Microsoft Word
WS	WordStar
WP	WordPerfect

Starting Programs in DOS Shell

DOS Shell's graphical interface makes launching programs easy. Refer to the following steps to start a PC program from within the DOS Shell operating interface:

1. Locate the program name from the list of directories and files.

2. Double-click the program name. The DOS Shell interface runs the program.

Starting Programs in Windows

Starting programs in Windows is similar to starting programs on the Macintosh. To start a program in Windows, follow these steps:

1. Open the disk on which the program is stored.

2. Locate the program icon.

3. Move the mouse over the program icon and double-click. The program is loaded into the computer's RAM.

Starting Mac Programs

Starting a program on a Macintosh is as simple as pointing and double-clicking. To start a Mac program, take the following steps:

1. Open the disk on which the program is stored.

2. Locate the program icon. (If necessary, open the folder that stores the program.)

3. Move the mouse pointer over the program icon and double-click the mouse button. The Finder loads and runs the program.

Shutting Down the Computer

The final section in this chapter explains how to end a work session.

Shutting Down the PC—DOS

When you are ready to end a work session with the PC, follow these steps:

1. If you are using an application program, make sure that you save the file on which you are working.

2. Return to the operating system level. (If you don't remember how to go to the main DOS, OS/2, or UNIX screen, look in the program's documentation for instructions on how to exit the program.)

3. When the operating system prompt appears, such as C> for DOS on a hard-disk system, you can safely turn off the system. If you use a power surge-protection strip, turn off the surge protector's master switch. Otherwise, turn off the monitor and then the system with the power switches.

Shutting Down a PC—DOS Shell

To end a session on the PC that is running the DOS Shell interface, follow these steps:

1. Exit the application program you are using and return to the DOS Shell.

2. From the File menu, select the Exit option.

3. DOS responds with the C:\ prompt, which indicates you may safely switch off the computer. If you use a power surge-protection strip, turn off the surge protector's master switch; otherwise, turn off the monitor and then the system with the power switches.

Shutting Down a PC—Windows

To shut down a PC after a session in Windows, take the following steps:

1. Exit the application program you are using and return to the Program Manager.

2. Click on the Control Box in the upper left hand corner of the active window.

3. Select the Close option.

   The C:\ prompt appears, and you now can safely turn off the system.

4. If you use a power surge-protection strip, turn off the surge protector's master switch. Otherwise, turn off the monitor and then the system with the power switches.

Shutting Down the Mac

To turn off the Macintosh, follow these steps:

1. If you are using an application program, quit from the program now. The desktop appears.

2. Close all open windows by clicking in the Close Box in the upper-left corner of the window.

3. Point to the Special menu in the menu bar at the top of the screen.

4. Open the menu and select the Shut Down option.

   Some Macintosh models just shut down. At this point, other models may display a Finder message that says you can power down the Macintosh safely. If you choose, you can start another session by clicking on the Restart button in the bottom left corner of the window.

5. Turn off the Macintosh either at the surge protector strip or on the back of the computer.

To close all the windows automatically, hold down the option key on the keyboard and click in the close box of the active window. All open windows will be closed by the Mac.

T I P

Troubleshooting

At the start of a computer session everything usually works. If, however, something goes wrong, the following examples give you a few possible problem areas to check:

Problem: The Macintosh displays a flashing ? (question mark) when the computer is turned on.

> **Solution:** The System files cannot be located. Insert the System Tools disk and reboot the computer. After the computer boots from the floppy, check the hard disk system folder. If the system is missing, you need to reinstall.

Problem: DOS displays the following message:

```
Not Ready reading Drive B
Abort, Retry, Fail?
```

> **Solution:** The disk in drive B is incorrectly placed in the drive or no disk was placed in drive B. Insert a disk into the drive and press R for Retry. If you continue to get the error press A to Abort the process, reinsert the disk, and start over.

Problem: DOS displays the following message:

```
General failure reading Drive B
Abort, Retry, Fail?
```

Solution: The disk in drive B cannot be read. Make sure that the disk is formatted. Press A to Abort.

Problem: The PC's monitor doesn't turn on when you turn on the system.

Solution: The computer may have a separate power source. Make sure that the power cord for the monitor is plugged in. If all is well, check the cable that connects the system unit to the monitor to make sure that this connection is secure.

Problem: You insert a disk that you know is formatted with Macintosh files. However, the Mac displays the message `Can't read disk--Initialize?`

Solution: The disk may be damaged. Try the following before re-initializing the disk (which deletes all information):

■ Slide the metal bar back and forth (it may be stuck).

■ Shake the disk softly (the disk may be stuck to the hard plastic and unable to spin).

■ Use a disk first-aid program (if available).

Problem: The Mac suddenly freezes in a work session. Your mouse and keyboard actions are not recognized.

Solution: Perform a warm reboot by pressing the reboot button on the front of Mac II computers or on the back left side of the Classics and the SE/30 computers.

Problem: You double-click on a Mac file and the system displays the message `The file "filename" could not be opened/printed (the application is busy or missing)`.

Solution: The software isn't loaded on the hard disk. Locate original software and reinstall.

Problem: The System doesn't respond to keyboard actions.

Solution: Tighten the keyboard cable that runs between the system unit and the keyboard.

Problem: You see the message `Non-system disk in drive A`.

Solution: You placed an unformatted disk in drive A. Format the disk and try again.

Problem: The disk whirs and spins but nothing happens.

> **Solution:** The disk may not be properly seated. Remove and reinsert the disk in the drive, make sure that the disk is placed in the drive correctly, and close the drive door.

Chapter Summary

This chapter introduced many of the procedures you encounter in daily computer use. Beginning with a basic discussion about working with disks, this chapter explained elementary procedures for preparing disks; organizing files; copying, erasing, and renaming files; and starting and shutting down a computer. The following chapter starts Part IV, which explores some of the more popular software programs for personal computers.

A Software Review

This Part provides you with an overview of the categories of software available.

The sections that follow each overview briefly introduce you to the software identified; for further reference, books are listed to which you can turn for more information.

Because this software review includes a mix of PC, Amiga, and Macintosh products, icons are used in the margins to highlight the individual software types. Look for the following model-specific icons in this book:

Symbol	For this type of hardware/software
C:>	Any IBM PC or PC-compatible
⊞	Windows applications
🍎	Any member of the Macintosh family
A	Any member of the Amiga line

Spreadsheets

Computers effortlessly perform a task many people find difficult or impossible: computing complex numerical data accurately and quickly. If you give a computer (more specifically, a spreadsheet program) a list of numbers, the computer can add the numbers faster than you can reach for a pencil. You can accurately compute numbers by hand, but if you work with a spreadsheet that contains hundreds of calculations, you make fewer mistakes.

If you aren't a numbers person, a spreadsheet program takes this worry off your shoulders. If you are numbers-oriented, the power of the electronic spreadsheet can help you accomplish a wide range of financial feats in a fraction of the time a conventional accountant's pad-and-pencil method takes. This chapter introduces several popular spreadsheet application programs.

Defining a Spreadsheet

A spreadsheet is an electronic on-screen representation of an accountant's columnar pad. Figure 12.1 shows an example of a typical spreadsheet program. The display is organized in columns and rows, similar to the paper spreadsheet's organization. The number of rows and columns available for the spreadsheet depends on the spreadsheet program you use. The intersection of each row and column is a cell. You enter data and formulas in the spreadsheet cells, in which you can perform myriad numeric operations, such as sorting, calculating, copying, moving, and formatting.

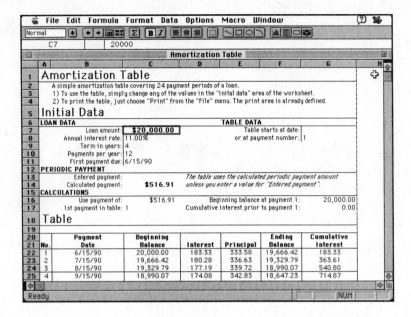

FIG. 12.1

An example of Excel for the Macintosh, a spreadsheet program.

Working with a Spreadsheet Program

Spreadsheet programs can replace every calculation you perform with a calculator. Whether you balance a checkbook once a month or handle the finances of a large company, a spreadsheet makes the work easier and more accurate. Specifically, you can use a spreadsheet for (among others) the following tasks:

- Creating a simple profit-and-loss statement
- Forecasting sales for the first quarter
- Computing bowling scores
- Balancing a checkbook
- Creating a household budget
- Monitoring payroll information
- Performing cost analysis of the production of a new product
- Doing a what-if analysis to see whether you can afford a new car
- Creating a graph showing stock trends
- Performing simple database functions

Besides the basic add-and-subtract features, most spreadsheets also can create and print graphs to visually represent the data in the spreadsheet. Spreadsheets also can print the data from the spreadsheet in a variety of report formats.

From a simple spreadsheet that adds and subtracts a few numbers to a complex spreadsheet that uses sophisticated built-in financial functions to produce results, these programs save time, trouble, and headaches when you work with financial data. These built-in functions, such as Net Present Value, Mean, Average, and so on, are formulas already set up to calculate values based on variables the user enters.

Gaining Benefits from Spreadsheet Programs

Spreadsheets are popular for many numeric applications, including the following tasks:

- Data entry can be automated and checked for errors.

- After you enter data, you can work with and modify the spreadsheet without reentering data or recomputing formulas by hand.

- You can set any cell or group of cells to show the data or values on-screen in a variety of ways (or formats). These formats include dollar signs, commas, percent signs, and so on.

- The column-and-row format is easy to understand and use.

- Formulas perform calculations and are saved with the spreadsheet.

- You can sort, copy, and move columns and rows with formulas intact.

- You can print a spreadsheet in a variety of formats for financial reports.

- Many spreadsheet programs have built-in graph generators, which enable you to create simple graphs from the data in the spreadsheet.

- Most spreadsheet programs enable you to perform *what-if* scenarios to determine the values needed to arrive at a certain result. Some spreadsheets also enable you to start with a result and work backward.

Using Spreadsheet Programs

Spreadsheets range from simple to complex and powerful. Likewise, spreadsheet users range from people who perform only a few calculations to people who need a sophisticated spreadsheet, capable of a wide range of functions. The following people can benefit from using spreadsheet programs:

- Small-business users who want a spreadsheet program to handle bookkeeping tasks

- Managers responsible for financial reports and projections

- Support staff responsible for maintaining departmental cost spreadsheets

- People responsible for accounts payable and accounts receivable

- Home users who want to create a budget

- Teachers who want to track grades

Examining Spreadsheet Programs

Although this section lists stand-alone spreadsheet programs, other popular spreadsheet programs are available in integrated packages. Many users who need only an easy-to-use spreadsheet may enjoy using the spreadsheet portion of the integrated package, PFS: First Choice. (Refer to Chapter 15 for information about integrated software packages.)

Hundreds of spreadsheet programs are available but only a handful of packages attract most of the users. These popular spreadsheets are included in the following sections.

Lotus 1-2-3

Lotus 1-2-3 is the definitive spreadsheet program available for PCs. Worldwide, more than 10 million people work with 1-2-3. Several versions of 1-2-3 are available, depending on the system you use (Macintosh, 386, and 486 machines have different versions available).

Although the spreadsheet feature gets more press than anything else, Lotus 1-2-3 is a combination of three main application programs:

- Spreadsheet
- Database
- Graphics

With 1-2-3, users can create simple or complex spreadsheets, use the spreadsheet as a database, or graph spreadsheet information. Figure 12.2 shows a simple spreadsheet created in Lotus 1-2-3.

A1: [W16]   READY

	A	B	C	D	E	F	G
1		Cash Flow Projections					
2							
3		Jan−93	Feb−93	Mar−93	Apr−93	May−93	Jun−93
4	Sales	$27,000	$13,500	$27,000	$27,000	$40,500	$81,000
5	Cost of Goods	$4,050	$4,050	$8,100	$8,100	$12,150	$24,300
6	Returns	$675	$675	$1,350	$1,350	$2,025	$4,050
7	Net Sales	$22,275	$8,775	$17,550	$17,550	$26,325	$52,650
8							
9	Rent	$1,313	$1,313	$1,875	$1,875	$2,438	$2,438
10	Utilities	$263	$263	$375	$375	$488	$488
11	Telephone	$290	$290	$520	$520	$750	$750
12	Salaries	$9,083	$9,083	$13,500	$13,500	$17,917	$17,917
13	Equipment	$12,000	$12,000	$6,000	$0	$8,000	$0
14	Inventory	$960	$960	$1,680	$0	$0	$4,320
15	Total costs	$23,909	$23,909	$23,950	$16,270	$29,593	$25,913
16	Net Income	($1,634)	($15,134)	($6,400)	$1,280	($3,268)	$26,737
17							
18							
19							
20							

CASHFLOW.WK1

FIG. 12.2

A simple spreadsheet created in 1-2-3.

From the inexperienced to the sophisticated, a wide range of people use 1-2-3. For accountants, financial planners, support staff, business owners, and managers, 1-2-3 is the PC user's spreadsheet application of choice.

1-2-3's many features include an easy-to-use worksheet layout, an understandable control panel, a wide range of functions, easy printing procedures, graph creation and printing techniques, and macro capability. (A *macro* is a series of stored keystrokes, saved in a disk file, that performs repetitive operations.)

The most recent versions of Lotus 1-2-3 are Release 2.4 for DOS, 1-2-3 for Windows, 1-2-3 for Home, and 1-2-3 for Mac include several add-on programs, such as WYSIWYG, a utility that enables you to change the look of the spreadsheet on-screen and in print; Auditor, for analyzing formulas; Viewer, for viewing file contents; and Macro Manager, for organizing macro files.

Que Corporation has a library of books devoted to Lotus 1-2-3. In these books, you can find everything you need to know about installing and working with all current 1-2-3 versions.

Address: Lotus Development Corp.
                 55 Cambridge Parkway
                 Cambridge, MA 02142

Price: $150 - $400, depending on the version

For Further Reference:

1-2-3 Release 2.2 QueCards, Que Development Group

1-2-3 for DOS Release 3.1+ Quick Reference, Que Development Group

1-2-3 for DOS Release 3.1+ QuickStart, Que Development Group

1-2-3 for Windows Quick Reference, Rosemary Colonna, published by Que Corporation

1-2-3 for Windows QuickStart, Greg Harvey, published by Que Corporation

1-2-3 Power Macros, Que Development Group

1-2-3 Release 2.4 Quick Reference, Joyce Nielsen, published by Que Corporation

1-2-3 Release 2.4 QuickStart, Rick Winter, published by Que Corporation

Easy 1-2-3, 2nd Edition, Shelley O'Hara, published by Que Corporation

Look Your Best with 1-2-3, David Ewing and Robert Perry, published by Que Corporation

Using 1-2-3 Release 2.4, Special Edition, Que Development Group

Using 1-2-3 for DOS Release 3.1+, Special Edition, Que Development Group

Using 1-2-3 for the Mac, Special Edition, Mark K. Bilbo and Christopher Van Buren, published by Que Corporation

Using 1-2-3 for Windows, Que Development Group

Using 1-2-3/G, Que Development Group

Quattro Pro

Quattro Pro is a professional yet easy-to-use spreadsheet fully compatible with Lotus 1-2-3. An electronic replacement for traditional

accounting tools, Quattro Pro enables you to easily create files and save spreadsheets in a variety of formats compatible with other applications. Figure 12.3 shows a Quattro Pro screen.

MouseStrap Sales Forecast

		Qtr1	Qtr2	Qtr3	Qtr4	Total
Sales						
	Response factor	0.8	1.1	0.9	0.7	
	Units sold	3230	4442	3634	2827	14,133
unit price	Sales revenue	$41,834	$57,521	$47,063	$36,604	$183,022
12.95	COGS	$26,489	$36,423	$29,800	$23,178	$115,890
	Gross margin	$15,344	$21,099	$17,262	$13,426	$67,132
Expenses						
	Commissions	$2,510	$3,451	$2,824	$2,196	$10,981
unit cost	Advertising	$4,000	$4,000	$4,000	$4,000	$16,000
8.20	Overhead	$5,020	$6,903	$5,648	$4,393	$21,963
	Total expenses	$11,530	$14,354	$12,471	$10,589	$48,944
	Profit	$3,814	$6,745	$4,791	$2,838	**$18,188**
	Margin	9.1%	11.7%	10.2%	7.8%	9.9%
Constraints						
	Advertising Budget	?	?	?	?	$16,000
	Production per qtr	5000	5000	5000	5000	20000

FIG. 12.3

An example of a Quattro Pro for DOS screen.

Quattro Pro offers all the standard spreadsheet features and includes easy-to-use printing and graphing techniques. You also can perform data management functions, create statistical applications, work with macros, and create your own menus.

Address: Borland International
800 Green Hills Road
Scotts Valley, CA 95067-0001

Price: $449

For Further Reference:

Easy Quattro Pro 4, Revised Edition, Shelley O'Hara, published by Que Corporation

Easy Quattro Pro for Windows, Shelley O'Hara, published by Que Corporation

Quattro Pro for Windows Quick Reference, Linda Flanders, published by Que Corporation

Quattro Pro for Windows QuickStart, published by Que Corporation

Quattro Pro 4 Quick Reference, Trudi Riesner, published by Que Corporation

Quattro Pro 4 QuickStart, Don Roche, Jr, published by Que Corporation

Using Quattro Pro for Windows, Special Edition, Brian Underdahl, published by Que Corporation

Using Quattro Pro 4, Special Edition, Patrick J. Burns, published by Que Corporation

Microsoft Excel

Microsoft Excel, the leading spreadsheet program in terms of popularity, was originally available only for the Macintosh. In keeping with Microsoft's make-it-easy-for-the-user philosophy, the program now is available for the PC.

Microsoft Excel for the PC works with Microsoft Windows (an environment that enables you to run similar programs in individual windows). Because this program was originally created in a Macintosh environment, Excel offers users an easy-to-understand on-screen menu system and gives PC users the capability of using the mouse. Many operations that require typing in other applications can be handled with the mouse in Microsoft Excel. You also have options for producing a variety of reports in different fonts, a feature usually limited—or unavailable—in PC spreadsheets.

The latest Mac and Windows version 4.0 combine an extremely fast spreadsheet with database and presentation features. Along with a standard toolbar are customizable toolbars that can be moved anywhere on the screen. New analytical tools come with the program that allow you to generate frequency tables, histograms, ranking in percentages tables as well as financial and engineering functions. This version also enables you to link together spreadsheets by pointing and clicking. Figure 12.4 shows an example of an Excel screen on the Macintosh.

Address: Microsoft Corporation
16011 NE 36th Way
Redmond, WA 98073-9717

Price: $335 (PC-DOS)
$350 (PC-Windows)
$350 (Mac)

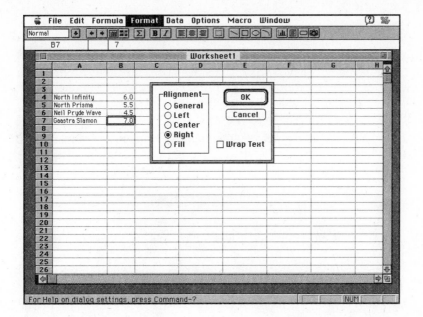

FIG. 12.4

An Excel screen
on the
Macintosh.

For Further Reference:

Easy Excel, Shelley O'Hara, published by Que Corporation

Excel 4 for Windows QuickStart, Sharel McVey, published by Que Corporation

Excel 4 for Windows Quick Reference, Don Roche, Jr, published by Que Corporation

Look Your Best with Excel 4 for Windows, Rick Winter and Patty Winter, published by Que Corporation

Using Excel 4 for Windows, Special Edition, Ron Person, published by Que Corporation

Using Excel 4 for the Mac, Special Edition, Christopher Van Buren, published by Que Corporation

Excel 4 for the Mac Quick Reference, Rita Lewis, published by Que Corporation

Quicken

Quicken is not a spreadsheet program, but rather a bookkeeping and financial package for personal or business use. Quicken can help you track your finances at home or on the corporate level. Some of Quicken's features include balance and budget sheets, a register, Billminder, and check writing.

Quicken is designed for people who need to manage personal or business finances. Many people who use Quicken are bookkeepers or accountants. Figure 12.5 shows an example of a Quicken screen.

Date	Num	Description / Memo / Category	Payment	C	Deposit	Balance
6/29 1992		Opening Balance [CB]		x	132,589 00	132,589 00
6/29 1992	103	Magic Jones	525 00			132,064 00
6/29 1992	104	Southern California Gas Co.	35 56			132,028 44
6/29 1992		Payroll Deposit			1,575 28	133,603 72
6/29 1992	105	AT&T	76 82			133,526 90
6/29 1992	106	Withdrawal	300 00			133,226 90
6/29 1992	107	California Water Service	45 62			133,181 28
6/29 1992	108	Nordstrom	450 00			132,731 28
6/30 1992						

Quicken for Windows - QDATA

File   Edit   Activities   Lists   Reports   Window   Help

CB

Save   Restore   Open Splits

Ending Balance: $ 132,731.28

FIG. 12.5

A Quicken screen.

With Quicken, you can generate income and cash flow statements and keep track of monthly inventory in a business. This program maintains a check register and deducts payments and adds deposits to a checking account. Quicken reduces the possibility of overdrawing an account because of miscalculations and enables the computer to generate checks. Quicken also tracks tax deductions and compares budget information. you can use the program to perform basic bookkeeping functions; manage assets and liabilities; and keep track of investments, receivables, credit lines, mortgages, and business payables. You can use Quicken as an accounting package, and you can compare and track budgets.

Address: Intuit Corporation
               155 Linfield Avenue
               Menlo Park, CA 94026

Price: $69.95

For Further Reference:

Easy Quicken, Shelley O'Hara, published by Que Corporation

Quicken 5 Quick Reference, Linda Flanders, published by Que Corporation

Quicken for Windows Quick Reference, Elaine J. Marmel, published by Que Corporation

Using Quicken 5, Stephen Nelson, published by Que Corporation

Using Quicken for Windows, Stephen Nelson, published by Que Corporation

Using Quicken 3 for the Mac, Stephen Nelson, published by Que Corporation

Chapter Summary

In this chapter you learned about spreadsheets, including an overview of some of the most popular spreadsheet programs. In the following chapter, you learn about word processing programs.

Word Processing

The introduction of word processing brought a great sigh of relief from typists all over the world. No more correction fluid. No more crumpled pieces of paper littering the floor around the wastepaper basket. No more carbon paper or erasable bond.

If you ever have typed and retyped until you produced a perfect document, you can appreciate the time and trouble word processing saves. All the text you type is saved in a file so that you can make changes without retyping a word. Just fix the error, print the document, and you're done.

Defining Word Processing

Word processing is an application program specifically designed to make creating, editing, formatting, and printing text easier. Word processing is the electronic replacement for the typewriter in your office. All the work you do on a typewriter or with pen and paper, you also can do with a word processor. In fact, with a word processor you actually can do some limited typesetting to produce printouts that rival professionally typeset text in terms of print quality and layout.

The following list provides some examples of word processing program capabilities:

- Write routine correspondence and save the file to reuse or modify as necessary
- Create business reports
- Write articles or books
- Generate lists
- Type term papers
- Compose any kind of business document
- Create a letterhead for your company
- Perform mail-merge functions

Gaining the Benefits of Word Processing

Besides replacing the standard tools of the trade, word processing brings you the following benefits:

- Reusable data; you first type and then store the document on disk to be used again
- Easy text entry and editing features
- On-screen formatting capabilities, such as bold text, underlining, and highlighting
- Usually, a spelling checker, thesaurus, and grammar checker
- A variety of print options that enable you to customize the program for your printer
- The capability of changing the font and style of text

Working with Word Processing

Anyone who works with words on a regular basis can benefit from a word processing program. If you ever had to retype a long document because of one misspelling, you understand the drastic savings in time and effort a word processing program can offer. Specifically, word processors are used by the following people:

- Writers who want a method of retaining text without retyping

- Editors who receive writers' word processing files and edit the entered text

- Managers who produce reports

- Support staff who create correspondence

- Home users who need a method of printing information from files

Identifying Different Word Processors

With word processing software, you have the easy and the not-so-easy and the powerful and the not-so-powerful. How do you select the best program? To help you make a decision, this section explains some differences in word processing software.

The qualities you need in a word processor depend on your goals. Are you using the word processor to create a couple of letters a month? Are you performing 80 percent of your work with the program, and creating documents, reports, and proposals? Are the documents you create used by your staff for in-house training programs, or do your publications go out to clients and prospective customers? (If so, the items you produce must be the highest quality possible.)

Word processors differ in the following areas:

Ease of use. An easy-to-use word processor attracts many people. If you use the program sparingly, you don't want to spend 40 hours learning how to use the program's features. Often, ease of use and range of features come into conflict, because programs with the most special features are the most complex to learn.

Quality of output. Quality printing is a consideration for many potential users. How professional do you want your letters to look? If you use a PostScript printer, special fonts, and high-resolution graphics to print correspondence, buy a word processor that enables you to create this kind of high-level output. If, however, you print only one report four times a year, a word processor that just puts words on paper may suffice.

Range of features. The number and complexity of features in most word processors is enormous. You can buy programs from the simplest words-on-paper program to a complex document-building program that does everything from entering text and creating elaborate tables of contents, indexes, and custom dictionaries to documents that can support sound and video. The higher the number of features, the higher the price. Between the simple and complex, however, are many intermediate programs with intermediate price tags.

Examining Word Processing Programs

This section introduces several popular word processing programs. This chapter also references word processors included in integrated packages. These programs are listed here and in the integrated packages chapter because many users purchase these packages only for the word processing application.

 ## Ami Pro

Ami Pro, created by the makers of Lotus 1-2-3, can perform with ease almost any word processing task. Besides standard text entry, this program can help you create charts, tables, equations, and graphics from the same window. Ami Pro's capability of producing collapsible outlines and long compound documents is complemented by the richest macro language of any Windows word processor (see fig 13.1).

One of the most helpful features of Ami Pro is the capability of displaying SmartIcons that give you one-click access to major functions. You can create the SmartIcons with the graphic of your choice and then can be moved anywhere on the screen. Ami Pro also provides easy style sheet manipulation, allowing you to insert with ease previously created style sheets into the current document. Ami Pro also includes a background printing feature that reduces the time you spend waiting for your document to print.

Address: Lotus Development Corp.
5600 Glenridge Dr.
Atlanta, GA 30342

Price: $495

For Further Reference:

Easy Ami Pro, Shelley O'Hara, published by Que Corporation

Look Your Best with Ami Pro, Que Development Group

Using Ami Pro, James Meade, published by Que Corporation

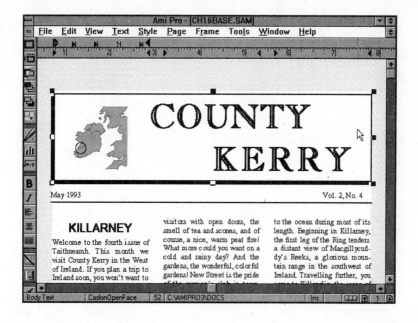

FIG. 13.1

The Ami Pro screen, showing text and graphics.

First Choice (Word Processor)

First Choice word processor is part of the PFS: First Choice integrated package. This word processor is popular in business applications because of its easy-to-use features and the integration between word processing and the other applications (spreadsheet, database, graphics, and communications).

The menu system in First Choice enables you to move in and out of the word processor without learning a long list of new commands. On-screen formatting, support for a variety of printers, and easy print routines enable you to become productive right away. The easy integration of applications gives you access to information from the database, spreadsheet, or graphics applications, that you can use in word processing documents. Figure 13.2 shows an example of the First Choice word processor screen.

Address: Spinnaker Software Corporation
                201 Broadway
                Cambridge, MA 02139

Price: $99

For Further Reference:

Using PFS: First Choice, Katherine Murray, published by Que Corporation

WordPerfect

WordPerfect is the most popular word processing program on the market today. A full-featured word processor with an extensive range of features, WordPerfect appeals to users who demand many sophisticated tasks from their word processor. The following list details some of WordPerfect's features:

- Easy text entry

- Powerful thesaurus and spell-checking routines

- Support for a wide range of fonts and printers

- The capability of creating custom dictionaries

- On-screen formatting

- Preview capabilities (you see on-screen how a document looks in print)

- The capability of importing and printing graphics

- Column capabilities that enable you to create documents in multiple column format

Figure 13.2 shows a sample document in WordPerfect 5.1 on an IBM PC.

```
Memo

To: All employees using WordPerfect

From: Ms. Rose

Re: Using the Block command to save time!

You can save time using the block command! With this command, you
highlight the area of text you want to change, move, copy, delete,
save, or print. You can use some features, like text enhancements,
while you type. But often it's easiest to type your whole document,
then go back through it and edit the text with the help of the Block
command.

Using the Block command is easy. Position the cursor at the beginning
of the block of text you want to highlight, and press Block (Alt-F4).
Then move the cursor to the end of the text. That's it!

Blocked text appears highlighted on your screen. In a sense, blocked
text is text that's identified as being "ready" for a second
operation.

Block on                                    Doc 1 Pg 1 Ln 3.12" Pos 1
```

FIG. 13.2

A WordPerfect
5.1 document.

Among its more sophisticated features, WordPerfect also offers a powerful macro language and macro editor. A *macro* is a small program assigned to one key combination. When you press the assigned key combination, the program carries out the macro, performing the operation you assigned to the keys. Suppose that you always end letters the same way. You can assign the closing lines to a key and then, when you reach this point in writing your correspondence, you press the macro key combination. WordPerfect inserts the lines.

WordPerfect also has a master document feature for assembling one large document from a series of subdocuments, and a tutorial to help the inexperienced user. You also can use WordPerfect to program, plan, and draft writing projects.

WordPerfect is popular in corporations and among programmers, college students, attorneys, consultants, professors, trainers, desktop publishers, and accountants.

Address: WordPerfect Corp.
1555 N. Technology Way
Orem, UT 84057

Price: $495

For Further Reference:

Easy WordPerfect, Shelley O'Hara, published by Que Corporation

Easy WordPerfect for Windows, Shelley O'Hara, published by Que Corporation

Look Your Best with WordPerfect 5.1, George Beinhorn, published by Que Corporation

Look Your Best with WordPerfect for Windows, George Beinhorn, published by Que Corporation

Using WordPerfect 2.1 for the Mac, Dave Reiser and Holly J. Morris, published by Que Corporation

Using WordPerfect 5, 3rd Edition, Charles Stewart III, et al., published by Que Corporation

Using WordPerfect 5.1, Special Edition, Que Development Group

Using WordPerfect for Windows, Special Edition, Que Development Group

WordPerfect 2.1 Quick Reference for the Mac, Trudi Reisner, published by Que Corporation

WordPerfect 5.1 Quick Reference, Que Development Group

WordPerfect 5.1 Office Solutions, Ralph Blodgett, published by Que Corporation

WordPerfect 5.1 QueCards, Que Development Group

WordPerfect 5.1 QuickStart, Que Development Group

WordPerfect 5.1 Tips, Tricks, and Traps, 3rd Edition, Charles Stewart III, Daniel Rosenbaum, and Joel Shore, published by Que Corporation

WordPerfect Quick Reference (Version 5), Que Development Group

WordPerfect for Windows Power Macros, Ken Chestek, published by Que Corporation

WordPerfect for Windows Quick Reference, Que Development Group

WordPerfect for Windows QuickStart, Que Development Group

Microsoft Word

Microsoft Word is a state-of-the-art word processing program with a wide range of powerful and easy-to-use features. Word is popular among both Mac (Version 5.0) and PC (Version 5.5 for DOS and 2.0 for Windows) users, and a large following of dedicated users prefer Word to any other word processor on the market.

With Microsoft Word, you can integrate text with graphics and revise information within a document. Microsoft Word has special features, such as print preview, side-by-side columns, built-in outlining, and automatic pagination. Word also enables you to open and switch between multiple documents quickly and easily. Word is designed to help you print reports, memos, and documents and performs all the basic word processing functions, such as deleting, italicizing, and highlighting. Word has a Table command to help you produce great-looking tables, and Word enables you to mix fonts and font sizes easily. Microsoft Word also features a spelling checker, thesaurus, grammar checker, and an Undo command. Finally, elaborate and well-written Word tutorials can take you through Word's features. Figure 13.3 shows a screen from Microsoft Word 5.0 on the Macintosh.

Many users prefer Word because of its compatibility with other programs. If your office uses both PCs and Macs, you have an advantage using a word processor available for both systems, and you can share data between systems. Many people also use Word because of the program's compatibility with PageMaker, a desktop publishing program. You can set up stylesheets in Word that you can bring directly into PageMaker, to make page layout as simple as flowing the text onto the pages.

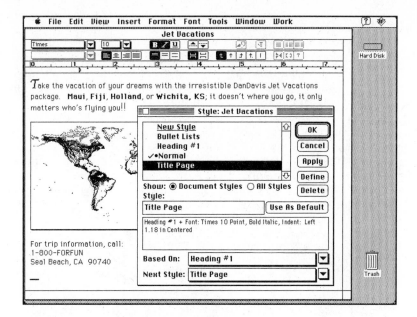

FIG. 13.3

A screen from Microsoft Word 5.0 on the Macintosh.

Address: Microsoft Corporation
                  16011 NE 36th Way
                  Redmond, WA 98073-9717

Price: $395

For Further Reference:

Easy Word for Windows, Shelley O'Hara, published by Que Corporation

Look Your Best with Word for Windows, Susan Plumley, published by Que Corporation

Using Microsoft Word 5.5: IBM Version, 2nd Edition, Brian Pfaffenberger, published by Que Corporation

Using Word for Windows 2, Special Edition, Ron Person and Karen Rose, published by Que Corporation

Using Word 5 for the Mac, Special Edition, Bryan Pfaffenberger, published by Que Corporation

Microsoft Word 5 for the Mac Quick Reference, Que Development Group

Word for Windows 2 Quick Reference, Trudi Reisner, published by Que Corporation

Word for Windows 2 QuickStart, Elaine J. Marmel, published by Que Corporation

Microsoft Word Quick Reference, Que Development Group

WordStar

WordStar has long been a favorite program of word processing enthusiasts. One of the original word processors, WordStar has been around for nearly a decade and has a dedicated group of users. Early versions of WordStar took criticism for the high number of Control-key combinations and menu sequences required to carry out some operations. Experience, however, proves the combinations are easy to use and to recall, and users are given the option of displaying the menu on-screen or removing the menu altogether. (You actually have three menu levels from which to choose: full menu, partial menu, or no menu.) WordStar also has an elaborate help system. Figure 13.4 shows a WordStar document screen.

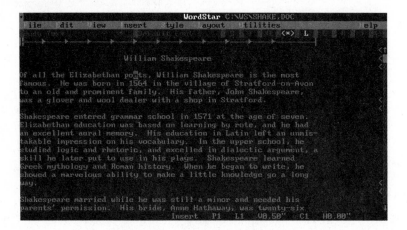

FIG. 13.4

A WordStar document screen.

The current version, WordStar 7.0, offers page preview capabilities with tiling (to show up to 15 minipage icons for preview), full font capability, enhanced printer support, and a full-featured spelling checker and thesaurus. Although WordStar is equal in power to WordPerfect and Microsoft Word, no version of WordStar is yet available for the Macintosh.

Address: WordStar International
               201 Alameda del Prado
               Novato, CA 94949

Price: $495 (Windows or DOS)

For Further Reference:

Using WordStar 7.0, Katherine Murray, published by Que Corporation

Professional Write

Professional Write is a word processing program designed for people who have no time to learn a complicated software program. This program can help you create documents, memos, reports, letters, and other business-related paperwork.

Professional Write is designed for many different kinds of people. In business, Professional Write is used for basic word processing tasks, such as writing correspondence and publishing reports. Professional Write also is helpful for business managers who must produce printed documents fast or for support people who may require on-line help and pull-down menus. This program can assist all who need a powerful, easy to learn and use word processor. Figure 13.5 shows an example of a Professional Write screen.

```
 F1-Help  F2-File/Print  F3-Edit  F4-Format  F5-Spell/Grammar  F6-Addresses
    program (again, at no additional cost) also was performed,
    which will control weed growth between the houses and 300
    feet beyond the property lines of the homes.

    Because the Andrews Co. helped the Association save a total
    of $3,976, the board hereby recommends that we place this
    firm on retainer for future tasks of this nature. To signify
    your acceptance or rejection of this recommendation, please
    place a mark in the appropriate box below and then return
    your answer to the Board:


    Should we retain Andrews Co.?


      ┌──────┐        ┌──────┐         ┌──────┐
      │      │        │      │         │      │
      └──────┘        └──────┘         └──────┘
        YES              NO             NO OPINION

    Thank you for taking the time to respond to this poll of the
    Association members.
 ┙┙┙┙┙┙┙┙╻┙┙┙┙┙┙┙┙╻┙┙┙┙┙┙┙┙╻┙┙┙┙┙┙┙┙╻┙┙┙┙┙┙┙┙╻┙┙┙┙┙┙┙┙╻┙┙┙┙┙┙┙┙
         [    ]T    2       3       4       5       6       7
TEXT.DOC     Inserting                        4%          Line 16
Esc-Main Menu
```

FIG. 13.5

A Professional Write for DOS screen.

With Professional Write, you can produce impressive reports, merge address files with documents, and import spreadsheets and graphs. Professional Write also has a spelling checker and a thesaurus. The current version, 2.2, includes a page layout mode that you can zoom to four levels, an icon bar you can customize for one-click access to major functions (Windows), and a grammar-checking utility. With this program, you can edit and enhance text, preview full pages before printing, display a help menu at all times, and import graphs. Finally, Professional Write has a context-sensitive help menu and macro capability that enables you to record frequently used keystrokes and menu selections.

Address: Software Publishing Corporation
1901 Landings Drive
Mountain View, CA 94039-7210

Price: $249

For Further Reference:

Using Professional Write, Katherine Murray, published by Que Corporation

Using Professional Write PLUS for Windows, George Beinhorn, published by Que Corporation

FullWrite Professional

FullWrite Professional, from Ashton-Tate, is a full-featured word processor available for the Macintosh. The most recent release, 1.5, includes page layout features that enable you to create columns and control the look of your document. Besides all the major features found in other word processors, FullWrite offers the following features:

- True WYSIWYG (what-you-see-is-what-you-get) capability
- Walk-down menus that enable you to bypass menu selections
- Capability of merge printing information from a database
- A variety of printing options
- Drawing
- Spelling checker
- Printing a background picture

Address: Borland International, Inc.
1800 Green Hills Road
Scotts Valley, CA 95067-0001

Price: $249

MacWrite Pro

MacWrite, popular with Macintosh users because of its ease of use and simple command structure, is being revised and upgraded and is scheduled to be released in the fall of 1992. MacWrite Pro, although still easy to use, includes significant upgrades in terms of power and flexibility. Besides standard word processing functions, such as text insert, spell checking, and style sheets, MacWrite Pro provides desktop publishing features that enable you to insert tables, charts, graphics, and sound. MacWrite Pro also has full System 7 functionality, supporting Publish and Subscribe, Balloon help, and TrueType fonts.

Address: Claris
                 5201 Patrick Henry Drive
                 Box 58168
                 Santa Clara, CA 95052-8168

Price: $249

ProWrite

ProWrite, a word processing program from New Horizons, gives full writing and editing capabilities to the Amiga. ProWrite includes a 100,000-word spelling checker; a 300,000-word thesaurus; the capability of wrapping text around graphics; support for IFF and HAM files; numerous fonts, styles, and sizes; and defaults that you can modify for all program settings.

Address: New Horizons
                 206 Wild Basic Road, Suite 109
                 Austin, TX 78746

Price: $99

Chapter Summary

In this chapter, you learned about word processing programs and explored some of the popular programs available for the PC, Macintosh, and Amiga. The following chapter covers popular database programs.

Data Management

Y ou are a data manager. When you make an entry in your check register, when you make a grocery list, when you add a new name to a Rolodex, you manage data. Depending on how much data you manage, you may benefit from using a database program on your new computer.

Defining Data Management

Data management software (*database* programs) gives you a way of entering and working with data on a computer, whether the data includes updating a client list or keeping a household inventory.

Different data management programs offer different capabilities. Although all database programs help you organize and access data, the features found in each program varies widely. You may need a simple database program that enables you to enter client names and addresses and print mailing labels. A low-end database program may meet this need. High-end database programs offer an extensive range of sorting, searching, and programming features that enable you to build intricate data management systems as far-reaching as your needs warrant.

Gaining the Benefits of Data Management

Whether you need a simple program or an elaborate system that enables you to design a complex database, you gain many benefits by using a database program to organize data. Consider the following benefits:

- *You can reuse data.* After you enter data into a database, you can access data easily. You can sort, search, and arrange the data; create reports; print labels; and perform other functions, all without reentering the information.

- *You can arrange data easily by using a database program's sort feature.* All database programs can sort the items in a database. You can sort a client's records alphabetically by last name, or perhaps you want to arrange all inventory items by the date of purchase.

- *You can quickly find the data you need by using a program's search capabilities.* Suppose that you cannot recall the name of a company, but you can remember the last name of the contact person. Enter the name of the person in the correct field on the data-entry form, press a key, and the database displays the correct record. (The keys and procedure for finding specific records vary from program to program.)

- *Printing features enable you to generate mailing labels and reports.* All databases provide some kind of print routine—whether you need to print complex reports, produce simple column-style printouts, or perform a variety of customized operations, such as hiding certain fields, calculating columns, or adding headers and footers.

Working with Data Management Programs

Database programs are used by a wide variety of people, from support people responsible for printing mailing labels to high-level managers who need to track personnel information. Specifically, database programs are used by (among others) the following people:

- Managers who need to record and work with data about products, people, and places

- Small-business owners who need to maintain a client list

- Buyers who need to create and maintain a supplier list

- Salespeople who keep in contact with specific customers

- Home users who want to organize household inventory

- Support staff who update name and address information

- Marketing people who create and send out mass mailings

- Business-information people who manage accounting, inventory, and job cost

Organizing the Database

The database is built on a simple concept: you need a method of organizing data so that you can retrieve the information later. A Rolodex, a telephone book, a shoe box of receipts, and a three-ring binder are examples of this concept. The benefits of the electronic database far outweigh the time spent learning to use the program. You save time not only in entering and maintaining the data but also in searching for and printing data from the records.

With all database programs, you enter data into a data-entry form (like filling out a paper form with a pen or typewriter). Figure 14.1 shows a data-entry form from a popular database program.

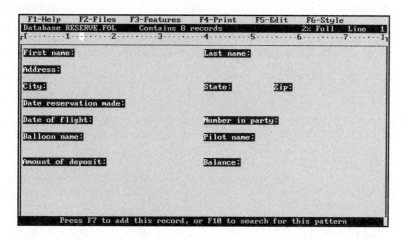

FIG. 14.1

A data-entry form.

Each data-entry form, or *record*, stores information about one particular subject—here, one client in a database. On a form, you enter the data in individual *fields* (the field names are Last Name, First Name, and so on.)

After you enter data in a database program, you can display, sort, such as alphabetically, search for specific records, or print the data. Some databases also enable you to search and copy subsets of data, such as creating a database of records with a 317 area code. Figure 14.2 shows several records displayed in table view.

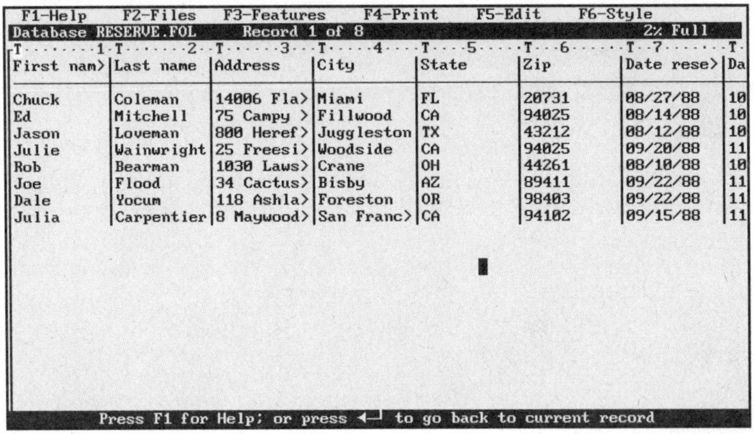

```
 F1-Help    F2-Files   F3-Features    F4-Print    F5-Edit    F6-Style
 Database RESERVE.FOL      Record 1 of 8                          2% Full
 T········1·T········2·T········3·T·····4····T····5····T···6·····T··7······T·
 First nam>|Last name |Address    |City      |State  |Zip     |Date rese>|Da

 Chuck     |Coleman   |14006 Fla>|Miami      |FL     |20731   |08/27/88  |10
 Ed        |Mitchell  |75 Campy >|Fillwood   |CA     |94025   |08/14/88  |10
 Jason     |Loveman   |800 Heref>|Juggleston |TX     |43212   |08/12/88  |10
 Julie     |Wainwright|25 Freesi>|Woodside   |CA     |94025   |09/20/88  |11
 Rob       |Bearman   |1030 Laws>|Crane      |OH     |44261   |08/10/88  |10
 Joe       |Flood     |34 Cactus>|Bisby      |AZ     |89411   |09/22/88  |11
 Dale      |Yocum     |118 Ashla>|Foreston   |OR     |98403   |09/22/88  |11
 Julia     |Carpentier|8 Maywood>|San Franc> |CA     |94102   |09/15/88  |11




                                        ▮


         Press F1 for Help; or press ◄┘ to go back to current record
```

FIG. 14.2

Displaying a list
of records.

In the following sections, you see two categories of databases, flat file and relational. A *flat file* database, the simplest form of database, stores, organizes, and retrieves information from one file at a time. Each record contains all the information related to one particular topic.

A *relational* database allows linking between databases. The program can work with two data tables at the same time, relating the information through links established by a common column or field. Suppose that you created an extensive inventory database that displays the number of items last ordered, sold, and on-hand. With a relational database, you can link to the inventory database a second database that tells you information about the manufacturer of the inventory item so that, when your stock runs low, you can contact the supplier to order more merchandise.

Databases span the range of capabilities from simple to complex. Depending on your needs, you can find programs that record names and addresses or that you can program to create customized screens and automate data-entry processes.

Examining Data Management Programs

The following sections introduce several popular database programs available for PC, Amiga, and Macintosh computers.

Q&A

Q&A is a sophisticated, easy-to-use database program for PCs that combines a data manager with a report generator and a word processor. Q&A also is the first database program to use an *artificial intelligence interface*, which enables users to type questions in easy-to-understand, English-style sentences. This interface (the Intelligent Assistant) enables you to enter a request, such as "Find all clients in Minnesota," and the database locates and displays all records that show MN in the State field. Figure 14.3 shows an example of a Q&A menu.

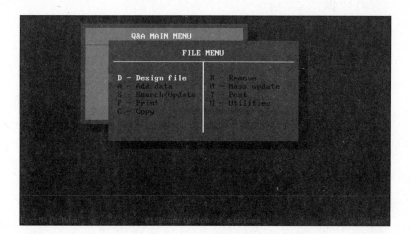

FIG. 14.3

An example of a Q&A database menu.

The database capabilities of Q&A are only part of the package. Q&A Write and Report are two other modules designed so that data you enter in the database part of the program (the Q&A File) can be used seamlessly with information in the Report or Write modules. Suppose that you want to create a business letter to send to 100 clients. You can create the letter in Q&A Write and then use the data from Q&A File to insert the names and addresses of the clients.

Q&A also enables you to include graphic images in the database and to employ an easily used import and export feature that can bring data into and out of Q&A with minimum effort. Q&A doesn't stop here; you also can create program and data-entry screens by using Q&A's programmable forms feature.

Q&A is flexible enough to meet the needs of people who have varying degrees of expertise. New users like the easy-to-use features of Q&A; experienced users find the capabilities of the program powerful enough to meet most sophisticated database needs.

Address: Symantec Corporation
10201 Torre Avenue
Cupertino, CA 95014

Price: $399

For Further Reference:

Q&A QueCards, Que Development Group

Q&A 4 QuickStart, Que Development Group

Q&A 4 Quick Reference, Que Development Group

Using Q&A 4, 2nd Edition, David Ewing and Bill Langenes, published by Que Corporation

dBASE IV

dBASE is the home-run hitter of PC database software. Long the standard in data management, dBASE first appeared on the market as dBASE II, the definitive database program for the PC. After dBASE II, other versions of the program evolved: dBASE III, dBASE III Plus, and dBASE IV.

Early versions of dBASE were difficult to use; detractors claimed the program was designed for programmers and that beginning users needed an expert to create databases. Today's dBASE is more user-friendly, offering a menu system for new users or the old dot-prompt commands for experienced dBASE users. Figure 14.4 shows an example of a dBASE IV screen.

dBASE IV has extensive data manipulation options that enable you to enter, search, sort, index, link, summarize, and create reports from records and subsets of records. dBASE IV also added *Structured Query Language*, a database management language developed by IBM primarily for mainframe and minicomputers. SQL gives you the power to link sophisticated database systems.

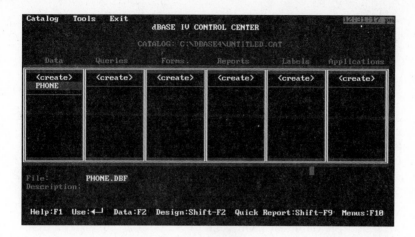

FIG. 14.4

A dBASE IV 1.5
for DOS screen.

dBASE IV brought the power of the sophisticated database program to new users. With the addition of the Control Center, even novice users can find their way around easily and perform needed data maintenance tasks. dBASE IV is used for many business applications and is capable of crunching even complex sets of data. Another high-level feature of dBASE IV is the batch processing mode, which enables you to select specific tasks, such as accounting transactions, while other processing operations are being performed. The networking capabilities of the program also make dBASE IV a good choice for all high-level business database needs.

A version of dBASE also is available for Macintosh users, dBASE Mac. This version combines the best of the Mac with the power of dBASE. One great feature of dBASE Mac is the easy linking capability of the program. Suppose that you created a database of personnel information. In one database, you store an employee's name, address, tax withholding information, and the hire and review dates. In another database, you track sick days, personal days, and earned vacation time. With dBASE Mac, for example, you can link the hire date field to the second database to calculate the data for the second database.

Address: Borland International, Inc.
              1800 Green Hills Road
              Scotts Valley, CA 95067-0001

Price: $795

For Further Reference:

dBASE III Plus Handbook, 2nd Edition, George T. Chou, published by Que Corporation

dBASE IV 1.5 Quick Reference, Que Development Group

Using dBASE IV 1.5, Special Edition, Steve Davis, published by Que Corporation

ORACLE

ORACLE is a relatively new database program for both the PC and the Macintosh and is elbowing its way into the fan clubs of many other existing database programs. ORACLE is a powerful package that offers you the option of using the program as a basic database with extensive query and reporting features or of totally customizing the package and programming your own forms and database interactions.

ORACLE is a relational database that enables you to easily link and access multiple databases. ORACLE for Macintosh 2.0 also includes a hefty set of end-user tools that enables users to create a graphical query and to export the results of the query to other Macintosh applications.

Address: Oracle Corporation
500 Oracle Parkway
Redwood Shores, CA 94065

Price: $699

4th Dimension

4th Dimension is a multiple-user relational database for the Mac. Although this program packs many diverse features, the basic design of the program is easy even for beginners to understand and use. The latest version of 4th Dimension, version 2.2.3, also includes graphing capabilities, which enable you to create visual output that shows data in area, column, pie, scatter, or picture graphs.

You won't find 4th Dimension lacking in size allotment, either; your database can store up to 16 million records in one file, with each record containing up to 511 fields. Besides these massive allowances, you can open up to 100 files at a time (depending on the memory in your computer).

Address: ACIUS
10351 Bubb Road
Cupertino, CA 95014

Price: $795

FoxPro

FoxPro is an award-winning relational database program available for both the PC and the Macintosh. Similar to the popular dBASE, FoxPro 2.0 is a user-friendly, intuitive program that operates up to 200 times faster than other database programs.

This program enables you to create forms, link databases, enter data, and easily design custom reports. You also can control the output results and add special touches by changing color, font, size, and style settings.

Address: Fox Software
                134 W. South Boundary
                Perrysburg, OH 43551

Price: $795

For Further Reference:

FoxPro Programmer's Reference Guide, John Hawkins, published by Que Corporation

Using FoxPro for Windows, Que Development Group

Using FoxPro 2, Lisa Slater and Steve Arnott, published by Que Corporation

SuperBase Professional

SuperBase Professional is a relational database program for Amiga users. This easily learned, user-friendly program covers a range of features, including form-design capabilities, application development, and a built-in project-management utility.

Address: Precision Software
                8404 Sterling Street
                Irving, TX 75063

Price: $399

Reflex

Reflex is a popular database program that started on the PC and moved to the Mac. This database program helps you record, track, organize, and analyze information. Used widely in business, Reflex and Reflex Plus enable you to analyze graphical, numerical, and textual data.

Reflex is used in businesses for a variety of tasks. If you are an experienced user, Reflex gives you the power to handle all data management needs. If you are a new user, Reflex's friendly interface can get you up to speed quickly.

Reflex combines two approaches to manage databases. In the traditional file folder method of organizing data, Reflex enables you to create data-entry screens, modify fields, and enter data. Reflex also provides an approach to organizing data similar to a spreadsheet, which can help you analyze data. Finally, Reflex includes the capabilities of creating custom reports and also boasts import and export features.

Address: Borland International
4585 Scotts Valley Drive
Scotts Valley, CA 95066

Price: $249

FileMaker Pro

FileMaker Pro, a database program from Claris (makers of ClarisWorks and HyperCard), is a hit with Macintosh users. FileMaker Pro, the latest version, appeared on the market in 1990 and provides users with an easy-to-use flat file database that allows picture fields and places no limit on the number of data records a database can store. Figure 14.5 shows an example of FileMaker Pro.

Address: Claris Corporation
5201 Patrick Henry Drive
Santa Clara, CA 95052

Price: $299

For Further Reference:

Using FileMaker Pro, Barrie Sosinsky, published by Que Corporation

HyperCard

HyperCard is an information manager available free with every Macintosh sold (you also can purchase the HyperCard Development Kit Version 2.1 for $199). HyperCard caused quite a stir in the development of database and applications software. Organized around a card-filing system like a Rolodex, HyperCard presents users with an easy method of designing, storing, and retrieving data from the systems.

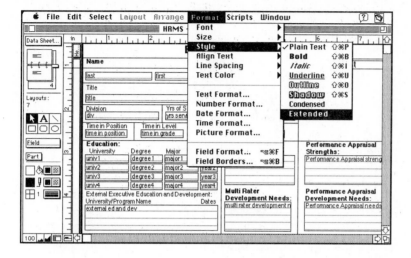

FIG. 14.5

A sample screen from FileMaker Pro.

The fun and flexibility of HyperCard is found in the capability of linking cards and stacks (the HyperCard word for database). You can move between cards by adding buttons to link the current stack to another stack. You then can move directly to the second stack by clicking the button. Figure 14.6 shows an example of a HyperCard stack.

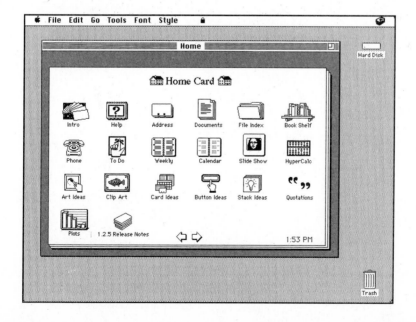

FIG. 14.6

An example of a HyperCard database card.

HyperCard includes several levels, from browsing (where you page through but change none of the cards) to scripting (in which the highest level enables you to use HyperTalk, HyperCard's accompanying programming language, to create special effects and program the way you want the database to work).

Address: Apple Computer, Inc.
20525 Mariana Avenue
Cupertino, CA 95014

Price: Free with new Macintosh
$199 for HyperCard Development Kit

For Further Reference:

HyperCard 2 QuickStart, Rebecca Gold, published by Que Corporation

Chapter Summary

In this chapter, you learned about database software. The following chapter introduces you to integrated software and explores popular packages for PC, Amiga, and Macintosh computers.

Integrated Software

A s you learned in Chapter 8, integrated software includes several programs in one package. Usually, an integrated package includes the following application programs:

- ■ Word processing
- ■ Spreadsheet
- ■ Data management
- ■ Communications

Often, individual integrated packages also include graphics, desktop publishing, and communications programs.

Many users purchase a computer application to solve a particular problem. If you need help working with words, for example, you buy a word processing program. What happens, however, when your business grows and you suddenly need a spreadsheet to help with the bookkeeping, or if you decide that you want to design and print fliers but you don't have desktop publishing capabilities?

If you don't have an integrated program, you must buy each additional program separately. Buying each piece of software independently poses two problems: cost and compatibility. Integrated packages cost less than the price of comparable stand-alone applications. In addition, finding stand-alone, yet compatible, programs can be difficult. Compatibility is more of a problem with PCs than with Macs. (*Compatible* programs can share information easily.)

This chapter highlights some popular integrated software packages.

Understanding the Benefits of Integrated Software

If you use a computer to perform a variety of tasks, you probably will benefit from buying an integrated software package. In the past, most people used computers for one task; you were either a wordsmith or a number cruncher. Wordsmiths used computers to operate word processing programs, and number crunchers used spreadsheet programs.

Today, applications are expanding beyond their original descriptions. Word processors are edging into desktop publishing markets. Spreadsheets include fine graphics. Jobs are becoming less defined and more flexible.

If you find that you must go where the work leads you, you probably use a word processor on Monday, a spreadsheet on Tuesday, and a desktop publishing program on Wednesday. Integrated software is definitely to your advantage. Not only can you exchange data between applications, you also can apply the commands you learn to operate one application to all other applications. The following list highlights a few of the benefits of integrated software:

- *Data is compatible among applications.* You can use information from the spreadsheet in word processing documents, data from the database in the spreadsheet, and parts of a letter from the word processor in a spreadsheet.

- *The menu system usually is the same, which reduces the number of menus and options you must learn.* Learning three or more programs at the same time can intimidate a new user. Most integrated software makers ensure that the same *look and feel* is consistently applied throughout the package. The applications use similar menus and options so that you can find your way through any application, whether you use a program daily or monthly.

- *Having an all-in-one package means that you spend less time loading, opening, and closing files.* Most integrated packages can load all needed files into RAM; you undergo no long delays as you move among applications. If you use stand-alone applications, you must exit one program before you can start another.

■ *Integrated software costs less than the same number of applications purchased individually.* When you strip away all the other benefits and look only at cost, the integrated program comes out the clear winner. If you think you may use the additional features in the integrated package, the investment is well worth the added cost. If you use only one of the applications, however, you may be better off if you invest in a lower-cost, stand-alone application that meets your needs.

A disadvantage of integrated packages is that the individual programs usually have fewer features than top-of-the-line, stand-alone applications. Most integrated databases are not as flexible as, for example, dBASE or Paradox. Most integrated spreadsheets have fewer functions than Lotus 1-2-3 or Excel.

Working with Integrated Software

Integrated packages are becoming more and more popular for a variety of business uses. Specifically, the following kinds of people are buying integrated software:

■ Owners of small businesses who want a single program that handles all bookkeeping, word processing, and data management tasks

■ Managers who need quick access to data in a variety of forms (data from a database, sums from a spreadsheet)

■ Support personnel who maintain client databases and correspondence lists

■ Users who want a program that grows as their needs grow

■ Users concerned about purchasing software compatible with their current system and software

Examining Integrated Software

This section highlights a few of the more popular integrated packages. Where possible, addresses of the manufacturers and retail costs are included.

GeoWorks Pro

GeoWorks Pro is a fully integrated software package that actually is an operating system and a graphical user interface separate from, yet with links to, DOS. GeoWorks Pro provides an array of file manipulation functions, Desk Accessories, and programs. Touting more programs than the standard integrated packages, GeoWorks is an ideal solution for varied business or personal computing needs. GeosWorks Pro offers the following programs:

- *Quattro Pro Special Edition*, a DOS-based spreadsheet program that includes 14 chart types, a database and a complete macro language, and is Lotus 1-2-3 compatible. For full font control and the capability of adding high-quality graphics, GeoWorks Pro supplies *Quattro Pro Viewer*, which enables you to export to GeoWrite as text or GeoDraw as a drawing.

- *GeoWrite*, a word processor that provides 7 text styles, multiple-column layouts, color character capability, a 100,000-word spell checker, and also the other standard word processing functions.

- *GeoDraw*, which enables you to create graphics by using 8 drawing tools, rotate images and text, and can import Quattro Pro *EPS* (Encapsulated PostScript, a special form of graphic) files.

- *GeoManager*, a file, directory, and disk management utility.

- *GeoDex*, similar to a Rolodex, you use this program to store names, addresses, and phone numbers. GeoDex enables you to print phone lists and mailing labels.

- *GeoPlanner*, a personal scheduler program.

- *GeoComm*, a communications program that enables you to connect to remote computers.

- *America On-Line*, a popular electronic information service.

GeoWorks Pro also includes six "Appliances" for beginners, including BannerMaker, and when you're ready to have fun, two games—Solitaire and Tetris—are included.

Address: GeoWorks
2150 Shattuck Avenue
Berkeley, CA 94704

Price: $199

For Further Reference:

Using GeoWorks Pro, Greg Shultz, published by Que Corporation

PFS: First Choice and WindowWorks

PFS: First Choice for DOS and WindowWorks for Windows are popular integrated packages for the PC, which combine the following applications:

- Word processing
- Spreadsheet
- Database management
- Graphics
- Communications

These applications follow an easy-to-use format so that you can learn quickly how to use each application.

PFS: First Choice and WindowWorks have a multitude of users from sophisticated business managers to the personal hobbyist. Some users include business people who type correspondence, balance books, and manage files, and business owners and managers who analyze and maintain information. Other users include support staff who work on data entry, create visual presentations, or produce reports. Many home users and hobbyists who want a complete package also choose PFS.

Both PFS: packages automate many business tasks traditionally done by hand. With these programs, you can perform accounting tasks, such as analyzing data and creating and printing spreadsheets. The word processor enables you to type correspondence, produce manuals, print documents, create presentations, and so on. First Choice and Window-Works also enable you to graph data, print graphs, plot graphs, create slide shows, and perform basic data-entry tasks. With the database management part, you can design database forms, create mailing labels, edit and analyze data, update files, retrieve files, and create and print database reports. The programs are so easy to use and so affordable that if you plan to use only two of the five applications, you get more than your money's worth.

Address: Spinnaker Software Corporation
201 Broadway
Cambridge, MA 02139

Price: $149 (WindowWorks)
$149 (First Choice, for DOS)

For Further Reference:

Using PFS: First Choice, Katherine Murray, published by Que Corporation

Using PFS:WindowWorks, Sean Cavanaugh, published by Que Corporation

Microsoft Works

Microsoft Works became so successful on the Macintosh that Microsoft wrote a version for the PC. Microsoft Works is an integrated program that combines the following applications:

- Word processing
- Spreadsheet
- Database management
- Communications

Microsoft Works has an enthusiastic following in both the PC and the Mac worlds. Because of easy-to-use features and friendly user interface (that is, a menu system), the applications in Microsoft Works are easy to understand and use. Both Mac and PC users use Works in business and at home, and both new and experienced users seem to find a niche with Works. Figure 15.1 shows a sample screen from Microsoft Works for the PC.

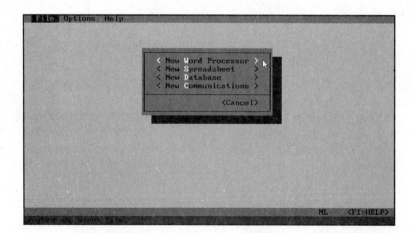

FIG. 15.1

A sample screen from Microsoft Works for DOS.

Microsoft Works' sturdy word processor enables you to enter, edit, save, and print text and reports. Specialized search-and-replace features, a thesaurus, and a spelling checker also help ensure the accuracy of your work.

With the Microsoft Works spreadsheet, you can create simple or complex worksheets, perform what-if calculations, and use Works' formulas to take the drudgery out of bookkeeping chores. The data manager gives you a great deal of flexibility in generating data-entry forms, working with fields, displaying data, and generating reports. The communications module accesses the world outside your computer by transferring files to and from remote computers. Finally, the features in Microsoft Works enable you to format data, merge data between applications, and exchange information with other programs and modules.

Address: Microsoft Corporation
              16011 NE 36th Way
              Redmond, WA 98073

Price: $95 (PC)
              $129 (Mac)

For Further Reference:

Microsoft Works Quick Reference (IBM version to 2.0), Douglas Wolf, published by Que Corporation

Using Microsoft Works 3 for the Mac, Greg Shultz, published by Que Corporation

Using Microsoft Works: IBM Version, Douglas Wolf, published by Que Corporation

Using Microsoft Works for Windows, Douglas Wolf, published by Que Corporation

Enable/OA

Enable/OA is a sophisticated integration of five software applications: word processing, spreadsheet, graphics, database management, and telecommunications. With Enable/OA, you can use a variety of these functions simultaneously. The Master Control Module manages the entire program and enables you to easily switch, change, and move between screens. Figure 15.2 shows a screen from the Master Control Module, which is the heart of the Enable/OA program.

Enable/OA appeals to a large audience of both experienced and new users. Although Enable/OA isn't difficult to learn and use, some features of the program may be too sophisticated for an average user. Therefore, many of the best applications for Enable/OA are found in business environments that demand a hard-hitting integrated package designed around the word processing applications program.

In Enable/OA, you can view up to eight files from any application, and you can stack these files behind one another for easy access. Enable/OA also has a mail-merge facility, multiple character sets, character transportation commands, and a built-in calculator. With the graphics application of Enable/OA, you can create pie graphs, line graphs, and two- or three-dimensional bar or stacked graphs. With the telecommunications module, you can transmit data and connect to host systems for electronic mail.

```
        <DIR> ..        2/28/91  23:49:10

     <DIR> ..                 2/28/91  23:49:10  [.D....]              (........)
     1QSMEMO  .WPF      880   3/03/91  21:42:34  [A.....]              (........)
     BOXES    .WPF      747   3/04/91   1:27:56  [A.....]              (........)
     COLUMNS  .WPF    6,225   3/01/91   1:52:28  [A.....]              (........)
     DEMOWORD.WPF     8,310   3/03/91  22:23:32  [A.....]              (........)
     DOCFORM  .WPF    6,272   6/01/90  17:40:44  [A.....]              (........)
     FONTS    .WPF    7,203   7/10/90   7:11:32  [A.....]              (........)
     HAWAII   .WPF    3,446   3/17/91  17:43:44  [A.....]              (........)
     HNGINDT  .WPF      896   3/03/91  22:52:50  [A.....]              (........)
     NONAME   .WPF      930   3/04/91   0:28:42  [A.....]              (........)
     QS3LTR   .WPF      521   2/12/91   2:17:42  [A.....]              (........)
     SAMPLE   .WPF      965   3/17/91  16:44:40  [A.....]              (........)
     SIDEWAYS.WPF     1,278  11/13/90   9:56:00  [A.....]              (........)
     T-PAPER  .WPF    3,923   3/04/91   1:03:34  [A.....]              (........)
     TABS     .WPF    1,675   3/01/91   0:32:10  [A.....]              (........)
     TEXT     .WPF    1,629   3/04/91   0:07:22  [A.....]              (........)
     WH7X     .WPF    2,606   3/04/91   1:02:24  [A.....]              (........)


     Select = Enter   PgUp   Home       Mark/unMark = F7
     Exit   = Esc     PgDn   End        Mark Range  = sft/F7
     View   = V       F10 = Top Menu    unMark ALL  = alt/F7
 #3 C:\4ODATA\*.WP*                                16 Files       47,506 bytes used
```

FIG. 15.2

A screen from the Master Control Module in Enable/OA.

Address: The Software Group
                 Northway Ten Executive Park
                 Ballston Lake, NY 12019

Price: $495

For Further Reference:

Que's Using Enable, Walter Bruce, published by Que Corporation

Claris Works

In November 1991, Claris Corporation entered the integrated software arena with Claris Works for the Macintosh. This robust package includes the following:

■ Word Processing

■ Graphics

■ Spreadsheets

■ Charts

■ Database Management

■ Communications

Unlike other integrated software packages, Claris Works supports each function within the same document. This seamless integration enables you to add text, graphics, or spreadsheet calculations to any document. From within any document, for example, clicking the spreadsheet tool enables you to perform calculations, clicking a drawing tool enables you to draw a box around the mathematical function, and adding text is performed by clicking the word processing tool. Figure 15.3 shows a screen from Claris Works on the Maintosh.

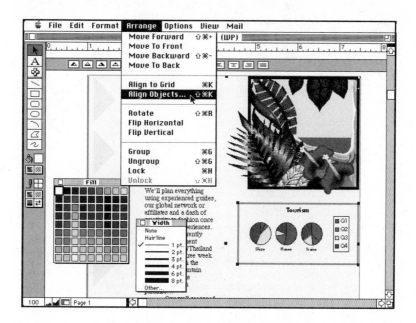

FIG. 15.3

A screen from Claris Works on the Macintosh.

Key features of Claris Works include word processing options of multiple columns and linked text frames. A mail merge feature is available as well as on-line spelling and thesaurus utilities. Spreadsheet options include 96 mathematical, statistical, financial and trigonometric functions; multiple level sort capabilities; and chart generation. The graphics function enables you to create and manipulate graphics with rotate, reshape, and duplication features. Claris Works also provides automatic alignment and colored pens and pattern tools. Database functions in Claris Works range from simple field definition to versatile search and sort features. Finally, the Communications extension provides automatic dialing and an extensive portfolio of connection settings, terminal emulation, and file transfer tools.

Address: Claris Corporation
                  5201 Patrick Henry Drive
                  Santa Clara, CA 95052

Price: $198

For Further Reference:

Using Claris Works, by Que Development Group

Chapter Summary

This chapter explained the benefits of integrated software and introduced you to some of the most popular integrated packages for the IBM
and Macintosh computers. In the following chapter, you learn about
desktop publishing programs.

Desktop Publishing

Not so long ago, producing publications was a painful task. If you were a casual publisher, creating simple bulletins, church or school event fliers, and so on, you assembled documents by typing the text and then pasting in graphics. If you were a professional publisher, creating the company newsletter or thick documentation, you used a typesetter to print the text, an artist to produce the art, a layout person to assemble the document, and a printer to produce the final pages. A great deal of work went into one publication, whether the publication was a 500-page book or a small advertising flier.

Desktop publishing brings an end to the hard work of publishing. With the right hardware and software, you can produce any document you could make the *old* way in a fraction of the time and at much less expense. Desktop publishing software packages are electronic page layout programs that enable you to combine text and graphics on a page to create the document you want.

This chapter helps you gain an understanding of what desktop publishing is and provides information on several popular desktop publishing programs.

Understanding the Benefits of Desktop Publishing

Although the introduction of desktop publishing came much later than the first of the three main categories of software (spreadsheet, word processor, and database), desktop publishing arrived in time to offer the business world a solution for the time-consuming and cumbersome task of publishing. Specifically, desktop publishing offers users the following benefits:

- *On-screen layout of text and graphics.* Desktop publishing enables you to see your work on-screen. (Many typesetting machines lack this feature.) The capability of placing text and graphics together on-screen also helps you fine-tune the page layout and design. Most desktop publishing programs offer different views that you can use to see a page in different sizes. For an overall effect, you can zoom out and view the whole page. If you want a close-up view, you can zoom in and see a portion of a page.

- *Assembling documents quickly and making changes easily.* Desktop publishing offers the power conventional publishing cannot by giving you the flexibility to make changes with little effort. Traditional publishing requires many steps to change a layout or a design. Often a change requires repasting one or several pages. With desktop publishing, you can put documents together quickly and, if you don't like what you see, you can make a change and then print the result. If you want to make more changes, just make the changes and print again.

- *Importing text from word processors or typing text directly in the program.* All desktop publishing programs enable you to import, or to bring in, text you created in word processing programs. The desktop publishing programs differ in the word processing programs they support. With the popular desktop publishing program PageMaker, for example, you can import files from most word processing programs. With less sophisticated desktop publishing programs, your word processor choices are more limited.

- *Printing on a variety of printers ranging from dot-matrix to PostScript laser printers.* Most desktop publishing programs support many popular printers. Most of the less sophisticated desktop publishing programs support a wide range of dot-matrix printers and supply many fonts. Thus, you can create professional publications whether you work with an expensive PostScript printer or a dot-matrix printer.

Working with Desktop Publishing Software

Although publishing once fell to a select few who were handy with type, scissors, and paste, today a great number of people are publishing. The following kinds of users regularly use desktop publishing software:

- Small-business owners who want to create letterhead and stationery for their companies

- Teachers who need handouts for training and classrooms

- Managers who must produce professional-looking reports

- Business people who need to publish corporate newsletters

- Writers, publishers, and editors who create camera-ready documents

- Ad agency specialists who compose graphics and text layouts

- Typesetting people who typeset and design layouts

Understanding Different Desktop Programs

Desktop publishing programs range from the simple to the complex. The simple desktop publishing programs (*low-end programs*) enable you to perform basic layout functions, such as placement of text and graphics, a limited number of columns, and support for a variety of printers. Many low-end programs also include *clip art*, which is art you obtain from another source and use in your document. Low-end programs can start as low as $130. Figure 16.1 shows the popular, low-end PC desktop publishing program PFS: First Publisher.

The more complex desktop publishing programs (*high-end programs*) include more sophisticated features such as table generation, indexing features, automatic page numbering, automatic text flow, and a wide range of other powerful features. High-end programs can cost $600 or more. Figure 16.2 shows a screen from Aldus PageMaker, which is one of the most popular high-end desktop publishing programs available.

An example of a
low-end desktop
publishing
program (PFS:
First Publisher).

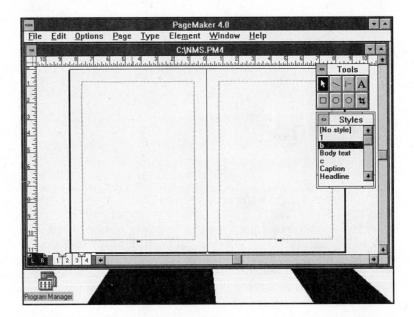

An example of a
high-end desktop
publishing
program
(PageMaker).

How do you determine the kind of software you need? If your desktop publishing needs are limited to an occasional flier or a simple newsletter, a low-end program may better fit your needs and budget. If you plan to produce elaborate professional-quality documents such as full-length books, training manuals, or visual support materials, you need a more powerful high-end program.

Examining Your Desktop Publishing Needs

Before you begin shopping for desktop publishing software, you first must identify your exact needs. Answer the following questions to help you define your search:

- Do your needs warrant a sophisticated program?

- Do you need a simple program you may use only occasionally?

- Do you need automatic page numbering?

- Is table generation or indexing important to you?

- Do you have enough memory to run this program?

- Do you need a mouse with this program?

- Does the program work with your current word processing program?

Examining Desktop Publishing Programs

The following sections introduce some of the most popular desktop publishing programs. The desktop publishing arena is bursting with new products, so don't expect to find every program listed here.

PageMaker

Aldus PageMaker is the most popular desktop publishing program on the market in terms of power and flexibility. Also known as a page-composition program, PageMaker enables you to combine text and graphics on the page to compose documents. PageMaker accepts text from a variety of popular word processing programs and graphics in popular file formats.

PageMaker is available for both the Macintosh and the PC. Within the past year, Version 4.0 has become available for the PC and version 4.2 for the Mac.

Although PageMaker is a high-end desktop publishing program, many people find the program easy to learn and use. Used with Microsoft Windows, PageMaker has familiar menus, pop-up dialog boxes, and a Mac-like display.

PageMaker enables you to format a page in a number of columns and formats; use different fonts; import sophisticated graphics; create on-screen graphics such as boxes, rectangles, and ovals; create master pages information that copies onto every page; and perform many other high-end functions.

Who uses PageMaker? Anyone who needs a high-end publishing program. Few people purchase PageMaker to create business cards—only those interested in power publishing spend this much money on desktop publishing. Among others, professional designers, publishers, and corporate sales departments use PageMaker to produce professional-quality documents.

Address: Aldus Corporation
                411 1st Avenue South
                Seattle, WA 98104

Price: $795 (PC)
                $595 (Mac)

For Further Reference:

Using PageMaker 4 for Windows, Diane Burns and Sharon Venit, published by Que Corporation

Ventura Publisher

Ventura Publisher and Ventura Publisher for Windows are high-end desktop publishing programs available for the PC. Ventura takes a different approach to desktop publishing. Rather than just entering text as you do in PageMaker, you assemble documents in Ventura by using frames and tags to build a publication.

Ventura offers sophisticated features that enable you to easily produce long and complex documents. Ideal for textbooks, technical manuals, and large projects that involve a number of operations such as indexing and special formatting, Ventura shines for difficult or involved publications.

Ventura is loved by a vast number of users. Especially in the technical publishing field, users appreciate the framework approach to building documents. After learning the basic concept, the menus become easy to maneuver and options easy to find. A few beginning users find the tag and frame approach cryptic, but for complex documents, Ventura's power outweighs the time you invest in learning how to use the program.

Address: Ventura Software, Inc.
15175 Innovation Dr.
San Diego, CA 92128

Price: $495 (PC)
$795 (Windows)

For Further Reference:

Que's Using Ventura Publisher 4 for Windows, Schuyler W. Lininger, published by Que Corporation

Professional Page 2.0

Professional Page 2.0 is a desktop publishing program for Amiga. With basic text layout, modification features, and other new perks, Professional Page surpasses other popular publishing programs. Professional Page 2.0 includes the capability of selecting more than one menu option at a time and provides a widened range of page views so that you can see a document at 200 percent size, at thumbnail size, and at several sizes in between.

Professional Page 2.0 includes two editing modes. You can select the ever-present text editor to make small changes and revisions, or you can work with the article editor—a large-scale editor that enables you to compose and revise long documents without leaving Professional Page. Version 2.0 also includes the Pantone Matching System, a feature that enables you to print color separations or to use a color PostScript printer or slide imager.

Address: Professional Page 2.0
Gold Disk
5155 Spectrum Way, Unit 5
Mississauga, Ontario
Canada L4W 5A1

Price: $395

PFS: First Publisher

PFS: First Publisher is a desktop publishing program designed to help you produce newsletters, brochures, booklets, and other documents.

This low-end program comes with all the tools you need to write, design, illustrate, and print documents. First Publisher also comes with a library of clip art that you can add to documents, and it supports more than 100 dot-matrix printers.

The most recent version of First Publisher of DOS, 3.0, was released in 1990 and version 1.1, first Publisher for Windows, was released in May, 1992. Both versions provide a special layout gallery feature that enables you to select the number and placement of columns from a library of over 20 different layout designs. Another important feature is a selection of special fonts that enhance printouts.

A wide audience exists for both PFS: First Publisher and First Publisher for Windows, ranging from business owners to PTA presidents to CEOs. Anyone who wants to publish something quickly and easily can put First Publisher to good use. Users with high-end publishing tasks should look at a more powerful desktop publishing program.

Address: Spinnaker Software Corporation
201 Broadway
Cambridge, MA 02139

Price: $129 (First Publisher for DOS)
$149 (First Publisher for Windows)

For Further Reference:

Using PFS: First Publisher, 2nd Edition, Katherine Murray, published by Que Corporation

Express Publisher

Express Publisher is a low-end desktop publishing program that enables you to produce professional-looking documents that combine text and graphics. Express Publisher can produce documents at 300 dpi resolution (or at the highest resolution of a dot-matrix printer). Express Publisher, however, lacks the advanced features needed for complex documents.

Express Publisher includes scalable fonts, which give you a wide variety of available fonts. The program also contains advanced page layout tools and more than 100 pieces of clip art.

Used mainly by business people who produce professional-looking brochures, newsletters, and stationery, Express Publisher has a variety of text-handling capabilities and page layout features. You can place text into frames that are connected to create a page layout. This program enables you to create the exact font size you need for each application, to draw boxes, and to import several kinds of graphics. Express Publisher flows text from a variety of word processing programs and has tracking and auto hyphenation to ensure uniform line length. Within this program are a number of powerful drawing and text-handling tools that enable beginners to create documents from scratch from within the program.

Address: Power Up Software Corp.
                 2929 Campus Drive
                 San Mateo, CA 94403

Price: $160

Publish It!

Publish It! is a low-end desktop publishing program available for PC and Macintosh computers. With Publish It!, you can design, lay out, and print professional-looking documents with a minimum of time and trouble.

Publish It! imports documents from a variety of popular word processors and supports graphics in several formats. Some features Publish It! offers are shown in the following list:

- Flexible page sizes and layout features

- A variety of built-in typefaces

- A startup package for adding additional fonts

- A built-in word processor

- Special typesetting functions, such as *kerning* (character spacing) and *leading* (line spacing) features

- The capability of creating master pages

Publish It! is used by many people from home users who produce garage-sale signs to business users who publish professional-looking documents. Special timesaving features such as page guides, quick keys, automatic page numbering, and style sheets enable you to automate the page layout process.

Address: Timeworks, Inc.
                 625 Academy Dr.
                 Northbrook, IL 60062

Price: $149 (Publish It! for DOS)
                 $179 (Publish It! for Macintosh)

QuarkXPress

If you need a desktop publishing program for the Macintosh, you may find the answer in QuarkXPress 3.1. Although easy to learn and use, this program gives all the publishing capabilities you need to produce documents from business cards to books.

With QuarkXPress, you can use style sheets, control leading to 1/1,000 of an inch, and scale type sizes from 2 points to 720 points.

Address: Quark, Incorporated
300 South Jackson, Suite 100
Denver, CO 80209

Price: $899

Chapter Summary

From a basic introduction of page layout to a specialized program-by-program account of popular desktop publishing products, this chapter explored many page layout packages. The kind of program you decide to buy will be based on your individual needs.

In the following chapter, you learn about programs you can use with desktop publishing programs—software packages that can put your creative energy on-screen in the form of graphics.

Graphics Software

I f you believe a picture is worth a thousand words, graphics software is right up your alley. Graphics software gives you the capability —electronically—of creating simple or complex artwork on your computer screen, and the great thing about graphics software is that you don't need artistic talent to create great looking graphics!

A variety of graphics programs is available to create almost any artwork you can imagine. Programs range from the simple and inexpensive to high-cost, state-of-the-art. Simple, or low-end, programs usually are easy-to-use freehand painting programs, while high-end programs use special technology to create perfectly curved lines and high-quality printouts.

This chapter introduces you to paint, draw, and presentation graphics programs and to computer-aided design (CAD) programs, which are more sophisticated than traditional graphics programs and are used for engineering, architectural, and other professional design tasks. Included in this chapter are several programs from each category to introduce you to the wide range of graphics software available.

Understanding Graphics Software

Graphics programs for the computer are becoming increasingly sophisticated. A specific graphics program exists for almost any artist's (or would-be artist's) needs. If you are new to computing, the myriad of graphics software packages from which to choose can be baffling. Understanding which graphics software performs which task is the first step in your purchase decision. The following section defines the basic graphics software categories.

What Is Graphics Software?

You can divide the category of graphics software into the following groups:

- Paint programs
- Draw programs
- Presentation graphics programs
- CAD programs

At the low end of the graphics spectrum, *paint programs* can provide you with a wide range of artwork. With a paint program, you have access to a variety of tools, colors, and patterns to *paint* the screen. This kind of graphic is easy to edit; just magnify the size of the graphic and change the color of individual pixels. The printed output may look choppy, however, and you may see the individual dots that make up the art. Figure 17.1 shows the screen of a paint program.

High-end graphics programs, or *draw programs*, usually incorporate some CAD features, which you learn about later in this section, and provide high-quality images you can export in a variety of formats, such as PICT (Picture), TIFF (Tagged Image File Format), and Paint. These sophisticated graphics programs offer an incredible range of features but are often difficult to learn. Figure 17.2 shows the screen of a high-end draw program.

Presentation graphics programs are relatively new packages that enable you to create charts easily. Popular for many business applications, presentation graphics software provides a wide range of options to create charts for display, printer, plotter, or film recorder output.

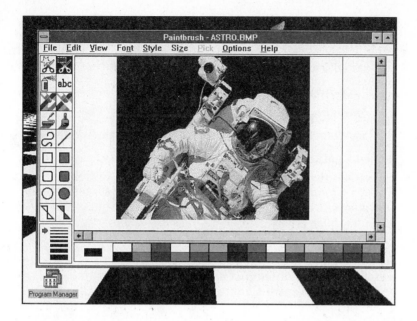

FIG. 17.1

A screen from a paint program.

FIG. 17.2

A screen from a draw program.

The final category of graphics programs you learn about in this chapter is often considered a category of its own. *Computer-aided design (CAD) programs* bring another dimension—literally—to graphics applications. CAD programs add the capability of showing, rotating, and modifying images in three dimensions, providing users with the tools to make images come to life.

CAD programs have become increasingly popular over the last few years. This software builds on the capabilities of draw programs and has features that simplify designing anything from the inside and outside of a house to highly complex machine parts. Computer-aided design is popular not only in architecture but also in many engineering, design, and graphic art areas. Figure 17.3 shows the screen of a popular CAD program.

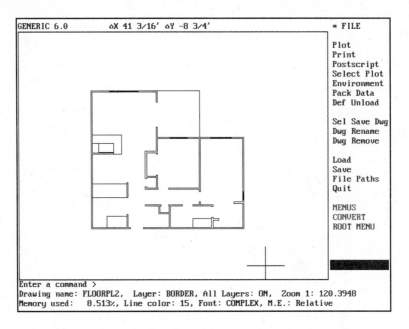

FIG. 17.3

A screen from a CAD program.

What Are the Benefits of Graphics Software?

Whether you work with art only when you must or you spend hours at the computer painting, graphics programs have several major benefits:

- You can use the art you create over and over again without losing the original quality.

■ With on-screen graphics, you don't have to go back to the drawing board each time. You can make modifications to the original art until you achieve the design you want.

■ You can create a variety of charts easily with presentation graphics software.

■ Most paint programs enable you to try a variety of shading and filling techniques.

■ The art tools in a graphics program give you control over the precision of your creations.

■ Draw programs produce graphics in PostScript printer format, providing you with higher quality output than is available with non-PostScript laser printers.

■ With many graphics programs, you can import art directly into popular desktop publishing programs.

Who Uses Graphics Software?

Graphics software is used by a growing number of business and home users. Specifically, the following users now work with graphics programs:

■ Graphic artists who create sophisticated artwork

■ Desktop publishers who want paint or draw graphics for their publications

■ Home users who create invitations and miscellaneous art

■ Owners of small businesses who want a company logo and letterhead

■ Business persons who want graphics to illustrate technical information

The following sections introduce some specific graphics packages. The categories are presented according to the complexity of the programs: first low-level paint programs, then high-level draw programs, followed by presentation graphics, and concluding with CAD programs.

Examining Paint Programs

Graphics programs are among the most important and the most enjoyable programs to learn and use. Graphics added to almost any report can enhance the point you are making. You also may find that using these programs is fun!

PC Paintbrush IV Plus

PC Paintbrush IV Plus is a graphics program used to create colorful pictures and images you can add to desktop publishing, word processing, and other software applications. PC Paintbrush is used by business persons who want professional graphics and illustrations in documents, brochures, and newsletters.

With this program, you have access to a wide array of drawing tools that help you generate sophisticated graphics. A comprehensive tutorial and manual help new users learn to use the program quickly. PC Paintbrush also enables users to scan and work with scanned images directly in the program.

PC Paintbrush has a wide selection of tools to assist you in creating detailed images and graphics. After you create or import the graphics, you can zoom in or out displaying different views; use a variety of cursor shapes and thicknesses; and add labels, titles, and banners to customized drawings.

Additional editing and customizing commands make PC Paintbrush one of the most popular PC paint programs currently available. Because of the program's capability of using expanded memory, you can scan and work with large images for more sophisticated graphics, as shown in figure 17.4.

Address: ZSoft Corp.
1950 Spectrum Circle, Suite A495
Marietta, GA 30067

Price: $115

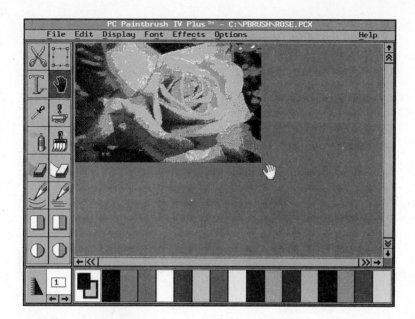

FIG. 17.4

The main screen
of PC Paintbrush
IV Plus.

Logitech Paintshow

Logitech Paintshow is a graphics program that can create and edit high-resolution pictures. Used by people who need graphics for desktop publishing or other business or personal applications, Paintshow is especially useful for businesses that want customized graphics to use in brochures, newsletters, or other documents.

Paintshow enables you to display a series of pictures on a screen in a slide-show like presentation. Because you can save files in a variety of popular graphics formats, importing files into desktop publishing applications is easy. With more than 20 tools, Paintshow gives you full capabilities for creating on-screen images. A full set of menu options enables you to perform all the basic editing procedures on your graphics.

This program also includes a utility with which you can present a slide show or enhance your graphics. Paintshow has speed keys and shortcut features that increase your efficiency when you work with the program.

Address: Logitech Inc.
6505 Kaiser Drive
Fremont, CA 94555

Price: $79

MacPaint

MacPaint was the first paint program available for the Macintosh. Today, the newest version of MacPaint (Version 2.0) is extremely popular. MacPaint offers you all the basic paint tools in the familiar Macintosh interface. Figure 17.5 shows a screen from MacPaint.

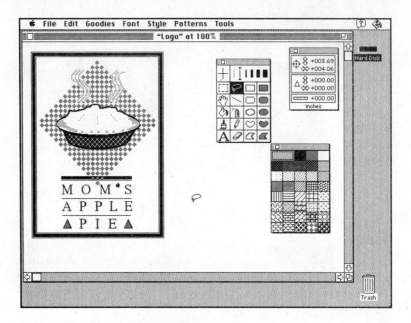

FIG. 17.5

A screen from MacPaint.

MacPaint is used by a variety of people who need to create artwork on a Macintosh. For many high-level applications, MacPaint doesn't pack enough punch. For simple or fun graphics, however, users like the features available with this program.

Address: Claris Corporation
5201 Patrick Henry Drive
Santa Clara, CA 95052

Price: $125

Examining High-Level Draw Programs

This section introduces several high-level draw programs available for PC and Macintosh computers. With these programs, you can produce more sophisticated results than you can with paint programs.

MacDraw Pro

MacDraw Pro is a drawing program that enables Mac users to create sophisticated graphics that demand a high degree of accuracy. Used by many designers, engineers, and architects, MacDraw Pro is a more sophisticated version of the old MacDraw, which was originally available on all Macintosh computers.

MacDraw Pro enables users to save graphics files in other popular formats, including PICT2 file format, used to save files in color. The program includes templates for frequently used designs, help features, graphics enlargement and reduction features, and an editor that enables you to create custom patterns for filled objects. Figure 17.6 shows a screen from MacDraw Pro.

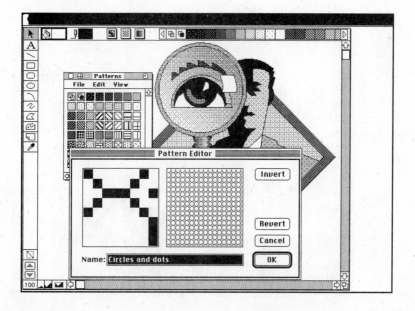

FIG. 17.6

The Patterns editing box in MacDraw Pro.

Address: Claris Corporation
                 5201 Patrick Henry Drive
                 Santa Clara, CA 95052

Price: $399

Micrografx Designer

Micrografx Designer is a high-level drawing program for PCs. Made specifically for PC users who need sophisticated, full-color, graphic-art illustrations, Designer offers many features not found in other PC products.

Designer's features include the items in the following list:

- A palette of up to 16 million colors
- A full selection of graphics tools, including tools for drawing ellipses, curves, lines, polylines, parabolas, and more
- A method to shape, smooth, and connect objects easily
- A way to rotate objects as little as one-tenth of a degree
- The capability of creating up to 64 separate layers
- A utility that makes Designer files compatible with AutoCAD

Figure 17.7 shows a Micrografx Designer screen.

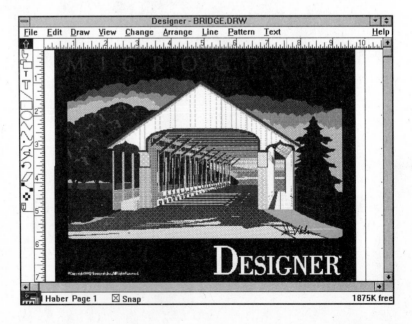

FIG. 17.7

A screen from Micrografx Designer.

Designer includes many clip-art files you can use in publications. Micrografx also offers several other clip-art packages and drawing and graphing programs.

Address: Micrografx
                  1303 Arapaho
                  Richardson, TX 75081

Price: $695

DesignWorks

DesignWorks is a graphics program for the Amiga that offers a wide range of features at a small price. With a variety of freehand tools and object-oriented tools, you can create sleek, sophisticated graphics without denting your pocketbook.

If you want a structured drawing program for the Amiga, DesignWorks provides the capability of creating Bézier curves, using an unlimited number of layers, creating unique patterns, and customizing colors. Special printing techniques gives you near-PostScript quality from a simple dot-matrix printer.

Address: New Horizons
                  206 Wild Basic Road, Suite 109
                  Austin, TX 78746

Price: $125

Adobe Illustrator

Adobe Illustrator is a popular, high-level graphics program. Originally available only for the Macintosh, this software also is now available for the PC. With Adobe, you can turn a simple line-art or paint-type artwork into something spectacular.

Perhaps the single biggest reason users purchase Adobe is the quality of the printed output. Adobe, like Micrografx Designer and Aldus Freehand, can output files in PostScript format, which gives you the highest quality possible for printed graphics images.

Adobe Illustrator includes the following features:

- Autotracing (the program's capability of *tracing around* the outside of edges, smoothing rough curves, and turning a paint image into a draw image)

- Color separations
- The capability of customizing patterns
- Tools for blending shapes, colors, and patterns
- Precise freehand drawing tools
- Previewing capabilities

Adobe Illustrator is perfect for technical designers or anyone needing near-CAD graphics capability. Figure 17.8 shows an Adobe Illustrator screen.

FIG. 17.8

A screen from Adobe Illustrator.

Like other high-end graphics programs, Adobe can output files in a variety of formats that other programs support.

Address: Adobe Systems
1585 Charleston Road
Mountain View, CA 94039

Price: $695

CorelDRAW!

CorelDRAW! is hailed as one of the best high-level graphics programs available for the PC. With many of the same features as Micrografx Designer and Adobe Illustrator, CorelDRAW! goes a step further with the capability of breaking letters into their natural curved elements. In CorelDRAW! you can manipulate letters as a graphic element. By using this feature, you can stretch and squash the letter B, for example, to your heart's content until you get just the right effect. You then can print the art with no loss in quality.

Graphics artists, designers, engineers, and illustrators work with CorelDRAW!. The following list shows some of CorelDRAW!'s features:

- 102 built-in typefaces

- Easy import and export routines for working with files from other programs

- Autotrace feature

- A variety of tools for creating sophisticated freehand graphics

- A large selection of clip art

- The capability of working with and converting familiar third-party fonts, such as fonts from Bitstream or Adobe

Address: Corel Systems
1600 Carling Avenue
Ottawa, Ontario KIZ 8R7
Canada

Price: $595

Examining Presentation Graphics Programs

Presentation software can help you make a dramatic statement, particularly when the way you communicate the information is important. Presentation graphics software replaces the sometimes dull overhead transparencies (although you can use these programs to create overhead transparencies). This software also takes the busy work out of preparing charts and materials used in presentations.

Here's how presentation graphics works. Imagine that you are sitting in a meeting, looking at the glaring white of a projection screen while the meeting leader places one transparency after another on the projector. He drones on while you look at boring black-and-white charts. Now, imagine sitting in a room with a large, color monitor that shows a variety of charts and animated images. Special effects enable the leader to fade between charts, and special pop-up notes appear to highlight important chart facts.

In this section, you learn about a few popular presentation graphics programs for the PC, the Amiga, and the Mac.

Harvard Graphics

Harvard Graphics is the definitive presentation graphics program for PC users. The latest releases of Harvard Graphics, version 3.0 and Harvard Graphics for Windows, make the program easier to use and add even more features than the already feature-laden 2.3. With Harvard Graphics, you can create charts from scratch or use the Chart Gallery—a huge library of already-created charts in which you plug your own data.

Used primarily in business, Harvard Graphics has many enhancement options, and most users can find their way around easily. A comprehensive help system (available on literally every screen except chart display) assists you as you learn how to use the software. The following list shows a few of the program's features:

- The Chart Gallery, offering nine chart types in a variety of formats

- The Draw utility, a graphics program built-in to Harvard Graphics that enables you to add customized art to charts

- Put charts you create in an automated slide show

- Animate art you create in Draw, which gives the illusion of real animation in presentations

- Support for data imported from a variety of spreadsheet programs, such as Lotus 1-2-3 and Microsoft Excel

- Output on display, printer, plotter, or film recorder devices

- The capability of creating and using macros for often-used procedures

- The opportunity to create templates for charts and frequently used chart settings

Address: Software Publishing Corporation
                    1901 Landings Drive, P.O. Box 7210
                    Mountain View, CA 94043

Price: $595

For Further Reference:

Easy Harvard Graphics, Shelley O'Hara, published by Que Corporation

Harvard Graphics Quick Reference, Que Development Group

Harvard Graphics 3 Quick Reference, Trudi Reisner, published by Que Corporation

Using Harvard Graphics, 2nd Edition, Steve Sagman and Jane Graver Sandlar, published by Que Corporation

Using Harvard Graphics 3, Jane Graver Sandlar and Steve Sagman, published by Que Corporation

Using Harvard Graphics for Windows, Bob Benedict, published by Que Corporation

SCALA

SCALA is a presentation graphics program for the Amiga. Offering a variety of special, built-in features, such as the 59 included background images, and a library of symbols you can use in presentations, SCALA makes communicating ideas easy. SCALA includes the following qualities:

- 17 built-in fonts
- Special text effects such as drop shadows, tilting, 3-D viewing, and special color effects
- 70 special effects to control the way one chart or slide flows into another
- Capability of animating graphics and text
- A way to send graphics files to a variety of sources, including display, printer, plotter, and film recorder
- Capability of creating templates for reuse

SCALA is ideal for who need professional-looking presentations.

Address: Great Valley Products, Inc.
                    600 Clark Ave.
                    King of Prussia, PA 19406

Price: $239

Wingz

Perhaps including Wingz in the presentation graphics category isn't fair; this program is really much more. The graphics portion of the Wingz spreadsheet, however, is powerful and offers up to 20 graph types, including 3-D, scientific, and engineering graphics. Because of this power, Wingz is often used to create charts and dazzling presentations.

Wingz is touted as a spreadsheet that enables you to create a worksheet of more than one *billion* cells (depending on the amount of memory available in your Mac). Because Wingz follows the Macintosh ease-of-use philosophy even beginners can learn this program easily. Specifically, Wingz incorporates these presentation graphics features:

- Enables you to create 20 kinds of graphs
- Special effects for 3-D graphs including rotation, elevation, and differing perspectives
- A palette of 16 million colors for graph display
- Capability of using draw tools to enhance charts
- Use of multiple fonts, sizes, and styles
- Capability of importing clip art or scanned images
- Easy steps for adding charts directly into spreadsheets

Address: Wingz
Informix Software, Inc.
16011 College Boulevard
Lenexa, KS 66219

Price: $399

PowerPoint

PowerPoint is one of the most popular business presentation tools available. Powerful, but designed for ease of use, PowerPoint provides drawing tools capable of producing color graphics, and high-end word processing options, such as special line spacing for outlines of text and automatic style sheets.

A built-in "slide show" feature gives your computer a slide projector look for on-screen presentations. Other PowerPoint features include the items in the following list:

- Slide and title sorter options
- A library of presentation templates
- Rulers and guides for precise drawing
- Date and time codes that update by reading the computer's internal clock

Address: Microsoft Corporation
16011 NE 36th Way
Redmond, WA 98073-9717

Price: $446 (Windows)
$268 (Mac)

For Further Reference:

Using PowerPoint, James G. Meade, published by Que Corporation

Examining CAD Programs

Computer-aided design (CAD) programs replace the drafting table and drafting tools used in engineering and architectural fields. Because of the high degree of accuracy needed in designing, computerizing the design of manufactured items reduces the time and effort you spend laboring over plans and schemes.

Although CAD and CAM (computer-aided manufacturing) programs are true applications software like spreadsheets and paint programs, these high-end programs often are used as sophisticated drawing tools. Many CAD programs go beyond basic high-level graphics programs and include statistical analysis capabilities and a variety of other scientific features.

AutoCAD

AutoCAD, the best-selling CAD program for PCs and Macs, runs on all Macs *except* the LC. Introduced in 1982, AutoCAD has gone through numerous revisions with each version of the program substantially more powerful than preceding versions. Specifically, AutoCAD offers the following features:

- An easy-to-use interface with pull-down menus and dialog boxes
- Support for a mouse or digitizer

■ Capability of layering, rotating, copying, mirroring, moving, stretching, and scaling

■ 3D wire-frame modeling

■ Up to 16 different views

Figure 17.9 shows an example of an AutoCAD screen.

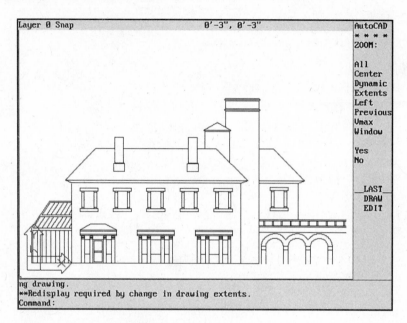

FIG. 17.9

A screen from AutoCAD.

Address:	Autodesk, Inc.
	2320 Marinship Way
	Sausalito, CA 94965

Price: $3,500

For Further Reference:

Using AutoCAD Release 12, Que Development Group

AutoCAD Release 12 QuickStart, Nancy Fulton, published by Que Corporation

AutoCAD Quick Reference, 2nd Edition, published by Que Corporation

Generic CADD

Generic CADD (Computer Aided Drafting and Design) is another popular CAD program originally designed for PCs and currently at Version 6.0. (The current version for the Mac is 2.0.) AutoCAD is used for high-end sophisticated engineering and architectural work. Generic CADD covers a broader base, giving users comparable power in an easier-to-use format than AutoCAD's format. Specifically, Generic CADD offers these features:

- Built-in symbol libraries

- Capability of displaying objects in different views

- Rotation capabilities

- Capability of printing on different printers or plotters

- Capability of working with a mouse or digitizing tablet

- Capability of adding dimensions

Figure 17.10 shows a screen from Generic CADD.

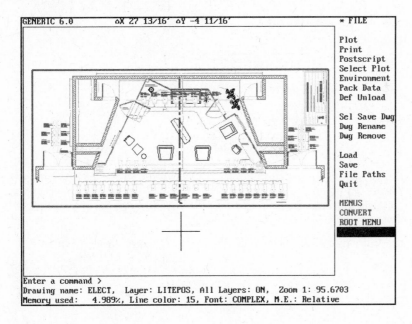

FIG. 17.10

A screen from Generic CADD.

Address: Autodesk Retail Products
11911 North Creek Parkway South
South Bothell, WA 98011

Price: $495

MiniCAD Plus

MiniCad Plus is a popular CAD program for the Macintosh. With a full array of tools in a variety of shapes and capabilities, MiniCad Plus gives users sophisticated CAD features in the easy-to-use Macintosh format.

MiniCad Plus enables users to handle the following tasks:

- Display objects in a variety of different views

- Show items on-screen in different colors

- Set measurement preferences

- Fill objects with colors or patterns

MiniCAD is ideal if you need CAD drafting quality but not all the full-blown CAD sophistication of the more expensive software packages.

Address: Graphsoft
8370 Court Avenue
Suite 202
Ellicott City, MD 21043

Price: $495

Chapter Summary

In this chapter, you learned about the variety of graphics programs available. From an introduction to paint, draw, presentation graphics, and CAD programs, you explored some currently popular graphics software packages.

In the following chapter, you learn about communications software.

Communications Software

So far in Part IV, you have learned about the various kinds of applications software. You learned how an application can automate a specific task, such as writing a letter (using a word processing application), balancing a checkbook (using a spreadsheet), or organizing an address list (using a database).

Although you can include communications software in the applications category, communications doesn't automate tasks. Communications does, however, provide you with added flexibility in managing, creating, and transmitting computer files.

This chapter introduces you to communications software—programs that allow you to connect and communicate with other computers. You can use communications software to transfer files (whether across the country or across the room), or send messages. In this chapter, you also explore information services, which take communications software one step further. Information services provide everything from on-line encyclopedias and advice panels to free software.

Understanding Communications

Many new users are wary of communications (also known as *telecom-munications*). Communications seems more intimidating to beginning users who often put off exploring this technology until put in a situation that requires it. In this section, you learn about communications and communications software packages and who benefits from using communications software.

Defining Communications

Communications with computers is no more complex than using the telephone. The only real difference is that communication takes place between two computers rather than between two people.

Communication between computers is possible because of two elements: the modem and the communications software. The first element, the *modem*, changes data into a form you can send through the phone lines. Modem is an abbreviation for *MOdulator/DEModulator*.

The modem can be a device outside the computer (an *external modem*) or inside the system unit (an *internal modem*). A modem receives data from your computer and *modulates* the information (that is, turns the data into electronic pulses). The information then is sent through the phone lines. The receiving modem at the other end of the transmission receives and *demodulates* the data (that is, turns the data from electronic pulses back to a form that the computer can use). To learn more about modems, see Chapter 3, "The Computer: A Closer Look."

Besides the modem, you must have communications software to communicate between computers. Communications software enables you to send data by activating the modem and sending the files. The receiver also must use communications software to receive the files.

Before you begin using communications software, become familiar with the following terms. This area of computer use has dozens of terms that you may find unfamiliar:

Baud. A measurement of the amount of information a modem transmits per second. A 2400-baud modem can send data at approximately 2,400 bits per second (bps). A bit is one of the eight pulses in a byte of information. A byte is roughly equivalent to one character.

Bulletin board. An electronic bulletin board used for leaving and receiving messages and files.

Downloading. The process of transferring a file from a remote computer to your computer.

Host. The computer that controls the communication. When a user calls a bulletin board and downloads a file, the computer that runs the bulletin board is the host.

Uploading. The process of transferring a file from your computer to a remote computer.

Defining Communications Software

When the field of communications was young, most communications software enabled you only to send and receive files. Today, a full range of capabilities is available in communications software, which makes selecting a software package to meet your needs difficult. Later in the chapter, you learn about several communications software packages with features that stand above the others, but most programs enable you to send and receive files.

With all communications programs, you can perform the following tasks:

- Select settings for the modem
- Connect to another computer that uses the same software or to a bulletin board service
- Send files
- Receive files
- Disconnect from the other computer or bulletin board service

Besides these features, the more popular communications software offers additional capabilities, which include the following:

- Easy to access help screens to assist you
- A wide selection of *file-transfer protocols* (the hardware and software standards used to send files so that the sending and receiving systems use the same setup)
- Macros that carry out complex operations with a simple keystroke
- Automatic *log-on* procedures (connecting to another system)
- Data compression utilities that compress the data you send to transmit files more quickly and with fewer errors
- Automatic retransmission features that resend any block of data that may have errors

■ The capability of sending files while you work on other applications on the computer

Who Uses Communications Software?

Communications software is used more in business than anywhere else. With the increase in the number of home offices, however, the line between business and home use is no longer clearly defined. The following list shows a few examples of people who use modems and communications software and the tasks they accomplish:

■ Sales managers who access and download sales information from outside sales points

■ Store managers who must send important information to the home office

■ Writers who research topics by using an information service

■ Travelers who want to make airline reservations

■ Office workers who transmit files to a central location

■ Hobbyists who communicate with other users about computers or software

Examining Communications Software

This section explores some of the popular communications software packages. You can find many low-cost communications programs that offer a variety of features (some software is even available on public bulletin board systems), but this section lists several of the most popular, currently available communications programs.

Note that many integrated software packages, such as PFS: First Choice, GeoWorks Pro, and ClarisWorks, offer communications as part of the entire package. For these integrated package users, sending a file is as simple as using another module of already-familiar software. For all others, however, finding and working with communications software involves more work.

The following sections give you an overview of the programs available. Specifically, you learn about PROCOMM PLUS 2.0, CrossTalk, PFS: First Choice, Microphone II, White Knight, and SmartCom III.

PROCOMM PLUS

As the definitive communications software for PCs, PROCOMM PLUS 2.0 and PROCOMM PLUS for Windows are easy-to-use communications programs that pack plenty of punch. DATASTORM TECHNOLOGIES, the makers of PROCOMM PLUS, adopted a new approach to the marketing of this product: the *test drive*. You can test the program before buying to make sure that the program does all you need. The test drive version is a working version of the program, minus a few of the features that make PROCOMM PLUS even more intuitive.

With the purchased version of the program, PROCOMM PLUS includes the following functions:

- Autodial features

- Comprehensive help screens

- An instructional manual and a tutorial

- A keyboard remapping program. (Keyboard remapping is redefining what the keys do. By remapping the keyboard, you can set up the system to work better while you are communicating with other systems.)

- A built-in text editor

- Samples of script files you can use to log on to frequently called services. (A script file consists of a series of commands stored as one command. Script files are used to perform repeated functions, such as logging on.)

- Free membership to several on-line information services

- 90 days of telephone technical support

PROCOMM PLUS is both flexible and powerful, and the features of the program are organized so that even beginners can navigate the program easily.

PROCOMM PLUS also includes a powerful script language that enables you to build add-on utilities for communications sessions, such as building a utility for logging on to another system or for downloading files. The language ASPECT script is available with the purchased version of PROCOMM PLUS along with examples of scripts written to automate tasks.

Address: DATASTORM TECHNOLOGIES, INC.
1621 Towne Drive, Suite G
Columbia, MO 65202

Price: $129 PROCOMM PLUS for DOS
$149 PROCOMM PLUS for Windows

For Further Reference:

Using ProCOMM PLUS, 2nd Edition, Walter R. Bruce III, published by Que
Corporation

  # CrossTalk

Crosstalk Communications has been a contender in the PC software
race since the early days of personal computing. Now, besides the
original CrossTalk for DOS, the company released a version of
CrossTalk specifically for use with Microsoft Windows.

CrossTalk for Windows offers the following features:

- The capability of sending and receiving files in the background;
you can send and receive files while working on another Windows
application

- The flexibility of cutting and pasting information from a communications session and using the data in another program running
under Windows

- A powerful programming language that enables you to create dialog boxes (a window the program displays on-screen to request or
display information) and automate tasks

- Support for all popular transmission protocols

- A phone book feature, which enables you to store and easily call
frequently used numbers

CrossTalk for Windows also supports all modems currently available
and provides 48 programmable function keys for macros or other customized features. You can use the customized pull-down menus, or on-
screen icon buttons with the mouse, to select menu items during the
work session.

Address: Digital Communications Association, Inc.
1000 Alderman Drive
Alpharetta, GA 30202-4199

Price: $195

PFS: First Choice (Communications)

With the communications module of PFS: First Choice, users can contact the outside world easily and receive data in a familiar form. Because the communications module has the basic look and feel of the other applications, First Choice users select only a few different options from the menu bar in the communications module. Figure 18.1 shows the option for beginning a First Choice communications session.

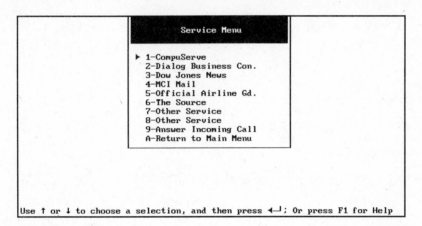

FIG. 18.1

The options for starting a First Choice communications session.

You do not find the wealth of powerful features in First Choice's communications module that you find in PROCOMM PLUS or CrossTalk. If you need only to send and receive an occasional file or perform simple communications procedures, however, First Choice may be all the communications software you need. First Choice communications offers the following features:

- Easy-to-use options in a familiar interface

- The capability of adding frequently called numbers to the Service menu

- Macros to dial numbers automatically

- The capability of cutting and pasting information from a communications session into other First Choice applications

- Speed keys for moving around the communications screen and for working with text received

First Choice enables you to connect to any remote computer, whether a mainframe, in the home office, another PC on the other side of the office, or an on-line information service, such as CompuServe. An advantage to using the entire First Choice package is that, no matter what application you use, the menus on-screen remain similar.

Of course, the best part of all integrated software packages is the integration. After you receive the information, you can work with the data in word processing, spreadsheet, database, and graphics applications.

Address: Software Publishing Corporation
                    1901 Landings Drive
                    Mountain View, CA 94039-7210

Price: $149

For Further Reference:

Using PFS: First Choice, Katherine Murray, published by Que Corporation

MicroPhone II

MicroPhone II is a powerful but easy-to-use communications program for the Macintosh. Specifically, MicroPhone II offers the following features:

- An easy-to-use icon system for logging on to services

- A series of specially designed setup files (or scripts) that enable you to log on to services easily

- The capability of working in the background (working on other applications while you send or receive files)

- A sophisticated scripting language that enables you to automate operations with written procedures that streamline communications sessions

Figure 18.2 shows the opening screen of MicroPhone II.

Address: Software Ventures
                    2907 Claremont Avenue
                    Suite 220
                    Berkeley, CA 94705

Price: $295

White Knight

White Knight (formerly Red Ryder) is another communications program for the Macintosh. White Knight was the first communications program developed for the Mac. In the current version, White Knight offers the following features:

- The capability of customizing a variety of features

- An easy-to-use menu and icon system

- Full communications features, including script support and automatic log-on procedures

- Macro capability that you can add as on-screen buttons

Address: FreeSoft
150 Hickory Drive
Beaver Falls, PA 15010

Price: $139

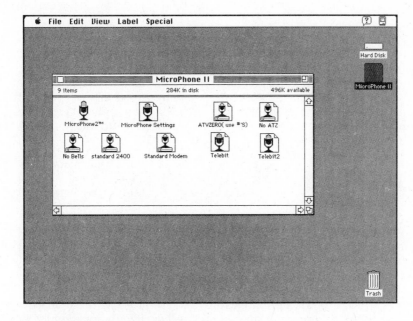

FIG. 18.2

The opening
screen of
MicroPhone II.

SmartCom III

SmartCom III was created by Hayes, one of the leading modem manufacturers. Versions of SmartCom III are available for the PC and the Macintosh. Specifically, the following features are included with SmartCom III:

- An easy-to-use menu system

- A displayable, scrollable buffer that enables you to read through previous sections of information you receive

■ Full-color capabilities

■ Autopilots, similar to scripts or macros, enabling you to stream-line communications operations

■ Start-up procedures that enable you to sign onto major informa-tion services

Address: Hayes Microcomputer, Inc.
5923 Peach Tree Industrial Park Boulevard
Norcross, GA 30092

Price: $105

Examining Information Services

Contacting an information service is just one of the many functions a communications program can handle. An *information service* consists of a large mainframe computer that stores information. The information may relate to a wide range of topics or may pertain only to a specific application. Most information services are available to Mac, Amiga, and IBM computers.

This section introduces several major information services and tells you a little about each service. Specifically, you learn about CompuServe, PRODIGY, Promenade, DIALOG, GEnie, Dow Jones, and BIX and America Online.

CompuServe

CompuServe is the information service almost every computer user knows about. If you want to investigate the weather in Tahiti, learn about cruises to Alaska, or check stock prices in Ecuador, CompuServe has the information. Whether you want to log on and read through in-formation or participate in an on-line forum of users, CompuServe opens up worlds of information for you to explore.

When you first subscribe to CompuServe, you receive a few hours of free time to help you learn the system's commands and menu struc-ture. You can find information in the following categories:

■ Arts and entertainment

■ News

■ Weather

- Sports

- Travel

- Electronic mail service

- Financial information

- Numerous bibliographic databases

- Industry news and reviews

- Games

- Productivity forums covering particular computers or applications

- Job markets

The preceding list gives only a few of the many services available on CompuServe.

Address: CompuServe
P.O. Box 20212
Columbus, OH 43220

Price: $39.95 (for start-up kit)

For Further Reference:

Que's Quick Guide to CompuServe, Mark K. Bilbo, published by Que Corporation

PRODIGY

PRODIGY is a large information service that links you to numerous outside resources. You can purchase items, make plane and hotel reservations, and find other connections throughout the world. Macintosh and PC computer users can log on to PRODIGY. Although PRODIGY is extremely popular as an information exchange, the program has a drawback: you cannot save files by downloading them to your computer. You can print only what you see on-screen.

If you are a PS/1 user, PRODIGY is included with the system. Another feature, the Users' Club (another bulletin board), is a division of PRODIGY created specifically for PS/1 users. In the Users' Club, you find information about how to use the new PS/1 and how to get tips and suggestions from other PS/1 users and PS/1 technical support staff.

PRODIGY is a large service that offers almost limitless access to information. You can find all kinds of different computer users and computer information in the larger-scale PRODIGY network. PRODIGY gives you the option of making connections far beyond the scope of PS/1 topics, such as the following areas that may interest you:

- Travel
- Shopping
- Financial information
- Educational software
- News
- Weather
- Stocks

Depending on the version of PRODIGY you use, you may be able to use a mouse. The version of PRODIGY packaged with most PS/1s may not be the current version (the old version doesn't support the mouse). If you have an old version, however, don't despair. After the initial sign-on to PRODIGY (or the Users' Club), the Prodigy company sends you an updated version that supports a mouse. The screens and the user interface also are improved in the new version.

Address: Prodigy Membership Services
                445 Hamilton Avenue
                White Plains, NY 10601

Price: Free trial period
                $12/month flat fee

For Further Reference:

Using Prodigy, Stephen Nelson, published by Que Corporation

Promenade

Promenade is another communications service included in the PS/1 package. Promenade offers a different mix of information—centered on PS/1 use—than you find in PRODIGY. The biggest benefit Promenade offers is the capability of uploading and downloading files.

Promenade offers users the following areas of interest:

- **Clubs and special interests.** Includes business and financial information and supports car, entertainment, hobby, career, veterans, sports, and other special information groups.

- **Entertainment and games.** Includes Center Stage Auditorium where special guests are included in forums, and users can type questions and join the conference. You also can play on-line games, such as Casino, MasterWord, and sports quizzes.

■ **Education and reference.** Includes the Academic American Encyclopedia and the Interactive Education Services, which enable you to enroll in courses, learn more about career opportunities, and access the Teachers' Information Network.

■ **Software and computing.** Includes access to the 10 top programs, contains a special PS/1 forum, special features, software highlights, and information from the developers of the PS/1.

■ **What's new and member services.** Contains information about membership, billing, customizing Promenade, and a directory of services.

Address: Promenade
8619 Westwood Center Drive, Suite 200
Vienna, VA 22181

Price: Free trial period
$.12 per minute after 6 P.M.
$.25 per minute before 6 P.M.

DIALOG

The DIALOG information service is available to both PC and Macintosh users and includes the following features:

■ Access to more than 300 databases

■ Business information

■ Chemistry article overviews

■ Information on humanities

■ Social science studies

■ Electronic mail network

■ DIALNETZ custom telephone service

■ The new ImageCatcher feature (for Mac users), which enables you to perform a variety of operations on images and text

Address: DIALOG Information Service, Inc.
3460 Hillview Avenue
Palo Alto, CA 94304

Price: $99 to $185 for start-up package

GEnie

GEnie, from General Electric, offers on-line time at a rate lower than that offered by other companies. GEnie offers information on the following topics:

- Business
- News
- Home shopping
- Travel
- Macintosh forums
- PC forums
- Bulletin board of games and miscellaneous utilities
- Computer industry news

Address: GEnie
Dept. 02B
401 N. Washington Street A
Rockville, MD 20850

Price: $29.95 registration fee

Dow Jones

Dow Jones News/Retrieval is the only information service devoted exclusively to business-related information. Whether you need stock quotes, current articles from the Wall Street Journal, or a piece of financial analysis software, you can find the information in Dow Jones. This program offers the following services:

- Business information
- Financial information
- Market prices
- Up-to-the-minute news
- A complete edition of the *Wall Street Journal*
- *Barron's* articles
- *Business Week* articles
- *Forbes* articles
- *Money* articles

Address: Dow Jones
P.O. Box 300
Princeton, NJ 08540

Price: $24 and up

BIX

BIX is a relatively new information service, a spin-off of *BYTE* magazine. BIX was first to stray from the norm set by other information providers by charging a flat fee. You access the service for an unlimited length of time for a set fee as opposed to the hourly amounts charged by other companies. Specifically, BIX offers the following forums:

- Amiga exchange

- IBM exchange

- Mac exchange

- Writers exchange

- Games exchange

- Up-to-the-minute computer industry news

- Support from major hardware and software manufacturers

Address: BIX
One Phoenix Mill Lane
Peterborough, NH 03458

Price: $59 (flat rate for three months)

America Online

America Online comes standard with the GeoWorks Ensemble and GeoWorks Pro integrated software packages or can be purchased separately. America Online features:

- A software library of more than 15,000 programs

- Live forums for advice and ideas exchange

- Electronic mail and message service

- On-line encyclopedia

America Online also allows you to copy and save files directly to your hard disk.

Address: America Online
8619 Westwood Center Dr., Suite 200
Vienna, VA 22182

Price: $7.95 monthly fee

Chapter Summary

In this chapter, you learned about communications and the various kinds of communications software available. The following chapter gives you a closer look at educational and recreational software.

Educational and Recreational Software

Computers don't have to be the no-nonsense workhorses they appear to be when used with some applications. Computers also can be the Indianapolis 500, Dodger Stadium, the home of the U.S. Open, the scene of a murder mystery, or the airway over Madagascar. Computers can perform more than operations alone. Computers also can teach you about worlds you have previously left unexplored—things like world geography, French, typing, or advanced chemistry.

This chapter provides a brief look at a few of the educational and recreational programs available in the PC and Macintosh markets.

Working with Educational and Recreational Software

Whether the objective is to learn something new or just to get away from tedium for awhile, the following people reach for educational and recreational programs:

- Users who want to learn something new, from typing to tax laws to Tennyson
- Children and adults who want to brush up on math and English skills
- Employees who want to review skills related to their jobs
- Adults, students, and children who want to hone their computer skills with interactive game software
- Adults and children who play arcade-style games

Examining Educational Software

This section introduces the popular educational programs World Atlas, Brøderbund Treehouse, and Where in the World is Carmen Sandiego?. Too many kinds of educational software exist to list them all, but these programs are representative of the selections available at local software shops.

World Atlas

The World Atlas program is a combination of maps and graphics and a staggering amount of information on populations, geography, governments, economies, and cultures. World Atlas includes world, continent, and individual country maps. Each map displays on-screen the major cities and their populations and important geographical features.

World Atlas is mouse-driven. Although you can use the keyboard, the program is extremely slow without a mouse. Because of the huge amount of information in the data files of the program—World Atlas eats up 8M of disk storage—the program is unusable without a hard disk. The program, however, runs with only 512K of RAM.

You can print a wide variety of charts with World Atlas. You also can use data, maps, and graphics to produce reports that you can import into desktop publishing or word processing applications.

Address: The Software Toolworks
60 Leveroni Ct.
Novato, CA 94949

Price: $80

Brøderbund Treehouse

Brøderbund Treehouse is ideal for 6-10 year olds. Children are exposed to math, music, science, and writing skills through an exciting and supportive environment. Treehouse consists of six basic activities: Theater, a language and drama arts development game; Road Rally, a chip and coin game that teaches math skills; Musical Keys and Musical Maze, musical appreciation games; and Animal Album and Guess My Animal, games that expose children to the sciences.

Address: Brøderbund
               17 Paul Drive
               San Rafael, CA 94903

Price: $59.95

Where in the World is Carmen Sandiego?

Explore the world's great cities while chasing Carmen's notorious gang of thieves. Use Interpol's Crime Computer to get arrest warrants. Where in the World includes a real world almanac with which to explore. Also available in the Carmen Sandiego series of educational software are the following programs:

- *Where in the USA is Carmen Sandiego?,* which includes a copy of Fodor's USA Travel Guide

- *Where in Europe Is Carmen Sandiego?,* which includes a Rand McNally Concise Atlas of Europe; an on-screen, fact-finder's database; and a crimestopper's notebook

- *Where in Time Is Carmen Sandiego?*

- *Where in America's Past Is Carmen Sandiego?*

Address: Brøderbund
               17 Paul Drive
               San Rafael, CA 94903

Price: $35-60 (depending on where Carmen is)

Examining Recreational Software

You do need spreadsheets, word processors, and database programs for serious work. Graphics programs can give you a creative break from data crunching, but for a really good time, find and play a game you like. (Some games even are available with a fake spreadsheet that pops down over the game—for those sticky moments when the boss walks up and looks over your shoulder.) This section examines a few games available for PC and Macintosh computers.

Chuck Yeager's Advanced Flight Trainer

Whether you are an armchair pilot or an aviation specialist, you will enjoy the ride with Chuck Yeager's Advanced Flight Trainer 2.0. To accomplish your mission, you can choose one of 18 aerodynamically correct planes complete with 3-D modeling. By using an unlimited number of camera angles, zooms, and pans, you can soar over your choice of landscapes as you cruise along different courses.

Address: Electronic Arts
1820 Gateway Drive
San Mateo, CA 94404-2496

Price: $24.95

Chuck Yeager's Air Combat

This combat flight simulator puts players in the cockpit of six elite fighter planes during some of the most historic combat of World War II, Korea, and Vietnam. With more than 50 actual historic missions from which to choose and the option to fly on either side, players get both the variety and broad perspective of air combat history. Players can fly an American F-4 Phantom against a World War II German Focke-Wulfe 190 and a North Korean Mig-15.

Address: Electronic Arts
1820 Gateway Drive
San Mateo, CA 94404-2496

Price: $59.95

Mah-Jongg

Mah-Jongg is the ancient game of Chinese tiles. It is similar to the American game of Concentration in which you match and remove similar patterns of tiles. Versions of Mah-Jongg are available for the PC and Macintosh, although you may see the game under different names, such as Shang-hi for the Mac. Figure 19.1 shows a screen of Mah-Jongg for the PC.

Address: Nels Anderson
92 Bishop Drive
Framingham, MA 01701

Price: Shareware, optional contribution

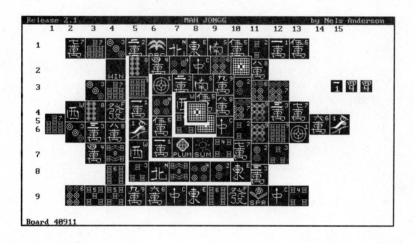

Fig. 19.1

A screen from
Mah-Jongg.

Monopoly

This popular board game has been rewritten for the PC. With the electronic version of Monopoly, you can make all the traditional Monopoly moves: buy and sell property, accumulate wealth, *and* go to Jail.

Address: Virgin Mastertronic International, Inc.
18001 Cowan, Suite A & B
Irvine, CA 92714

Price: $50

Hard Ball III

No more slow-pitching from the mound, Accolade's Hard Ball brings professional baseball right into your computer. You can choose a traditional 9-inning game (or go into extra innings if the competition is tight), select teams, change the position of players, and control the type and direction of pitches.

Address: Accolade
5300 Stevens Creek Blvd.
San Jose, CA 95129

Price: $60

Windows Entertainment Pak Volume II

This collection of games for Windows contains two solitaire games and a game that enables you to create jigsaw puzzles that you draw with a paint program. Also included is a tiles game and an apple-eating snake game. Pipe Dream complements this package with a race to lay pieces of pipe before the green goop begins to flow!

Address: Microsoft Corporation
One Microsoft Way
Redmond, WA

Price: $29.95

Casino Pak

This Windows package is a typical Las Vegas style game—but without the worry of losing money. The Pak contains Video Poker, Keno, and Black Jack. The features are what you would expect from any big casino with double downs and splits. Overall, the Casino Pak gives you the thrill of Las Vegas or Reno without the strain on your pocketbook.

Chapter Summary

In this chapter, you looked at some of the popular educational and recreational software programs available for PC and Macintosh computers. The next chapter concludes your trek through applications software with an exploration of utility programs that make your work environment more efficient.

Utility Programs

By now, you have probably set up your computer, purchased a few application programs, and, perhaps, even created and saved some project files. So, the next step may lie in simply making the work processes faster, easier, and more efficient. You can achieve these improvements with utility programs.

Suppose that you want to speed up the rate at which application programs run. A memory management utility can perform this task. If the system starts to crash a lot, or files mysteriously vanish, you may have a computer virus. Antivirus utilities can solve this problem. To keep a hard disk defragmented, you may want to purchase a hard disk optimization utility. To add organization to your life, you may consider a time management tool. To add spice and fun to the work environment, background screens and sounds are available.

Defining Utility Programs

Utility programs are designed to meet specific needs. These programs, however, don't always behave like other programs that produce text or graphical illustrations—although utilities can enhance these applications. Foreign language dictionaries that run parallel with most word processors, for example, are available and sold under the label of a utility program. On-line thesauri and grammar checkers also are utilities that run with most word processors. Adding sounds and visual elements to an existing application also is now possible with select utility programs.

Besides complimenting applications, utilities also can enhance and aid the operating system of a computer. System (or *operating environment*) utilities run in either the background or foreground. A background utility, known as an *init* (initialization program) on a Macintosh and as a *TSR* (Terminate and Stay Resident) on a PC, is activated when the computer is started. The program then runs in the background and is accessed with a menu command or an action performed by the user. Most virus checkers are initialization programs that run in the background. When a disk is inserted, the antivirus utility scans the disk for computer viruses and displays a warning if a virus exists. Sound utilities also are inits, called forward when the user performs certain actions.

Utilities that run in the foreground behave like any other application on the computer. The program is opened and menu (or typed) commands perform certain tasks. Hard disk repair, defragmentation, and some antivirus utilities can be opened like other programs. Most time and date scheduling tools also are utility programs that are accessed like other applications.

Understanding the Benefits of Utility Programs

Whether you are a system administrator for a large network of computers or simply use the computer for infrequent personal work, there is probably a utility program to make work easier and more efficient. The following lists some of the major benefits a utility program can bring:

- Optimized work environments
- Clean and organized disks
- Audio and visual interactions from your computer
- A longer life for the hardware
- Time and date management tools for personal organization

Reviewing Utility Programs

Due to increasing popularity, utility programs are establishing their own place in the computer software realm. Most retailers even have a separate listing for utilities. This section highlights the following utility categories and provides information on various software packages available, including the addresses of manufacturers and retail list prices.

- AntiVirus Programs
- Compression, Backup, and File Management Utilities
- Utility MultiPacks
- Personal Organization and Productivity Programs
- Sounds and Screens

AntiVirus Programs

Computer viruses, created by ingenious but misguided programmers, now are commonplace in most computer systems. A computer virus is much like its biological cousin, which attacks the human body and which can spread and mutate. The programmer writes the virus code and then attaches this code to seemingly harmless files. After the infected file is copied to the computer's hard disk, the virus can spread to infect other files. Suppose that a friend gives you a computer game that, unbeknownst to either of you, is infected with the nVIR virus (nVIR is a common but treatable computer virus). The virus lies dormant until the file that loads the game file *and* the virus is loaded in computer RAM. All other files you launch become infected after loading the files into RAM. If left untreated, you can see how the virus eventually can spread to, and infect, all the files on a computer.

So many different viruses exist that do so many different things, listing all these viruses in this book is impossible. Some viruses simply display messages on specific dates, other viruses can destroy or hide data, and—if left untreated—some of the more lethal viruses can actually ruin hardware.

Because viruses cannot be seen, you need to use utility programs to combat the possible infection of the computer. Antivirus utilities can run in the background to scan each disk you insert into a floppy drive and programs as they load into RAM. Any known viruses are detected by the utility and a warning is displayed. Most virus utilities also come with virus detection programs that run like other normal programs, allowing you to manually scan and search files, folders, and disk drives. Virtually all virus utilities can eradicate viruses and repair infected files. The following sections cover several popular antivirus programs for the Mac and PC.

Virex

Virex antivirus for both Macintosh and the PC is designed to keep the computer applications, system, and files *germ free*. Background monitoring enables Virex to detect infected files when a disk is inserted or a file is launched. An audible virus alarm sounds upon detection and you can then have Virex remove the viral code and restore the file to its original condition. Figure 20.1 shows the Virex introduction screen.

To guard against new viruses as they are introduced, registered users are notified of updated versions of Virex. You also can subscribe to the Virex "Annual Update Service" and receive the updates through the mail.

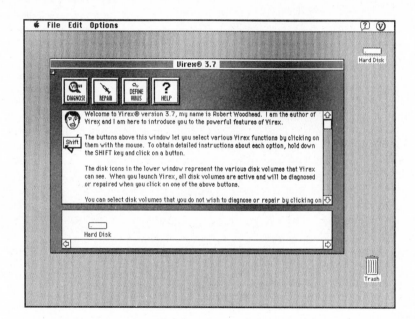

FIG. 20.1

The Virex introduction screen.

Address: Microcom, Inc.
                    P.O. Box 51489
                    Durham, NC 22717

Price: $99

You also can purchase Virex as part of the MVP Package by Microcom for $259.

Symantec AntiVirus for the Macintosh

Symantec AntiVirus for the Macintosh (SAM) is a comprehensive antivirus utility that protects a Mac from the harmful effects of computer viruses.

As disks are inserted or files are launched, SAM scans the files for viruses. If a virus is found a warning is displayed. You then can use the Virus Clinic to eradicate the offending virus. Virus Clinic works like other Mac programs to scan individual files or complete hard drives or network servers.

Current versions of SAM combat known viruses (WDEF, nVir, Scores, and ZUC_), and also detect file irregularities, which may be unknown strains of virus.

Address: Symantec Corporation
10201 Torre Ave.
Cupertino, CA 95014-2132

Price: $99

Compression, Backup, and File Management Utilities

Data compression is important when disk space is limited, a situation that affects most computer users. Compression programs reduce files to a fraction of the original size. If you have a 100K word processing file, for example, you can (depending on the compression program you use) reduce the size of the file down to 40K. Compressing files is especially helpful when you want to send a file over a modem.

Compressed files must be uncompressed before use so, depending on the program, you must either decompress the file manually, or the file is decompressed automatically when opened. The time needed to compress and decompress files is the only drawback associated with these popular programs.

You must understand the importance of making backups of files. Making a copy of one file is a small matter and requires little time, but what if you want to back up *all* the files (and programs) on your hard disk? At this point, file backup utilities can help. Most backup programs can reduce the copying task to a few simple keystrokes or mouse clicks.

The following sections list several popular compression and backup programs. Also included in these sections are file management utilities, which help you organize and access files quickly.

AutoDoubler

AutoDoubler saves on disk space by compressing files to nearly half their original size. Options are available to compress specific files and folders, or you can have AutoDoubler compress the entire contents of a disk. One of AutoDoubler's nicest features is the capability of decompressing quickly. When a file is opened, AutoDoubler decompresses the file directly into RAM and the file is opened almost as quickly as an uncompressed file. Figure 20.2 shows the AutoDoubler Main Control window.

The AutoDoubler Main Control window.

Address:	Salient Software, Inc.
	124 University Ave., Suite 300
	Palo Alto, CA 94301
Price:	$79

Fastback Plus

Fastback Plus is a backup utility for both the PC and Macintosh. You can use Fastback's high-speed, easy to use file backup capability for virtually any device. The Quicktag option marks files for fast backup and data compression, which reduces the number of disks needed. Also included in Fastback Plus are English language macro's for automatic backups, a scheduler for timed backups, and full copy and erase functions.

Address: Fifth Generation
             10049 N. Reiger Road
             Baton Rouge, LA 70809-4562

Price: $189

DiskLock

DiskLock is a security utility for files and disks. The features found in this utility are password protection, locking, and encryption schemes. The "load and forget" operation makes DiskLock easy to use and security measures are stringent. This program is ideal for anyone who works with sensitive data.

Address: Fifth Generation
             10049 N. Reiger Road
             Baton Rouge, LA 70809-4562

Price: $189

DiskTop

DiskTop is a file management tool that enables you to easily find, list, delete, copy, rename, or move files from within the current application. You also can launch other programs, shut down and restart without leaving the current program. Also included with DiskTop is GOfer 2.0 for sophisticated and detailed file searches and DT Launch, which allows for easier and faster application loads. Figure 20.3 shows an example of a DT Launch screen.

Address: CE Software
             P.O. Box 65580
             West Des Moines, IA 50265

Price: $99

System Resource Utilities

Several system management tools exist for the Macintosh. These tools enable you to organize system resource files, such as font, sound, and init files to save memory and create a cleaner, streamlined System folder. The following two sections cover Mac System resource utilities.

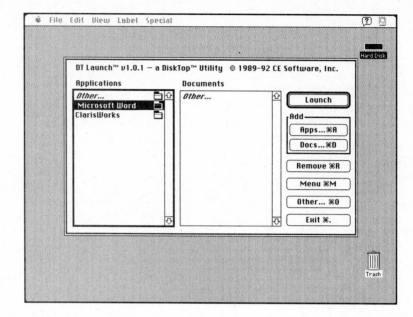

FIG. 20.3

An example of
a DT Launch
screen on the
Macintosh.

Suitcase II

Suitcase II, a resource management utility, is designed for anyone operating more than the bare system resources. Suitcase II enables you to
organize fonts, sounds and FKeys into folders. When you launch an
application, you can then load only the necessary resource folders.
This capability saves on memory and speeds up processing. Suitcase II
also can compress font and sound files down to 60 percent of original
size. Suitcase II also displays fonts in their own typeface so you can see
what each font looks like without first typing with the font selected.

Address: Fifth Generation Systems
                  10049 N. Reiger Road
                  Baton Rouge, LA 70809-4562

Price: $79

MasterJuggler 1.57

MasterJuggler offers timesaving and fun resource management tools.
You can apply various sounds, for example, for the Macintosh to use
instead of the standard beep. You also can link programs so that all
programs launch with one command. You can purchase MasterJuggler

separately or as part of the ALSoft Power Utilities package, which also includes disk management and recovery tools.

Address: ALSoft, Inc.
                 P.O. Box 927
                 Spring, TX 77383

Price: $49

Utility MultiPacks

If you need more than one utility program, you may want to consider buying a multiple-utility package. These packages include several full-blown utilities, bundled in one box at a considerable cost savings. The following sections cover utility multi-packs for the PC and Macintosh computers.

Norton Utilities

The Norton line of Utilities for the Macintosh and PC are integrated file management and productivity packages. Norton Utilities for DOS, version 6.0, provides data recovery tools, such as Disk Doctor, UnErase, File Fix, and Disk Editor. Norton for DOS also comes with tools for defragmenting drives, locking files, and reducing the amount of memory required by DOS. Also included is a sophisticated directory control, a powerful file searching program and a tool to completely erase files from a disk.

Norton Utilities for Windows enhances the File Manager and also provides backup and restore tools. Also included is a "Shredder" to completely erase files, a screen saver; quick launching and access paths; a batch builder to automate common tasks; and the Emergency Disk to UnErase, UnFormat, and repair damaged disks.

Finally, Norton Utilities for the Macintosh provides Mac users with the Norton Disk Editor to locate and fine-tune disk information, the Speed Disk with advanced algorithms so that even sudden power losses won't destroy data, and Visual Data Map for graphically showing data fragmentation. Several tools for data recovery and repair also are provided, as well as an advanced Find utility.

Address: Symantec Corporation
                 10201 Torre Ave.
                 Cupertino, CA 95014-2132

Price: $149 (Windows)
                 $179 (DOS)
                 $129 (Mac)

For Further Reference:

Using Norton Desktop for Windows, Michael L. Miller, published by Que Corporation

Using Norton Desktop for DOS, Que Development Group

Using Norton Utilities 6, Alan C. Elliott, published by Que Corporation

Norton Utilities 6 Quick Reference, Edmond X. DeJesus, published by Que Corporation

Using Norton Utilities for the Mac, Bob Benedict, published by Que Corporation

911 Utilities

911 is a combination utility package designed by Microcom, Inc. 911 starts with an extensive Troubleshooting Guide to help you isolate and identify problems. If your Mac is down, consulting the Troubleshooting Guide can walk you through the steps necessary to get up and running again.

Included in the 911 package is 1stAid, a file management tool that examines files and disks to determine their status and recover lost information. Complete Undelete is a control panel device that maintains a log of all deleted files that you can retrieve if necessary. For virus protection, a copy of Virex also is included in 911 (refer to the Virex section of this chapter for more information).

911 provides the Sector Collector to isolate and prevent bad disk sectors from being used. Using this program reduces the chance of losing precious data due to disk errors. Finally, the FileKnit optimization tool rounds out the 911 Utilities package. FileKnit improves performance by defragmenting files on either hard or floppy disks. Data is reformed into contiguous files that you then can access and read more quickly. Figure 20.4 shows an example of defragmentation in progress, using FileKnit.

Address: Microcom, Inc.
P.O. Box 51489
Durham, NC 22717

Price: $149

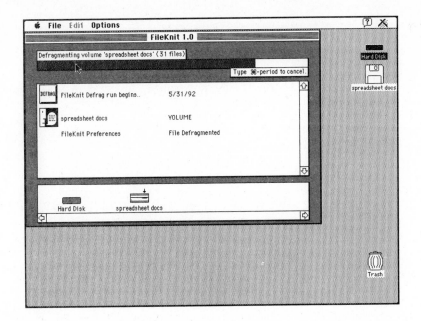

FIG. 20.4

An example of a FileKnit defragmentation in progress.

PC Tools

PC Tools is an integrated utility package that includes Windows Backup for backing up files to disk or tape drives, Windows UnDelete for recovering deleted files, and Windows Launcher for starting DOS or Windows programs from the system menu. PC Tools also includes virus protection, FileFix and DiskFix for repairing damaged files and disks, the Application Menu System to quickly move from one application to another, and Commute—a remote communications program. Rounding out the collection of utilities is Wipe, a program that completely erases files; Filefind for detailed searches; a data compression option; and a system monitoring program that lists available memory, operating information, and peripherals.

Address: Central Point Software, Inc.
15220 N.W. Grendrier Pkwy., Suite 200
Beaverton, OR 97006

Price: $179

For Further Reference:

Using PC Tools 7.1, Walter Bruce, published by Que Corporation

PC Tools 7 Quick Reference, Edmond X. DeJesus, published by Que Corporation

Personal Organization and Productivity Programs

If you use your computer often, you may want to invest in organization and productivity programs. These utilities provide calendars, schedulers, clocks, and other time-management functions to help keep your activities on track. The following sections cover these helpful organization and productivity utilities.

Alarming Events

If you have a hard time arriving at appointments on time, try a time management utility, such as Alarming Events. Alarming Events helps you track your events by creating reminder notes that can consist of up to 29 characters for subject titles and 255 characters for note titles. You then assign events a type; timed events, such as meeting appointments, or untimed events, such as a to-do list.

When the specified time of an event occurs, a pop-up notification box shows you the subject and notes associated with the event. You then can postpone notification, mark the event completed, delete the event, or simply dismiss the dialog box with no action. You also can print events in Report format, showing subject, body, and date. You can store past events in an archive file or appointment file for easy reference.

Address: CE Software
P.O. Box 65580
West Des Moines, IA 50265

Price: $129

CalendarMaker

This program provides a quick and efficient way to create monthly calendars that display events and information. Calendar options include 1 or 2 months per page (tall or wide), pictorial styles, and date icon reminders. You also can create floating notes to print in unused boxes or across multiple dates, which are useful for multiple-day events, and large reminders of forthcoming events. Figure 20.5 shows an example of a CalendarMaker screen.

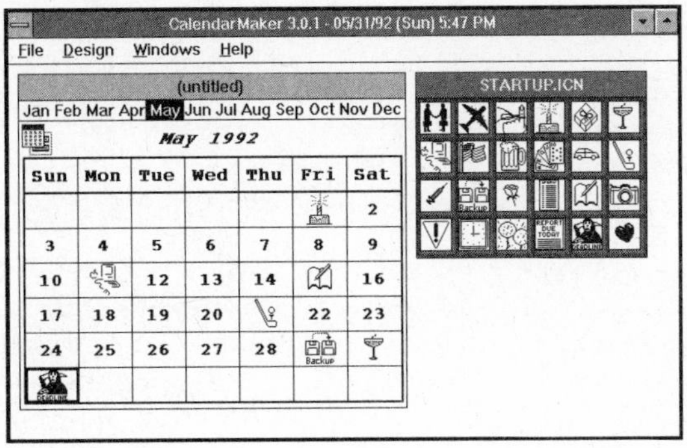

FIG. 20.5

An example of a
CalendarMaker
screen.

Individual days can be viewed in edit boxes, allowing you to add text
(up to 254 characters per date box) with a choice of text style, print
colors, and monthly icons. Also included with CalendarMaker is
IconMover, a utility program that enables you to move, edit, or design
icons.

Address: CE Software
                 P.O. Box 65580
                 West Des Moines, IA 50265

Price: $69

Sounds and Screens

If you leave a computer on but unattended, the image on the monitor
may eventually burn into the screen. Screen saver programs ensure the
life of the monitor by blacking out the screen after a specified time
passes with no keyboard activity or mouse movement. As soon as the
keyboard or mouse is touched, the screen saver goes away and the
computer image reappears.

Many different kinds of screen savers are available with a multitude of
animated pictures that appear when the screen saver is activated.

Sound programs don't save your hardware but do add some spice to
your computing experience. Sound programs, such as ScreenGems, can
replace your simple computer "beep" with any of a multitude of other
sounds.

ScreenGems

ScreenGems by Microseeds is a collection of four separate screen utilities. ColorDesk enables you to replace the standard desktop pattern with any PICT format graphic. This program requires a fair amount of memory though, approximately 300K on a standard Apple (640x480) 256-color monitor.

If you switch the monitor between black & white and color often, Switch-A-Roo reduces this task to a simple key combination, which eliminates the need to go through the Control Panel. Also included in ScreenGems is Dimmer, a screen-saving device. Dimmer works by slowly dimming the monitor when the computer is unattended. You can customize the dim with a time delay (1-120 minutes) and a dimming level (0 to 100 percent).

The fourth utility in ScreenGems is TN-3 which enables you to *redecorate* the finder with color sets for menu titles and commands. A bonus utility, known as Globe, also is included. Globe, a little spinning sphere that resembles earth, replaces the standard wristwatch the Mac displays while the computer is processing.

Address: Microseeds Publishing, Inc.
              5801 Benjamin Center Drive, Suite 103
              Tampa, FL 33635

Price: $79

After Dark

After Dark for both Macintosh and Windows PCs provides a large and unusual number of screen-saving modules in the package, including the Flying Toasters and Fish! You can set the time that passes before the program automatically invokes and hot spots to instantly turn on or off the program also can be specified. Also available is More After Dark, which provides 25 add-on displays and also virus scanning and a game module.

Address: Berkeley Systems
              2095 Rose Street
              Berkeley, CA 94709

Price: $49
              $69 with More After Dark

Pyro!

Pyro! is an entertaining screen saver for the Macintosh and PCs running DOS. Thirteen modules for the Mac and forty-one displays for the PC are provided, including a fireworks spray, a kaleidoscope, and a bouncing clock. Helpful messages also can be displayed so that you can leave information on-screen while you're gone. Even an entry-level password protection option is available so that only you can remove Pyro! from the screen. Figure 20.6 shows an example of the Pyro! configuration screen.

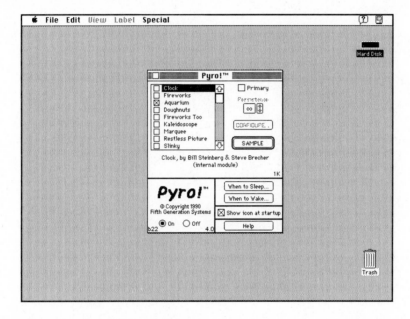

Address: Fifth Generation
             10049 N. Reiger Road
             Baton Rouge, LA 70809-4562

Price: $39 (Mac)
             $49 (PC)

SoundMaster

"I'm tryin' to think, but nothin' happens!" Imagine these immortal words from Curly of the Three Stooges replacing the simple beep of the computer. If you don't care for the Stooges, how about HAL 9000 from 2001, informing you "I'm sorry Dave, I'm afraid I can't do that" when you reach a Macintosh limitation. These sounds are possible with

SoundMaster by Bruce Tomlin. SoundMaster is a simple control panel device that enables you to add a multitude of pre-recorded sounds to the system folder. Figure 20.7 shows the SoundMaster Control Panel window.

The best feature of SoundMaster is the cost—free! You can down-load SoundMaster from most bulletin board services but to keep the shareware spirit alive, send a donation to creator Bruce Tomlin at the following address.

Address: Bruce Tomlin
                    15801 Chase Hill Blvd. #109
                    San Antonio, TX 78256

Price: Free (donations accepted)

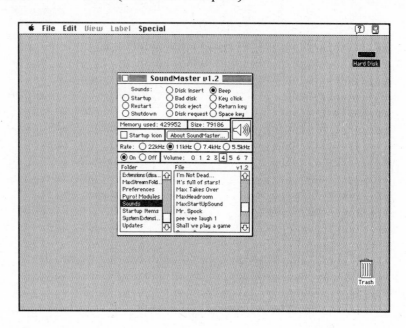

FIG. 20.7

The SoundMaster Control Panel window.

Chapter Summary

This chapter concludes an exploration of utility programs and ends *Introduction to Personal Computers*, 3rd Edition.

This book introduced you to the various makes of computer and software programs and showed you a large selection of the wide variety of computer products currently available. From a basic introduction to hardware and software, you progressed to exploring different kinds of hardware and software products. For the prepurchase user, this book also includes important elements to consider as you explore the computer options and select the right system and software. Remember that, although this book touches on all major areas of personal computers, because the scope of computer information available is so broad, some of the finer points aren't covered. If you didn't find an answer to a specific question or need within these pages, consult other Que publications for more information.

Glossary

5 1/4-inch disk. Also known as a *floppy* or *minifloppy* disk, this disk is a flexible piece of mylar plastic, encased in a protective covering, that records data.

3 1/2-inch disk. A smaller, sturdier floppy disk, known as a *microfloppy*, encased in a hard plastic housing.

Access light. The light on the front of the system unit that glows when the computer is reading from or writing to a disk.

Access time. A measurement of how quickly the computer can read and write information from and to disk drives and send data to various chips in the computer.

Address. The number assigned to a bit of data so that the computer can store and retrieve this data.

Analog. An electronic signal that is a combination of varying intensities. In personal computing, analog often refers to a specific monitor type and to the way the monitor receives video signals.

Application. A class of software, such as word processing, spreadsheet, or database applications.

ASCII. An acronym for American Standard Code for Information Interchange. ASCII is an international standard for representing letters and numbers.

Backup. An extra electronic copy of important programs and data.

Backup copy. A copy of a program or data disk that you use for daily use to protect the originals from damage.

Bit. The smallest measurement of data. Taken from the term *binary digit*, a bit is an electrical representation that is either 0 or 1.

Board. Originally known as *circuit boards*, these boards house computer chips. Chips are attached to the surface of the board, and the board is plugged into the appropriate slot in the system unit. See also *motherboard*.

Booting. The process of starting the computer.

Bundled software. Software included with the purchase of a computer; the software is *bundled in* as part of the deal.

Byte. A measurement of computer memory or disk space. Roughly one character, or the equivalent of eight *bits*.

Cable. A collection of wires twined together to form a cable that connects computer peripherals to the system unit.

Cache memory. Extra sections of memory the computer sees as a specialized segment.

CAD (computer-aided drawing). A highly specialized drawing program used in architectural and engineering work.

Capacity. The total amount of usable storage space on a disk.

Card. See *board*.

Chips. Computer chips, technically known as *integrated circuits* (or ICs). Although most computer chips have a similar appearance, different kinds of chips perform different operations: the micro-processor (CPU) chip is responsible for all operations performed by the computer; the memory chips store programs and data; other chips, such as a math coprocessor chip, enable the computer to more efficiently perform other operations.

Clip art. Art images packaged with some computer programs (and also offered separately from software companies) that you can *cut-and-paste* and place in your publications.

Cold boot. Also known as *powerup*, the procedure of initially turning on the computer for the current work session.

Compatibles. Machines created with a technology similar to IBMs. Also referred to as *IBM clones* or *IBM compatibles*.

Cooling fan. A small fan used in many computers that keeps the boards and ICs cool.

CPS. Acronym for characters per second; used to measure the speed of printers.

CPU. The "brain" of the computer, also known as the *microprocessor,* which is a small chip of electronic circuits responsible for all the data processing done by a computer.

Cursor. A small on-screen indicator that shows you where the next operation will take place if, for example, you type a character, click a mouse button, and so on.

Database programs. Software programs that enable you to enter, organize, and update information.

DDE (Dynamic Data Exchange). A Windows 3.1 feature that allows programs to pass information to documents in other Windows programs that support DDE.

Default. A setting or value the program assumes if you do not supply a new setting or value.

Density. The amount of data that can be stored on a disk, relative to the size of the disk surface. High density disks, for example, can hold more than double density disks, even though the total surface areas of both disks are equal.

Desktop publishing. The capability of creating a typeset-quality document, from start to finish, by using a personal computer and desktop publishing software.

Directory. In the PC world, a directory is similar to the conventional filing cabinet drawer in which you store individual files related to a certain subject of your choosing.

Disk drives. Devices that read and write the data to and from disks.

DOS. An acronym for disk operating system. This term usually refers to IBM's PC DOS or Microsoft's MS-DOS.

DOS prompt. The on-screen indicator displayed by DOS to show you that the system is ready to accept commands. If the current disk drive is C, the DOS prompt is displayed as C>.

Drivers. A software program included with peripheral devices you may buy, such as a printer or a mouse. The device driver communicates necessary information about the component to the system. For DOS systems, the DOS file CONFIG.SYS stores information about device drivers.

Execute. To run a program.

Expansion ports. The plug-in receptors in the back of the system unit that enable you to attach other devices, such as a printer, modem, and other add-on devices.

Expansion slots. Slots built into the motherboard that enable you to expand the system.

File. A named collection of information stored as a unit. (You create and save a letter in a file, for example, with a unique file name, on a disk.)

Finder. The graphical interface of an operating system used by the Apple IIgs and Macintosh computers.

Floppy disk drives. Devices that enable you to store and read programs and data from a removable disk that you place in the computer.

Folder. In the Apple IIgs, Amiga, GeoWorks Pro, and Macintosh worlds, a folder is similar to a conventional drawer in a filing cabinet. Each folder can store many individual files.

Font. A collection of letters, numbers, and other characters that appear in one typeface, size, and style.

Formatting. The process of preparing a disk to store data.

Function keys. The special keys on IBM and some Macintosh keyboards that enable you to assign special functions to the keys. (Software programs, however, often control this feature; many programs by default assign functions to these keys.)

Hard copy. A printed copy of a file.

Hard disk. A data storage device that provides a large amount of storage space for programs and data. (Hard disks are housed in the system unit or are available as an external or removable unit.)

Head. The part of the disk drive that reads data from and writes data to the disk.

Hierarchical directories. The organizational method of arranging files in a DOS tree structure or in the file-and-folder method of Apple IIgs and Macintosh computers.

Highlight. The process of selecting an object on-screen. The item changes visually (usually appearing in inverse video), showing that you have selected the item.

Icon. An on-screen graphical element, or symbol, that represents certain items, such as a file or folder.

Index hole. A small hole in a floppy disk that the computer uses to control the spinning of the disk.

Information services. Communications services that run on huge mainframe computers, which store a wealth of information about a variety of topics.

Initialize. The process, usually in Apple IIgs and Macintosh applications, of preparing a disk to store information.

Inkjet printer. A category of printer that places characters on the page by squirting ink onto the page.

Installation. The process of placing programs on a computer hard disk (occasionally used when explaining loading programs on disk-based systems as well).

Keyboard. A typewriter-like component you use to input data, issue commands, and generally interact with the computer and software.

Kilobyte. 1,024 bytes (or, roughly, characters) of information. 640K is read as "640 thousand bytes."

Local area network (LAN). A group of computers linked by a network of cables.

Logged drive. The disk drive to which the operating system goes when looking for files to retrieve or save. Also known as *default drive* and *current drive*.

Mail merging. The process of merging information from a database with text created in a word processing program, usually to create personalized form letters.

Megabyte. One million bytes of information.

Memory. The area in the computer where information is stored. See also *RAM* and *ROM*.

Menu bar. The horizontal bar across the top of the screen that shows menu titles (in Apple IIGS, Macintosh, and some PC applications).

Microprocessor. The "brain" of the computer, also known as the *CPU*, a small chip of electronic circuitry responsible for all the data processing done by a computer.

MIDI interface (Musical Instrument Digital Interface). An add-on device used to connect an electronic musical instrument to the computer. With the proper software, the sounds are turned into electric pulses that can be stored as a file in the computer.

Modem (short for *MOdulator DEModulator*). An add-on (or add-in) device used to connect one computer to another remote computer or to an information service through use of the telephone line and communications software.

Monitor. The computer's display screen.

Monochrome. A single-color monitor.

Motherboard. The main board in the system, housing the computer's microprocessor chip.

Mouse. A hand-held device that enables users to manipulate a menu and icon system for selecting commands and options instead of typing commands at the keyboard.

Mouse button. The button on the mouse (there may be one, two, or three, depending on the model of mouse) that you press (or *click*) to perform operations and make selections.

Multitasking. The capability of opening and working with several programs at the same time.

OCR software (Optical Character Recognition). A program used with a scanner to convert text from a graphics image (as the text is originally scanned) into usable text for applications.

OLE (object linking and embedding). The capability of some Windows programs (running under Windows 3.1) to share or store data in two or more different documents.

Operating system. A different type of software that enables a computer to communicate with you and the application programs. To work properly, every computer must have an operating system.

Parallel. A method computers employ to transfer more than one bit of information at the same time.

Path. The route the operating system or program takes to a specific directory or folder to locate or save a specific file.

Peripheral. A component you connect to the system unit, such as a printer, mouse, modem, scanner, and graphics tablet.

Pointer. The small cursor on-screen that is controlled by the movement of a mouse.

Port. A socket-like receptacle on the back of a computer, where you plug cables that connect peripheral devices.

Power supply. The device that channels electricity needed to power the computer and add-on devices.

Printer. The device used for printing a variety of computer-generated items (such as mailing labels, reports, letters, and so on).

Prompt. A message displayed by the computer to signal the user that the system is ready for input.

RAM (random-access memory). Random-access memory chips store the programs and data you load during a current work session; when you turn off the computer, the information in RAM is erased.

Resolution. A term used to refer to the clarity of images displayed on-screen or characters printed on the page.

ROM (Read-Only Memory). Read-only memory chips contain important information that a computer needs to perform basic functions and run built-in programs. This category of memory is permanent and retains the information recorded on the chip after you turn off the computer's power.

Scanner. A device that enables you to digitize a picture, line drawing, text, or other graphic element into a form usable by the computer.

Serial. A method computers use to transfer one bit of data after another.

Software. Programs that work with a computer to help you perform specific tasks, such as creating a spreadsheet, writing a report, or drawing graphics.

Soldered. The method in which chips are placed on circuit boards. Chips are soldered to the board with melted metal; this technique seats the chips securely in place. (Some boards now have snap-in chips, making the addition or replacement of chips easier for end users.)

Spreadsheet programs. Software programs that replace the accountant's pad, pencil, and adding machine, giving you an efficient and accurate method of working with numbers.

Subdirectory. With PCs (the Apple II and the Mac use folders for this purpose), subdirectories are directories within other directories. You can create many subdirectories and many levels of subdirectories within a single directory.

System 7. An entirely new operating system for Macintosh computers with added features, such as a new file system display, a Finder utility to search devices for items, a customizable Apple menu, a simple networking capability, and more.

System unit. The main box of the computer that includes the hardware that performs all data-processing operations, houses power supply and internal disk drives, and contains other important hardware devices.

Warm boot. Restarting the computer while the power is on. On DOS computers, you perform a warm boot (also known as *rebooting*) by pressing Ctrl-Alt-Del.

Word processing programs. Software programs that enable you to work with words in a way not possible with typewriters, giving you reusable text, easy editing features, on-screen formatting, and good-quality printouts, among other features.

Write-protecting. The process of protecting a disk from receiving new—or modifying existing—information. Write-protecting prevents accidental erasure and overwriting of files. Use this important procedure to protect disks that store important information, such as programs and operating systems.

Symbols

A

P

X–Y–Z